GENDER, CRIME, AND JUSTICE

GENDER, CRIME, AND JUSTICE

LEARNING THROUGH CASES

ERIN KATHERINE KRAFFT

UNIVERSITY OF MASSACHUSETTS, DARTMOUTH

JO-ANN DELLA GIUSTINA

BRIDGEWATER STATE UNIVERSITY

SUSAN T. KRUMHOLZ

UNIVERSITY OF MASSACHUSETTS, DARTMOUTH

ROWMAN & LITTLEFIELD

LANHAM • BOULDER • NEW YORK • LONDON

Published by Rowman & Littlefield
An imprint of The Rowman & Littlefield Publishing Group, Inc.
4501 Forbes Boulevard, Suite 200, Lanham, Maryland 20706
www.rowman.com

86-90 Paul Street, London EC2A 4NE, United Kingdom

British Library Cataloguing in Publication Information Available

Library of Congress Cataloging-in-Publication Data

Names: Krafft, Erin Katherine, 1979– author. | Della Giustina, Jo-Ann, author. | Krumholz, Susan T., 1953– author.
Title: Gender, crime, and justice : learning through cases / Erin Katherine Krafft, Jo-Ann Della Giustina, Susan T. Krumholz.
Description: Lanham, Maryland : Rowman & Littlefield, an imprint of the Rowman & Littlefield Publishing Group, Inc., [2021] | Series: Learning through cases | Includes bibliographical references and index. | Summary: "In Gender and Justice, each chapter opens with a compelling case study that illustrates key concepts, followed by a narrative chapter that builds on the case study to introduce essential elements. This book is distinctive in its inclusion of LGBTQ experiences in crime, victimization, processing, and punishment"—Provided by publisher.
Identifiers: LCCN 2021017412 (print) | LCCN 2021017413 (ebook) | ISBN 9781442257856 (cloth) | ISBN 9781442257863 (paperback) | ISBN 9781442257870 (epub)
Subjects: LCSH: Victims of crimes. | Sex discrimination in criminal justice administration. | Women—crimes against. | Sexual minorities—Crimes against.
Classification: LCC HV6250.25 .K73 2021 (print) | LCC HV6250.25 (ebook) | DDC 364.3081—dc23
LC record available at https://lccn.loc.gov/2021017412
LC ebook record available at https://lccn.loc.gov/2021017413

♾™ The paper used in this publication meets the minimum requirements of American National Standard for Information Sciences—Permanence of Paper for Printed Library Materials, ANSI/NISO Z39.48-1992.

CONTENTS

The workings of the criminal justice and legal systems have perhaps never been as central to mainstream discourse in the United States as they are today. Debates about law enforcement, incarceration, methods of reform, transformative justice, and many other aspects of the justice system reach the nation through such varied sources as political statements, news outlets, podcasts, reality television, documentaries, nonprofit campaigns, grassroots organizing and social movements, and social media. As such, there is an increasingly visible need for thoughtful engagement with and deep study of the criminal justice and legal systems, and this book is a unique and critical contribution to that effort.

Gender, Crime, and Justice: Learning through Cases takes two large and complicated concepts—"gender" and "justice"—and explores key aspects and concrete manifestations of both, as well as how they affect one another. Using a highly accessible format, we explore the ways in which changing notions of gender impact the treatment of individuals within the criminal justice and legal systems and provide an opportunity for students to consider the relationship between social norms and stereotypes and the law.

Crucially, this book does not treat "gender" as simply a stand-in for "women." It does explore many gender-based obstacles faced by cis women within the criminal justice and legal systems, but it also examines multiple manifestations of gender: social norms and stereotypes surrounding concepts of femininity and masculinity; the relationship between race and gender and intersecting forms of discrimination; particular obstacles faced by those who are trans, nonbinary, gender nonconforming, and intersex; and more. Our central question—How does gender impact the criminal justice and legal systems, and how does the justice system impact contemporary understandings of gender?—requires that we look beyond binary understandings, not only of sex or gender, but of crime and justice. As a result, this book is necessarily interdisciplinary and could be as at home in a women's, gender, and sexuality studies course as in a justice studies, legal studies, or criminal justice course.

Our hope is that this book provides an opportunity for instructors and students to engage in critical dialogue that considers both gender and the criminal justice and legal systems as constantly in flux. After all, it has only been about 150 years since women were allowed to practice law in the United States; fifty-five years since all women were able to access the right to vote (after the Voting Rights Act of 1965); forty years since the first woman sat on the Supreme Court of the United States; and a handful of years since trans, nonbinary, and gender nonconforming individuals have been able to have state identification that reflects their gender identities (still unavailable in the majority of states).

Understanding the roots of these changes—and the possibilities for further changes—requires examining both the workings of the criminal justice and legal systems as well as the transformation of gender-based stereotypes and forms of discrimination in society at large. This book provides the opportunity to engage with this study through case studies, analyses, and discussion guides that demystify the tangled relationship between gender and justice.

LEARNING THROUGH CASES: THE STRUCTURE OF THE TEXT

Each chapter in this book opens with clear **Learning Objectives**, followed by a detailed **Case Study** drawn from historical and contemporary instances in which gender intersects with the criminal justice and legal systems. In this way, students are able to contextualize their understandings of the relationship between gender and the criminal justice and legal systems through a real-life narrative. Each case study closes with a short set of questions, **Thinking Critically about the Case**, which prepare students to critically engage with the histories, policies, precedents, and processes that inform the interplay between gender norms and legal norms. The following section, **Context and Analysis**, guides students through the significant elements of each case, illuminating historical backgrounds, fundamental concepts, and key laws and policies that are relevant to not only the case at hand, but the larger topic of the chapter. **Review and Study Questions** allow students to reflect on the central concepts of each chapter, followed by **Going Further**, a selection of readings and other media that students may choose to explore in order to deepen their knowledge of each chapter's topic. Finally, **Key Terms** provide a quick overview of terminology that may be new to students.

This format provides the opportunity for students to become invested in the narratives that open each chapter, which then allows for deeper acquisition of the concepts and analyses that follow. The case studies in this book were carefully chosen for their ability to reveal particular aspects of the position of gender and sexuality within the criminal justice and legal systems. As such, each case is unique and yet creates an entry point into larger questions and concepts. The historical, sociological, political, and legal contexts of each case are made accessible via storytelling that animates what may otherwise be abstract, and students are able to see the concrete applications and manifestations of the legal, political, and social norms that are woven through not only the cases presented in the book, but through the complicated and evolving tapestry of understandings of gender and their bearing on individuals, communities, and the law. The case-study approach also creates the opportunity for classroom discussions and assignments that extend beyond academic exercises into personal and intellectual engagement with students' own relationships to notions of gender and justice.

OVERVIEW OF THE CHAPTERS

Chapters 1 and 2 provide material that serves as a foundation for what follows. Chapters 3 through 11 examine categories of behaviors defined as crimes, while exploring the gendered nature of both the acts and the social response to them. Chapters 12 through 14 focus on the lived reality of the criminal legal response to the acts and the people, as well as ideas for alternatives to existing systems.

Chapter 1: Gender and the Law—Case #1: Myra Bradwell. This chapter begins with a story about one of the early women pioneers in the legal field. Then we explore the history of the relationship between gender and law in practice and in theory, including the emergence of feminist, critical race, and queer legal theories.

Chapter 2: Crime Theory—Case #2: The Central Park Five. Following a case that explores the darkest places for race, masculinity, and the law, this chapter provides an overview of criminology, methodology, and stereotyping of both victims and offenders.

Chapter 3: Intimate Partner Violence—Case #3: Hedda Nussbaum. The case featured in this chapter illuminates both the history of responses to intimate partner violence and the contradictions and complications present when the criminal legal system delves into our most personal relationships. The content that follows expounds on the successes and failures of the law, and the community, in understanding and responding to these harmful behaviors.

Chapter 4: Sexual Assault—Case #4: The Steubenville Football Team. This chapter presents the legal and social intricacies of sexual assault and rape. The case, from Steubenville, Ohio, illustrates the unique challenges of experiencing sexual assault and of the community and legal response.

Chapter 5: Gendered Hate Crime—Case #5: Elliot Rodger. This chapter examines the destructive power of hate, focusing particularly on hate based on gender and difference. The case exemplifies the dangers posed when that hate intensifies in the absence of reasoned intervention.

Chapter 6: At Risk: Youth, Race, and Gender—Case #6: Tamir Rice. The case study addresses how a police officer perceived a twelve-year-old African American male who was playing as a threat, and the ensuing legal processes. The chapter then contextualizes these issues within the history of the juvenile justice system, the connections between victimization and offending, and the different impacts on girls, LGBTQ youth, and young people of color. Finally, the school-to-prison pipeline and changes in punishment of young offenders are discussed.

Chapter 7: Traditional Street Crime: Nonviolent—Case #7: Alva Mae Groves and Dorothy Gaines. The seemingly separate stories of Alva Mae Groves and Dorothy Gaines explore the formidable, often disproportionate, manner in which the so-called war on drugs has impacted women's lives. This chapter provides supporting data on women's involvement with "street crime" and the overcriminalization of women, particularly women of color.

Chapter 8: Traditional Street Crime: Violent—Case #8: Stanley Tookie Williams. The Williams case raises important questions about masculinity, violence, redemption, and the death penalty. This chapter expands on these themes, adding discussions on gangs, guns, and domestic terrorism.

Chapter 9: Sex Work and Trafficking—Case #9: Rachel Lloyd and GEMS. This case study looks at the risks of violence and exploitation that a young person on the streets faces, and the way that Lloyd ultimately used that experience to provide a safe haven for others. The case informs the chapter content, which includes a history of laws and a debate about the criminalization of prostitution.

Chapter 10: Crimes of Power: State and Corporate—Case #10: Stonewall. Stonewall has become analogous with LQBTQ rights. As the case study illustrates, it is also emblematic of the state's use of power against its citizens. This chapter presents information and ideas about policing, immigration, and corporations as sites of power employed differentially toward women and LGBTQ people.

Chapter 11: Pregnancy, Birthing, and Rearing: "Damned If You Do, Damned If You Don't"—Case #11: Regina McKnight. So many of our intimate interactions have become the subject of laws. This chapter addresses some of those that have resulted in criminalization. One example is the McKnight case, where she was charged with homicide by child abuse after suffering a still birth. The case allows us to explore the variety of ways parenting has been regulated and the disproportionate impact it has on women of color and the LGBTQ community.

Chapter 12: Incarceration as a Reproduction of Masculinity—Case #12: Kalief Browder. This chapter explores how theories of masculinity interact with incarceration, from the prison-industrial complex, the male "prison code," solitary confinement, and the impact of masculinity on prison correction officers and staff. Prison programming, related to the role of masculinity, is discussed. The case study incorporates much of the chapter's content as it reveals the negative effects of pretrial imprisonment on young males.

Chapter 13: Unique Populations in Prison—Case #13: CeCe McDonald. This case offers a singular story, the life of a transgender woman, her victimization, and her eventual incarceration. Her story serves as a jumping-off point to an exploration of the impact and consequences of incarceration, beyond masculinity.

Chapter 14: Trending Issues and Future Directions—Case #14: Marissa Alexander. The case study in the final chapter returns to a reflection on the complicated face of intimate partner violence in a story about a woman's abuse, trial, imprisonment, and release. This chapter explores intersectional forms of oppression, with a focus on the current movements to reform or radically alter the criminal legal system. Several forward-looking programs and initiatives are discussed, including the emerging sphere of restorative and transformative justice.

THE FUTURE OF GENDER

A final word before we begin: Social, cultural, and legal treatments and understandings of gender, sexuality, and justice continue to evolve. This text, therefore, cannot be final or empirical any more than the position of gender within law and society is final or empirical. Instead, it captures a period in the evolution of notions of gender, sexuality, and justice and prepares students to not only examine contemporary notions and norms but to develop the tools and critical frameworks for understanding—and perhaps even affecting—this continuing evolution.

ACKNOWLEDGMENTS

We must begin by thanking Carolyn Boyes-Watson. It was her wisdom, dedication, and wonderful skill at storytelling that initially created the series Learning through Cases. We are excited that we are now presenting the third book in the series. I personally want to thank her for providing me with this opportunity to share my visions of this field of study. We also offer our sincere gratitude to the staff and editors at Rowman & Littlefield who we have had the privilege of working with during the long time it took to get this book to fruition. We'd especially like to thank Sarah Stanton for recognizing the value of the Learning through Cases approach from the beginning; Kathryn Knigge for working closely with us through the development of the book; Becca Beurer, who inherited us in the middle of this stressful year (2020) and who guided—and put up with—us through the final stages of big decisions (what photos to use) and painful tedium (the bibliography) of getting a book into print; and Nicole Carty, our patient production editor.

I'd like to thank Jo-Ann, who has long been a colleague and friend and was an important part of this book from its inception. And I know Jo-Ann will agree that most of our appreciation goes to Erin. She arrived just in time to save this project from the dust pile. Her energy, commitment, generosity, and just sheer brilliance got us working again and focused on producing a powerful, contemporary textbook. And finally, to Jack with love, for taking care of me at all those times I seem incapable of doing it myself.

Susan

My deepest gratitude goes to Susan, who had the wisdom to launch this project, to Erin, who was instrumental in propelling it forward, and to everyone who has been invaluable to my research, including the incarcerated men at the Old Colony Correctional Center, my Inside-Out students (both incarcerated students and Bridgewater State University students), and everyone involved with the Alternatives to Violence Project.

Jo-Ann

My gratitude and appreciation go to my colleagues and students in the Department of Crime and Justice Studies at UMass Dartmouth, whose thoughtful approaches to teaching, learning, and critical engagement consistently inspire me and brought life to this project. Thanks, too, to Luke, for slowly building a house around us while I worked on this book. And, finally, thanks to Susan and Jo-Ann for their insights, for their tireless commitment, and for embodying a kind of mentorship and collaboration that is all too rare in the academic world.

Erin

Gender and the Law

In this chapter, you will learn about the history of gender in law. We begin with a case that looks at the women who were first admitted to the practice of law in the United States. After the case study, you will read about women's roles in many facets of the legal system, as well as the gendered theories that impact the relationship we all have with the legal environment.

LEARNING OBJECTIVES

After reading this chapter, you should be able to do the following:

- Explain the history of feminism and feminist theory.
- Identify the roots and branches of critical theory.
- Describe women's role in developing theories of criminology and methodology.
- Explain intersectionality.
- Articulate women's changing role in law.

Case #1: Myra Bradwell

In 1981, Sandra Day O'Connor became the first woman appointed to serve as a U.S. Supreme Court justice. Such a momentous appointment would not have been possible without the earlier efforts of a number of women who had fought for—and created—rights for women to practice law. More than a century before O'Connor took her place on the bench, Myra Colby Bradwell (1831–1894) was determined to become the first woman in the United States to enter the practice of law.

Born in Vermont in 1831 and raised in Illinois, the young Myra Colby showed an early penchant for learning. Single-mindedly devoted to furthering her education, she eventually enrolled in the Elgin Female Seminary. The number of female seminaries across the nation was growing exponentially in the first half of the nineteenth century; more women were choosing to pursue a secondary or even postsecondary education, but they were still commonly denied entry into colleges and universities. The seminaries were often rigorous, focused on both education and self-discipline, and they offered their students opportunities that were still very new for women. Women were seen as intellectually weaker than men, and as students, they were often taught only what was considered necessary at the time: social skills, proper etiquette, and housekeeping. Education at the seminary represented a radical shift in women's learning and in the opportunities open to them; as literacy rates rose quickly and steadily and women were able to learn from professional teachers in challenging environments, more women were prepared for—and determined to enter—professions. Seminaries, several of which later emerged as leading educational institutions for both women and men and transformed into four-year colleges and universities, played an indispensable role in the growing movement toward women's equality. That movement, however, was still in its infancy during Myra's time.

Legal education was similarly in its early stages of development. Until the nineteenth century, many lawyers in the United States were either educated in Great Britain or learned the law through apprenticeship. In the 1800s, small professional law schools began to emerge, but initially they were principally geared toward practitioners and were generally more vocational than theoretical. It was not until the late nineteenth century—and in some areas even the early twentieth century—that institutionalized, university-based legal education became the norm. This new standard was brought about in part because of the creation of the American Bar Association (ABA), a national organization of lawyers, in 1878. The ABA pushed for formal legal education, and by the early 1930s, most states mandated a legal education, rather than an apprenticeship, as a necessary qualification for admitting anyone to the practice of law. There are today still four states—California, Vermont, Virginia, and Washington—that allow for lawyers to be trained through apprenticeships in lieu of the typical three-year university-based curriculum. All aspiring practitioners, however, whether emerging from an apprenticeship or law school, are required to take bar examinations before they are allowed to practice law on their own.

In 1852, Myra married James Bradwell. James was a polymath and a supporter of Myra's aspirations; he himself was a teacher and would soon enter the practice of law. When he passed the bar in the mid-1850s, Myra's nascent law career also began; for the next decade, she worked as an apprentice in his Chicago law office, learning all she could, with an eye on eventually being admitted to the bar herself. As an apprentice, she was able to learn the law through research, observation, and legal writing, but because of restrictions placed on married women, Myra was unable to perform some particular duties. For example, she could not legally notarize documents. To notarize, or to certify the legality of a document, administer oaths, or witness the validity of a signature, you must be a notary public, and Myra was prevented by the laws of coverture from holding such an appointment.

Coverture was a legal doctrine or common-law rule that dictated that when a man and woman married, they were no longer two but one, and that one was the man (husband). This rule meant that once a woman married, she lost her individual legal existence. As a result, she could no longer enter into contracts, buy or sell property, execute a will, or sue or be sued. The husband had absolute rights to the children, to any income the woman earned, and even to his wife's actual physical being, as coverture meant that a wife had no right to her own body. A man was legally incapable of raping his wife, according to the marital rape exemption, as they were considered one legal entity. A man was also fully within his rights to beat his wife, so long as he did not beat her to death. Given these grim realities, Myra's inability to act as a lawyer or even as a notary public was representative of her position as a second-class citizen, and she was unwilling to accept such restrictions. She continued to learn the law, and to focus on other pursuits as well.

In 1868, Myra became founder, manager, and editor of the *Chicago Legal News*. The first legal publication in the United States to be edited by a woman, the *Chicago Legal News* was an early incarnation of what would become a busy tradition of legal journalism. It was a well-regarded publication, and alongside its summaries of laws, court opinions, and ordinances, it had a special focus on laws relating to women. Myra's work for women's rights was not contained solely in the *Legal News*; instead, the paper was only a small part of her continuing efforts on behalf of women's liberation. In particular, she was focused on securing the right of married women to have control over their own property and earnings, and she had a hand in drafting the Illinois Married Woman's Property Act of 1861 and the Earnings Act of 1869. She also participated in drafting legislation that would give all people the right to pursue any profession they choose, and she drafted a bill that gave women the right to run for office within the Illinois school system. She was a staunch lobbyist and, with the assistance of her husband, shepherded the passage of these and other bills surrounding greater rights for women.

In August 1869, Myra passed the Illinois law examination and promptly applied for admission to the bar. She was not admitted, however, and refusing to accept such a decision, she appealed to the state of Illinois. During the same year, Arabella Mansfield of Iowa became the first woman to be admitted to the bar, in the first state that allowed women admission to the bar. Mansfield had at first been denied admission as well, and like Myra, she appealed. In response to her appeal, the state of Iowa determined that she could not be denied admission to the bar. Mansfield, however, did not go on to practice law; the dream of a woman law practitioner was still unrealized.

After a yearlong deliberation, the Illinois Supreme Court affirmed their denial of Myra's admission to the bar, saying in 1870 that as a married woman, she was not fit to practice law. In an opinion written by Chief Justice Charles B. Lawrence, the court ruled, "God designed the sexes to occupy different spheres of action, and that it belonged to men to make, apply and execute laws, was regarded as an almost axiomatic truth."

Not being easily discouraged, Bradwell appealed this decision as well and took her appeal all the way to the U.S. Supreme Court. There, her attorney argued that she had the right to pursue a livelihood and that the rights granted to her by the privileges and immunities clause of the Fourteenth Amendment were being violated. Amendment XIV, Section 1, Clause 2 of the Constitution states, "No State shall make or enforce any law which shall abridge the privileges or immunities of citizens of the United States." Again, after a yearlong deliberation, the Court issued its ruling, and in an 8–1 decision, they determined that the Fourteenth Amendment did not guarantee the right to practice a profession. Justice Joseph Bradley, in a concurring opinion, wrote, "The natural and proper timidity and delicacy which belongs to the female sex evidently unfits it for many of the occupations of civil life. . . . The paramount destiny and mission of women are to fulfill the noble and benign offices of wife and mother. This is the law of the Creator."[1] The Court was concerned that by granting Bradwell admission to the bar, they would be opening the doors for women to gain in numbers in the legal profession, that women would have a negative effect on the administration of justice, and that "brutal" cases would not be proper for women to hear.

While awaiting the Court decisions, Bradwell made good use of her time; in 1872, with Alta M. Hulett, an eighteen-year-old woman with similar aspirations to be admitted to the bar, Bradwell participated in successfully pushing a new law through the Illinois legislature that assured that women in the state, regardless of marital status, could enter the bar or any other profession they chose (with the exclusion of the military). After the Supreme Court's disappointing verdict, Bradwell chose not to apply to the bar again, and in 1873, Hulett became the first woman actually admitted to the Illinois bar. Her practice was, unfortunately, cut short; Hulett would pass away from poor health only a few years later, in 1877, at the age of twenty-two.

Myra never again attempted to join the bar, but in 1879 the Illinois State Bar Association granted her an honorary membership, along with Ada Kepley, who in 1870 had become the first woman in the country to graduate from law school, from the Old University of Chicago (which subsequently became Northwestern University). Also, in 1879, Belva Ann Lockwood, who had been fighting very similar battles around Maryland and Washington, DC, saw legislation that she had drafted be signed into law: women were no longer to be prohibited from practicing law in federal courts.

Throughout the 1870s and 1880s, Myra continued her work with the *Chicago Legal News*, and she continued to help other women blaze their own trails into the profession. It had been just over twenty years since she had submitted her application to the bar, and in the intervening years, she had also emerged as an active member of the women's suffrage movement, fighting for women's right to vote. Suddenly, in 1890, despite the fact that she was no longer pursuing admittance to the bar, acting on its own motion, the Illinois Supreme Court approved her original application, making Myra the first woman to have submitted an application for admission to the bar that was—eventually—approved.

Myra Bradwell died only three years later, but her legacy lives on. Her daughter, Bessie Bradwell Helmer, graduated from law school in 1882 and continued publishing the *Chicago Legal News* until 1925, just two years before her own death. Bradwell's sustained efforts helped to carve out new spaces and new paths for women to enter not just the legal profession, but different spheres of public life in new capacities. Her vision was one of gender equality, and work toward that vision still continues.

THINKING CRITICALLY ABOUT THE CASE

1. What are the benefits or drawbacks of allowing aspiring lawyers to gain qualifications through apprenticeship rather than formal education in law school?

2. Where do we see remaining vestiges of coverture?

3. Women may no longer be legally disallowed from attending law school on the basis of gender. Does this mean that all individuals have equal access to law school? Where and how might barriers arise?

REFERENCES

This case is adapted from the following sources:

Barry, Margaret M., Jon C. Dubin, and Peter A. Joy. "The Development of Legal Education in the United States." PILnet. Accessed February 16, 2016. https://www.pilnet.org/resource/the-development-of-legal-education-in-the-united-states.

Danilina, S. "Who Was Myra Bradwell: America's First Woman Lawyer." The Law Dictionary. Accessed February 16, 2016. https://thelawdictionary.org/article/who-was-myra-bradwell-americas-first-woman-lawyer.

Lewis, Jone Johnson. "Separate Spheres Ideology: Women and Men in Their Own Places." ThoughtCo., September 11, 2019. https://www.thoughtco.com/separate-spheres-ideology-3529523.

Morello, Karen Berger. *The Invisible Bar: The Woman Lawyer in America, 1638 to the Present*. New York: Random House, 1986.

Sweet, Leonard I. "The Female Seminary Movement and Women's Mission in Antebellum America." *Church History* 54, no. 1 (March 1985): 41–55.

CONTEXT AND ANALYSIS

During the past several decades, the fields of sociology and criminology have witnessed an explosion of texts purporting to study gender and the criminal/legal system. The vast majority of these books address issues of women and the criminal/legal system but fail to address the complicated array of situations and factors that truly reflect the gendered nature of society and of the criminal/legal system. This text attempts to fill that void by not only addressing how the criminal/legal system impacts women, but also how it acts toward men and LGBTQ[2] people.

Since Europeans arrived in what was to become the United States, laws have not been favorable to girls and women. Females were branded as witches in the colonies and were not considered "people" for purposes of the Constitution. They had no right to vote and were deemed to be the property of their fathers or husbands. As we saw in the Myra Bradwell case, women could not practice law. And for much of the history of the United States, women could not make laws. The first woman was elected to the House of Representatives in 1917, the first to the Senate in 1932. A great deal of progress has been made, much of it quite recent. Women were granted "personhood" and therefore the right to vote in 1920. **Coverture** finally and fully legally ended in 1981, the same year the first woman was appointed to the Supreme Court. As of January 2019, women comprise 25 percent of the U.S. Senate and 23.4 percent of the U.S. House of Representatives. At this writing, we have yet to see a woman president, and the Equal Rights Amendment, first introduced to the legislature in 1971, has not been ratified.

Let's take a look at the history.

Patriarchy

Studies have traced the concept of **patriarchy** back through four thousand to six thousand years of human history. In the most basic terms, patriarchy means a society controlled by men, one where men have power over women. But in order to truly understand patriarchy and the patriarchal society, it is necessary to delve more deeply into its meaning. A patriarchal society is one in which men hold the power and privilege, men hold the positions of authority, and men make rules and enforce them. According to this theory, in the rare instances where women hold positions of power, they do so by conforming to the constraints of the system, thereby not posing a real challenge to the patriarchal superstructure.

While we recognize that humankind existed in earlier millennia without evidence of patriarchy, it has shaped society, with few exceptions, for at least five thousand years. As such, we consider patriarchy a social construct, not a status that exists in nature (though some theorists consider the dichotomy of culture versus nature to be itself a product of patriarchy). Maintaining control of another requires constant attention, and so the structure underlying patriarchy is based on an emphasis on rules, domination, subordination, exclusion, and coercion.

Patriarchy maintains control within systems of **hierarchy**, not just between men and women, but among men as well. Historically these hierarchies were based on age, a system where elder men held power over younger men. In more contemporary societies, hierarchies are based on other measures of status—economic wealth, the color of one's skin, and how well a person performs the expectations of masculinity, among other statuses. Men with more power and status have control over the lives of less powerful men. All are more valued than women, though women experience different degrees of control and manipulation as well. Many of these distinctions will become clearer as you read explanations and illustrations throughout this text.

Coverture and the Separate Sphere

As patriarchy finds its power within hierarchies, patriarchal societies base their beliefs on a system of duality, a system where one side is given a position above the other. These dualisms divide the world into opposing pairs, pairs that are gendered and value laden

COVERTURE
A legal doctrine that said that when a man and woman married, they became one legal person: the man. Therefore, a married woman had no independent legal identity to sue or be sued, contract, or retain or control finances.

PATRIARCHY
A system in which men hold primary authority and control over role definitions and power.

HIERARCHY
Any system of dominance that prioritizes one thing, or one person, over another.

and that themselves confer privilege. Examples of these dualisms include culture versus nature, as noted above, as well as man versus woman, good versus bad, and reason versus emotion. Coverture is a concept borne out of patriarchy; the separate sphere is a clear example of a dualism.

As noted in the Myra Bradwell case study, coverture prevented women from having a legal identity apart from a man—a father or husband. But what exactly is coverture? The literary definition means protective or sheltering. The legal concept emerged from a need to protect, or control, the behavior of women within marriage. Single women were free to sue or be sued, sign contracts, and otherwise control their own property. Once married, however, the husband and wife became one legal entity: the husband. He had primary decision-making authority; he could contract, sue, and execute a will—for both of them. Coverture was the law until it began facing legal and legislative challenges during the nineteenth century. Legal remnants of coverture continued to exist until the twenty-first century but have largely vanished in recent years. But as much as the legal constraints might be shrinking, the social norm of separate public and private (domestic) spheres persists.

The **separate sphere** is more of a social construct than a legal one. The concept can be traced back as far as the ancient Greeks, who had described the *polis* as the political or public space that men inhabited. In the United States, the concept took on new meaning with the advent of industrialization. Prior to industrialization, most work took place in and around the home—farming, for example—and was often shared by all members of a family. With the advent of the Industrial Revolution, the primary center of work—the place where income would be generated—moved away from the home. In the process, women's work, which continued to revolve around the home and family and did not generate income, quickly became socially devalued. As we will see in chapter 3, the relative power contained in the separate spheres is key in theories of intimate partner violence. The construct of separate spheres has proven to be more intractable than the actual legal constraints.

It is important to note that the construct of the domestic sphere, sometimes referred to as the "**cult of domesticity**" that dictated that women were delicate and therefore should not work outside the home, has always been applied differently to wealthier white women. Women who are poor, immigrants, or women of color are often stereotyped as physically stronger than men and have always been expected to work both inside and outside the home.

Women and Juries

Pursuant to common law, women could not be jurors. The ancient doctrine of *propter defectum sexus*, or "defect of sex," meant that women were physically and temperamentally unfit to serve on a jury. The essence of that doctrine was confirmed by the U.S. Supreme Court in the 1879 case of *Strauder v. West Virginia* (100 U.S. 303). In something of an irony, the court in *Strauder*, a case that involved the trial of an African American man accused of killing his wife, found that excluding African Americans from juries violated the constitutional right to be tried by a jury of one's peers, while affirming that women could be excluded.

Women were first allowed to serve on juries in Utah in 1898, but the change caught on slowly. Though women acquired the right to vote in 1920, it would take until the late 1930s for the attitude that women were incompetent, easily swayed, and too emotional to serve as jurors to begin to change. As recently as 1961, the Supreme Court case of *Hoyt v. Florida* (368 U.S. 57) unanimously upheld a Florida law that automatically "exempted" women from jury duty (though they could "opt in" by taking some affirmative action to do so). These opt-in policies were found unconstitutional in the 1979 case of *Duran v. Missouri* (439 U.S. 357); the attorney arguing to overturn these policies, Ruth Bader Ginsburg, was to become a Supreme Court justice.

SEPARATE SPHERE
A social construct that separates the public parts of life from the private and, by definition, restricts women, and whatever occurs within a family, to the private sphere.

CULT OF DOMESTICITY
Another term for the sphere occupied by women.

FEMINISMS AND THEORY

Feminism, and therefore feminist theory, has evolved over the past 250 or so years and is said to have arrived in "waves." Though the roots of feminism can be found in the eighteenth-century writings of Wollstonecraft, Austen, and Mills, **first-wave feminism** is considered to have formally begun with the **Seneca Falls Convention** in 1848 and to have continued until 1920. During that time, women fought for the right to vote and the right to divorce, issues that defined women's voice in society. With the passage of the **Nineteenth Amendment** in 1920, women in the United States were granted the right to vote in national elections (though the rights of women of color were not legally protected until the passage of the **Voting Rights Act** of 1965). First-wave feminists were also active in the U.S. temperance and abolitionist movements. Activists of the time, such as Elizabeth Cady Stanton and Sojourner Truth, were demanding that their voices be heard.

The second wave of feminism technically began in the 1920s but didn't emerge with force until the 1960s. Arriving at a time when society was witnessing significant social turmoil, **second wave feminism** was energized by the anti–Vietnam War, civil rights, and Chicano rights movements. Initially marginalized within those movements, feminists responded by creating their own organizations. The issues that initially dominated the second wave were reproduction, sexuality, and body image, but as the movement developed its theoretical construct, broader issues of race, class, and oppression emerged.

> The second wave was increasingly theoretical . . . [associating] the subjugation of women with broader critiques of patriarchy, capitalism, normative heterosexuality, and the woman's role as wife and mother. Sex and gender were differentiated—the former being biological, and the latter a social construct that varies culture-to-culture and over time.[3]

Second-wave feminism is said to have moved from the streets to the academy. And the theories that emerged have formed the basis of the third and fourth waves.

Third-wave feminism, which emerged in the 1980s, is most notable for breaking boundaries. Following along on the second-wave introduction of intersectionality, the third wave emphasized the diversity of "womanhood" on the basis of race, class, and ethnicity, but also gender, sexuality, and the notion of **heteronormativity**. One of the more interesting aspects of third-wave feminism was the reclaiming of representations of femininity such as makeup and high heels that had been rejected by second-wave feminists as objectifications. Also notable was the hesitancy of third wavers to identify as feminist. Theories that emerged during this period focus on decentering what was considered by some to be the largely white, middle-class feminism of the second wave and on breaking down gender norms.

Sometime after the turn of the twenty-first century, **fourth-wave feminism** materialized. Though it remains to be fully formed, the fourth wave is characterized by empowerment, inclusion, and activism. Nowhere is this "wave" more completely represented then in the rash of movements publicly calling out sexual harassment, sexual assault, and male privilege in the workplace. With the fourth wave came a reclamation of the term "feminist," now proudly displayed on T-shirts that say, "This is what a feminist looks like."

The History of Feminist Theory

In introducing a text on *Feminist Thought* in 1994, sociologist Charles Lemert stated, "Feminist thought . . . has emerged in the last generation as *the* [emphasis in original] single most creative and challenging source of social thought there is." Since feminists began to inhabit the academy in the 1970s, there has been a rapid development of feminist theory. To a significant extent, legal theory has followed in the footsteps of the broader feminist theories. What follows is a brief history of contemporary feminist theory, legal theory, and how these theories have impacted the field of criminology. It is important to

FIRST WAVE FEMINISM
If the movement known as "feminism" could be defined by points in time, or waves, the first wave began with the Seneca Falls Convention in 1848 and continued into the 1920s.

SENECA FALLS CONVENTION
This convention brought together three hundred men and women who rallied for the equality of women to be recognized.

NINETEENTH AMENDMENT
The amendment to the U.S. Constitution that gave women the right to vote.

VOTING RIGHTS ACT
An act signed into law in 1965 to prohibit discriminatory voting practices.

SECOND WAVE FEMINISM
The period of the feminist movement from the 1920s through the 1970s.

THIRD WAVE FEMINISM
A period of feminism beginning in the 1980s that decentered the movement, recognizing racial and gender diversity.

HETERONORMATIVITY
The belief that heterosexuality, or relations between people of the opposite sex, is the cultural norm.

FOURTH WAVE FEMINISM
The contemporary feminist movement, emphasizing empowerment, inclusion, and activism.

keep in mind that there is no unified "feminist theory" but that over time feminists have developed a wide range of theories, and there continues to be divergence between those feminists who might consider themselves conservative, liberal, progressive, or radical.

The first phase of feminist theory was dominated by liberal notions of equality. This theory argued that women would be made equal by granting them access to male institutions such as law, politics, and the workplace. **Equality theory** is the basis upon which legislation has granted women equal access to education and work and equal pay. At the same time that equality feminism was playing out, a more radical version of feminism was evolving. This too had a tremendous impact on future theories. **Radical feminism** posited that there needed to be a radical restructuring of society, criticizing **neoliberalism** (though that term would not enter the language of critique for a decade or two) as a social and economic framework dominated by patriarchy, where men are privileged and women are oppressed.

While this era (the 1960s to 1970s) gave women many rights, equality theory has been criticized by many for being "assimilationist" because it did not challenge existing societal structures. Instead, it expected women to change in order to be successful. Critics say that any definition of feminism must recognize the prevalence of patriarchy and the ways in which men benefit and women are oppressed. Despite its flaws and critics, equality feminism has persisted as a broadly accepted notion within liberal societies. Among feminists however, theory must respond to critique. And so, in the 1980s, feminist theories emerged that recognized the importance of difference.

At least in part as a response to the backlash against feminism and the media-fueled idea that now that women are "equal" there is no longer a need for feminism, feminists argued that women are different from men and that equality does not, indeed cannot, mean simply inserting women into roles dominated and defined by males. One criticism of this **difference feminism** is that it is essentialist, that it glorifies traditional roles of male and female.

Standpoint theory also grew out of this second phase of feminist theory. As much an **epistemology** or methodology for acquiring knowledge as a theory, standpoint theory proposes that we make women's experiences the lens for understanding rather than men's. The idea is that instead of understanding the world as described and explained by the dominant, we will have a fuller understanding when the voices of the marginalized are included. Feminist standpoint theory in particular has influenced theories of other marginalized groups, as we will see in the discussions of critical race and queer theory below.

The theories to emerge from the third and fourth waves of feminism, those that have dominated feminist thinking since the 1990s, emphasize diversity and intersectionality. As the voices of Black women especially entered the discussion, the unique perspective they offer has shown how race and gender oppression not only coexist but layer in ways that compound the oppression. **Intersectional theory** helps us acknowledge the ways in which the lives of women are shaped by race, class, heteronormativity, age, and so forth.

Intersectionality

Gender, race, and class are integral to the behavioral influences, role expectations, and life experiences that structure people's lives and their responses to their surroundings. A person's actions emanate from the totality of his or her life experiences. In the United States, very different life experiences shape men and women, white people and Black people, and the rich and the poor, gender specific or not.

During the nineteenth century, Black feminists such as Sojourner Truth explained the lives of Black women as being a combination of racial and gender oppression.[4] That perspective reemerged in the 1960s and 1970s when feminists of color (Black, Latina, Asian, and Native American feminists) analyzed their oppression as the multiple oppressions of gender, race, class, and sexuality as a response to the inability of mainstream feminist and racial inequality theories to address the oppression of women of color. Historically, both the feminist and antiracist movements suppressed the ideas of women of color. Antiracist

---

EQUALITY THEORY
A theory that states that all people should be treated equally, no matter one's gender.

RADICAL FEMINISM
A theory suggesting that without radically altering society and social relations, gender equality can never be achieved.

NEOLIBERALISM
A social and economic philosophy that advocates for an extreme version of free-market capitalism, deregulation of markets, and elimination of the role of government, as in welfare.

DIFFERENCE FEMINISM
A response to equality theory, difference theory posits that only by recognizing gender differences, or what makes us unique, can we address gender inequality.

STANDPOINT THEORY
A theory that suggests we need to change the lens through which we view, describe, and understand the world from a patriarchal or hierarchical lens to one that is more accepting of differences.

EPISTEMOLOGY
The philosophy of knowledge or how we acquire and make sense of what we learn; how we know what we know.

INTERSECTIONAL THEORIES
Theories that recognize that our lives are shaped by many aspects of our identification, including race, class, gender, and heteronormativity.

strategies tended to flow from the racism experienced by men of color, and the sexism experienced by white women tended to set the agenda of the feminist movement. Due to the exclusion of women of color in leadership positions, those movements failed to reflect the ideas and lives of women of color, who experience racism differently than do men of color and sexism differently than do white women.

In the past decade the conversation of oppression has been extended to sexual preferences and gender representation. The multiple oppressions perspective (also known as multicultural feminism, Third World feminism, multiplicative identity, multiple consciousness, among others) rejects the idea that women must decide whether they are more affected by racial oppression, gender or sexual oppression, or gender inequality. Instead, a combination of gender, race, sexuality, and class, and not any one of these alone, forms a woman's identity, status, and circumstance. Focusing exclusively on patriarchal domination, as traditional feminist thought does, obscures the reality of the lives of these women, who are differently situated in the economic, social, and political worlds than are white women. A woman's social context is created by interconnecting systems of power (e.g., patriarchy, race subordination, capitalism) and oppression (racism, sexism, classism).

FEMINIST LEGAL THEORY

Women began to study law in growing numbers during the 1970s and 1980s. Concurrent with this growth was the development of what became known as feminist legal theory. In the 1970s, during the early stages of this development, there began to appear a feminist legal theory, though at the time it was generally not labeled as such. As women entered the legal profession in greater numbers, advocates for women's rights began to challenge traditional legal assumptions, such as the "reasonable man" theory described below. Much as with feminist theory in general, during this period most of the arguments focused on women's equality. It was not until the 1980s, when the theoretical work being done in other disciplines reached the law, that feminist legal scholarship began to develop.

Core Concepts

Like feminist theory itself, there is no singular approach or methodology, no single definition of feminism. But there are several core concepts that form the basis of the feminist perspective. First is the centering of women's experience. Women's experiences had long been decentered. In other words, history told men's stories. Women's stories only entered public knowledge when a woman stepped out of her expected role. Legal and social theories ignored what might be important in women's lives because there was little shared. Beginning to bring those experiences to light created the chance for change. For example, it was only by listening to women's experience that sexual harassment was recognized. Out of that recognition came the development of laws.

The second concept is the implicit male bias of the law. We noted earlier that patriarchy functions by creating and enforcing gendered and valued dualisms. Olsen notes that these dualisms privilege the characteristics associated with men (i.e., reason over emotion, abstraction over contextualization).[5] Thus, the law itself, and the law as applied, favors men and disadvantages women. This disadvantage is not necessarily deliberate. As an example, for centuries the standard by which actions were judged by a court to be reasonable rested on the "reasonable man" theory; what would a reasonable man do? This became particularly important in self-defense cases where what a woman—often smaller, not as strong, and not skilled in the fighting arts—might reasonably do would not meet the reasonable man standard. The fact that the law has changed in recent years to refer to the "reasonable person" and in some instances "reasonable woman" has not moved the judgment of the court far from the male-centered standards.

The third concept has been labeled by feminist legal scholars as dilemmas of difference. When challenging the sexism of the law, women are often put in a position where there are no "good" options. An example of this is family leave. Women, and men, have been fighting for fair family leave policies in the United States for several decades. To the extent that fight has been successful, family leave is most often taken following the birth or adoption of a child, and mostly taken by the mother. But in practice taking family leave shows vulnerabilities and an unwillingness to value work over family, both of which are penalized when assessing job performance for raises and promotions.

A fourth concept that is generally recognized in feminist legal theory is the general intractability of patterns of male domination. For instance, when women move into jobs that are predominantly male, they are either isolated in a subfield (i.e., women in medicine are most likely to be family practitioners or ob-gyns, and much less likely to be surgeons), or the job itself loses status, as has occurred in the legal profession.

Lastly, we must explore when a choice is a choice. Here again, the law is a good example. It is often said that women don't become partners in law firms at the same rate as men because women choose to prioritize their lives outside work. But choices are not made in a vacuum. When a woman with a young child doesn't work a one-hundred-hour week, that is hardly a choice. Compound the practical aspects of her life with the powerful social messages of what it means to be a "good" mother, and we can see that the choices we make are often quite constrained.

Feminist Legal Theory Develops

The equal rights approach that dominated feminist theory in the 1960s and 1970s was useful in establishing some rights for women. For example, the Civil Rights Act of 1964 gave women equal access to employment (Title VII) and education (Title IV), both of which have proved to be significant steps toward equality for women. By the 1980s, with talk of women's differences, feminist legal scholarship turned to matters of notable biological difference, such as pregnancy and sexual violence.

Not all feminist legal scholars focused on difference theory. A more progressive critique emerged among feminists focusing on male dominance. Dominance legal theorists critiqued liberal equality theories in many of the same ways radical feminist scholars did, asserting that by employing arguments for individual rights, privacy, and legal objectivity, more traditional scholars were simply extending the status quo. What is really necessary, according to **dominance legal theory**, is to transform the law so that control or dominance of others is no longer acceptable. An example of the agenda of dominance legal theorists was the fight against pornography, which they saw as objectifying women and making them more vulnerable to sexual violence.

The 1990s brought to feminist legal theory what some have called the diversity stage. In contrast to the three earlier decades, feminists began to resist the idea of essentialism, noting that women's experiences are not monolithic. Indeed, experiences, and therefore oppressions, vary and are impacted by race, class, sexual preference, and physical abilities. There has also been a recognition among legal scholars that women not only have different experiences but that they also respond to their oppression in different ways. Therefore, pursuing legal remedies requires acknowledgment of and sensitivity to these various modes of coping. For example, there has been increased recognition that legal and societal responses to intimate violence need to include a range of acceptable remedies.

Late in the 1990s and into the twenty-first century, a critical legal scholarship emerged that focused on a theory first introduced in a 1976 article by Owen Fiss.[6] This theory has come to be known as **antisubordination theory**. Balkin and Siegel explain antisubordination theory as arguing that "guarantees of equal citizenship cannot be realized under conditions of pervasive social stratification and that law should reform institutions and practices that enforce the secondary social status of historically oppressed groups."[7]

The antidiscrimination framework, that which is most commonly used by contemporary courts in addressing, for example, affirmative action cases, can lead to individual members of aggrieved groups receiving differential treatment, without addressing the needs of many and without doing justice to the intent of the equal protection clause of

DOMINANCE THEORY
Similar to radical theory, this theory suggests that to transform law, we need radical restructuring; in this case, we need to remove constructs of control or dominance.

ANTISUBORDINATION THEORY
An early critical legal theory that law should be used to reform institutions of oppression.

the U.S. Constitution. Pursuit of this theory led to another theory, that of **identity performance**. Identity performance focuses on the ways that discrimination can target certain individuals within a group more so than others on the basis of their conduct, dress, and self-presentation. Both of these theories are indicative of what could be the most significant move in feminist legal theory since the turn of the century, which is to join with other critical legal theories—race theory and queer theory, in particular—to posit collective arguments and actions.

Feminists in Criminology

Criminological theory, like law, was (and is) predominantly male oriented. Men comprised a majority of the practitioners and, like law, a majority of those subjected to the system. Feminist theories initially emerged in criminology to explain female offending. Some of the earliest theories incorporated notions of equality theory, stressing that once women are "equal" to men, their offending will mirror men's as well. But as feminist theories moved to examine the unique ways in which women are socialized and by which women perform gender roles, those early theories were dismissed.

While feminist criminology does not focus solely on women but also includes discussions of masculinities, patriarchy, and gender/sexuality, it puts women's lived experiences in the center of inquiry. A unique **feminist methodology** or approach to research has developed in criminology, as it has among feminist theorists in general. This is further explained in chapter 2, but for introductory purposes it is sufficient to understand that the particular mode of research, whether qualitative or quantitative, is less important than, first, listening to women and, second, allowing the mode or method to emerge from the questions asked, rather than letting the chosen method dictate the context and content.

Feminist research in criminology has examined the profound connections between victimization and offending. **Feminist pathways theory** is an example of how, by examining the various ways that life experiences affect the chances of engaging in illegal behaviors, feminist criminologists seek to expand our understanding of all those individuals who find themselves identified as "criminal." Look for more on feminist pathways and other feminist criminological theories as they are presented throughout this text.

Critical Race Theory

Critical legal studies was organized in law schools in the late 1970s as a challenge to "orthodox ideas about the inviolability and objectivity of laws that oppressed minorities and white women for centuries."[8] Because the perspectives of people of color and white women were often excluded by segments of the critical legal studies movement, critical race theory and feminist legal theory developed as separate entities, although they remain in accordance with the critical legal studies perspective. Critical race feminism is an extension of those concepts in that it is a feminist intervention in race discourse and a race intervention in feminist discourse.

Critical race theory, often referred to as the CRT movement, examines the relationships of "race, racism, and power." In contrast to feminist legal theory, which grew out of the seeds of feminism in the academy, CRT began as a movement in the law. In the tradition of critical feminist theory, CRT challenges the basic assumptions of the neoliberal state. Much as we've seen with feminist legal theory, CRT challenges the assumptions of equality theory, questions whether legal reasoning is actually impartial, and asserts that the so-called neutral principles of constitutional law are only neutral for those who created it.

Like feminist theory, CRT contains an element of activism. Some of the particular issues addressed by critical race scholars include the failure of so-called color blindness in law to, for example, successfully integrate and equalize education; examining the ways in which race and class collide as factors subjugating people of color, impacting, for example, the ability to accumulate wealth when restrictions limit access to real estate ownership;

IDENTITY PERFORMANCE
A theory that explores the ways that discrimination can target certain individuals within a group more so than others on the basis of their conduct, dress, and self-presentation.

FEMINIST METHODOLOGY
A model of epistemology that suggests we give voice to that which we seek to understand.

FEMINIST PATHWAYS THEORY
A theory that explores how our lived experiences impact our life course or path.

CRITICAL RACE THEORY
A collection of theories that examine the relationships of race, racism, and power.

and power, especially that used by the criminal/legal system to profile, incarcerate, and disenfranchise people of color.

Queer Theory and the Law

Queer theory builds on feminist theories that challenge whether gender is at the core of our identity and examines the socially constructed nature of sexuality and our sexual identities. Queer theory suggests that gender and sexuality are fluid, not fixed, and that one may have different experiences of gender and sexuality over the course of one's life. As with feminist and race theories, queer theory examines discourse and our choices and use of language. The very label of "queer" is the result of an evolution in the nature of language.

Queer legal theory is, more specifically, a body of scholarship that gives a voice to the interests of sexual minorities in the pursuit of ending sex/gender subordination and to help promote egalitarianism and equality. Part of the agenda for queer legal theory includes challenging heteropatriarchal norms, including diverse voices and narratives in legal decision making, and moving beyond the constitutional notion of sexuality as privacy by showing the very public economic, social, and political impacts of discrimination on the basis of gender and sexual representation, a good example being the situation of LGBTQ people in the military.

These critical legal theories are seeing growing recognition as their perspectives appear increasingly in law review articles and in legal opinions issued by the courts.

THE GENDERED PRACTICE OF LAW

The number of women attending law school has grown exponentially in the past several decades. In 1968, women were 6 percent of law students. That number grew to 16 percent in 1973 and 42 percent by 1988. In 2016, the number of women enrolled in law schools exceeded the number of men; that trend continues. Of law students in 2018, 18.5 percent were "minority" women. Approximately 7 percent defined themselves as African American and 7 percent as Hispanic. It is notable, however, that women are still below 50 percent in fourteen of what are considered the twenty best law schools, and as low as 41.3 percent at Duke University.[9]

The first woman admitted to the bar in the United States was Arabella Mansfield, admitted to the Iowa bar in 1869. In 1872, Charlotte E. Ray became the first African American female lawyer. Today almost half of the associates in law firms are women, and about 15 percent of those are women of color. All of this might suggest that women have overcome obstacles impeding their success in the practice of law. But that seems not to be the case. In 2019, women comprise 22.7 percent of partners, and less than one in five, or 19 percent, of equity partners, those people entitled to share the profits, are women. Women of color face an even steeper climb; for them, those numbers are 6 percent and 3 percent, respectively.[10]

In the past thirty years, many books and articles have been published addressing issues of sexual harassment, discrimination, and inhospitable working conditions faced by women in the legal profession. Studies indicate that there is widespread discontent among lawyers, especially women, and more so for women of color. But when asked if gender discrimination is an issue, most lawyers—mostly male lawyers—say it is no longer a problem. In contrast, a study published in 2017 found that, controlling for all other variables, female lawyers arguing before the U.S. Supreme Court were interrupted earlier in their argument, interrupted more often, and given less time to respond between interruptions than their male counterparts.[11] It appears that despite the addition of female justices, discrimination is not just a thing of the past.

Attorneys leave the profession in fairly high numbers. Exact data on the numbers is difficult to find, but one study found that of lawyers who passed the bar in 2000, about 24 percent were not practicing law in 2012.[12] Research on why this might be the case involves

QUEER LEGAL THEORY
A body of scholarship that gives a voice to the interests of sexual minorities in the pursuit of ending sex/gender subordination and to help promote egalitarianism and equality.

two broad topics. Most common are studies that examine working conditions within the practice of law—the long hours, the lack of accommodation for family, the continuing presence of sexual harassment, and the glass ceiling or missed opportunities for advancement. According to a 2006 study done by the American Bar Association,

> Thirty-two percent of women of color and 39 percent of white women reported missing out on desirable assignments because of gender; 46 percent of women of color and 60 percent of white women reported that they were denied informal or formal networking opportunities because of gender; 32 percent of women of color and 55 percent of white women reported having missed client development and client relationship opportunities because of gender; and 14 percent of women of color and 28 percent of white women reported that they were denied advancement and promotion opportunities because of gender.[13]

One particular example is work-life balance, something that has put more pressure on women's professional choices than on men's.

A second line of research examines the nature of law as a masculinist endeavor and explores the manner in which women do or do not adapt. Studies range from an observation of the emotional life of a law firm to studies of women in particular fields of practice, most notably as defense lawyers or in large private law firms. The former study says of emotional work that it is "directly related to Marx's theory of alienation. That is human beings pay a piece of their emotional selves when they work for others."[14] The emotional work referred to in these studies includes relationship building, rationalizing choices, and sometimes conscious distancing from others. Most of this emotional work seems to fall on women. As one researcher notes, "male lawyers tended to talk about themselves and their feelings as if they were separate entities."[15] Many of the women in these studies have developed strategies for adaptation, many others strive to emulate the traditional "male lawyer," and many choose to leave the profession. As with any other discussion that teeters on the verge of essentialism, these studies walk a delicate balance. A prominent feminist legal scholar warns that focusing on women's different approach to resolving disputes risks continuing the stereotypes that suggest that women can't be aggressive enough to be litigators. It could be argued that the issue isn't whether women "can" be sufficiently aggressive to litigate (to take the most commonly used example) but whether they might choose to do so, and at what personal cost.

In the next chapter, we will review a range of criminological theories, including mainstream theories, critical theories, and emerging theories such as LGBTQ theory (queer theory), masculinity, and feminist pathways.

REVIEW AND STUDY QUESTIONS

1. How does intersectionality theory help us understand the impact of gender in our lives?
2. Why is it important to include race in our consideration of gender? In what ways do race and gender intersect? How are they similar? How are they different?
3. Of the various feminist theories presented in this chapter, which makes most sense to you and why?
4. Can you think of specific times when your gender or gender identification affected the way you were treated? What were the circumstances surrounding that occasion? How did you react? Did it have an ongoing impact on you?

GOING FURTHER

Readings:

Wollstonecraft, Mary. *A Vindication of the Rights of Woman*. First published in 1792.

Websites:

Twelfth Annual Women in the Law Conference. Links to other articles of interest. https://www.northeastern.edu/law/alumni/news/women-law.

Videos/Movies:

RBG. a documentary about the life of the second female to serve on the U.S. Supreme Court, Ruth Bader Ginsburg. Magnolia Pictures, 2018.

On the Basis of Sex. A fictionalized movie about Ginsburg's early career. Focus Features, 2018.

KEY TERMS

antisubordination theory An early critical legal theory that law should be used to reform institutions of oppression.

coverture A legal doctrine that said that when a man and woman married, they became one legal person: the man. Therefore, a married woman had no independent legal identity to sue or be sued, contract, or retain or control finances.

critical race theory A collection of theories that examine the relationships of race, racism, and power.

cult of domesticity Another term for the sphere occupied by women.

difference feminism A response to equality theory, difference theory posits that only by recognizing gender differences, or what makes us unique, can we address gender inequality.

dominance theory Similar to radical theory, this theory suggests that to transform law, we need radical restructuring; in this case, we need to remove constructs of control or dominance.

epistemology The philosophy of knowledge or how we acquire and make sense of what we learn; how we know what we know.

equality theory A theory that states that all people should be treated equally, no matter one's gender.

feminist methodology A model of epistemology that suggests we give voice to that which we seek to understand.

feminist pathways theory A theory that explores how our lived experiences impact our life course or path.

first-wave feminism If the movement known as "feminism" could be defined by points in time, or waves, the first wave began with the Seneca Falls Convention in 1848 and continued into the 1920s.

fourth-wave feminism The contemporary feminist movement, emphasizing empowerment, inclusion, and activism.

heteronormativity The belief that heterosexuality, or relations between people of the opposite sex, is the cultural norm.

hierarchy Any system of dominance that prioritizes one thing, or one person, over another.

identity performance A theory that explores the ways that discrimination can target certain individuals within a group more so than others on the basis of their conduct, dress, and self-presentation.

intersectional theories Theories that recognize that our lives are shaped by many aspects of our identification, including race, class, gender, and heteronormativity.

neoliberalism A social and economic philosophy that advocates for an extreme version of free-market capitalism, deregulation of markets, and elimination of the role of government, as in welfare.

Nineteenth Amendment The amendment to the U.S. Constitution that gave women the right to vote.

patriarchy A system in which men hold primary authority and control over role definitions and power.

queer legal theory A body of scholarship that gives a voice to the interests of sexual minorities in the pursuit of ending sex/gender subordination and to help promote egalitarianism and equality.

radical feminism A theory suggesting that without radically altering society and social relations, gender equality can never be achieved.

second-wave feminism The period of the feminist movement from the 1920s through the 1970s.

Seneca Falls Convention This convention brought together three hundred men and women who rallied for the equality of women to be recognized.

separate sphere A social construct that separates the public parts of life from the private and, by definition, restricts women, and whatever occurs within a family, to the private sphere.

standpoint theory A theory that suggests we need to change the lens through which we view, describe, and understand the world from a patriarchal or hierarchical lens to one that is more accepting of differences.

third-wave feminism A period of feminism beginning in the 1980s that decentered the movement, recognizing racial and gender diversity.

Voting Rights Act An act signed into law in 1965 to prohibit discriminatory voting practices.

NOTES

[1] *Bradwell v. The State*, 83 U.S. 130, 141–42 (1873).

[2] Lesbian, gay, bisexual, transgender, queer. The currently extended acronym is "LGBTQIAAP," which includes intersex, asexual, ally, and pansexual, but this book mainly examines intersections between the justice system and LGBTQ communities and individuals. Therefore, "LGBTQ" will be used.

[3] Martha Rampton, "Four Waves of Feminism," *Pacific Magazine*, 2008.

[4] Sojourner Truth, "Ain't I a Woman?," in *Feminism: The Essential Historical Writings*, ed. M. Schneir (New York: Random House, 1972).

⁵ Fran Olsen, "The Sex of Law," in *The Politics of Law: A Progressive Critique*, David Kairys, 2nd ed. (New York: Basic Books, 1998).

⁶ Owen M. Fiss, "Groups and the Equal Protection Clause," *Philosophy and Public Affairs* 5, no. 2 (Winter 1976): 107–77.

⁷ Jack M. Balkin and Reva B. Siegel, "American Civil Rights Tradition: Anticlassification or Antisubordination?," *Issues in Legal Scholarship* 2, no. 1 (2003).

⁸ Cornell West, foreword to *Critical Race Theory: The Key Writings That Formed the Movement*, ed. Kimberlé Crenshaw, Kendall Thomas, Gary Peller, and Neil Gotanda (New York: New Press, 1995).

⁹ "Law School Data, Class Enrollment by Gender and Race/Ethnicity (Aggregate)," American Bar Association, Fall 2018, https://www.americanbar.org/groups/legal_education/resources/statistics.

¹⁰ Commission on Women in the Profession, *A Current Glance at Women in the Law* (Chicago: American Bar Association, April 2019), https://www.americanbar.org/content/dam/aba/administrative/women/current_glance_2019.pdf.

¹¹ Dana Patton and Joseph L. Smith, "Lawyer, Interrupted: Gender Bias in Oral Arguments at the US Supreme Court," *Journal of Law and Courts* 5, no. 2 (Fall 2017).

¹² Debra Cassens Weiss, "'After the JD' Study Shows Many Leave Law Practice," *ABA Journal Magazine*, April 1, 2014.

¹³ "Law School Data, Class Enrollment by Gender and Race/Ethnicity."

¹⁴ Cynthia Siemsen, *Emotional Trials: The Moral Dilemmas of Women Criminal Defense Attorneys* (Boston, MA: Northeastern University Press, 2004), 163.

¹⁵ Jennifer L. Pierce, *Gender Trials: Emotional Lives in Contemporary Law Firms* (Berkeley: University of California Press, 1995), 132.

Crime Theory

In this chapter we review criminological theories, with a particular focus on critical, gender, and intersectional theories. You will read about how we create knowledge and the profound role media plays in shaping our understanding of the world around us.

LEARNING OBJECTIVES

After reading this chapter, you should be able to do the following:

- Explain basic concepts in criminology theory.
- Describe how criminology theory has moved from classical theorists to critical race theories.
- Distinguish feminist methodology from traditional methodology.
- Analyze the impact media has on how we define crime and criminals.

Case #2: The Central Park Five

Late evening, April 19, 1989: Trisha Meili went for a jog after a long day at her job as an investment banker at Salomon Brothers, taking her usual route through Central Park in Manhattan. Trisha could not envision how the night would end.

At the same time, a group of teenagers was entering the park—there were between thirty and forty boys—and during the course of the evening, police responded to multiple reports of teenagers threatening, robbing, and physically harassing and attacking other park-goers, including joggers. Scattered among this large group were five boys— Antron McCray, Kevin Richardson, Yusef Salaam, Raymond Santana, and Korey Wise. The boys were from Harlem, typical high school students that liked sports and music. Some of them knew each other; some of them didn't. All of them were between fourteen and sixteen years old.

Later that night, Meili was discovered by passersby, brutally beaten and lying limp and unconscious in a ditch. Ambulances that arrived on the scene found her tied up, bleeding from several serious lacerations on her head and elsewhere, and clearly in critical condition. It was later found that Meili had been knocked out and then violently sexually assaulted. Doctors would report that it was a near miracle that she had survived. She had lost the majority of her blood and had several skull fractures from blunt force blows to the head, as well as a shattered eye socket and severe damage to the eye within it. She would be in a coma for nearly two weeks.

When police received the call about Meili in the wee hours of April 20, their suspicions turned to the teenagers about whom they had been receiving reports all night. McCray, Richardson, Salaam, Santana, and Wise were all picked up by the police on April 20, and after a long period of questioning in separate rooms, four of them confessed to the rape and assault of Meili; all but Salaam eventually provided written or recorded confessions. Being that most of the boys were only fourteen or fifteen years old, the law required that their parents or other responsible adults were present for interrogation, but even their parents were not quite clear what was at stake. The initial hours of the interrogation were not recorded, and so the lines of questioning that resulted in the boys' confessions, as well as their willingness to eventually commit their confessions to video recording, are unclear. What was clear, however, was that the details that each boy provided contradicted the facts of the case, the details given by the others, and even their own stories of what happened. Their stories—about their own actions, about the actions of the others, and about the details of the case, including what Meili had been wearing and what sorts of injuries she suffered—continued to change. Nevertheless, within a week, all of them would face various charges, including rape, assault, rioting, and

attempted murder, and they would be endlessly attacked by the press and the public.

The boys and their parents would later report that they had been told that if they would simply confess, they would get to leave, and that they were not informed of the potential severity of the charges they faced. All of them would later withdraw their confessions. The initial confessions were enough, however; the police, as well as public opinion, determined that the boys were guilty. Media coverage of the story began almost immediately, and when the public got the story that was unfolding, they were fed stories of violent young boys of color and an innocent victim. The boys were referred to as a "wolf pack," as "monsters," and as men, despite the fact that they were all in their mid-teens.

New York City was experiencing a spike in violent crime in the 1980s, especially in the latter part of the decade. With the growing presence of crack cocaine, homicide rates hovering around two thousand per year, and increasing tension between the rising wealth on Wall Street and the deepening poverty of other city neighborhoods, the case involving a young, white investment banker and the boys of color that allegedly attacked her channeled this tension like a lightning rod. There were more than three thousand reported rapes in New York City that year. There had been another report of sexual assault in the park only a few days earlier, and more than two dozen in the past week alone, but Meili's case got the most prominent position in the headlines, perhaps because of the brutality of the crime, or perhaps because the case reflected the deeply complicated dynamics of gender, race, and criminal justice that were playing out across the city.

After nearly two weeks, Meili emerged from her coma. Her recovery would be incredibly slow, physically and cognitively; simple acts such as walking would have to be relearned, both because of her musculoskeletal injuries and because of the traumatic brain injury she had suffered, which impacted her balance and coordination. Meili remained in the hospital for months for all sorts of treatment and rehabilitation, including physical therapy and specialized treatment for survivors of sexual assault. Incredibly, despite her shattered eye socket and the damage that had been done to her eye itself, surgeons were able to restore her vision, and over the course of several months, she was able to not only walk but begin to run. Despite her milestones toward recovery, however, she was unable to remember anything that happened on the night she was attacked and was only able to piece it together based on information from others. In fact, Meili has no memory of the hours leading up to the attack, nor of more than a month that followed it.

Meanwhile, the following year, New York City assembled a team of prosecutors that were known for being efficient and effective. In the summer of 1990, McCray,

Salaam, and Santana went to trial, and the case built by the prosecutors relied heavily on the taped confessions, as they had no concrete physical evidence or any DNA tying the boys to the scene of the crime; there was DNA from the attacker found on Meili, but it did not match any of the five boys. The defense asked the jury to consider the absence of physical evidence and the validity of the confessions, as well as the contradictions and inconsistencies that might suggest that the confessions were false. In the middle of August 1990, after a trial that had lasted for several weeks and jury deliberation of ten days, all three were convicted of rape and assault. In early December, after a trial that closely mirrored the first, Richardson was also convicted of all counts of rape and assault, while Wise was convicted of sexual abuse, assault, and rioting. All but Wise were sentenced to five to ten years and sent to juvenile detention facilities; at sixteen, Wise was treated as an adult and sentenced to up to fifteen years to be served at Rikers Island. Half of the city rejoiced, feeling that justice had been done; the other half mourned, feeling that injustice, rather than justice, had marked the case from beginning to end. This, however, was not the end of the story.

The four youngest boys—Antron McCray, Kevin Richardson, Yusef Salaam, and Raymond Santana—each served about seven or eight years, and each of them were released at different points in the late 1990s. Korey Wise remained in prison until 2002, when the story of the Central Park Five, which had largely disappeared from public memory, reemerged.

In 2002, a man by the name of Matias Reyes came forward to confess to the crime. He was already a convicted rapist who had, in the same year that the Central Park incident had taken place, been dubbed the "East Side Rapist." The case shot back into national media as the New York City district attorney's office reopened the case to examine the potential validity of Reyes's confession. When they did, it was found that his DNA matched the DNA that was found on Meili thirteen years earlier. It was also found that Reyes matched the description of an attacker that had been given to police by a woman who had been sexually assaulted in the park on April 17, 1989, just two days before Meili was attacked. The survivor of the attack on April 17 had told police that her attacker had visible stitches on his chin, and though a detective had heard from a local hospital that they had seen a man who fit that description and had even been provided Reyes's name, there was no follow-up, and the case had not been connected to the events on April 19. It would later be discovered that Reyes had assaulted and raped several more women, murdering one of them, before he was eventually arrested in mid-June 1989. All this took place while McCray, Richardson, Salaam, Santana, and Wise were in detention and awaiting trial. Reyes was moved to confess, he said, because he had experienced a spiritual awakening in prison, and when he had crossed paths with Wise in 2001, he discovered that he could not abide by these five men being imprisoned for a crime that he had committed. Reyes's confession, unlike the confessions that had once been given by McCray, Richardson, Santana, and Wise, reflected accurate details about Meili's attack. Asked what this new confession meant to her, Meili—who up to this point had been known only as the "Central Park jogger" but decided to reveal her identity in 2003—responded, "If he is telling the truth, it's a horrible thing if innocent people are sent to prison and—it only adds to the tragedy of that evening."[1]

In response to this new evidence, District Attorney Robert Morgenthau, who had worked on the original case, recommended that all the convictions be vacated, and in 2002, the convictions were indeed overturned. Again, however, the story does not end there.

Representatives of the New York City Police Department, after an internal investigation, maintained that their investigation had been sound and that there had been no coercion meant to elicit confessions from the boys. Some members of the district attorney's office were also reluctant to acknowledge the overturning of the convictions as a judgment of innocence. Meili shared that she was also skeptical of Reyes's story, particularly his assertion that he had acted alone. Reflecting on the various layers of the case that continued to be exposed, Meili said, "I always knew that there was at least one more person involved because there was unidentified DNA. . . . So when I heard the news that there was an additional person found whose DNA matched, that wasn't a tremendous surprise. But when he said that he and he alone had done it, that's when some of the turmoil started, wondering 'Well, how can that be?'"[2] Her memory of the attack remains irretrievable to this day.

The vacated convictions and renewal of the discussion about the case brought out its deeper dimensions once again. Salaam, discussing the recorded confessions, explains: "If you take an individual that's fifteen years old, and you put that individual in a room by themselves with two to four to six officers, some of them wanting to attack you, that individual would be terrified. It could be almost tantamount to someone having a gun to your head."[3] Others agree, recalling the ways that their respective interrogators coerced them to provide confessions: they report that they were told that there was evidence implicating them, that others had confessed, or that if they pointed fingers at each other, they would get to leave. Salaam also addresses the question of race in the way that their case played out: "I think race played a big role. Had we been white youths, they probably would have, you know, contacted the legal aid people and probably had some lawyers down there to speak to us, but because we were from Black and Latin communities, because we were from—some of us—impoverished homes, it's like 'hey—who's gonna mind that another Black youth or another Latin youth is off the street? They're criminals anyway.'"[4]

McCray, Richardson, Salaam, Santana, and Wise pushed forward to initiate a federal lawsuit on the grounds that their civil rights had been violated. The lawsuit was slow to immobile for the better part of a decade, until attention to the case reignited. A book about their case by writer and filmmaker Sarah Burns was released in 2011, and a documentary film to accompany the book was released the following year by Sarah Burns, Ken Burns, and David McMahon. The book and the film were instrumental in drawing attention back to the case and compelling New York City to settle, and McCray, Richardson, Salaam, Santana, and Wise were finally awarded a settlement of $41 million in 2014. Some members of city law enforcement and prosecutors that had been with the case for decades were outraged by this decision, and Meili herself was not comfortable with the settlement. Meili said, "I so wish the case hadn't been settled. I wish that it had gone to court because there's a lot of information that's now being released that I'm seeing for the first time. I support the work of law enforcement and prosecutors at the time. They treated me with such dignity and respect."[5] Others—among them lawyers and legal scholars, activists, reporters and journalists that have covered the story since its beginning, and more—see the settlement as a major victory for civil rights and an acknowledgment of years of unjust imprisonment and condemnation of innocent boys.

Trisha Meili released a memoir in 2003 called *I Am the Central Park Jogger*, and she now advocates for survivors of sexual assault and traumatic injury. She returned to banking after the attack but realized after a few years back on Wall Street that she felt called to support the rehabilitation and healing of others.

The discussion about sexual assault, race, racism, and civil rights was a central feature of the public response to their case when it occurred, and the discussion continues at every reemergence of the case. In fact, the discussion still continues. In 2015, the Colorado School of Law's Innocence Project, which provides legal support and advocacy for those who maintain that they have been wrongfully convicted, was renamed the Korey Wise Innocence Project after Wise donated enough to provide for a full-time director of the project. And, in 2019, acclaimed filmmaker Ava DuVernay released a docuseries about the case, *When They See Us*, which once again brought the story into the public eye.

THINKING CRITICALLY ABOUT THE CASE

1. Why were law enforcement officers and prosecutors willing to overlook the lack of evidence to convict the Central Park Five?

2. What may have compelled the boys to confess to a crime they did not commit?

3. Why was the language used about the boys in media coverage important to the case as a whole?

REFERENCES

This case is adapted from the following sources:

"The Central Park Jogger: After 14 Years, Woman at Center of Famous Case Reveals Identity." *Dateline NBC*, December 8, 2003. http://www.nbcnews.com/id/3080050/ns/dateline_nbc-newsmakers/t/central-park-jogger/#.XPaY6ohKg2x.

Cobb, Jelani. "The Central Park Five, Criminal Justice, and Donald Trump." *New Yorker*, April 19, 2019. https://www.newyorker.com/news/daily-comment/the-central-park-five-criminal-justice-and-donald-trump.

"'I So Wish the Case Hadn't Been Settled': 1989 Central Park Jogger Believes More than 1 Person Attacked Her." ABC News, May 23, 2019. https://abcnews.go.com/US/case-settled-1989-central-park-jogger-believes-person/story?id=63077131.

Welsh, Susan, Keren Schiffman, and Enjoli Francis. "Looking Back at the 1989 Central Park Jogger Rape Case That Led to 5 Teens' Conviction, Later Vacated." ABC News, May 24, 2019. https://abcnews.go.com/US/back-1989-central-park-jogger-rape-case-led/story?id=63084663.

"Wrongfully Convicted 'Central Park Five' Defendant Makes Gift Renaming Innocence Project." University of Colorado Law School, December 9, 2015. https://www.colorado.edu/law/2015/12/09/wrongfully-convicted-central-park-five-defendant-makes-gift-renaming-innocence-project.

CONTEXT AND ANALYSIS

In chapter 2, we review a range of criminological theories, some generally applicable and others specifically designed to address variables such as gender, race, and power. For many of you, this will be a review, but it is useful to reexamine these theories.

You will read about feminist methodology. All research begins with a problem. Your methodology is defined by how you understand the world (**ontology**), how you create knowledge (epistemology), and the model you use for gathering data (research design). There is no one definition of feminist methodology, just as there is no one definition of feminism, but you will learn about the characteristics that distinguish feminist research from more traditional methodologies.

Lastly, you will get an introduction to the role media plays in creating and stereotyping victims and offenders. As you read in the Central Park Five case study, the media has extraordinary power to influence both the public's perceptions and the criminal/legal system's responses.

As you're reading about these theories, think about which ones were used to explain the behaviors in the Central Park Five case.

REVIEW OF CRIMINOLOGICAL THEORIES

What follows is not a comprehensive look at criminological theories but an overview to familiarize those who have not studied these theories in depth, and a refresher for those who have. We begin with classical theories and progress toward more contemporary theories, especially those reflecting the values of intersectionality and gender inclusivity.

Individual/Psychological Perspective

The earliest "theories" of crime assigned criminal behavior to the devil, much like what we saw in the Salem witch trials (detailed in *Crime and Justice: Learning through Cases*). While those ideas, and the inquisitions that accompanied them, were debunked, we continue to see them practiced, for example in the so-called war on drugs being carried out by the president of the Philippines, where the national police have killed thousands.

The 1700s saw a period of social theorizing and scientific development that came to be known as the Enlightenment. It was during this time that the classical school of criminology emerged (though it is notable that the actual use of the term "criminology" did not enter the lexicon until the twentieth century). A characteristic of that time was the social contract, and along with it the belief that individuals were **hedonistic**, that is, they would naturally maximize pleasure and minimize pain. The most notable contributors to the development of classical criminology were Cesare Beccaria and Jeremy Bentham. Beccaria claimed authorship of an essay titled *On Crimes and Punishments* that became very successful. In it he wrote that punishment should be proportional, that it should be "swift and certain," and that the death penalty was evil and should be avoided. Bentham agreed with Beccaria in many ways and stressed that deterrence should only be used to the extent that it will prevent someone from acting; it should not be used in excess, needlessly, or to punish. What Bentham is most famous for is the **panopticon**,

> a building circular . . . the prisoners in their cells, occupying the circumference—The officers in the centre. By blinds and other contrivances, the Inspectors concealed . . . from the observation of the prisoners: hence the sentiment of a sort of omnipresence—The whole circuit reviewable with little, or . . . without any, change of place. One station in the inspection part affording the most perfect view of every cell.[6]

Classical theory reemerged in the 1980s in what is referred to as neoclassical theory. This theory focuses on deterrence, claiming that if punishment is harsh enough, people will use a cost-benefit analysis and determine that it is not worth following through with

ONTOLOGY
A branch of philosophy that studies the nature of existence, things, and their being or identity.

HEDONISTIC
A person who seeks only to maximize pleasure and minimize pain.

PANOPTICON
Literally meaning "all seeing," it is a building created with a central observation tower and surrounding wings that can be observed from the central point. Today it is a model for jails and prisons, but also schools and other institutional buildings.

whatever criminal act they are contemplating. This theory persists, despite a large body of research that suggests punishment does not deter crime. Indeed, for most acts that violate the law, it is unlikely that consequences enter the calculations for most individuals when contemplating certain behaviors that have been deemed criminal.

Among the theories that place the nexus of criminal behavior with the individual are ones that contend that the individual suffers from physical or psychological defects. From the earliest biological theories that relied on the bone structure of a person's skull, the "science" of **phrenology**, to contemporary theories such as "low IQ" or the "presence of XYY chromosomes," scientists have sought to attribute criminal behavior to one's biology. This science has been largely debunked, but that hasn't stopped popular culture from imagining that a sugar imbalance could make you commit a crime. (In the 1970s, Dan White, who killed San Francisco mayor George Moscone and supervisor Harvey Milk, got a reduced sentence for what became known as the "Twinkie defense.")

Psychological theories are also about the individual's (versus society's) characteristics. The first psychological theories were Freudian and explain criminal behavior, as all other behavior, as a result of conflicts between the **id**, the **ego**, and the **superego**. Other psychological theories identify personality disorders as the cause of criminal behavior. There are numerous variations on this idea, the most commonly referenced being **sociopathy** and **psychopathy**; both are considered antisocial personality disorders. Mood disorders such as depression, mania, and schizophrenia are often thought of as being predictive of criminal behavior. Since the deinstitutionalization of mental health services, the number of individuals with mood disorders in the criminal/legal system has grown exponentially. Yet data indicates that there is no correlation between mental illness and crime, with the possible exception of sociopathy and psychopathy, which by definition include an inability to live within the norms and laws of society.

Sociological Theories

Social Ecology

Social ecology theorists suggest that crime is not rooted in the individual but arises out of the physical, social, and cultural contexts of human activity. These theories derive from the early work of social ecologists Shaw and McKay, who sought to understand a person's relationship to his or her social and physical environment. Their social disorganization theory limited its focus to poverty, racial/ethnic heterogeneity, and residential mobility as measures of deteriorating neighborhoods. Contemporary social ecologists have reanalyzed this approach to reflect a changing society. This newer perspective constructs the social disorganization/social ecology model more broadly, defining the internal dynamics of a community and its ability to regulate behavior. The variables that researchers identify as most important in understanding social disorganization are median family income, percent below poverty rate, percent people of color, percent of children under eighteen years old, percent of children not living with both parents, and population density.

Strain

One of the earliest social theories of why crime occurs came from one of the most significant sociological thinkers of the late nineteenth and early twentieth centuries, Émile Durkheim. Durkheim believed crime was inevitable and natural in a society. He referred to it as a "social fact." He believed that some, but not all, crime served a function in society, that it helped society to define and affirm its norms and values. In this analysis, crime will never completely disappear. As we "decriminalize" one behavior, we will create a new one to set the social boundary. And as we condemn one actor for unacceptable behavior, we reinforce our social bond.

Crime is likely to increase, according to Durkheim, when individuals, and more so society as a whole, experience a state of normlessness, or what he called **anomie**. Durkheim created the concept while studying suicide. He found that in periods of social anxiety and disruption, such as war or economic disaster, individuals were more likely

---

PHRENOLOGY
A branch of science that examines cranial (skull) structure to determine a range of characteristics; at one time used to determine a predisposition to crime, also used by the Nazis to determine ethnicity.

ID, EGO, AND SUPEREGO
A concept developed by Sigmund Freud that describes three elements that together comprise the human personality.

SOCIOPATHY
Considered to be the result of environmental factors, sociopaths tend to be erratic and impulsive and have difficulty forming attachments. Sociopaths have difficulty holding down a job and conforming to societal norms.

PSYCHOPATHY
Believed to be a genetic predisposition resulting in underdeveloped brain regulation of emotions. As a consequence, psychopaths have little or no ability to form emotional attachments or feel empathy. They can often appear to be living within social norms. While some of the most well-known serial killers are believed to be psychopaths, some are CEOs of major corporations.

ANOMIE
A state of social unrest or rapid social change, when social norms are unclear or not enforced.

to feel adrift and more likely to kill themselves. But anomie could also arise from rapid social change, as he saw in the move from traditional agrarian society to an industrial one, and, as we have witnessed, in the increased role that technology plays in defining our social relationships. He explained how this led to suicide—or crime—by saying that being in a state of anomie increased the likelihood of experiencing **strain**, which then led to norm-violating behaviors.

Durkheim's idea of strain was further developed, and significantly altered, by Robert K. Merton in a work first published in 1938 and in the lifetime of work that followed. Unlike Durkheim, who saw the flaw that resulted in violating norms as often personal, arising from critical breakdowns in society and an individual's failure to adapt, Merton believed that crime was rooted in the larger society and was in fact pervasive. This belief was reinforced by examining the widely variant crime rates across countries and in the violent culture that existed (and continues to exist) in the United States.

Merton saw two essential elements that defined social structure: goals and means to achieve those goals. Goals are those things that are socially defined expectations. For instance, in the United States, the belief in the American dream dictates a definition of success that is measured by your monetary status. Institutionalized means, as Merton defined them, represent the socially acceptable or legitimate ways we provide for individuals to achieve goals. In a perfect world, everyone would have access to institutionalized means, but that is often not the case. The disjuncture between goals and means creates anomie.

According to Merton, there are five possible ways for an individual to adapt, what he refers to as the modes of adaptation. Each measures the extent to which goals and socially defined means are accepted or rejected. Each results in different individual outcomes. *Conformity*, which is the most common, refers to those individuals who accept the goals and the idea of legitimate means, even if they may not have access to those means. *Innovation* describes those individuals who believe in the goal but, believing they cannot access it by legitimate means, devise illegitimate avenues. Recognizing that this occurs at all levels of society, Merton believed that this is the most common adaptation among the working class. For example, if you believe in the socially defined goal of making money as the measure of success but have no access to jobs that can help you acquire wealth, you might "innovate" by thievery or drug dealing. Innovators are typically defined as **deviant**. *Ritualism* describes individuals who accept the social means, thereby following the rules, though they reject the goal. Ritualism is tolerated by society, though often viewed as deviant due to the individual's rejection of widely held values and expectations. *Retreatism* defines those who reject both the goal and the means. Merton defined this group as dropouts, vagrants, and drug addicts, although as some theorists point out, these individuals might not have retreated if they'd had access to success. Lastly, Merton presents *rebellion*. Rebellion describes those people who reject socially accepted goals and means, but rather than "dropping out," rebels create new goals and new means by which to achieve them.[7]

TABLE 2.1	Modes of Adaptation	
Mode of Adaptation	**Cultural Goals**	**Institutionalized Means**
Conformity	accept	accept
Innovation	accept	reject
Ritualism	reject	accept
Retreatism	reject	reject
Rebellion	reject/replace	reject/replace

STRAIN
The anxiety or uncertainty an individual might experience in a state of anomie.

DEVIANT
A term used to describe anyone who deviates or differs from the social norm.

Merton's theory has been criticized for not addressing all crime, though he says that was never his intent. One critic, Albert K. Cohen, suggested that Merton's ideas only applied to adults and that most juvenile crime was not innovative, as Merton described, but expressive. Cohen describes juvenile motivations as hedonistic, nonutilitarian, malicious, and negativistic. He also notes that juveniles, unlike adults, regularly engage in destructive acts as a group, rather than individually. Youth, he posits, who are otherwise denied status (his term is **status frustration**), create their own subcultures, such as gangs, where they can redefine status that is achievable. Cohen's theory is described as a strain-subculture theory. Cohen's theory is largely criticized as only being a theory that applies to working-class male behavior.

One further development in the strain theories we have just reviewed is that made by Richard Cloward and Lloyd Ohlin. Their theory is called differential opportunity theory. Differential opportunity theory attempts to combine Merton and Cohen. It states that it isn't just legitimate opportunities that are differently available, but also illegitimate ones. Individuals living in communities with limited opportunities will adapt to those limitations by resorting to illegitimate opportunities, but only if those illegitimate opportunities are available. They define three distinct deviant subcultures: criminal subculture, where career criminals already have a stake in the community and can interact with youth; conflict subculture, where gangs are created by the juveniles; and retreatist subculture, where individuals cannot access either legitimate or illegitimate opportunities and therefore drop out. As with other such theories, Cloward and Ohlin's theory is criticized for only focusing on the criminalization of working-class males.

While Merton and Cohen focus on structural limitations to success, Robert Agnew, in his general strain theory, focuses on individual sources of strain, highlighting the failure to achieve positive goals, the loss of positive influences, and the introduction of negative influences as precursors to deviant behaviors among boys and girls. The first strain theorist to include girls, Agnew (in a work he coauthored with Lisa Broidy) noted that it is important to remember that females often have different sources of strain than males, as they are more likely to experience violence in the home, for example, and that they react differently than males, with girls more likely to internalize their anger. Agnew's theory, especially as it applies to females, has been the subject of much research in the past decade. Researchers have examined the link between strain and daily substance abuse, for example, and have found that relationships are a major source of strain for females.[8]

Economic Deprivation

Economic deprivation theory is yet another contemporary interpretation of strain theory, suggesting that the value of money in American society is associated with power and success. It is a measure of achievement beyond its utility for buying goods for consumption. As a result, attaining money is an ongoing goal in itself. A large body of research has examined the relationship between crime and economic deprivation, both **absolute deprivation** and **relative deprivation**. That research has been diverse and complex and often inconclusive.

Absolute deprivation theory maintains that increased poverty, or absolute economic deprivation, produces high rates of crime because the struggle to obtain basic life necessities likely produces strain that may encourage hostilities to escalate, often resulting in violence. The deprivation associated with limited economic resources can also weaken social controls because extreme economic deprivation is demoralizing, leading to a decline in confidence in the conventional order and social controls.

On the other hand, relative deprivation theory argues that greater relative deprivation, or economic inequality, is responsible for conflict and hostilities that may lead to violent crime. The *income inequality approach* focuses on the differences of income distribution within a community. This approach suggests that some people measure their economic position in relation to others so that their absolute poverty is not as important to them. According to this view, frustration, which leads to violence, occurs when an individual believes that other people have more desired social and economic resources.

STATUS FRUSTRATION
An expression to describe when a person, especially youth, are unable to obtain status in a manner that is socially acceptable.

ABSOLUTE DEPRIVATION
A term used to describe a situation when a person is so poor they are unable to obtain such basic necessities as food and shelter.

RELATIVE DEPRIVATION
A term used to describe a situation when, in an affluent society, a person does not have access to the measures of comfort or affluence available to many.

Interactionist Theories

Interactionist theories are based on the idea that actions are not meaningful until we define them. In other words, it is our interaction with others that gives our choices meaning. Theories that fall within this subcategory include *differential association* theory, which says that criminal behavior, as with all other behavior, is learned from others and from our environment. The extent to which we incorporate it depends on the "frequency, duration, priority, and intensity" of our exposure. Another popular interactionist theory is **labeling**. According to labeling theory, our identity is formed by how others see us, so when a child is told at a young age that they are stupid, for example, they incorporate this into their sense of self. The same would be true if a person was labeled as a criminal. Labeling theorists are therefore critical of the juvenile justice system, arguing that if we didn't allow the system to label so many children as "juvenile delinquents," most youth would simply age out of their antisocial behaviors.

Conflict Theory

Conflict theory is the name given to a view of crime based on the writings of two classic social theorists, Karl Marx and Max Weber. While there are many versions of conflict theory, for our purposes we will review the core principles. First, law is not neutral, nor does it exist in nature. Rather, it is an instrument of power designed to maintain the status quo. Second, no person or behavior is inherently criminal. People or acts are labeled as criminal by those with the power to do so. For example, even killing is accepted when committed by certain people with the authority to kill, for example in the death penalty or during war. And third, the social structure is not something everyone consents to, but rather the result of struggles to create structures and laws that represent one's own interests.

Integrated and Critical Theories

Feminist Pathways Perspective

Since the 1970s, research has compared the distinct pathways toward criminal offending experienced by women and men. For female offending, a leading theory is feminist pathways theory, which maintains that risk factors for female offending are often shaped by gender. In examining girls' and women's offending behaviors, institutional race, class, and gender discrimination impact the lives of females. It is argued that victimized girls become offenders as a survival or resistance strategy. Girls run away from home because of victimization in the family and risk living on the streets, where they may turn to alcohol, drugs, or prostitution to cope with the mental health consequences of their victimization. Moreover, they may turn to crime, including violent crime, in response to further harm.

One pathway focuses on the institutional race, class, and gender discrimination that results in young Black women's structural dislocations from their family, education, and employment.[9] Another pathway for young women is rooted in past victimization. It focuses on abuse, both child abuse and intimate partner abuse, and trauma as factors that can influence women to commit noncriminal status offenses and later criminal behavior.[10] Yet another pathway to female criminal behavior is extreme poverty, homelessness, and educational/vocational inequality, which highlights the complex intersection of gender, race, and class with extreme marginalization.

Racial Inequality and Critical Race Theory

Racial inequality has been a focus of criminological research, since Black people and other people of color are overrepresented as both offenders and victims. Some argue that crime may be an adaptive response of Black people to institutionalized racism, which continues to be prevalent in American society. One influential explanation of the racial inequality hypothesis argues that the variation in crime rates is due to the economic advantage of one racial group over another. Although studies have had mixed results,

LABELING
A theory that says that someone who is identified by those in authority—teacher, parent, police—as criminal is likely to incorporate that identity.

several studies of violence by Black people have emphasized its connection to economic inequality as described above. Racial disadvantage variables that represent a measure of institutional racial discrimination include unemployment, underemployment, and marginal employment as well as access to opportunities to acquire the education needed to become gainfully employed. Racism, joblessness (unemployment and unstable employment), poverty, and forced reliance on a punitive welfare system have created disadvantages among people of color in the form of family disruption, community chaos, and disintegrating public schools.

A person's lifestyle may be affected by the nature of his or her work or lack of work. Within a disadvantaged group, those who achieve professional status have the best chance of attaining economic security, occupational autonomy, and power, which are pathways to success. Moreover, stable, substantial employment is important not only for the "perquisites" or benefits associated with a middle-class income, but also for the dignity and pride that come with being able to be responsible and support oneself and one's family.

Education is an important indicator of a community's level of racial inequality. Education, especially college education, is an essential requirement for entry into high-status, high-paying jobs. In addition, education provides the means to explore social realities and to challenge traditional gender roles and power differences. Theory suggests that blocked access to education and employment opportunities created by racial discrimination has produced a **chronic frustration syndrome** among many Black men, who may direct their anger against society.

Critical theorists contend that the laws are written specifically to criminalize the behaviors of Black people and other people of color. Examples are most apparent when looking at drug laws. Drugs generally used by the white population (alcohol, prescription drugs) are legal, and their use and abuse are considered socially reasonable, whereas the history of the criminalization of opium and marijuana is dominated by racist imagery. It is notable that when drug use in the Black community becomes excessive, as we saw in the 1980s crack cocaine "epidemic," it is defined as evil and is criminalized. Yet when what is presently defined as the opiate "epidemic" overwhelmingly impacts white America, it is considered largely a public health matter. This bias is just as relevant in the enforcement of laws, or rather the laws we choose to enforce. Street crime, which has a relatively minor impact on society overall in terms of money and lives spent (the FBI calculates the cost at $15 billion annually), is heavily policed, whereas corporate and so-called white-collar crime, which the FBI says costs society $1 trillion a year, is hardly prosecuted. This is discussed in more detail in chapter 10.

In the past decade, a movement has emerged posing the necessity of creating a unique theory of African American offending. James Unnever and Shaun Gabbidon argue that not all offending emerges from similar circumstances and that to truly understand African American offending, the theory must explain the unique, though not universal, experience of African Americans. In their groundbreaking book *A Theory of African American Offending*,[11] they critique traditional theories while recognizing the distinctive experiences of African Americans in relation to the criminal/legal system, racism, and socialization. Racism and negative encounters create anger and ultimately weaken social bonds, those very bonds that encourage a person to live within the rules of society. Toward the end of the book, they present a theory that posits that the greater the experience of racism, marginalization, and injustice at the hands of the criminal system, the higher the likelihood of individual offending.

Intersectionality and Black Feminist Criminology

Intersectionality theory is located within the critical race feminist perspective. Critical race feminism developed from the legal theoretical perspectives of critical legal studies, critical race theory, and feminist legal theory as explained in chapter 1. Although this theory was originally developed in the context of women of color, race is also part of the lives of white women, who experience privileges based on their skin color, as well as multiple other factors, such as ableism, gender representation, and sexual preference.

CHRONIC FRUSTRATION SYNDROME
A theory that expands upon the idea of status frustration, suggesting that when all avenues of success or power are consistently denied, the response may be social anger.

A recent theoretical development emerging from feminist criminology and critical race theory is called Black feminist criminology.[12] According to Hillary Potter, "it extends beyond traditional feminist criminology to view African American women (and conceivably, other women of color) from their multiple marginalized and dominated positions in society, culture, community, and families."[13]

Intersectionality is changing how researchers approach the study of violence against women as well as women affected by the criminal/legal system. There is an increasing focus on disaggregating victims and offenders by race and ethnicity. Not all women are similarly situated, so treating them in the same way may obscure important distinctions that could help to explain the impact of the criminal/legal system. You will read more about intersectionality throughout this text.

Queer Theory

Queer criminology is defined as a field of study that focuses on the intersections of gender, sexual representation, and criminology. The most recent among the fields of study presented here, queer criminology is said to be in its infancy. The first mention of the need for a queer criminology was in the mid-1990s, but most of what has been written defining the field has been more recent. Most of these writings are theoretical; few research studies have been conducted.

As with queer legal theory, one of the foci of queer criminology is the use and intention of language, specifically "gender" and "transgender." According to one theorist, "the transgender definition is not related to sexuality but gender and that gender is a non-binary concept, even though people tend to identify themselves using mostly the categories male and female."[14]

There can be no doubt that developing a further understanding of the relationship between LGBTQ people and the criminal/legal system is necessary. As we show elsewhere in this text, LGBTQ people are more often victimized than non-LGBTQ people and are often victims of the system itself.

Masculinity

Masculinity has become an important concept for understanding trends in crime. Masculinity is defined as the complex socially constructed expectations of appropriate gendered behaviors, beliefs, expressions, and styles of social interaction for men. In a patriarchal culture, masculine characteristics are strength, power, control, and the suppression of emotion. Gender role expectations for males are that they should be confident, exhibit assertiveness, demonstrate sexual prowess, and hide any and all vulnerable emotions. In addition, the dominant view of gender roles for men embraces fearlessness by engaging in risk-taking behavior and dominance through aggressive and violent behavior. Gender socialization begins in early infancy, starting with the family, school, media, video games, and community interactions, then continues through adolescence with guided gender assignment and peer relationships. There is a significant link between masculinity and violence, which is discussed in chapter 8.

FEMINIST METHODOLOGY

As Joanne Belknap points out in her seminal work, *The Invisible Woman: Gender, Crime and Justice*,[15] first published in 2006, when women and girls are excluded from studies about crime, none of the available knowledge can contribute to our understanding. And though women and girls have been increasingly present in studies of crime over the past two decades, the same can't be said for other marginalized populations. If they have been studied, it is often through a dominant (i.e., white male) lens.

Feminist methodology, which is not, and never was, intended to be exclusive to women or feminist researchers, means a lot more than "add females and shake." Instead, it is designed as a model that espouses best practice. Since the mid-1980s, feminist theorists have asked the question, is there a feminist methodology, and if so, what does it look like? Most feminists would agree that the answer to the first part of this question is a loud yes. The second part of the question is more complicated. First of all, as Belknap pointed out, there is no knowledge of women and women's lives without women's voices. Inclusion is critical. Second, there is no universal "woman" and no single "woman's" experience. There are many, and we must remain willing to listen to all those experiences. Third, women may not want to be the subject of inquiry. As Harding said of oppressed groups, the questions they want answered are about "how to change [their] conditions; how [their] world is shaped by forces beyond it; [and] how to win over, defeat, or neutralize those forces."[16]

Beyond the theory of inquiry, there are several threads that draw feminist research methodology together.[17] Researchers must be able to understand the pervasive role that gender plays in defining and viewing women's lives. They must realize the problem of power dynamics, in life as well as in the research-subject relationship; they must understand how to frame questions to allow the subjectivity of the researched to emerge; and they must appreciate that all research is political, and the best research intentionally so—shedding light so as to empower. Feminist researchers have found that by employing a variety of methods, integrating both elements of qualitative and quantitative methodology, they are able to conduct viable research that allows for some broad determinations, while being truer to the voice of the research subject.

THE ROLE OF MEDIA IN STEREOTYPING VICTIMS AND OFFENDERS

From newspapers, to television and movies, to, more recently, social media, images of crime, "criminals," and "victims" are pervasive. How these images are presented in media and popular culture controls to a large extent how we as individuals perceive crime.

Three points must be made here. First, our perception of the amount of crime in society and our own vulnerability are broadly impacted by our exposure to representations of crime. For example, violent crime in the United States has decreased almost every year since the 1980s. One notable example is that between 1990 and 2014, the homicide rate in New York City has dropped by 85 percent.[18] Yet, since the growth of the all-news, all-the-time cable channels on television and cell phone videos on the internet, we are continuously barraged with images of crime, which leads to a misconception about the crime level that exists. When a killing in Arizona is on the television in our living room in Massachusetts and the images are replayed over and over for hours or even days, it is difficult for even the most knowledgeable and critical viewer to not feel emotionally and physically vulnerable.

Second, when images associated with those crimes are presented in racially biased ways, those too become the images we associate with crime. Even when reporting about the ongoing crisis of the criminal/legal system targeting, and even killing, young men of color, the images that are associated with that reporting are not the images of law enforcement, but those of the young victims.

And third, even the images of victims are widely misrepresented, leaving many angry and scared. For example, the media portray women and the elderly as being particularly vulnerable to crime. Though almost every murder mystery or television drama concerns a woman victimized by violence, according to the National Crime Victimization Survey published by the Bureau of Justice Statistics, in 2017, women and men experience violent victimization at about the same rate of twenty per one thousand. And after the age of twenty-four, the risk of violent victimization falls precipitously—to 6.5 per thousand for those sixty-five and older.[19]

Mainstream media presents images that follow and encourage the ideology that crime is committed by poor, estranged people of color; that women, especially white women, are all at risk of being victimized at any moment; and that the only way to protect ourselves is to have a strong police presence and harsh punishment. To the extent that this is largely based on biased information, we need to be even more diligent in educating ourselves and others about the realities.[20]

In the next chapter, intimate partner violence is discussed. Included in that chapter is a discussion of the legal history, theories of domestic abuse, policy considerations, and the battered women's movement.

REVIEW AND STUDY QUESTIONS

1. Which theory of crime would the New York City police have used to explain the Central Park Five case? What does this say about theories that try to explain behavior defined as criminal?

2. Explain Merton's modes of adaptation theory, with an example of each type of adaptation. Which type of adaptation best describes how you relate to society?

3. Looking at a recent newspaper, find all the ways the media shapes our view of crime in society. Do they use photos? Articles? Data?

GOING FURTHER

Readings:

Burns, Sarah. *The Central Park Five: A Chronicle of a City Wilding*. New York: Knopf, 2011.

Duggan, L. "Queering the State." *Social Text* 39 (1994): 1–14. http://doi.org/10.2307/466361.

Websites:

Media Representations and Impact on the Lives of Black Men and Boys. https://www.opportunityagenda.org /explore/resources-publications/social-science-litera ture-review.

Videos/Movies:

Burns, Ken, Sarah Burns, and David McMahon. *The Central Park Five*. Florentine Films, WETA Television, 2012.

KEY TERMS

absolute deprivation A term used to describe a situation when a person is so poor they are unable to obtain such basic necessities as food and shelter.

anomie A state of social unrest or rapid social change, when social norms are unclear or not enforced.

chronic frustration syndrome A theory that expands upon the idea of status frustration, suggesting that when all avenues of success or power are consistently denied, the response may be social anger.

deviant A term used to describe anyone who deviates or differs from the social norm.

hedonistic A person who seeks only to maximize pleasure and minimize pain.

id, ego, and superego A concept developed by Sigmund Freud that describes three elements that together comprise the human personality.

labeling A theory that says that someone who is identified by those in authority—teacher, parent, police—as criminal is likely to incorporate that identity.

ontology A branch of philosophy that studies the nature of existence, things, and their being or identity.

panopticon Literally meaning "all seeing," it is a building created with a central observation tower and surrounding wings that can be observed from the central point. Today it is a model for jails and prisons, but also schools and other institutional buildings.

phrenology A branch of science that examines cranial (skull) structure to determine a range of characteristics; at one time used to determine a predisposition to crime, also used by the Nazis to determine ethnicity.

psychopathy Believed to be a genetic predisposition resulting in underdeveloped brain regulation of emotions. As a consequence, psychopaths have little or no ability to form emotional attachments or feel empathy. They can often appear to be living within social norms. While some of the most well-known serial killers are believed to be psychopaths, some are CEOs of major corporations.

relative deprivation A term used to describe a situation when, in an affluent society, a person does not have access to the measures of comfort or affluence available to many.

sociopathy Considered to be the result of environmental factors, sociopaths tend to be erratic and impulsive and have difficulty forming attachments. Sociopaths have difficulty holding down a job and conforming to societal norms.

status frustration An expression to describe when a person, especially youth, are unable to obtain status in a manner that is socially acceptable.

strain The anxiety or uncertainty an individual might experience in a state of anomie.

NOTES

[1] "The Central Park Jogger: After 14 Years, Woman at Center of Famous Case Reveals Identity," *Dateline NBC*, December 8, 2003, http://www.nbcnews.com/id/3080050/ns/dateline _nbc-newsmakers/t/central-park-jogger/#.XPaY6ohKg2x.

[2] Susan Welsh, Keren Schiffman, and Enjoli Francis, "Looking Back at the 1989 Central Park Jogger Rape Case That Led to 5 Teens' Conviction, Later Vacated," ABC News, May 24, 2019, https://abcnews.go.com/US/back-1989-central-park -jogger-rape-case-led/story?id=63084663.

[3] Welsh, Schiffman, and Francis, "Looking Back."

[4] Welsh, Schiffman, and Francis, "Looking Back."

[5] Welsh, Schiffman, and Francis, "Looking Back."

[6] Jeremy Bentham, *Proposal for a New and Less Expensive Mode of Employing and Reforming Convicts* (London, 1798).

[7] Robert K. Merton, "Social Structure and Anomie," *American Sociological Review* 3 (October 1938): 672–82.

[8] Susan F. Sharp, B. Mitchell Peck, and Jennifer Hartsfield, "Childhood Adversity and Substance Use of Women Prisoners: A General Strain Theory Approach," *Journal of Criminal Justice* 40, no. 3 (June 2012): 202–11.

[9] Regina A. Arnold, "Processes of Victimization and Criminalization of Black Women," *Social Justice* 17 (1990): 153–66.

[10] Crystal A. Garcia and Jodi Lane, "Dealing with the Fall-Out: Identifying and Addressing the Role That Relationship Strain Plays in the Lives of Girls in the Juvenile Justice System," *Journal of Criminal Justice* 40, no. 3 (June 2012): 259–67.

[11] James D. Unnever and Shaun L. Gabbidon, *A Theory of African American Offending: Race, Racism, and Crime* (New York: Taylor & Francis, 2011).

[12] Katheryn K. Russell, "Development of a Black Criminology and the Role of the Black Criminologist," *Justice Quarterly* 9, no. 4 (1992): 667–83.

[13] Hillary Potter, "An Argument for Black Feminist Criminology: Understanding African American Women's Experiences with Intimate Partner Abuse Using an Integrated Approach," *Feminist Criminology* 1, no. 2 (2006): 106–24.

[14] Lemos A. Prezepiorski, "What Is Queer Criminology?," University of Oxford, accessed July 29, 2019, https://www.law .ox.ac.uk/centres-institutes/centre-criminology/blog/2018/06 /what-queer-criminology.

[15] Joanne Belknap, *The Invisible Woman: Gender, Crime and Justice*, 4th ed. (Stamford, CT: Cengage Learning, 2015).

[16] Sandra Harding, "Introduction: Is There a Feminist Method?," in *Feminism and Methodology: Social Science Issues*, ed. Sandra Harding, 1–14 (Bloomington: Indiana University Press, 1987).

[17] Mary Maynard, "Methods, Practice and Epistemology: The Debate about Feminism and Research," in *Researching Women's Lives from a Feminist Perspective*, ed. Mary Maynard and June Purvis, 27–48 (Bristol, PA: Taylor & Francis,1994).

[18] Reid Wilson, "In Major Cities, Murder Rates Drop Precipitously," *Washington Post*, January 2, 2015, https://www .washingtonpost.com/blogs/govbeat/wp/2015/01/02/in-major -cities-murder-rates-drop-precipitously/?utm_term=.e2c5bf86 a4ab.

[19] Rachel E. Morgan and Jennifer L. Truman, "Criminal Victimization, 2017," NCJ 252472, Bureau of Justice Statistics, December 2018, accessed July 31, 2019, https://www.bjs .gov/content/pub/pdf/cv17.pdf.

[20] Lisa A. Kort-Butler, "Content Analysis in the Study of Crime, Media, and Popular Culture," *Oxford Research Encyclopedia of Criminology* (2016), https://oxfordre.com/criminology /view/10.1093/acrefore/9780190264079.001.0001/acrefore -9780190264079-e-23.

Intimate Partner Violence

This chapter introduces readers to intimate partner violence. Among the topics covered are legal history, theories of domestic abuse, policy considerations, and the battered women's movement.

LEARNING OBJECTIVES

After reading this chapter, you should be able to do the following:

- Explain the history of social responses to violence between intimate partners.
- Describe the patterns of intimate abuse.
- Identify the laws that have been created to address intimate partner violence (IPV).
- Articulate the impact of IPV on various populations.

Case #3: Hedda Nussbaum

Hedda Nussbaum first began to experience intimate partner violence in 1978, before the notion of the "battered woman" had moved into the consciousness of popular culture. The violence would continue for the next nine years, only coming to an end when, in 1987, police arrived at Nussbaum's home to find her daughter so severely injured that she was unconscious and barely breathing; she would die a few days later. Finding herself blamed for the murder, it was only at trial that the true extent of the physical and psychological abuse Nussbaum had suffered was revealed.

In 1978, the first shelter for battered women in New York had been open for only one year. It would be six years before the creation of the first federal law to deter family violence and sixteen years until the passing of the Violence Against Women Act. "Domestic violence" was not yet a part of public parlance. Meanwhile, Hedda Nussbaum, still in the early years of what she then felt was a promising partnership, found herself caught within an abusive relationship that would eventually change the national conversation about domestic violence, its effects, and the policies surrounding it. In these early years, however, Nussbaum could not foresee the effects that this abuse would have on her life, the lives of her children, or the legal system's approach to intimate partner violence, nor could she foresee that the very abuse that she was suffering would one day lead to her being labeled a murderer.

BACKGROUND

Nussbaum's early life was relatively unremarkable. Born in 1942, she grew up in a pleasant neighborhood in Manhattan, achieving success in school and going on to major in English before eventually becoming an elementary school teacher. In the 1960s, this was a relatively common career trajectory for women of Nussbaum's background, but Nussbaum turned her sights elsewhere. She began writing children's books, and by the mid-1970s, she was working as an editor of children's and young adult books at a major New York publishing house.

Her life began to change—she thought, initially, for the better—when she met Joel Steinberg in 1975. Nussbaum had always been rather shy and reserved, and she felt that Steinberg, an attorney, was her opposite: attractive, charismatic, and gregarious. They soon began dating. Nussbaum felt that Steinberg built her up and increased her confidence, both with his own outgoing nature and his concerted efforts to guide her on how to carry herself in order to advance in her career. Nussbaum later recalls, "I thought he was godlike."[1] Not long after they began dating, Nussbaum moved in with Steinberg, into his Greenwich Village brownstone. So began her slow and painful evolution: from

creative and ambitious to harrowed, secretive, fearful, prematurely graying, and frequently showing signs of injury. According to later reports, Steinberg first struck Nussbaum in 1978; that year she had a dozen or more black eyes and suffered an injury to a tear duct that became a chronic condition. Over the next few years, Steinberg's violence against Nussbaum increased exponentially, and in 1982, due to absence and erratic behavior, she effectively lost her job. The loss of her job and Steinberg's increasingly controlling behavior meant that Nussbaum became more isolated than ever.

Steinberg took advantage of the isolation. According to friends and family, it was nearly impossible to get in touch with Nussbaum, and even in the rare instances that she could talk on the phone, Steinberg was constantly monitoring her conversations. He reportedly told her that she could neither use the phone nor open the door of their apartment unless he was present. She could barely eat without his permission. When her parents, William and Emma Nussbaum, tried to visit her in 1983, they were not even able to enter the apartment; instead, Nussbaum spoke to them hurriedly through a crack in the door and told them that they would have to arrange it with Steinberg if they wanted to visit. She then sent them away. Their next glimpse of her would not be until 1987, when they saw her on television after her arrest. Prior to her arrest in November 1987, Nussbaum had not left her home for almost a year and a half.

VICTIM OR VILLAIN?

Nussbaum, however, was not alone in the apartment during those years of captivity. In the early 1980s, Steinberg had unofficially adopted a baby girl, Lisa. He had been contracted to simply handle her adoption to another family but instead opted to take in the girl himself. In 1986, Steinberg again unofficially adopted an infant, this time a baby boy named Mitchell. Both had been born to young women who chose to give their babies up for adoption, neither of whom could imagine the home that their children would end up in. Only one of those mothers would see her child again.

Records suggest that Steinberg focused his violence and rage on Nussbaum, but when he began using cocaine, the physical abuse began to be directed at Lisa as well. Nussbaum, alternately afraid of and in awe of Steinberg, was incapable of intervening. She had been at his mercy for more than a decade when, on November 1, 1987, Steinberg beat Lisa so badly that she lost consciousness. For hours, Lisa lay motionless on the floor while Nussbaum, terrified of angering Joel and vaguely hoping that he could somehow heal Lisa, was not able to call 911. Around twelve hours passed before Steinberg finally agreed that they should call the police.

Nussbaum initially told police that her daughter had gotten food lodged in her windpipe and was unable to breathe, but when police arrived at the apartment, they found Lisa unclothed, unconscious, and barely alive, with clear signs of injury. Mitchell was somehow tied to his playpen, with only rotten milk to drink, but was found upon later examination to be in good health. The apartment itself was filthy—inspection of the house would later turn up blood on the walls, cocaine, crack pipes, thousands of dollars in cash, and human waste. Nussbaum's private nightmare was about to become a public spectacle.

Lisa was rushed to the hospital, and Mitchell was immediately and permanently removed from the custody of Steinberg and Nussbaum. Despite the fact that Nussbaum also displayed obvious signs of physical and psychological trauma, both she and Steinberg were arrested.

The doctors who examined Nussbaum following her arrest noted that she was "anemic, debilitated, malnourished, wasted, limping and hunchbacked."[2] By this time, the abuse had been going on for nearly a decade, during which time Steinberg had ruptured her spleen, fractured several of her ribs, broken her nose multiple times, burned her, and caused several more forms of damage, physically, emotionally, and psychologically. The doctors were in fact in awe that Nussbaum was even still alive given the severity of her condition. The same could not be said for Lisa; she was declared brain dead approximately three days after the initial injury and passed away on November 4, 1987. Steinberg and Nussbaum were charged with her murder.

The ensuing murder trial was televised, and the public watched in rapt attention. The stories of violence, squalor, and drugs seemed to be at such odds with the couple's affluent and comfortable background. Steinberg, maintaining his innocence, detailed his frustration with Nussbaum's feebleness and detachment and took no responsibility for his own part in breaking her down in such a way. Nussbaum herself was initially unwilling to testify against Steinberg; she was still attached to him and did not want to play any part in making him out to be a monster. Betty Levinson, Nussbaum's lawyer, was mystified by Nussbaum's continued efforts to downplay Steinberg's cruelty. Recalling Nussbaum's resistance to testifying, Levinson said, "It was so awful to hear her say he was a healer. . . . It was spooky, terrifying."[3] Only when Nussbaum learned that she might be held responsible for Lisa's death did she finally agree to take the stand against him. There, she testified that she worshipped Steinberg, obeyed him, and believed that he had the power to heal. Nussbaum's demeanor as she testified unsettled viewers; her voice was flat and emotionless, and she would occasionally lapse into long moments of silence. One reporter stated that it was as if she was in a sort of trance.

The New York City district attorney ultimately determined that at the time that Lisa died, Nussbaum had likely been incapable of either causing her harm or saving her because of her own debilitated physical and mental state, and in exchange for her testimony and cooperation in his case against Steinberg, he offered to drop the charges against Nussbaum. The public's response to this was extremely polarized: some (including prominent feminist Gloria Steinem) believed that Nussbaum, too, was a survivor of abuse and could not be held responsible for the suffering that both she and Lisa had endured, while others (including prominent feminist Susan Brownmiller) believed that, despite the abuse that she suffered, she still had the personal responsibility and agency to extract herself and the children from the abusive environment. Despite Nussbaum's clearly debilitated state, many viewers and commentators were unable to forgive her for the seeming failure of her maternal instinct. Decades later, we have learned a great deal more about the traumatic effects that intimate violence may have, and we now recognize the extreme psychological attachment that some may have to their abuser, as well as the ways in which trauma may lead to an inability to respond in self-defense.

After a lengthy trial, Joel Steinberg was found guilty of first-degree manslaughter, and it came with a sentence of eight to twenty-five years in prison. Nussbaum herself spent the next year receiving intensive inpatient psychiatric care.

THE CIVIL TRIAL

The picture of abuse that unfolded during the criminal trial was not the extent of Nussbaum's effect on the legal system's treatment of intimate partner violence. Despite the ongoing physical and psychological obstacles she faced, she filed a civil suit against Joel Steinberg, again with the help of Betty Levinson. What she sought: $3.6 million in damages for the decade of abuse.

New York and many other jurisdictions had a one-year statute of limitations on civil claims arising from physical assaults. For survivors of intimate partner violence, however, this time frame is frequently unrealistic. As with Nussbaum, many survivors of abuse are not able to bring suit against their abuser because of multiple internal and external factors. The Nussbaum case, visible as it was, was well positioned to take advantage of a provision in the law that lifted the one-year statute of limitations if the person with standing to sue (the victim) was prevented from suing due to "an overall inability to function in society."[4] A nation of viewers had witnessed Nussbaum's "inability to function" and had heard the details of what brought her to such a state, so Levinson went ahead and filed the suit, this time with the support of more than a dozen women's groups from New York City and beyond. At stake was not only Nussbaum's case, but the cases of many future survivors of abuse.

At the trial, testimony from experts on psychiatry and psychology made it clear that such sustained trauma affects victims of abuse in ways that may make them incapable of making active decisions in their own defense. They may become detached, shut down, and unable to plan for even the near future. Levinson built her argument: "It was true in Hedda's case . . . and it is true for other battered women, that when your surroundings are limited by your captor, you become focused on the tiny, tiny events of your life, like 'Will I eat today? Will I sleep on the floor today? Will I sleep at all today?'"[5] Levinson's approach to building the case was successful, and the New York State Supreme Court ruled in Nussbaum's favor. In the decision, it states that not just for Nussbaum, but for survivors of intimate partner violence, "the destructive impact of violence in such an intimate relationship may be so complete that the victim is rendered incapable of independent judgment even to save one's own life."[6] The verdict in this case established a legal precedent that made it possible for survivors of abuse in New York and elsewhere to bring suits against their abusers and was a crucial building block in growing understandings of the cycle of abuse and the effects of trauma.

THE AFTERMATH

In the decades following the case, Nussbaum has been proud to acknowledge her part in changing legal and social treatments of intimate partner violence, but her wounds—both physical and psychological—are still present. Perhaps equally disruptive is the infamy of her name and the fact that she cannot quite leave the case behind; finding work and establishing normalcy are difficult when one was the centerpiece of one of the first televised criminal trials. Joel Steinberg was released from prison in 2004, after which Nussbaum all but retreated from public life. She did publish her memoir, *Surviving Intimate Terrorism*, in 2005, but otherwise she has chosen—perhaps as an act of self-defense or self-protection—to disappear.

THINKING CRITICALLY ABOUT THE CASE

1. What may be the core arguments arising from both sides of the debate about Nussbaum's part in the abuse of the children? What suggests that she was at fault, and what suggests that she was a victim?

2. In cases such as this, are those suffering from abuse within their rights to physically strike back against their abusers? What determines if such an act is lawful or unlawful?

3. How did Nussbaum's physical, mental, and emotional condition affect the outcome of the criminal trial?

REFERENCES

This case is adapted from the following sources:

"The Advocates for Human Rights: Stop Violence against Women." Stop Violence against Women. Accessed August 1, 2018. http://www.stopvaw.org/state_and_federal_domestic_violence_laws_in_the_united_states.

Hampson, Rick. "The Metamorphosis of Hedda Nussbaum: 'Beyond Understanding.'" Associated Press, November 16, 1987. https://apnews.com/2e647d4a1cf9394d2689bad7b47aa8d0.

Jones, Ann. *Next Time She'll Be Dead*. Boston, MA: Beacon, 1994.

Mehren, Elizabeth. "A 6-Year-Old's Tragic Death." *Los Angeles Times*, November 25, 1987. https://www.latimes.com/archives/la-xpm-1987-11-25-vw-16336-story.html.

Russo, Francine. "The Faces of Hedda Nussbaum." *New York Times*, March 30, 1997. https://www.nytimes.com/1997/03/30/magazine/the-faces-of-hedda-nussbaum.html.

Sherbill, Sara. "Thirty Years Later, Can We Finally Forgive Hedda Nussbaum?" *Slate.com*, October 24, 2018. https://slate.com/human-interest/2018/10/hedda-nussbaum-joel-steinberg-abuse-trial-anniversary.html.

CONTEXT AND ANALYSIS

Historical Overview

Evidence offered by researchers indicates that men have beaten their wives for centuries. Such beatings were condoned from the moment humankind discovered that men played a role in the creation of a child. Men quickly assumed the power that women, as bearers of children, had held, and "the strictest fidelity was demanded of the wife in order to guarantee and authenticate the husband's fatherhood."[7] And so began patriarchy. The feminist view of violence against women proposes that violence is an extension of patriarchy, or men's need to maintain their control over women. Note that there is indeed no monolith that can be called a "feminist view." Indeed, as discussed in greater detail in chapter 1, there are many fully articulated feminist perspectives. Liberal feminism, radical feminism, and standpoint feminism are but a few. However, for the limited purpose of explaining **intimate partner violence (IPV)**, there is some agreement from which generalizations are drawn.

The emergence of patriarchal religions, Christianity and others, reinforced the role of man as the head of the family. Women were not to be trusted. They were "inferior, childlike and mindless . . . suitable only for conjugal duties."[8] It was man's duty to assure that his wife, like his children and livestock, obeyed. If they did not, he was to use "reasonable chastisement" to assure obedience. This made women the "appropriate victims" of family violence for many hundreds of years. The Puritans, who occupied much of New England, brought with them the humanitarian belief that it was immoral for a husband to beat his wife. This prohibition became a part of the Massachusetts Bay Colony criminal code. Nevertheless, the prohibition did not extend to what was considered to be "reasonable" punishment, which did not leave scars or do permanent injury. When cases were brought, judges often inquired as to the wife's responsibility in inciting the violence. Consequently, no one was ever convicted.

During the nineteenth century, a middle-class belief began to emerge that resorting to violence was plebian and therefore unacceptable. This was reinforced by the cult of domesticity, which became prominent at the end of the century. As men increasingly worked outside the home, women and the home were seen as places of refuge from the evils of the outside world. Neither of these influences was sufficient to counter the belief in the sanctity of the home or to erode the notion of the separate spheres of public and private. An 1874 North Carolina court decision said, in part, "It is better to draw the curtain, shut out the public gaze, and leave the parties to forget and forgive."[9] This became known as the **curtain rule** and was relied upon to justify the failure to provide legal or social remedies.

By the late nineteenth century, a public debate about women's social and legal status had begun and the stage was set for women to speak. North Carolina became the first state in the new nation to curtail a man's right to whip his wife, rejecting the argument that provocation could be a justification for beating.[10] The court qualified the prohibition, however, suggesting that, for the protection of the family, courts should not intervene "unless there existed permanent injury or extreme violence."

In the early 1900s, the **interspousal immunity rule** appeared in court decisions. This rule prevented one spouse from testifying against the other. It also assured that battered women could not bring tort actions against their husbands. Women were thus silenced, and it would take almost a century before the voices of the victims of intimate violence would be heard.

The Second Wave of Feminism and Wife Beating

Some researchers and activists trace the emergence of women's struggle against abuse by their male partners as a societal problem to a march of five hundred women and children in Chiswick, England, in 1971. Others say that it seems as if the issue of battered women came out of nowhere in the early 1970s. We do know that in 1971 the first hotline for battered women was established, and the first shelters followed. Prior to this time, few were

INTIMATE PARTNER VIOLENCE (IPV)
Replaces the term domestic violence, especially among researchers and scholars. This is the terminology we will use in this text whenever it makes sense to do so.

CURTAIN RULE
A legal idea that reinforces separate spheres (chapter 1) by ensuring that the court will not interfere with that which happens in the private sphere.

INTERSPOUSAL IMMUNITY RULE
A legal rule that prevents one spouse from testifying against the other, effectively restricting one spouse from seeking legal assistance when the other spouse is abusive.

even aware that such a problem existed. Even the women being abused, most of whom accepted or resisted the violence in silence, were not aware of the others who shared their experiences. It is generally agreed that the women's movement, the so-called second wave of feminism of the late 1960s and the 1970s, brought women together in record numbers. They began to share their own experiences and to recognize the extent to which those experiences were shared.

Due to pressure from activists, researchers, and others, policy makers began to focus on domestic violence as a national problem, which led to police responsiveness, domestic violence legislation, and public health responses to intimate partner violence against women. In 1978, the U.S. Commission on Civil Rights held a two-day "Consultation on Battered Women," which was organized in anticipation of the passage of a national Domestic Violence Prevention and Treatment Act. Ultimately, the bill did not pass, but in the interim, President Jimmy Carter established an Office of Domestic Violence within the Department of Justice. That office has since then disbanded.

Along with the increasing public awareness of violence against women in their homes, changes in the criminal/legal system played a role in the emergence of domestic violence as a social problem. The 1980s emerged with a newfound emphasis on the victim, emanating from the public and political mood of law and order, accompanied by increased demands for more protection for victims and more aggressive actions by law enforcement. Government awareness of the seriousness of domestic violence grew. In 1984, law enforcement officials, prosecutors, judges, victim assistance advocates, health care providers, and educators testified before the Attorney General's Task Force on Family Violence, which made several recommendations, including treating assaults within the family as seriously as assaults between strangers and coordinating efforts between the criminal/legal system, victim assistance agencies, and the entire community.

Also important in changing consciousness was the influence of international women who argued that violence against women is a violation of basic human rights. A dialogue between international women concerned with violence against women and women from the United States began at the 1975 United Nations conference on International Women's Year in Mexico City, Mexico, the first of its kind. The International Tribunal on Crimes against Women met in Brussels, Belgium, the following year. At that conference, over two thousand women from thirty-three countries heard testimony by women who had been battered by intimate partners. A resolution calling for the establishment of battered women's shelters, economic aid, and legal protection for battered women was sent to governments in every country. International organizations such as the United Nations and the World Health Organization made violence against women a focal concern. The Declaration on the Elimination of Violence against Women, adopted by the United Nations General Assembly in 1993, recognizes violence against women as an unacceptable violation of basic human rights. It declares that violence against women (in society and in the family) is an obstacle to achieving equality, development, and peace. It states, in part,

> Violence against women is a manifestation of historically unequal power relations between men and women . . . and . . . is one of the crucial social mechanisms by which women are forced into a subordinate position compared to men.[11]

The Law Changes

Today, IPV is recognized as a crime in all fifty states and the District of Columbia, but that was not the case prior to the mid-1970s. Domestic abuse was viewed as a private matter, and legal protections were limited to a handful of unusually brutal cases. Law enforcement officials maintained an explicit "hands-off" policy, and prosecutors were discouraged from actively pursuing cases. One of the limited options available to women, **civil injunctions**, carried no criminal penalty and therefore offered little protection. In addition, civil injunctions applied only to women who were married to their abuser

CIVIL INJUNCTION
A court ruling ordering an individual to do or not do some specific act.

and often were available only to women who had filed for divorce or legal separation. It was primarily the work of feminist legal scholars that made IPV the subject of extensive reforms.

A series of court cases set the stage for the legal changes that were to come. In 1976, two class-action lawsuits were filed on behalf of women on opposite sides of the country. The first, *Scott v. Hart*,[12] was filed against the police chief of Oakland, California, on behalf of Black victims of IPV, who were, according to the complaint filed, getting "less adequate police responses than were white victims." The complaint alleged a denial of equal protection pursuant to the Fourteenth Amendment. The second case, *Bruno v. Codd*,[13] was filed on behalf of married battered women against the New York City Police Department and the New York Family Court, alleging failure to protect. Both cases resulted in **consent decrees**, agreements between the parties detailing the manner in which the problems would be remedied.

As IPV gained visibility in the public domain, pressure began to intensify over the inadequate response of law enforcement. At the same time, societal attitudes toward crime and the response to crime were changing. Politicians and the public began to demand stricter enforcement, more actions were deemed criminal (criminalized), minimum or mandatory sentences became the norm, and time served was increasingly punitive. In a political climate that favored control, it became possible for battered women's advocates and social conservatives to become allies in demanding police action in instances of IPV.

The state of Oregon was the first to require police to arrest for domestic assault, passing the Abuse Prevention Act in 1977. By 1983, thirty-three states and the District of Columbia had passed legislation permitting warrantless arrests, and forty-three states had new laws relating to orders of protection for battered women. The next year, the Attorney General's Task Force on Family Violence issued a report recommending that law enforcement agencies establish arrest as the preferred response to domestic violence.

Then came the landmark case of *Thurman v. City of Torrington, Conn.*[14] In that case, the court found that the city's police policy of inaction constituted negligence for failing to protect Tracey Thurman from the violence of her husband. She and her son were awarded $2.3 million. In conjunction with the *Scott* and *Bruno* cases, *Thurman* alerted police departments nationally to their potential liability if they did not review their policies (both formal and informal) addressing IPV. That concern for liability prompted many police departments to reassess their domestic violence policies.

Despite some reported problems of police underenforcing, and at times overenforcing, IPV laws, by 1992 arrest was mandatory in fourteen states and in many cities and towns. Some of the other statutory changes included requiring police to provide women with information about legal options and available services, providing transportation for the women to a safe location, making violation of protective orders a criminal offense, and adding surcharges on marriage licenses and divorce decrees to help support services for battered women.

Another legal evolution of direct relevance to IPV was in the area of marital rape. Until the late 1970s, American law did not recognize marital rape as a crime. As recently as 1991, only nineteen states had completely abolished the marital rape exemption. Today, all fifty states and the District of Columbia recognize at least the possibility that marital rape can exist under the law. This represents a shift in the legal status of married parties, such that the man no longer has the nearly unfettered authority to impose his will.

Federal Law

Though the federal government played a role in funding research and recommending policy, little was done to address domestic violence in federal law until the passage of the Violence Against Women Act (VAWA) in 1994.

Prior to passage of VAWA, Congress had defeated several pieces of legislation aimed at domestic violence and passed only two. The two pieces of federal legislation addressing domestic violence were the 1984 Family Violence Prevention and Services Act, which

CONSENT DECREE
An agreement between parties to a legal action that resolves the underlying complaint.

provided limited grant money to shelter programs and police training programs, and the 1984 Victims of Crime Act, which provided money for victims of crime.

VAWA was first presented to Congress in 1990, where it was not well received. Senator Jesse Helms critiqued providing any federal support to domestic violence shelters because they constituted "social engineering," challenging the husband's place as "head of the family."[15] When VAWA was reintroduced by Senator Joseph Biden in 1994, it met with much more limited resistance.

VAWA, which finally passed as part of a larger crime bill, provided $1.62 billion over six years to fund a wide range of programs, from public park improvements to education for judges. In addition to the funding, the act contains provisions that provide some protection for battered immigrant women and their children, as well as the ability to bring a civil lawsuit for damages for victims who can prove that the violence inflicted on them was motivated by their gender.

The Violence Against Women Act was reauthorized in 2000, 2005, and again, after a fairly contentious debate, in 2013. In 2005, language was added to clarify that male victims were also included. And in 2013, violence in same-sex relationships was included. In 2019, the U.S. House of Representatives voted to reauthorize VAWA, but at this time the U.S. Senate has failed to do so.

DYNAMICS OF ABUSE

Scope of Intimate Partner Violence

As awareness of intimate partner violence grew, researchers gathered information about the scope of the problem. Early research in the 1970s and 1980s involved gathering information about the prevalence and characteristics of intimate partner violence in an effort to understand the scope of the problem. Researchers faced numerous obstacles: large numbers of those funding and publishing research believed that violence against women did not occur within the family, while others simply regarded the topic as trendy and theoretically unimportant. Questions about the extent of the problem dominated the research and policy agenda. Eventually, through the efforts of researchers and political activists, there was widespread recognition of the pervasive problem of intimate partner violence against women in the United States.

According to data from the 2015 **National Intimate Partner and Sexual Violence Survey (NISVS)** conducted by the Centers for Disease Control and Prevention (CDC), approximately one in four women (27.3 percent) and one in ten men (11.5 percent) experience some form of IPV in their lifetimes. Current annual estimates are that 5.5 percent of women, or one in eighteen, and about 5.2 percent of men, or one in twenty, experienced IPV in the year prior to the study. For female victims who experienced sexual or other physical violence or stalking by an intimate partner, over one quarter (25.8 percent) had their first experience before the age of eighteen, and many others (47.9 percent) between the ages of eighteen and twenty-four. The report found that these victimizations were not evenly distributed throughout society, with evidence suggesting that multiracial and Native American women have the highest rates of experiencing IPV. The rates reported for multiracial women were estimated at 26.8 percent and for men at 18.2 percent.[16] The overall numbers for Native women and men are too small to be statistically interpreted.

NATIONAL INTIMATE PARTNER AND SEXUAL VIOLENCE SURVEY (NISVS)
A unit of the national Centers for Disease Control, NISVS is an ongoing survey that collects state and national data about intimate partner and sexual violence.

"Abuse," the occurrence of one or more of the following acts between family or household members:
   (a) attempting to cause or causing physical harm
   (b) placing another in fear of imminent serious physical harm
   (c) causing another to engage involuntarily in sexual relations by force, threat, or duress
(MGL 209A§1)

Same-Sex IPV

Intimate violence among same-sex partners was not something that was publicly acknowledged throughout most of the twentieth century. The first research study on the subject was published in 1978, but the body of research didn't begin to grow until the mid- to late 1980s. Even today, there is significantly less attention paid to same-sex IPV than to violence among heterosexual couples. Several factors have led to the limited recognition of same-sex IPV, including discrimination, a belief that male-to-female violence was more problematic, a reluctance within the LGBTQ community to expose the extent of same-sex IPV, and perhaps among those interested in LGBTQ research, a preference for research in other areas, such as HIV/AIDS. Additionally, the early philosophy of the **battered women's movement** that patriarchy and sexism could only lead to male-on-female violence has required reframing the issue surrounding intimate violence in terms of the violence inherent in a patriarchal system, where power over others defines one's worth. This has allowed for the acknowledgment of a much more widespread problem.

Because many studies, such as the NISVS cited above, do not ask about sexual orientation, it is difficult to provide accurate data comparing IPV among LGBTQ couples with that of heterosexual couples. The data that does exist suggest that the lifetime chance of being a victim of IPV is much higher for lesbian women (43.8 percent) and gay men (26 percent) than for heterosexual women and men. The people most vulnerable to IPV, according to these statistics, are bisexual women (61.1 percent) and bisexual men (37.3 percent).[17] We engage in some analysis of why these numbers are so high in the discussion of theory below.

The Experience of Abuse

Most state laws define IPV, as does the law in Massachusetts, as physical harm, fear of physical harm, and/or sexual assault. The requirement of physical injury limits the usefulness of the law in addressing abuse.

Abuse itself is much more complicated and includes emotional control and manipulation, actions designed to limit self-esteem and agency, economic control, and isolation. The effects, as we saw in the case of Hedda Nussbaum, are often debilitating.

These effects are just as profound in same-sex IPV, where a person's social vulnerabilities can be used to the abuser's advantage. Fear of being "outed" to one's family or workplace might be used by the abuser to keep a victim from leaving or reporting the abuse. The myth of mutual combat in male homosexual relationships leads to less acceptance of the reality of the abuse, especially by law enforcement. The emergence of HIV has further complicated abuse, providing an additional element of shame and manipulation by suggesting that a victim is unable to negotiate safe sex. Moreover, there is a mistaken belief (another myth) that it is easier for gay men to leave an abusive relationship, which arises from yet another myth that gay men easily change partners and are not as stable as heterosexual or lesbian relationships.

Bisexual people are doubly marginalized and thereby more vulnerable, resulting in, as the statistics above indicate, much higher rates of abuse. Though research on the subject is limited, it is hypothesized that this vulnerability derives from increased isolation—not being recognized by lesbian and gay people as part of their community and, simultaneously, being stigmatized by heterosexuals.

Femicide

Femicide, also called gender-related homicide, is the ultimate form of violence against women. The term was first used by the feminist writer Diana Russell in the early 1970s to describe the "killing of women by men because they are women." Since the beginning of Russell's use of the term "femicide," it has been adopted and used more broadly to mean the murder of women, whether by men or by other women, for any reason. Femicide is

BATTERED WOMEN'S MOVEMENT
A movement that began in the 1970s to protect the rights and interests of women in abusive relationships, often combined with victims of sexual assault.

FEMICIDE
The killing of women; originally used to mean the killing of women by men as an act of hatred toward women.

a leading cause of death of women, with between three and four thousand women and girls murdered each year in the United States. Although it occurs among women of all ages and among all races and ethnicities, young women of color are disproportionately affected. According to the Centers for Disease Control and Prevention, it is the second-leading cause of death for African American women between the ages of fifteen and twenty-four, the fourth-leading cause of death for white women between those ages, and the leading cause of on-the-job deaths for all women. Since the 1970s, the rate of femicide in the United States has fluctuated between 3.8 and 4.5 deaths per one hundred thousand women. Non-Hispanic African American and American Indian/Alaska Native women experience the highest rates of homicide (4.4 and 4.3 per one hundred thousand population, respectively), which is about twice the rate of white women.[18]

An early study of victim-perpetrated homicides by Wolfgang found that 41 percent of female victims in Philadelphia were killed by their husbands.[19] Since that time, studies have found that intimate partner femicide is between 29 percent and 50 percent of femicide victims. Moreover, 5 to 8 percent of all murders committed by male perpetrators are cases of intimate partner homicide.[20]

ABUSE IN THEORY

Over the years, numerous theories have emerged to explain intimate personal violence. Two early approaches to domestic violence dominated the discussion through most of the twentieth century. These are identified in the literature as the feminist approach and the family violence perspective, also referred to as social control theory. The feminist view focuses on men's use of violence to control women. The purpose of such violence would be to maintain the existing social order. Feminist theorists emphasize the fact that women are the usual victims, and their primary goal is protecting women. The family violence, or social control, view employs the social work model of family systems to illustrate how family interactions can result in violence. Social control theorists often refer to mutual combat, suggesting that the use of violence is similar for men and women. This family violence is viewed as resulting from a breakdown in the social order. While all theorists share the goal of reducing the amount of violence in the family, feminist theorists fear that social control policies ignore the larger issues of gender inequality and the distribution of power.

During the 1970s and 1980s, psychological studies primarily focused on the individual pathologies of batterers and women who use violence against their batterers. The inquiry into women victims of intimate partner violence largely focused on the question, "Why doesn't she leave?" One of the most important theories to develop at that time was the **battered woman syndrome**. Prior to the 1970s, women who remained in abusive relationships were thought to be insane or to have a serious pathology that included a masochistic need to be hurt or punished (a belief that sadly continues to persist within society, especially among individuals not schooled in IPV). One early study concluded that battered wives were frigid and had other personality characteristics that made them undesirable as wives, while another study found that battered women's psychological profiles were similar to those of other emotionally disturbed women, particularly those with schizophrenia or borderline personalities. This began to change with the 1979 publication of *The Battered Woman* by Leonore Walker, in which she introduced the battered woman syndrome.[21]

The battered woman syndrome is a combination of two concepts, **learned helplessness** and the **cycle of violence**. Walker theorized that battering is neither random nor constant but occurs in repeated cycles, each having three phases: the tension-building stage, the acute battering stage, and the honeymoon stage. The tension-building stage is comprised of minor battering incidents that may be handled by the woman through nurturing, compliance, anticipation of the batterer's whims, or staying out of his way. If he explodes, she accepts responsibility for his actions. She uses denial and rationalization because anger would escalate the harm. The acute battering incident occurs when the woman's coping techniques fail, the woman withdraws from the batterer due to exhaustion, and the

BATTERED WOMAN SYNDROME
A term coined by Leonore Walker to explain why some women remained in abusive relationships.

LEARNED HELPLESSNESS
An element of battered women's syndrome that explained the state where a person might try, repeatedly, to break a pattern of abuse, to change a partner's behaviors, or to modify their own to reduce what they perceived as their chance of being harmed, only to find that their actions did not reduce those harms.

CYCLE OF VIOLENCE
A pattern of behaviors, sometimes used by abusers, where harm is followed by apologies and contrition, followed in turn by a repeat of the harmful acts.

batterer reacts with an uncontrollable discharge of tension. Both the man and the woman minimize and rationalize the seriousness of the attack. The third stage, kindness and contrite behavior, occurs immediately after the acute battering incident ends. This last stage is not necessarily one in which the man expresses regret and promises to change. Instead, it may simply be a time when violence and the threat of violence are absent.

Walker has described learned helplessness as an early response reinforcement that teaches what can and cannot be controlled or a psychological condition that causes women to feel powerless to effect positive control over their lives. It has also been described as a subcategory of **posttraumatic stress disorder (PTSD)**, which develops from prolonged or severe trauma. This theory also helps explain why women kill or injure their abusers instead of leaving the violent relationship.

The battered woman syndrome has been criticized because it tends to blame the woman for her own victimization and fails to explain why some women finally act and strike back. As a result, feminist scholars have continued to propose alternative theories. One such theory, the survivor theory, emphasizes the abused woman's strengths and help-seeking behaviors while simultaneously recognizing some of the barriers that can impede help seeking. This theory suggests that severe abuse prompts innovative coping strategies and efforts to seek informal and formal help, but the failure of the help sources to intervene in a decisive way allows the abuse to continue and escalate. Another variation of the survivor theory incorporates learned helplessness, focusing on the woman's inability to escape her situation and her passive acceptance of abuse. Here we recognize that the battered and abused woman may experience low self-esteem, self-blame, guilt, depression, and anxiety as the violence worsens, but nevertheless the woman actively begins to seek help. Despite her efforts, society's general disinterest and inadequate resources routinely force her to return to the batterer. The failure of society to provide the woman with a viable alternative and society's lack of active intervention on her behalf allows the abuse to continue and even escalate.

Typologies of Intimate Partner Violence

A common thread that runs through all these theories is an attempt to explain why the victims of IPV respond with such varied behavior patterns: sometimes leaving, sometimes staying quietly, and sometimes fighting back aggressively. In 2008, researcher Michael Johnson published a book titled *A Typology of Domestic Violence*,[22] building on earlier work in which Johnson had collaborated with Kathleen Ferraro.[23] According to Johnson, IPV takes a variety of forms. The one that we have been called "battering" he now calls **intimate terrorism**. Intimate terrorism, which Johnson observes in heterosexual relationships, largely perpetrated by men against women, is recognized as one person seeking to control another through the use of force, intimidation, and power. He adds that there are other kinds of IPV that may still injure a person but don't reproduce power and control in the way intimate terrorism does. He classifies these other types of violence as "violent resistance," where the acting is most often the woman trying to protect herself in an otherwise abusive situation, and "situational couple violence," which is not a matter of control but arises out of situational anger and is often mutual combat. This latter form of violence, Johnson says, is the most common form of IPV.

Intersectionality

As you're read in chapters 1 and 2, intersectionality involves theories that combine the multiple ways in which society impacts individual lives. Any analysis of violence against women in the United States must consider this country's racial history. Black feminists locate their analysis of the oppression of Black women in the United States in a long history of sexual abuse, racial oppression, class exploitation, and social control, which situates them differently from white women (and other women of color). For Black feminists, a feminist critique of rape, incest, and battering necessarily includes an analysis of racist

POSTTRAUMATIC STRESS DISORDER (PTSD)
A mental disability resulting from prolonged or severe trauma.

INTIMATE TERRORISM
Primarily perpetrated by a male against a female partner, intimate terrorism is rooted in a general pattern of control, jealousy, patriarchal beliefs, power, and stalking, whereas situational couple violence, in which either partner can be the aggressor, is embedded in a specific situation where conflict is settled with violence.

oppression rooted in the slave system, the lynchings of Black men, and the Jim Crow legal system. The history of African American women *is* the history of slavery, which brought the vast majority of the ancestors of American Black women to this country to work as slaves. Enslaved women suffered violence at the hands of their husbands, other enslaved men, and slave owners. Raping an enslaved woman was legal, whereas raping a white woman was a crime.

The traditional feminist analysis of wife beating focuses on marriage as the institution in which the wife is the property of her husband and the husband dominates over his wife on the basis of male ownership, property distribution, and control of subsistence goods. That type of marriage did not exist for enslaved women, who were the property of the slave owner. Since the enslaved husband had no property of his own to control, any power or control he had over his wife could not be based on his providing food, clothing, or shelter, which came from the slave owner. Moreover, intrafamily relationships had to conform to the work and social patterns of the slave system, including the sale and separation of husbands from their families.

This feminist theoretical construct has been applied to violence against women of color in Kimberlé Crenshaw's intersectionality theory,[24] which, as discussed in chapter 1, diverges from the narrow feminist emphasis on gender inequality as the primary factor responsible for intimate partner violence against women. Intersectionality goes beyond gender inequality theory by arguing that gender inequality intersects with other structures of power and oppression, such as racial oppression and class exploitation, to prompt intimate partner violence.

In addition, Crenshaw suggests that the link between patriarchy and racism may contribute to the cycle of intimate partner violence. She argues that the violence of men of color against their intimate partners may be a reaction to being denied the power and privilege white men have throughout all spheres of their lives.

BATTERED WOMEN'S SELF-DEFENSE

Research indicates that many women who commit crime have experienced abuse. This research is discussed in later chapters. But what happens when, as we saw in the Nussbaum case, victims of IPV are accused of serious crimes, such as homicide? Indeed, in this sense, the Nussbaum case is exceptional. Most often when an abused woman is charged with homicide, it is for killing her abuser.

As recently as 2016, Penal Reform International (www.penalreform.org) found that almost no jurisdictions have an avenue for women to present a history of abuse in their defense. How does she show that she was abused? Self-defense laws are not designed to help. Most self-defense laws require that the force or threat be "imminent" or immediate. Considering differences in size, strength, and power, most victims of abuse reasonably wait for a moment of weakness that may no longer make the threat of violence objectively imminent. But the battered woman is living with the ever-present threat. Women who are sentenced for killing their male partner are incarcerated for an average of three times as long as men who kill female partners.

One attempt to address these incongruities is the battered woman's defense. The defense arises from the battered woman syndrome, and those presenting it contend that a woman is a virtual prisoner in the relationship, from which she believes she is unable to escape. The perceived threat is constant, and when that threat becomes overwhelming, the action needed to stop it may result in killing. While there is little evidence that this defense deters conviction, courts that allow the defense to be presented are more likely to hear testimony regarding the experience of abuse.

SHELTERS AND THE BATTERED WOMEN'S MOVEMENT

According to *Women's International News*, millions of women around the world and tens of thousands of women in the United States have been physically abused, devastating individuals and communities, destroying health, and impeding national development. In the late nineteenth century, Protestant social reformers joined with feminists to establish shelters for battered wives, such as the Chicago-based Protective Agency for Women and Children. Those shelters generally disappeared in the twentieth century, and it was not until the 1970s that violence against women again became a focal concern of social agencies and feminists. The issue first emerged as women, nonfeminists and feminists, worked to heighten public awareness of rape and to establish rape crisis centers. Women who came to the crisis centers for help spoke of widespread sexual and physical violence by intimate partners, as well as their physical and sexual victimization as children. These conversations led to the development of the grassroots battered women's shelter movement.

Feminist activists and nonfeminist mainstream social service organizations, such as the YWCA and Salvation Army, established battered women's shelters. In the early stages, safe houses for battered women were offered to women seeking refuge. Those safe houses were private homes where the occupants were willing to provide a safe haven for a woman escaping an abusive partner. A porch light of a particular color would indicate its status as a refuge. In parts of Massachusetts, a home with a lit blue porch light meant that a battered woman could knock on the door to get help; in Baltimore, the color of the porch light was green. Other than those private homes, the first freestanding battered women's shelter in the modern-day United States was probably Women's House, started in 1973 in St. Paul, Minnesota, by the Women's Advocates collective. In 1975, the National Organization for Women adopted wife abuse as a priority issue and established a National Task Force of Battered Women/Household Violence. The National Coalition against Domestic Violence was established in 1978. Slowly, shelters were established around the country. There were only thirty shelters in the United States in 1977, but by 1983, there were almost five hundred shelters. Three years later, there were well over seven hundred shelters, and by 1995, there were more than twelve hundred shelters.[25]

The early battered women's movement was committed to women's self-determination, self-organization, and democratic participation. Its strategies for change focused on the battered women, their experiences, and their need for safety, refuge, social resources, and economic resources. Believing that battering occurs because a social hierarchy condones male violence against women, feminists argued that the logical response was social transformation. There were debates within the feminist movement between those who focused on legal and service reform and those who were committed to a radical transformation of the patriarchal system, which emphasized the connection between the male-dominated nuclear family and woman battering.

Shelters have long struggled with how to effectively accommodate lesbians in shelters designed around the issues of heterosexual women. While the vast majority of shelters say they welcome lesbians, few have specific programs to welcome them or specific knowledge to meet their needs. As so little IPV outreach has been done in the LGBTQ community, people are often not aware of the services that do exist and may fear that the stigma involved will be compounded if they reach out for services. Additionally, there is a heightened distrust of the criminal/legal system.[26] While significantly more outreach is being done in the LGBTQ community today, there is a long way to go before there is equal access to resources.

According to the National Domestic Violence Hotline, approximately 9 percent of those calling for assistance identify themselves as male.[27] Yet news reports in 2017 identify only two shelters that have been created exclusively for men. The men who are sheltered there report being victims of abuse by their male or female partners, as well as by other family members. Some shelters house both males and females, but this is rare. Most men in need of shelter are housed in hotels.

SYSTEM RESPONSES

Policing

As noted above, when domestic violence first emerged as a criminal/legal issue, it was the policy of most police departments, whether official or not, to separate the parties and calm the situation. Following on the heels of the Thurman verdict, and after the U.S. attorney general issued a report recommending that arrest be the standard law enforcement response to cases of misdemeanor domestic violence, mandatory arrest and pro-arrest policies were instituted in most jurisdictions. The attorney general's report also followed the 1984 **Minneapolis domestic violence experiment**,[28] the first scientifically controlled experiment to test the effect of arrest on incidents of domestic violence. This study concluded that mandatory arrest was the foremost deterrent against future domestic violence incidents. Subsequent replication studies have had varying results. Nevertheless, by 1989, 84 percent of all urban police agencies had mandatory or pro-arrest policies for domestic violence cases. As of 2011, nineteen states had arrest policies that are categorized as "officer's discretion." The remaining states have some combination of discretionary, pro-arrest, and mandatory arrest.[29]

Those who support the case for mandatory arrest cite five arguments. First, if, as some feminist theories suggest, battering is rooted in sexual inequality, then everything about the violence, including the response, reflects the power of men over women. Battering denies women their civil rights. A pro-arrest policy, on the other hand, aids women in their effort to achieve greater equality by redistributing justice on behalf of women. Second, mandatory arrest laws are a method of controlling and directing police behavior. Policy dictates what the police are expected to do if certain criteria exist, and they can then be held accountable if they fail to take the required action. Police discretion in these matters would no longer be politically expedient. Third, mandatory arrest of offenders of domestic violence does provide immediate protection for the victim. Mandatory arrest gives the victim time to consider her options, get an order of protection, and make arrangements to leave if she chooses to do so. Fourth, mandatory arrest assures that police service is available to women on a more equal basis. And finally, a pro-arrest policy makes clear that domestic violence is a crime. A clear message is thus sent to the abuser, the victim, and the community that domestic violence will not be tolerated. This strengthens and reinforces informal social controls.

There is a continuing debate on the efficacy of these policies. Concerns about mandatory arrest include the possibility of **mutual arrest**, differing outcomes for different populations, and the efficacy of the victims. Early research concluded that if the police are mandated to arrest upon a reasonable allegation of abuse, they may be unable (or unwilling) to determine who is the aggressor and so choose to arrest both parties. As one might expect, this has a chilling effect on the likelihood of victims calling the police. Some states that have mandatory arrest specifically state that mutual arrest is discretionary. Other states actively discourage mutual arrest. For example, in Massachusetts, police who arrest both parties must file a report justifying that action. The same requirement is in place for judges when ordering **restraining orders**.

Another connection between policing and IPV is the higher than average rate of IPV in police households. This is addressed in chapter 10.

Domestic Violence Courts

From the time the laws surrounding IPV changed in the late 1970s until the early 1990s, the number of cases reaching the legal system soared. The courts were feeling the pressure of the volume of cases, and judges were often dissatisfied with their lack of options and apparent inability to effect a change. Advocates for battered women also believed that specialization was needed. Studies found that the lack of education of court personnel resulted in victim blaming, which often left the victim feeling vulnerable or even revictimized by the process. Domestic violence courts were believed to be a reasonable

MINNEAPOLIS DOMESTIC VIOLENCE EXPERIMENT
The first large-scale experiment to test the impact of arrest on repeated incidents of domestic violence. There have been numerous follow-up studies, and the results remain controversial.

MUTUAL ARREST
A concept employed by some police departments where, rather than determining who was the person who initiated the violence or presented the greatest threat, both parties are subject to arrest.

RESTRAINING ORDER
Like a civil injunction, but with possible criminal penalties; a court order requiring one person to stop an action or stay away from another person or persons.

response to these concerns. Domestic violence courts first appeared in 1993 in Miami, Florida. By 2004, there were almost three hundred such courts.[30]

Changes sought by the battered women's movement include giving voice to women who have been battered by making them active participants in shaping a remedy, effecting a change both in society's attitudes and in behaviors toward violence against women and moving beyond patriarchy or a model of top-down power and control. There has been a good deal of concern in the movement that the legal system itself reinforces the existing power hierarchy. Domestic violence courts might attempt to address these concerns but are also limited by the needs of the state for speed, effectiveness, and expediency. As a result, the unique challenge faced by domestic violence courts is to increase efficiency while addressing the needs of both offenders (participants) and victims. Supporters suggest that creating dedicated teams of judges and prosecutors will lead to more knowledgeable personnel who can use their expertise to attend to the needs of victims even while processing the offender through the court.

Some research has found that both overall arrests and arrests for domestic violence were lower for offenders who had participated in the specialized court. Others found a lower rate of recidivism toward the same victim. For example, in a Miami court, the chance of having a misdemeanor dismissed was 37 percent lower for cases processed in the domestic violence court. But the participants do not always agree with the conclusions of researchers. In a study of Florida's domestic violence courts, victims reported a "general lack of assistance"[31] with the court process, which was associated with a frequent turnover in staff. Victims also reported that they did not feel sufficiently protected or that their need for privacy was respected.

A comprehensive study of domestic violence courts across the United States found that the vast majority of domestic violence courts shared the goals of victim safety and offender accountability. Beyond these goals, however, the study found that there was little consistency in the structure or implementation of the courts. In general, the researchers found that the commitment and involvement of court personnel and of community organizations designated to provide ongoing services was key to a successful domestic violence court.

Among activists and other stakeholders, there remain concerns that these courts will be viewed as panaceas. In addition, there are concerns that dedicated teams of community service providers run the risk of being marginalized in the process, that consistency among the courts can be a disadvantage if the judge or prosecutor assigned to the court is not an enthusiastic participant, and that resistance among court personnel may be high when they need to rely on an extensive network, including prosecutors and defense lawyers, community programs, law enforcement officers, and judges, any of whom might not be understanding or sympathetic to a victim's actions.

Batterers Intervention Programs

The first **batterers intervention programs (BIPs)** began in the 1970s as recognition of the problem of battering began to enter the public sphere. Early programs were modeled after mental health and substance abuse programs. Some even chose to employ couple's counseling, a model that subsequently raised concerns about potential power imbalances and increased risk for the abused. In the 1980s, the focus shifted to the **Duluth model** BIP based on recognition of power and control motivating factors, as provided on the power and control wheel. The wheel provides a tool for men to identify the ways in which their behavior is intentional and by which they use power and control to maintain dominance over their victim. The equality wheel was later developed to illustrate characteristics considered desirable and nonabusive.

While the Duluth BIP is still considered to be the best practice available, it is far from a panacea. Research on the effectiveness of programs for batterers continues to indicate inconsistent and not very optimistic results. Dropout rates are high. For those who do not drop out, recidivism in the form of rearrest is reduced as compared with those not

**BATTERERS
INTERVENTION
PROGRAMS (BIPS)**
Programs designed to
prevent batterers from
reoffending; typically
court mandated.

DULUTH MODEL
Otherwise known as
the power and control
wheel, this has become
the generally accepted
model for education
regarding IPV and for
creating curricula for
BIPs.

Figure 3.1. Power and Control Wheel. *Domestic Abuse Intervention Programs, 202 East Superior Street Duluth, MN, 55802, (218) 722-2781, www.theduluthmodel.org*

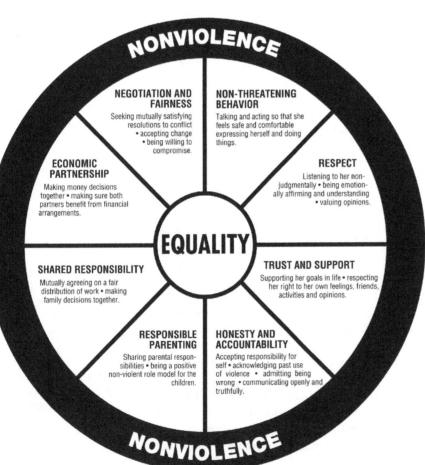

Figure 3.2. Equality Wheel. *Domestic Abuse Intervention Programs, 202 East Superior Street Duluth, MN, 55802, (218) 722-2781, www.theduluthmodel.org*

completing a program, but studies indicate that changing a batterer's attitudes is much more difficult. Not surprisingly, then, reports by partners of escalating verbal abuse suggest that batterers may have simply discovered less overt means of control.

In an effort to affect some of the shortcomings of BIPs, experts have recommended that these programs be coupled with community-based intervention and resources that go beyond punishment.

Coordinated Community Response

At the same time that domestic violence courts were developing, so was a parallel movement of coordinated community response to intimate partner violence. **Coordinated community response teams** are umbrella organizations that bring together domestic violence courts, prosecutors, and community advocates to provide coordinated services. Most initial efforts to address the criminal/legal system's response to domestic abuse were aimed at the actions of police. However, if police make arrests but the court system fails to follow through, that effort may simply aggravate the situation. Since the late 1970s, several models have been developed to bring together court and community actors—specifically prosecutors, victim-witness advocates, and community-based services for battered women—in an effort to encourage prosecution. Early examples include the Domestic Abuse Intervention Project in Minnesota and the Alexandria Domestic Violence Intervention Project in Virginia. These projects offered new promise by creating a dialogue between community advocates and prosecutors and effecting ongoing victim support.

An early example of such a coordinated response is the Santa Barbara Family Violence Program, considered an integrated model program. In most instances these are coordinated efforts that include the district attorney's office, the local police department, and the community, often represented by grassroots women's groups and/or the local shelter. This program was primarily championed by the district attorney's office, which then drew in the local police and the county sheriff. Community groups were not directly involved, though the district attorney, as an elected official, represented a community where grassroots feminist organizations wielded some power. The goals of the Family Violence Unit (FVU) that was established within the district attorney's office were to improve the reporting practices of the police by instituting an educational program and to prosecute cases more aggressively. Researchers believed that the unit itself succeeded, largely because of its independence from the rest of the district attorney's office. At the same time, the recognition of the importance of IPV from the district attorney gave the unit respectability in the eyes of law enforcement.

Duluth, Minnesota, was one of the first cities to establish a community intervention project (CIP), which is a coordinated community response that typically included mandatory arrest and treatment. Since that initial project, the CIP has become a popular model, with over twenty such projects in Minnesota alone. CIPs are founded on a shared philosophy representing a feminist construct of battering. First, no one has the right to use violence against another except in self-defense. Second, social norms have allowed men to use violence to maintain control in the family. And third, if society allows violence to continue, then the systems representing that society must provide the response.

Results of evaluations done in these and other program models are mixed. In general, research finds that no statistically significant difference in reabuse is evident. On the positive side, researchers found promise that a coordinated effort can produce greater levels of victim satisfaction and can ultimately reduce the rate of domestic homicides. One large-scale study demonstrated that women in the advocacy outreach program were more likely to be engaged in the prosecution of their abuser than women who went directly into the criminal/legal system.[32]

Since the passage of the Violence Against Women Act in 1994, funding has been provided for new collaborative efforts and for those projects to be evaluated on an ongoing basis. A component of VAWA, STOP (Services-Training-Officers-Prosecutors), required that states applying for grants encourage collaboration between law enforcement,

COORDINATED COMMUNITY RESPONSE TEAMS
A model of intervention to address IPV through the coordination of various services for victims and offenders, including police, courts, and service providers.

prosecution, and victim services. In the late 1990s, the U.S. Department of Justice designed the Judicial Oversight Demonstration (JOD) and selected three jurisdictions to serve as sites for criminal/legal system and community-based agency collaboration.[33] The success or failure of such programs was largely determined by the method of coordination. JOD emphasized the central role of the judge in directing the collaboration and bringing accountability to the process. The model employed was not very different from domestic violence courts, though the circle was drawn wider. As with previous studies of domestic violence courts, the evaluations of JOD sites were encouraging but largely inconclusive. Victims reported more involvement with service agencies, greater satisfaction with the process, and a lower level of fear than did a comparison group of victims. And while JOD increased offender compliance during their period of involvement with the court, it did not change expectations of negative consequences on their future behavior. Regarding recidivism, in two of the JOD courts, victims reported lower levels of revictimization than comparison victims, while in the third court, there was no significant difference. Based on offender self-reporting, there was no difference between the JOD offender and the comparison offender in either frequency or severity of violence. Some conclusions drawn from the evaluations of JOD projects are that the most successful programs have a diverse group of justice practitioners and community agencies. Building a well-managed group, where all partners play a role in articulating policies and practices, creates the most promising collaboration for addressing domestic violence.

POLICY CONSIDERATIONS

In recent years there have been several policies that are designed to move IPV away from the criminal/legal system, which fails many victims and perpetuates discriminatory practices. Considering the possibility of preventing acts of violence is not new, but some of the programs and methodologies are. One policy consideration for same-sex IPV would be to use more inclusive language and specifically targeted education, thus focusing on individuals rather than gender. Further, an important shift has been to consider IPV as a public health rather than criminal issue, thus focusing on prevention as key.

Since about 2005, the national CDC has made IPV a focus of its work. The CDC suggests a multipronged approach that identifies key risk factors and proceeds to address them by reducing the associated risks. In a 2017 report, the CDC identified several strategies, including ideas such as education, engagement, creating safe spaces, and improving financial security.

Education is an important tool for prevention, especially among young people, who are at significant risk for IPV. According to an analysis of the 2013 Youth Risk Survey, researchers determined that among students who had dated in the past year, 21 percent of girls and 10 percent of boys reported either physical violence, sexual violence, or both forms of violence from a dating partner.[34] Other studies, including the NISVS discussed above, indicate that the vast majority of people who experience IPV had their first experience before age eighteen. Programs that aim to educate young people have been emerging around the country. One such program is the Katie Brown Education Program (KBEP), based in Massachusetts. KBEP defines its mission as "promot[ing] relationships" through teaching students beginning in fifth grade "what healthy relationships look and feel like."

While few of the CDC suggestions offer radical solutions, it is worth noting their conclusion that economic security for families plays a key role in prevention. At a time in our history when providing public assistance has become an enigma, it is important to remind ourselves that financial security offers people relief from anxiety and anger, a decrease in gender income (and therefore power) disparity, and improved opportunities to protect themselves and others.

In addition to prevention, in recent years there has been an effort to reexamine the use of alternative dispute resolution models to respond to IPV. **Mediation** in situations of IPV has long been of concern to feminists, who argue that the inherent power imbalance

MEDIATION
A model of alternative conflict resolution that requires a neutral party to aid those in conflict in a conversation to resolve the underlying conflict.

negates the use of a tool that relies on relative equality between the parties. But in an effort to offer the victim more control and more choice, mediation has reentered the picture—with increased awareness and certain modifications that include preparations to secure the safety of the parties, prescreening for evidence of manipulation, and offering variations on mediation when necessary.

Feminists have raised similar concerns about the use of **restorative justice** in IPV situations. While restorative justice is not appropriate in all IPV situations, its use can be helpful in some cases with careful preparation and procedures. The positive aspect of using restorative justice is that the process is victim centered, the perpetrator accepts accountability and responsibility, and the support systems of both parties and the community are involved in determining the proper sanctions going forward. This approach avoids demonizing the abuser and can empower the victim. This is especially important in marginalized communities that already suffer the wrath of the system, including communities of color and LGBTQ people. Building on restorative justice principles, some communities have developed creative alternatives, often called **transformative justice**. One such program is Creative Interventions, a California-based program intended to "create and promote community-based interventions to intimate and interpersonal violence,"[35] and the Harm Free Zone Movement, coming out of the southern United States, that seeks to "repair the damage of racism and oppression of poor people of color" by giving the community the skills to both "confront and transform harm."[36] These programs are representative of what can be created when communities are able to more closely control how violence among intimate partners is defined, prevented, and condemned.

In the next chapter, we review definitions of sexual assault, legal issues, and the #MeToo movement. We also address sexual misconduct against specific populations, such as children, those in the military, and those in colleges and universities.

> **RESTORATIVE JUSTICE**
> A victim-centered response to harm that seeks accountability and responsibility from perpetrators of harm rather than punishment.
>
> **TRANSFORMATIVE JUSTICE**
> An extension of restorative justice that focuses on healing harms within the community, including racism, gender-based oppression, and environmental harms, among others.

REVIEW AND STUDY QUESTIONS

1. Describe how society's understanding of battering and abuse has changed over the past century.

2. If all women, and some men, are at risk of abuse, why are some populations more susceptible than others?

3. What response to IPV do you think is most useful? Least useful? Explain why you choose those responses.

National Intimate Partner and Sexual Violence Survey (NISVS). https://www.cdc.gov/violenceprevention/datasources/nisvs/index.html.

Videos/Movies:

Gibson, Brian. *What's Love Got to Do with It?* The story of Tina Turner. Touchstone Pictures, 1993.

GOING FURTHER

Readings:

Sipe, Beth N., and Evelyn J. Hall. *I Am Not Your Victim: Anatomy of Domestic Violence.* Los Angeles: Sage Publications, 2013.

Websites:

Exploring restorative justice models to address sexual harm and domestic violence. https://impactjustice.org/resources/how-can-restorative-justice-be-used-in-cases-involving-sexual-harm.

KEY TERMS

battered woman syndrome A term coined by Leonore Walker to explain why some women remained in abusive relationships.

battered women's movement A movement that began in the 1970s to protect the rights and interests of women in abusive relationships, often combined with victims of sexual assault.

batterers intervention programs (BIPs) Programs designed to prevent batterers from reoffending; typically court mandated.

civil injunction A court ruling ordering an individual to do or not do some specific act.

consent decree An agreement between parties to a legal action that resolves the underlying complaint.

coordinated community response teams A model of intervention to address IPV through the coordination of various services for victims and offenders, including police, courts, and service providers.

curtain rule A legal idea that reinforces separate spheres (chapter 1) by ensuring that the court will not interfere with that which happens in the private sphere.

cycle of violence A pattern of behaviors, sometimes used by abusers, where harm is followed by apologies and contrition, followed in turn by a repeat of the harmful acts.

Duluth model Otherwise known as the power and control wheel, this has become the generally accepted model for education regarding IPV and for creating curricula for BIPs.

femicide The killing of women; originally used to mean the killing of women by men as an act of hatred toward women.

interspousal immunity rule A legal rule that prevents one spouse from testifying against the other, effectively restricting one spouse from seeking legal assistance when the other spouse is abusive.

intimate partner violence (IPV) Replaces the term "domestic violence," especially among researchers and scholars. This is the terminology we will use in this text whenever it makes sense to do so.

intimate terrorism Primarily perpetrated by a male against a female partner, intimate terrorism is rooted in a general pattern of control, jealousy, patriarchal beliefs, power, and stalking, whereas situational couple violence, in which either partner can be the aggressor, is embedded in a specific situation where conflict is settled with violence.

learned helplessness An element of battered woman syndrome that explained the state where a person might try, repeatedly, to break a pattern of abuse, to change a partner's behaviors, or to modify their own to reduce what they perceived as their chance of being harmed, only to find that their actions did not reduce those harms.

mediation A model of alternative conflict resolution that requires a neutral party to aid those in conflict in a conversation to resolve the underlying conflict.

Minneapolis domestic violence experiment The first large-scale experiment to test the impact of arrest on repeated incidents of domestic violence. There have been numerous follow-up studies, and the results remain controversial.

mutual arrest A concept employed by some police departments where, rather than determining who was the person who initiated the violence or presented the greatest threat, both parties are subject to arrest.

National Intimate Partner and Sexual Violence Survey (NISVS) A unit of the national Centers for Disease Control, NISVS is an ongoing survey that collects state and national data about intimate partner and sexual violence.

posttraumatic stress disorder (PTSD) A mental disability resulting from prolonged or severe trauma.

restorative justice A victim-centered response to harm that seeks accountability and responsibility from perpetrators of harm rather than punishment.

restraining order Like a civil injunction, but with possible criminal penalties; a court order requiring one person to stop an action or stay away from another person or persons.

transformative justice An extension of restorative justice that focuses on healing harms within the community, including racism, gender-based oppression, and environmental harms, among others.

NOTES

[1] Francine Russo, "The Faces of Hedda Nussbaum," *New York Times*, March 30, 1997, https://www.nytimes.com/1997/03/30/magazine/the-faces-of-hedda-nussbaum.html.

[2] Ann Jones, *Next Time She'll Be Dead* (Boston, MA: Beacon, 1994).

[3] Russo, "The Faces of Hedda Nussbaum."

[4] Russo, "The Faces of Hedda Nussbaum."

[5] Russo, "The Faces of Hedda Nussbaum."

[6] Russo, "The Faces of Hedda Nussbaum."

[7] Maggie Humm, *The Dictionary of Feminist Theory* (Columbus: Ohio State University Press, 1990), 159.

[8] Del Martin, "The Historical Roots of Domestic Violence," in *Domestic Violence on Trial*, ed. D. J. Sonkin (New York: Springer, 1987), 6.

[9] As cited in Angela Browne, *When Battered Women Kill* (New York: Free Press, 1987), 167.

[10] *State v. Oliver*, 70 N.C. 60 (N.C. 1874).

[11] Declaration on the Elimination of Violence against Women," United Nations General Assembly, 1993, https://www.un.org/en/genocideprevention/documents/atrocity-crimes/Doc.21_declaration%20elimination%20vaw.pdf.

[12] *Scott v. Hart*, No. C-76-2395 (N.D, Cal., filed Oct. 28, 1976).

[13] *Bruno v. Codd*, 396 N.Y.S.2d 974 (S.Ct. 1977).

[14] *Thurman v. City of Torrington, Conn.*, 595 F.Supp. 1521 (Dist. Conn. 1984).

[15] 126 Cong. Rec. 24, 120, 1980.

[16] Sharon G. Smith et al., "The National Intimate Partner and Sexual Violence Survey (NISVS): 2015 Data Brief—Updated Release," National Center for Injury Prevention and Control, Centers for Disease Control and Prevention, 2018, https://www.cdc.gov/violenceprevention/pdf/2015data-brief 508.pdf.

[17] Luca Rollè, Giulla Giardina, Angela M. Caldarera, Eva Gerino, and Piera Brustia, "When Intimate Partner Violence Meets Same Sex Couples: A Review of Same Sex Intimate Partner Violence," *Frontiers in Psychology* 9 (2018): 1506, http://doi.org/10.3389/fpsyg.2018.01506.

[18] "Leading Causes of Death (LCOD) in Females, United States, 2015," Centers for Disease Control and Prevention, accessed July 7, 2019, https://www.cdc.gov/women/lcod /2015/index.htm.

[19] Marvin E. Wolfgang, *Studies in Homicide* (New York: Harper & Row, 1958).

[20] Wolfgang, *Studies in Homicide*; Jo-Ann Della Giustina, *Why Women Are Beaten and Killed: Sociological Predictors of Femicide* (New York: Edwin Mellen Press, 2010).

[21] Lenore Walker, *The Battered Woman* (New York: Harper & Row, 1979).

[22] Michael Johnson, *A Typology of Domestic Violence: Intimate Terrorism, Violent Resistance, and Situational Couple Violence* (Boston, MA: Northeastern University Press, 2008).

[23] Michael Johnson and Kathleen J. Ferraro, "Research on Domestic Violence in the 1990s: Making Distinctions," *Journal of Marriage and Family* 62, no. 4 (November 2000), http:// doi.org/10.1111/j.1741-3737.2000.00948.x.

[24] Kimberlé W. Crenshaw, "Mapping the Margins: Intersectionality, Identity Politics, and Violence against Women of Color," *Stanford Law Review* 43, no. 6 (July 1991), https://doi .org/10.2307/1229039.

[25] Elizabeth M. Schneider, *Battered Women & Feminist Lawmaking* (New Haven, CT: Yale University Press, 2000).

[26] Christine E. Murray and A. Keith Mobley, "Empirical Research about Same-Sex Intimate Partner Violence: A Methodological Review," *Journal of Homosexuality* 56, no. 3 (2009), http://doi.org/10.1080/00918360902728848.

[27] "National Domestic Violence Hotline," accessed October 15, 2013, https://www.thehotline.org/is-this-abuse.

[28] Lawrence W. Sherman and Ellen G. Cohn, "The Impact of Research on Legal Policy: The Minneapolis Domestic Violence Experiment," *Law & Society Review* 23, no. 1 (1989).

[29] "Domestic Violence Arrest Policies by State, June 2011," Commission on Domestic Violence, American Bar Association, accessed May 18, 2019, https://www.americanbar.org /content/dam/aba/images/domestic_violence/Domestic%20 Violence%20Arrest%20Policies%20by%20State%202011%20 (complete).pdf.

[30] Susan Keilitz, "Specialization of Domestic Violence Case Management in the Courts: A National Survey," NCJ 199724, National Institute of Justice, 2004.

[31] Martha L. Coulter, Abigail Alexander, and Victoria Harrison, "Specialized Domestic Violence Courts: Improvement for Women Victims?," *Women & Criminal Justice* 16, no. 3 (2005).

[32] Anne P. DePrince, Joanne Belknap, Jennifer S. Labus, Susan E, Buckingham, and Angela R. Gover, "The Impact of Victim-Focused Outreach on Criminal Legal System Outcomes following Police-Reported Intimate Partner Abuse," *Violence against Women* 18, no. 8 (2012), http://doi.org /10.1177/1077801212456523.

[33] National Institute of Justice, "The Judicial Oversight Demonstration: Culminating Report on the Evaluation," by Adele Harrell, Christy Visher, Lisa Newmark, and Jennifer Yahner, NCJ 224201, U.S. Department of Justice, 2009, accessed May 18, 2019, https://www.ncjrs.gov/pdffiles1/nij /224201.pdf.

[34] National Institute of Justice, "The Judicial Oversight Demonstration."

[35] Mimi Kim, "Alternative Interventions to Intimate Violence: Defining Political and Pragmatic Challenges," in *Restorative Justice and Violence against Women*, ed. James Ptacek (New York: Oxford University Press, 2010), 195.

[36] Harm Free Movement Zone, "Forward Justice," accessed October 18, 2018, https://forwardjustice.org/harm-free-zone -movement.

Sexual Assault

This chapter shifts the focus from intimate violence to sexual assault and rape. You will read about a range of behaviors, the impact on victims, and movements designed to bring attention to both victims and perpetrators.

LEARNING OBJECTIVES

After reading this chapter, you should be able to do the following:

- Describe the legal history of rape and responses to rape.
- Identify the various categories of sexual assault.
- Articulate the impacts sexual assault has on victims.
- Describe the history and impact of the #MeToo movement.

Case #4: The Steubenville Football Team

In the small city of Steubenville, Ohio, on the very eastern edge of the state where a little sliver of West Virginia jumps up to separate Ohio from Pennsylvania, many residents of the town spent the morning of August 11, 2012, watching the high school football team's preseason scrimmage. Football is popular in Steubenville and all of Jefferson County, and Big Red, the Steubenville High football team, is central to the town. Steubenville had once had a thriving industrial economy and an attendant unsavory nightlife, but as industry collapsed, so had local businesses and the city's population. Poverty, drugs, and increasing crime rates accompanied this decline, and the population of the city in the twenty-first century has fallen to approximately 18,500 people, half of its historic high. For this reason, Big Red, which won state championships in 2005 and 2006, is often seen as the single feather in Steubenville's cap. Despite the city's small population, the football stadium seats ten thousand, and devotion to the team and to attending the Friday night games is a given for many Steubenville residents.

Big Red football players, for all of these reasons, are treated like heroes for the life they bring to the city. Trent Mays and Ma'lik Richmond were two players that stood out at the scrimmage that August morning; they were in a position to become the new idols of the town. Mays was sixteen years old, a quarterback for the team and a wrestler for the school who lived in nearby Bloomingdale, Ohio. Richmond, also sixteen, was a wide receiver who also played basketball and served on the school's track team; he lived with guardians because of a troubled family history. It was after this successful scrimmage and full of hope and praise that Mays and Richmond headed out to parties that night. High school students from Steubenville and the surrounding towns came out in large numbers to revel in the end of summer and make the most of the last couple of weeks before school was to begin. Jane Doe, also sixteen, from Weirton, West Virginia, a city just across the river from Steubenville, also attended the parties that evening. She too was an athlete, but not a student at Steubenville High.

The first party that Mays, Richmond, and Jane Doe attended that night was fairly large, with around fifty people in attendance. The party was hosted at the house of a football coach; there was a lot of alcohol, and it was only the first in a string of parties across town.

According to later testimony from both Jane Doe and others that took the stand for the prosecution, Jane Doe was drunk by about ten o'clock and had blacked out by midnight. Apparently others took advantage of her inability to take care of herself; according to testimonies, a Steubenville High baseball player was trying to convince people to urinate on her. She would go to a couple more parties that night, but not of her own volition—Mays and Richmond allegedly led or carried her from party to party, as she could not walk on her own. At one point, she vomited in the street; she reportedly had no top on at the time. In a car on the way to another party, Mays exposed the passed-out Jane Doe to others in the car and allegedly put his fingers inside her—this was recorded by someone who later testified on behalf of the prosecution, saying that he had filmed it on his phone but later deleted the recording.

As the night wore on, Jane Doe became increasingly incoherent and unable to stand or walk, and she vomited several times, but even still, Mays reportedly tried to get her to perform oral sex on him. A fellow football player who testified for the prosecution said that no one objected because it did not seem at the time as if there was forceful coercion happening. At some point, she ended up totally naked and lying on the ground, allegedly with Mays next to her with his penis exposed and Richmond digitally raping her. Another Steubenville athlete who provided testimony for the prosecution, a good friend of Mays, reported that he tried to tell them to stop before they did something regrettable, but they didn't heed his words. This person took photos of the episode, supposedly so that Jane Doe would be able to see what had been happening to her, but he later deleted the photos after showing them to a small handful of people.

Jane Doe slept on a couch at the location of the final party of the night, with Mays sleeping next to her, until at some point he moved to the floor. By the time Jane Doe woke up on August 12, photos of the night were already circulating widely via text and social media; she had no recollection of any of it. A photo posted by a Steubenville High student, allegedly Jane Doe's ex-boyfriend, showed her being carried by wrists and ankles, hanging limp as a ragdoll. The rest of the town also found their social media littered with explicit accounts of the night. "Rape" and "drunk" were notable keywords in several posts. Posting on one social media platform, a former Steubenville athlete wrote, "Song of the night is definitely Rape Me by Nirvana"; he also wrote, "Some people deserve to be peed on."[1] It turned quickly into town gossip, and people who had no real knowledge of what had happened started immediately aligning themselves with either the victim or the perpetrators. Some argued that Jane Doe herself was irresponsible for getting so drunk and she was the one who was dragging the football players into something unsavory. Some shared their fears that the football players were so beloved that they would be allowed to get away with anything.

It was less than one day before Jane Doe's parents saw photos and posts about what had happened, along with insinuations about rape and urination. By late in the night of August 13 and the early hours of August 14, Jane Doe's parents took her to the hospital to have a rape kit done, and they took all the digital evidence they had collected to the police. Because two days had passed, the police foresaw difficulties collecting physical evidence, either of rape or of common date rape drugs such as Rohypnol. Jane Doe herself still remembered nothing—all she had was the evidence from social media and the stories in the newspaper.

On August 22, police revealed that Mays and Richmond had been arrested. The charges were rape and kidnaping, as they had taken Jane Doe to several parties when she was not in a position to make her own decisions. While awaiting trial, which was projected to begin on February 13, 2013, the boys spent two months in jail and were then released to guardians in order to spend the rest of the waiting time under house arrest, complete with ankle monitors and uniforms. Their families maintained that they were innocent.

The case against Mays and Richmond was slow to build, partially because the city was so small and so close-knit that it was difficult to get witnesses to come forward. It became a battle waged publicly in the town, not just in the courtroom. As prosecutors compiled evidence for their case, three Steubenville athletes testified against Mays and Richmond in October 2012; the divisions were deepening. Jane Doe and her family had to have law enforcement patrol their neighborhood because of threats against them. William McCafferty, the city's police chief, maintained that as far as he was concerned, the football players would not get any special treatment, despite the fact that many people had been complicit in what happened both on that particular night and in the following silence that was threatening to cover it up. "The thing I found most disturbing about this is that there were other people around when this was going on. . . . Nobody had the morals to say, 'Hey, stop it, that isn't right.' . . . If you could charge people for not being decent human beings, a lot of people could have been charged that night," McCafferty said.[2]

The saga began to develop in different directions, and many lives became wrapped up in the occurrences of that night and the public debate that followed. One particularly significant development was a blog post by Alexandra Goddard, a former resident of Steubenville who blogged about crime; Goddard took screenshots of the social media evidence and posted it all two days after the arrest of Mays and Richmond. She was concerned that the police would not fully pursue the case because of the importance football held in the town, and she named several football players in her post. She called out the head football coach, explicitly condemning him for essentially condoning such behavior by letting the players stay on the team. She also railed against the police for not doing more to pursue leads on people who had been accessories to the crime. She was not alone in her anger—many people commented on her blog, and an online petition was started to get the school to publicly apologize for their cavalier and dismissive behavior in the wake of the allegations.

On the other side, there were many local residents who believed that the blog was irresponsibly smearing innocent people, and still others who believed that there had not been an assault at all and that the accusations of rape had arisen only because Jane Doe had regretted her decisions and was refusing to take responsibility for her actions. This view was shared by a volunteer coach for the football team, who had himself been on the team about a decade earlier. "The rape was just an excuse, I think. . . . What else are you going to tell your parents when you come home drunk like that and after a night like that? . . . She had to make up something. Now people are trying to blow up our football program because of it," he said.[3] Because of the city's love for the team, many of those who believed the accusations and were critical of the way the town idolized the football players were afraid to share their thoughts, as they felt that being open with their opinions would lead to potential ostracism from the local community or even threats to their personal safety. One person who was open about these thoughts was Bill Miller, who had himself played on the team in the 1980s; he felt that the players had always been given a pass for bad behavior and that the whole culture of the team needed to change.

Reno Saccoccia, the head coach of the football team, had been at the helm since the early 1980s. He had led the team to three state championships and many victories during his years with the team; the practice field was even named after him. He did not suspend anyone who was at the parties except for two players who testified in a pretrial evidence-gathering hearing. Steubenville High's principal and the city's school superintendent gave Saccoccia free rein to determine how to move forward, and he was the only person in charge of deciding if there would be academic or sports-related consequences for the players. The principal and superintendent took a totally hands-off approach; they did not talk to any students, and both claimed to have little knowledge of what was going on.

Despite the number of witnesses, it was difficult for the police to find physical evidence of rape. No semen was found in Jane Doe, and though there were photographs of her retrieved from Mays's phone, they did not portray rape. Other phones that the police collected also returned no useful photographs or videos. McCafferty, the police chief, was frustrated—his department was being labeled as lazy and perhaps incompetent, as they were unable to find more evidence, but at the same time, their inability to build a case was partially due to the fact that only one person who had attended the parties came forward following requests for witnesses.

During pretrial hearings, Saccoccia and the basketball coach at the school both stood as character witnesses on behalf of Mays and Richmond, along with several other community members. In these hearings, it was determined that because neither of the boys had any previous offenses, they would be tried as juveniles rather than adults. By the end of the year, both the prosecution and the defense were putting their cases together. Meanwhile, Jane Doe was struggling to do such simple things as attend school and interact with friends.

The lawyers representing Mays, Brian Duncan and Adam Lee Neeman, argued that the case lacked real evidence and that it was essentially about whether consent had been given; they argued that Jane Doe had been aware enough to verbally convey accurate information after the rape was said to have taken place, so according to them, she would have been cognizant enough to consent. Richmond's lawyer, Walter Madison, was concerned that the court of public opinion had already made their decision, which made the case more difficult. He argued that Jane Doe herself was no angel, based on her past social media posts and evidence of promiscuous behavior. Both lawyers felt that the players who had testified against Richmond and Mays were undependable witnesses, as they might have only agreed to testify in order to distract from their own possible criminal behavior, as at least two of them had reportedly taken videos or photographs of the event. The special prosecutors assigned to Jane Doe, Marianne Hemmeter and Brian Deckert, argued that consent had clearly not been given. They said, "The bottom line is we don't have to prove that she said no, we just have to prove that when they're doing things to her, she's not moving. She's not responsive, and the evidence is consistent and clear."[4]

The case was moving slowly, and it did not immediately become national news. It was partially the work of the disorganized body called Anonymous, which operates as a sort of digital vigilante fact-finding, hacking, and exposure project, that brought Steubenville to wider public attention. A friend of Goddard's, Michelle McKee, was one of the first Anonymous operatives to begin to highlight Steubenville. She had seen the posts on social media that disparaged Jane Doe, joked about rape, and contained images of the night, and her first effort was to try to appeal directly to national media outlets to get them to pick up the case. Sexual assault is so common, as is online bullying, that the case did not stand out to media outlets as worthy of special attention. The *New York Times* did finally publish an article about it in December 2012, but it went mostly unnoticed. Frustrated with the lack of attention to the case, McKee reached out to Anonymous on Twitter, and she soon began an online campaign against not only the Steubenville high schoolers that were thought to have been central to the rape, but those who were protecting them. Using the hashtag #OpRollRedRoll (in reference to the high school football team's website, RollRedRoll.com), McKee created a campaign that then passed from her hands to a larger Anonymous crew called KnightSec, led by a user named KYAnonymous, who had already engaged in several hacking and doxing campaigns against, among others, the Westboro Baptist Church and a revenge porn site. KnightSec not only hacked the football team's home

page but also posted a video in which they named several of the players, showed screenshots of several incriminating posts, and threatened to post the names, addresses, phone numbers, Social Security numbers, and known relatives of all the people that Anonymous felt were implicated in the case. They were demanding public acknowledgment and an apology.

There was much unrest but very little response, and on January 2, 2013, Anonymous posted another video—this time, it was a video from the night of the party showing a graduate of Steubenville High laughing about the rape of Jane Doe. This garnered considerably more attention than the first video. A rumor began to circulate that Saccoccia would resign as well, but this never came to pass. The Anonymous campaign also led to an actual rally in Steubenville that was attended by about two thousand people, furious at what had happened and the city's slow response to it; MC, an Anonymous operative and organizer of #OpRollRedRoll, was also in attendance. The rally was not just a response to what had happened to Jane Doe but a community acknowledgment of the prevalence of—and silence around—rape and sexual harassment. The increased attention meant that more awareness of the event led to negative publicity and even online threats against the potentially culpable witnesses. Other online crusades against them began to question the actions of the county sheriff, Fred Abdalla, whom they accused of deleting digital evidence; Saccoccia, for his devotion to the players; and the county prosecutor, Jane Hanlin, at whose house one of the parties on that August night might have occurred, and who allegedly tried to discourage Jane Doe and her family from bringing charges against the boys.

By January 3, national news turned its attention to Steubenville. Anonymous was joined by other online campaigns against the perpetrators and potential colluders. Despite the readily available evidence for the assault, many people in the town still maintained that the victim was to blame due to irresponsible behavior, and continued to support the players.

A pretrial was held in mid-February, and the case finally officially went to trial at Jefferson County Juvenile Court in March 2013; it lasted five days. The divided allegiances in the town resulted in a rearranged cast of characters in the courtroom. The county prosecutor, Jane Hanlin, as well as the judge in charge of juvenile crime, Samuel W. Kerr, recused themselves because of their connections to the football team. Judge Thomas Lipps came out of retirement to serve on the trial. A lawyer for the prosecution, Jennifer Brumby, was also removed from the case because of a connection to the county prosecutor.

Both to the media and in the trial, Richmond stated that he thought Jane Doe was attracted to him. The question of consent, as it had been in the preparation of the two sides, was at the center of the trial. The defense argued that because Jane Doe had been planning on meeting Mays that night, consent was implied. They also argued that there was no evidence that Jane Doe had definitely said no at any point and that the fact that Jane Doe had texted Mays the day after the party suggested that nothing non-consensual had happened. The photo of an unconscious Jane Doe being carried around by Mays and Richmond was presented as evidence; Richmond claimed it was taken as a joke, at least at the time, and the defense attorneys argued that the photo was simply staged and taken with the consent of all involved. This stance was refuted by three Steubenville High football players from the party who contradicted these claims.

On the fourth day of the trial, Jane Doe herself took the stand. She said that she had liked Mays and had trusted him prior to the party. She recounted what she had to drink that night and stated that she felt it was not a normal buzz and that she had never blacked out from drinking before. She had only fuzzy recollections until she woke up the next morning, confused about her whereabouts and unable to find her shoes, phone, and underwear. A couple of friends picked her up, along with Mays and Richmond, and after they dropped off Mays and Richmond, her friends told her about the picture that social media was painting about the night. She had told her mother when she got home that she could not remember anything, and her parents soon took her to a doctor. Over the next few days, she says, Mays and Richmond sent her several panicked texts, and this was part of what compelled her and her family to go to the police. She recounted how it was not until she saw video that she began to understand the extent of what had happened. Because she could not remember much, a lot of the discussion around her state that night hinged on the difference between being blacked out and being unconscious; in the former case, it was argued, she may have offered consent, but the photographic evidence argued strongly for the latter. As the case wrapped up, Hemmeter stated that "the things that made [Jane Doe] an imperfect witness . . . made her a perfect victim."[5]

On Sunday, March 17, the trial came to an end, with the judge declaring that Mays and Richmond were delinquent—in other words, guilty. Richmond was found guilty of rape and sentenced to a minimum of one year and a maximum of the time that would elapse until he turned twenty-one. Mays was also found guilty of rape, as well as distribution of nude photos of a minor, and was sentenced to a minimum of two years and a maximum of the time that would elapse until he turned twenty-four. Mays and Richmond cried as they heard the final verdict, while crowds outside the courthouse celebrated. Both of them apologized to Jane Doe and to her family in the flush of emotion following the verdict.

The trial was not the conclusion of the town's ordeal—the Ohio attorney general revealed that a grand jury would be brought together and that more charges against others might follow. Individuals as well as official bodies—Steubenville High School and the city's school board—were likely to be investigated for cybercrimes, tampering with evidence, neglecting to report a crime, and more. In November 2013, the Steubenville school superintendent was charged with several felony counts of obstructing justice. In addition, a school principal and a football coach were charged with misdemeanor counts of failing to report child abuse, and a volunteer football coach was charged with several misdemeanor counts, including contributions to juvenile delinquency. Many of the charges were eventually dropped.

Ma'lik Richmond was released from juvenile detention in January 2014, just ten months after his conviction; later that year, he returned to the football team. As a Tier I sexual offender, he will need to check in with a county sheriff every year for ten years. Trent Mays was released from juvenile detention in January 2015, after slightly less than two years of imprisonment. As a Tier II sexual offender, Mays will be required to confirm his address and whereabouts with a county sheriff every six months for twenty years from his conviction date. Jane Doe finished high school and continued on to college.

In March 2017, Deric Lostutter, otherwise known as KYAnonymous, was sentenced to two years in federal prison for hacking and for lying to the FBI.

THINKING CRITICALLY ABOUT THE CASE

1. How did the popularity and status of the alleged perpetrators affect the progress of the case and the trial itself?

2. Why was it important to the progress of the case that attention was drawn to it, both locally and online?

3. What sorts of factors affected the court's understandings of consent in this case?

REFERENCES

This case is adapted from the following sources:

Abad-Santos, Alexander. "Everything You Need to Know about Steubenville High School's 'Rape Crew.'" *The Atlantic*, January 3, 2013.
———. "Look Who's Already in Trouble over the Steubenville Rape Case." *The Atlantic*, January 4, 2013.
Abad-Santos, Alexander, and Matt Sullivan. "Enter the Trial in Steubenville, Where the Cast Is Not Merely Football Players." *The Atlantic*, March 13, 2013.
Blake, Andrew. "Deric Lostutter, Hacker, Sentenced to 2 Years in Prison for Crimes Tied to Steubenville Rape Case." *Washington Times*, March 8, 2017.
Harkinson, Josh. "Exclusive: Meet the Woman Who Kicked Off Anonymous' Anti-Rape Accusations." *Mother Jones*, May 13, 2013.
Jablonski, Ray. "Steubenville Rape Convict Trent Mays Released from Juvenile Detention." Cleveland.com, January 8, 2015.
Kushner, David. "Anonymous vs. Steubenville." *Rolling Stone*, November 27, 2013.

Macur, Juliet, and Nate Schweber. "Rape Case Unfolds on Web and Splits City." *New York Times*, December 16, 2012. https://www.youtube.com/watch?v=1wfuy-vnpWY.

Muskal, Michael. "School Superintendent, 3 Others Charged in Steubenville Rape Case." *Los Angeles Times*, November 25, 2013.

Simpson, Connor. "The Steubenville Verdict Is In, and These Boys Are Guilty." *The Atlantic*, March 17, 2013.

———. "The Steubenville Victim Tells Her Story." *The Atlantic*, March 16, 2013.

Warsinskey, Tim. "Steubenville Rape Case: Ma'lik Richmond Returns to Football Field and Hears Cheers." Cleveland.com, August 28, 2014. https://www.cleveland.com/metro/2014/08/steubenville_rape_case_malik_r.html.

CONTEXT AND ANALYSIS

Historical Overview of Rape

The history of defining and criminalizing rape in the United States is a tangled one. Long before questions of what precisely constitutes consent became central to sexual assault trials, many more basic questions, such as whether or not women had a right to refuse to consent at all, were at the heart of discussions around rape. During the era of **chattel slavery**, for instance, there were absolutely no prohibitions against the rape of enslaved people; it was, in fact, an extremely common practice. And even until late in the twentieth century, **marital rape** (also known as spousal rape) was not recognized as a form of rape at all. The law operated with the idea that a wife had no civil or human right to refuse to consent to her husband, and it was not until 1993 that every state in the nation recognized that rape within the confines of marriage is a punishable offense under certain circumstances.

There are no federal laws regarding rape. Instead, since the nineteenth century, each state has been responsible for creating and subsequently updating their own definitions of what constitutes rape. The language of state laws varies considerably. Some states are very detailed about what may or may not constitute consent and the array of acts that constitute assault, while others provide broader definitions that hinge to a greater degree on the use of physical force. However, the Federal Bureau of Investigation (FBI) aggregates all reports of rape nationwide through their **Uniform Crime Reporting (UCR)** Program and **National Incident-Based Reporting System (NIBRS)**, and the descriptive language used in their reporting system acts as a federal guideline or model. On January 1, 2013, the FBI changed the definition of rape within the UCR program from "the carnal knowledge of a female forcibly and against her will" to read, "penetration, no matter how slight, of the vagina or anus with any body part or object, or oral penetration by a sex organ of another person, without the consent of the victim." This definition no longer hinges on the use of force. The NIBRS defines rape (with the exception of statutory rape) as "the carnal knowledge of a person, without the consent of the victim, including instances where the victim is incapable of giving consent because of his/her age or because of his/her temporary or permanent mental or physical incapacity."[6] The process for law enforcement agencies and state UCR programs differs from state to state, but in the majority of states, law enforcement agencies report to their state UCR program, and the data travels from there to NIBRS.

Despite the fact that defining and criminalizing sexual assault is the domain of each state, the federal government is active in attempting to create policies and funds that aid in these efforts. In 1984, Congress passed the Victims of Crime Act, which created the Crime Victims Fund. This fund provides crime victims who seek retribution or support with monetary assistance that can help them with physical and mental health services or loss of wages resulting from the trauma of victimization. The funds are generally channeled through organizations that provide support to victims, such as rape crisis centers or shelters for those experiencing domestic or intimate partner violence, and is, in some cases, also distributed directly to victims. A victim of crime may also be able to work with a victim advocate, who may help the victim to identify services that can help with recovery. The advocate may also advise about legal processes and offer support during court proceedings, along with other services specific to the victim's needs. The availability of this assistance varies from state to state.

In 1994, Congress passed the Violence Against Women Act (VAWA), which increases access to services for victims of violence, including sexual violence. VAWA provides the structure and resources for interagency coordination in response to reports of violence, which means that victims of violence ostensibly have access to not only immediate protection and shelter if necessary, but also to longer-term assistance that recognizes the practical and financial difficulties of escaping an abusive situation. This assistance may come directly from state agencies or from organizations funded by grants established by VAWA. VAWA also introduced mandatory arrest policies, meaning that law enforcement agencies are mandated to make an arrest when responding to, or investigating, reports of

CHATTEL SLAVERY
System where people are treated as the owner's chattel, or personal property, and are bought and sold as possessions.

MARITAL RAPE
Sexual intercourse with one's spouse without the spouse's consent.

UNIFORM CRIME REPORTING (UCR)
Summary-based reporting of crimes to the FBI from law enforcement agencies that voluntarily participate.

NATIONAL INCIDENT-BASED REPORTING SYSTEM (NIBRS)
FBI statistics that go into much greater detail than the UCR.

sexual violence or assault. These policies have been controversial because of the potential for unnecessary arrests and because they may dissuade victims from calling emergency services or reporting a crime. For a variety of personal, political, and financial reasons, victims may need immediate assistance but may not want their attacker or abuser to be arrested or incarcerated.

VAWA also attempts to address the particular problems of what it refers to as "underserved populations," meaning those who are at a disadvantage because of geographical lack of access, race or ethnicity, language, citizenship status, disability, age, or anything else that presents undue obstacles. It also attempts to study and address the specific needs of indigenous women. Violence against indigenous women in the United States is often difficult to address because of the relationship between the federal government, state agencies, and tribal governments. Indigenous women who attempt to report violence often find that their reports fall into a gap in jurisdiction, particularly if their attackers are not indigenous and therefore are not accountable to tribal courts. Indigenous women are much more likely to be victims of violence than other groups of women in the United States, and the legal loopholes that prevent them from accessing support and protection leave them particularly vulnerable socially and legally. VAWA has done little to reverse this.

Current laws for every state, including the mandated punishment for different forms of assault, are available in detail through the Rape, Abuse, and Incest National Network (RAINN). RAINN, founded in 1994, is the largest antiviolence organization in the United States, working on everything from public policy and collaboration with different branches of the federal government to hotlines and direct services for victims.

Categories of Sexual Assault

Law enforcement agencies, both state and federal, as well as the criminal/legal system, recognize several different types of sexual assault. Along with the broader definition of rape as described by the FBI, the federal government also recognizes sodomy, sexual assault with an object, and statutory rape.

The NIBRS defines sodomy as "oral or anal sexual intercourse with another person, without the consent of the victim, including instances where the victim is incapable of giving consent because of his/her age or because of his/her temporary or permanent mental or physical incapacity." Sexual assault with an object is defined as "to use an object or instrument to unlawfully penetrate, however slightly, the genital or anal opening of the body of another person, without the consent of the victim, including instances where the victim is incapable of giving consent because of his/her age or because of his/her temporary or permanent mental or physical incapacity." The definition of statutory rape, according to the NIBRS, is "nonforcible sexual intercourse with a person who is under the statutory age of consent," which means that even if a person has given consent, the consent is nullified in the eyes of the state and federal government if the person is under the age of consent, which varies by state between sixteen and eighteen years of age. The definition goes on to clarify, "If the victim was incapable of giving consent because of his/her youth or mental impairment, either temporary or permanent, law enforcement should classify the offense as Rape, not Statutory Rape."[7]

It is only within the last three decades that sexual assault within marriages has been recognized as a criminal act. Under the legal system of coverture, which was discussed in chapter 1, wives essentially became an appendage of their husbands upon marriage, which was understood to extend not only to their legal status, but also to their physical bodies. Under such circumstances, the law did not recognize the rights of wives to refuse to consent to sex with their husbands but instead recognized the "conjugal right" of the husband, or his absolute right to sexual relations with his wife. Rape outside of marriage was recognized and criminalized, but in the case of marriage, there was a **marital rape exemption**. This legal possession of wife by husband was a topic of debate throughout the nineteenth century, and with the emergence of the first-wave feminist movement in the

MARITAL RAPE EXEMPTION
Recognizes the "conjugal right" of the husband, or his absolute right to sexual relations with his wife.

second half of the nineteenth century, concerted attention turned to the conjugal rights of husbands, which feminists argued were perhaps legal but unethical. However, even as wives throughout the twentieth century became granted increasing degrees of legal personhood, and even as scholars and public intellectuals began to recognize that a husband's conjugal rights were outdated and women, even within the bounds of marriage, had a right to refuse to consent, it was not until the second-wave feminist movement reinvigorated the debate in the 1970s that actual legal changes were instituted. Social relations had been changing; divorce was becoming more common, as were sexual relations outside the bounds of marriage, and the marital rape exemption came increasingly under fire, particularly as more women entered the legal professions. In 1971, the Supreme Court decided in *Eisenstadt v. Baird*, that equal protections must be given to married and unmarried individuals.[8] Although the decision was explicitly about extending rights to contraception to unmarried individuals to the same extent as to married individuals, it became a precedent in cases of marital rape as well. In 1980, California removed the marital rape exemption, and in 1984, the New York State Court of Appeals ruled in *People v. Liberta*[9] that there was no basis for exemption of marital rape.[10] Since the 1980s, all fifty states have overturned the marital rape exemption, but there is still great variability in each state's recognition of what comprises nonconsensual contact within marriage.

Though marital rape is now recognized as a crime, it is not always easy, due to a complicated variety of reasons, for victims to want to press charges. For example, if victims come from marginalized communities and know that by pressing charges their partners may face outsized punishment, or if victims depend on their partners in other social or economic ways, victims may see more danger in reporting rape than in simply keeping quiet. It is further complicated if there are questions of nationality, valid citizenship, or language.

Another recognized category of sexual assault is date rape, including acquaintance rape. The term "date rape" was first coined by second-wave feminist Susan Brownmiller in her 1975 book *Against Our Will: Men, Women, and Rape.* The emergence of the idea of date rape was important. The popular imagination often sees rapists as shadowy strangers lurking in corners or parks, waiting to attack an unsuspecting passerby, but the vast majority of rapes are not committed by strangers and are instead committed by people that are already known to the victim. Though date rape is not treated as a separate category of sexual assault by states or courts, it is much more difficult to prosecute than assaults by strangers, for a variety of reasons detailed below.

Legal Issues

It is very difficult to know precisely how many women have experienced rape in their lifetimes. The way data is collected, the sample sizes of studies, differences in the definitions of rape and sexual assault, and the reticence of victims all make it very difficult to gather accurate data to reflect the prevalence of rape and sexual assault.

Perhaps the largest difficulty stems from the fact that many rapes go unreported, likely because there is so much opposition to victims at every level, from first reporting a rape to law enforcement to seeing it all the way through to a rape conviction. There is a widespread social belief that many rape allegations are false, which contributes to the difficulty of trials for victims, where their characters are often assassinated. In most cases of reported crimes, police believe the victims; they do not doubt someone who says they have been robbed. This is not always the case with allegations of sexual harassment or assault. Also, law enforcement agencies and prosecutors might not think they have a good chance of ultimately securing a conviction in such cases, so they may be unlikely to pursue them. Prosecutors are able to decide whether or not they will take on any particular case. They can reject cases if they believe there is not enough evidence to convict the accused, which means that, with such a low conviction rate, many prosecutors will not take a case unless it is absolutely watertight, a relatively very rare occurrence. There is evidence to suggest that white victims are given the opportunity to press charges and go to trial at a greater rate than victims of color. The 2010 Lisak et al. study suggests that between 64 and 96 percent of rapes go unreported because victims fear the follow-up.[11] These statistics correlate with an article published by Kimberly A. Lonsway and Joanne Archambault, which argues that only 5 to 20 percent of forcible rapes are reported to the police.[12] Part of the key here is the fact that in the United States, we use the **adversarial system** in trials, which means that the evidence presented is sometimes less important during a trial than the ability of both prosecution and defense to dismantle their opponents' arguments; this adversarial system allows aggressive questioning of both the accused party and the victim, and this is another deterrent for victims who are considering taking their cases to trial.

There are several studies published that seem to argue that false rape allegations are very common. A 1994 study by E. J. Kanin titled "False Rape Allegations" was published in the *Archives of Sexual Behavior*; in it, Kanin argues that 41 percent of rape allegations are false.[13] His study was based on a single police department's handling of rape cases over a nine-year period, and he argues that the fake accusations arose from victims who were primarily seeking revenge or sympathy. Despite the extremely limited scope of his sample size (109 allegations over the nine-year period) and the fact that his evidence was collected exclusively from the police department itself rather than from victims, his article has been cited by more than 150 studies and articles and continues to be cited by trial lawyers. Several of those studies and articles, however, have criticized his methods, and researchers such as Lisak and others provide evidence that false rape allegations are actually between 2 and 10 percent of overall allegations.

Though these different forms of rape (such as date rape and marital rape) are now generally recognized by courts, rape and harassment convictions continue to be difficult due to disagreements over what constitutes consent, as well as different understandings of the meaning of forcible rape. As we can see in the Steubenville case, semantic debates about these terms may overshadow the realities of an assault in a court case, particularly in the adversarial system of law.

One consequence of the lack of convictions for rapists is the high likelihood that they will reoffend multiple times. A 2002 study by Lisak and Miller shows that more than 60 percent of rapists are repeat offenders,[14] while a 2009 study by Stephanie K. McWhorter et al. shows that that number may be higher than 70 percent.[15]

Sexual Assault in Colleges and Universities

Despite the fact that it is difficult to know how many women experience sexual assault, there are many different studies that show that women between the ages of eighteen and twenty-four are at a particularly high risk. This means that not only law enforcement and legal systems but also colleges and universities must be attentive to rape. In 1972, the federal government under Richard Nixon passed the Education Amendments of 1972 (often referred to as the Higher Education Amendments). One of its most prominent components was the creation of **Title IX**, which states, "No person in the United States shall, on the basis of sex, be excluded from participation in, be denied the benefits of, or be subjected to discrimination under any education program or activity receiving federal financial assistance." One of the driving factors behind Title IX was to establish gender equality within athletics, but it more frequently has been associated with college and university responses to allegations of sexual assault.

Generally, when allegations have been made, Title IX urges colleges and universities to respond quickly to the allegations, to move quickly to an adjudication process, and to make sure that students are safe by quickly removing any person found guilty of assault or harassment. However, because the harshest possible punishment is dismissal from the institution, the guidelines for their adjudication procedures are quite different from civil or criminal trials. Further, colleges and universities have a responsibility to protect the innocent against false allegations. As per a "Dear Colleague" letter issued by the U.S. Department of Education's Office for Civil Rights in 2011, adjudication processes initially mandated by Title IX required only a preponderance of the evidence to determine that

ADVERSARIAL SYSTEM
A system, as the U.S. legal system, where the judge acts as a referee between the prosecution and the defense, who zealously represent their party's case.

TITLE IX
Law that states that no person can be discriminated against by a federally funded education program on the basis of sex.

someone is guilty, rather than "clear and convincing" evidence. As we have seen, the way that evidence is treated in civil and criminal trials allows key pieces of evidence to be suppressed, and educational institutions are determined first and foremost to keep their campuses and students safe, so such suppression of evidence would be contrary to their stated goals. The "Dear Colleague" letter states, in part,

> Sexual violence, as that term is used in this letter, refers to physical sexual acts perpetrated against a person's will or where a person is incapable of giving consent due to the victim's use of drugs or alcohol. An individual also may be unable to give consent due to an intellectual or other disability. A number of different acts fall into the category of sexual violence, including rape, sexual assault, sexual battery, and sexual coercion. All such acts of sexual violence are forms of sexual harassment covered under Title IX.[16]

This clearly outlines the Title IX understanding of "consent"—the victim may not be able to clearly say no, but the lack of a clear no should not be taken to mean that consent has been given. The letter also states,

> In order for a school's grievance procedures to be consistent with Title IX standards, the school must use a **preponderance of the evidence** standard (i.e., it is more likely than not that sexual harassment or violence occurred). The **clear and convincing** standard (i.e., it is highly probable or reasonably certain that the sexual harassment or violence occurred), currently used by some schools, is a higher standard of proof.

From September 2017, the U.S. Department of Education Office for Civil Rights has been revisiting this issue and issuing new guidelines, with sweeping new changes coming into effect in the summer of 2020. The new guidelines create further protections for those accused of sexual harassment, assault, or misconduct. Among other things, the new regulations require colleges and universities to allow cross-examination of complainants, reduce institutions' responsibility for off-campus incidents (even if said incidents may effectively impede a student's ability to receive education in a nondiscriminatory environment), and allow institutions to adhere to a "clear and convincing" standard rather than a "preponderance of the evidence" standard. As always, these regulations may continue to evolve.

Sexual Assault in the Military

Sexual assault in the military is a problem that has become more visible in the last two decades. The Department of Defense (DoD) began to collect statistics on rates of sexual assault across all four branches of the military—Air Force, Army, Navy, and Marine Corps—in 2006. The DoD asserts that rates of reporting have risen since 2006, partially because of greater efforts toward prevention and response. In 2006, for instance, the DoD estimates that only one in fourteen assaults was reported, and by 2016, one in three assaults was reported. The DoD attributes this dramatic rise in reporting to the Sexual Assault Prevention and Response Office. Moreover, they report that the majority of those who report would recommend that others report sexual assaults as well, based on satisfaction with the post-reporting process.

The central work of the U.S. Navy's Sexual Assault Prevention and Response (SAPR) Office falls into five categories—prevention, assistance to victims, investigation into reports, accountability for offenders, and assessment of the presence of sexual assault in the military overall—and there are dedicated victim advocates and attorneys as a part of the program. The DoD's Annual Report for Fiscal Year 2017 indicates that there were nearly 6,800 reports of sexual assault over the course of the year, nearly 10 percent more than in 2016, and if they estimate that only one in three assaults is reported, the number may be closer to twenty thousand assaults in 2017.[17] The changes in reporting rates make it difficult to know the rate of sexual assault in the military.

PREPONDERANCE OF THE EVIDENCE
Standard of legal proof used in noncriminal cases, where the evidence indicates that the fact is more likely than not (more than 50 percent likely) to be true.

CLEAR AND CONVINCING EVIDENCE
Standard of proof that is more stringent than the preponderance of the evidence but not as high as beyond a reasonable doubt.

Despite the rise in reporting and victims' satisfaction with follow-up reported by the Department of Defense, the SAPR program has no actual authority and is able to do little more than make suggestions and launch awareness campaigns. In reality, there is evidence suggesting that sexual assault in the military is a deeper problem than the DoD report reveals. Since the early 1990s, occasional large-scale investigations into every branch of the military have made national news and reached the halls of Congress. There are estimates that more than one in five female veterans experienced sexual assault during their tenure with the military. The strict hierarchy of the military creates an environment where service members feel powerless to defend themselves when superiors harass or assault them, and women who experience sexual assault find that male colleagues close ranks against them, ignore their claims, or actively threaten them to deter reporting. Because of this insular world, there are also ample opportunities for retaliation against victims who report or even complain—the retaliation may be physical, or it may take the form of demotion or disciplinary action for the victim. As with complaints to city and state law enforcement, reports of assault are often dismissed or not taken seriously by military security and law enforcement, or the credibility of the victims may be brought into question. Unlike civilian reports, service members must report to commanding officers, who may have no incentive to take the reports seriously. Female service members report that their cases were handled poorly, that they were accused of making false allegations, that they were threatened with demotion, and that assistance and advocacy, including assistance from the Department of Veterans Affairs for injuries and posttraumatic stress, were unsatisfactory or entirely missing, despite the fact that people who suffer sexual assault while serving have rates of posttraumatic stress disorder that exceed the levels of PTSD in combat veterans.

Men are not immune to being victims of sexual assault in the military. Since men greatly outnumber women in the military, the actual number of men who have suffered sexual assault is much higher than for women, even though the proportion of men who have suffered sexual assault may be lower. There is evidence that up to 1 percent of men in the military have suffered sexual assault.[18]

In 1950, the U.S. Supreme Court decision in *Feres v. United States*[19] created the Feres doctrine, which prevents service members from holding the military or federal government responsible for anything they experience during service, including sexual assault. A 2011 lawsuit against the Department of Defense led by several service members who had been assaulted, *Cioca v. Rumsfeld*,[20] was ultimately dismissed, but since 2012, greater attention to the problem has led to certain reforms, such as requiring that officers higher up in the chain of command, such as captains and colonels, rather than commanding officers, receive reports, but initiatives led by Congress and others are hoping to eventually move investigation and prosecution to fully civilian bodies.

IMPACT OF VICTIMIZATION AND TRAUMA ON RESPONSES/BEHAVIORS

One of the complicating factors in sexual assault proceedings is the psychological impact on assault victims, who often exhibit signs of posttraumatic stress. Posttraumatic stress manifests in neurobiological and physiological ways and can lead to both short-term and long-term difficulties in physical and mental health. Dr. Judith Lewis Herman has written extensively on such effects, arguing that the proceedings around sexual assault are often dangerous to the physical and mental health of victims. The healing of victims often requires the ability to feel heard, to feel in control, to feel that they can own their own stories and receive acknowledgment and support. Not only does the criminal/legal system make each of these needs unattainable, but often the opposite of each of these needs is present. Victims regularly find that court proceedings, rather than acting as a catharsis, end up worsening their posttraumatic stress syndromes. As seen in the Steubenville trial and the social media storm around it, the victim found herself on trial as well. Her character and actions were attacked, her story was doubted, and she had to deal with her experiences in a very public way, all of which are antithetical to the healing and recovery process that benefits victims. She also did not see her entire community as a support due to the divided allegiances. Those experiences can have negative effects on mental health, as the victim feels increasingly isolated from strong social supports that can be key to coping with the pressures of the stressful court process. Further complications and obstacles arise if victims arrive in court with prior negative experiences with the legal system, or if there are communication barriers arising from language or culture. All of these obstacles are responsible for making victims decide not to press charges or to follow a trial through to its end.

The Role of Shame

When victims do decide to press charges and go through a trial, conviction of the perpetrator may have a positive impact on the mental state of the victim, in the sense that the act has been acknowledged and the aggressor has been identified and punished in some way. They may also feel that they have played a part in protecting others from the perpetrator. However, there is little conclusive evidence to show whether or not going to trial leads to overall positive or negative results for the victim, no doubt due to the extreme variability in experiences and outcomes. It is clear, however, that victims benefit psychologically and physiologically when they sense that their cases have been treated with attention and respect, particularly in states where strong supports and advocacy for victims are available. Conversely, it is clear that victims who feel that their cases are wrongfully declined by prosecutors or handled clumsily and unfairly suffer negative psychological and physiological consequences.

Another obstacle facing victims, potentially preventing them from reporting or recovering from an assault, is the likelihood that they will blame themselves or otherwise feel shame for their own assault. Victims may blame themselves for not doing enough to prevent their assaults or believe that they somehow "brought it on themselves." This shame may result in not seeking assistance, in beginning to engage in self-destructive behaviors, or in long-term anxiety and depression, among other things. The fact that vulnerable populations are often surrounded by messages that essentially blame victims for their own assaults ("What were you wearing?" "Were you drunk?") increases the likelihood that victims will feel shame or blame themselves.

Greater awareness of the myriad difficulties of rape trials and the hurdles facing victims (both external and internal) has created a push for more understanding among legal professionals. The National Center for the Prosecution of Violence against Women, for instance, which is a program within the National District Attorneys Association, focuses on skills and practices that allow for advocacy and representation of victims that is sensitive to the internal psychological impact of assault, as well as the external impact of the assault and subsequent legal processes. They also offer resources and training for effective and supportive practices that recognize the **neurobiology of trauma** and its effect on victims at every stage of sexual assault cases.

SEXUAL ASSAULT OF CHILDREN

The sexual assault and abuse of children is described and treated much differently than the assault of adults. Children are a much more vulnerable population, and along with physical sexual assault, punishable offenses can include such behavior as any sexual contact with a child, exposing one's genitals to a child, masturbating in the presence of a child, showing a child pornographic materials, creating or being in possession of pornographic materials featuring children, or having sexual online interactions with children.

Sexual abuse and assault of children is reported as infrequently as sexual assault of adults. There are studies that have shown that the reporting rate may in fact be even lower

NEUROBIOLOGY OF TRAUMA
Scientific study of how stress changes a person's neurobiology, including the brain.

than the already-low reporting rate for adults, perhaps because so much of the abuse of children takes the form of **incest**. Because children are vastly more likely to be abused by family members, friends of the family, or others who are charged with their care, and because they lack the knowledge or resources to report such abuse themselves, children lack the basic ability to protect themselves. Though parents are more likely to report sexual abuse of a child if the abuser is neither a family member nor a friend, or if the abuse is particularly violent, overall reporting rates may be as low as 2 to 6 percent for the sexual abuse of children.[21]

As with adults, children who experience sexual trauma may undergo a number of posttraumatic mental, psychological, and behavioral changes. Children who have experienced sexual abuse are at much higher risk than their peers when it comes to suicidal ideation, self-harm (such as cutting oneself or eating disorders), depression, anxiety, poor performance in school, running away from home, and many other psychological and behavioral responses that arise not only from suffering abuse but from suffering abuse at the hands of adults who are supposed to be trusted and responsible.

BULLYING/CYBERBULLYING

Another particular danger facing children (and increasingly adults as well) is the rising prevalence of bullying and cyberbullying. Though bullying in schools has been a known hazard for decades, cyberbullying is in many ways much more difficult to prevent because of the constant presence of digital and social media and the invisibility of those digital worlds to those who are outside of them. Teachers and parents, for example, may have been able to witness bullying in the past when it occurred in the physical world, but with bullying moving into the digital world, it is much more difficult to see for those who are unconnected, despite the fact that it is a form of bullying or harassment that can occur twenty-four hours a day due to the nature of digital media and social networks.

Cyberbullying has become such a problem that even the federal government has begun to address it. StopBullying.gov, an online resource of the U.S. Department of Health and Human Services, reports that cyberbullying may include "sending, posting, or sharing negative, harmful, false, or mean content about someone else . . . [or] sharing personal or private information about someone else causing embarrassment or humiliation." Moreover, it indicates that some forms of cyberbullying constitute criminal behavior. As we have seen in the Steubenville case, posting pictures of a minor engaging in sexual behavior is much more than cyberbullying; it is the distribution of pornographic material featuring a minor and is therefore a criminal offense.

The Centers for Disease Control and Prevention (CDC) report in their Youth Risk Behavior Surveillance System (YRBSS) that in 2017, nearly 15 percent of high school students were electronically bullied. Girls were twice as likely as boys to experience cyberbullying.[22] The important thing to remember about cyberbullying is that while it happens online, its effects spill out of the digital world into the real world. Victims of cyberbullying, like childhood victims of abuse, may begin to suffer severe psychological trauma that may lead to such behavioral changes as suicidal thoughts, self-harm, and depression and anxiety.

Some states have laws that explicitly address cyberbullying, but many do not. Instead, many state laws against bullying, intimidation, and harassment are understood to address cyberbullying as well.

#METOO

The online environment can also be a tool for resisting assault, harassment, abuse, and bullying. Recently, a major wave of public acknowledgment of sexual harassment and assault began when the Hollywood producer Harvey Weinstein was accused of sexual

INCEST
The crime of having sexual intercourse with a parent, child, sibling, or grandchild.

harassment and assault by numerous women in the film industry. The phrase "me too" in reference to sexual harassment and assault had first been used by the activist and organizer Tarana Burke as early as 2006, as she worked on her own nonprofit called Just Be Inc., which provides support to victims of harassment and assault, but it became a rallying cry around the world when the actress Alyssa Milano sent out a tweet in the fall of 2017 urging all those who have been victims to use the hashtag **#MeToo** in order to highlight the depth and pervasiveness of the problem. This "hashtag activism" reached out from the digital world and manifested in the real world. In November 2017, an open "Dear Sisters" letter was released by the Alianza Nacional de Campesinas, which represents seven hundred thousand female farmworkers. The letter expressed solidarity with women in the film industry who had been victimized and highlighted the extreme vulnerability of female farmworkers, who have even less recourse and resources to respond when victimized.[23] In response, an open "Dear Sisters" letter from more than three hundred women within or adjacent to the film industry was then sent from a coalition calling itself "**Time's Up**."[24] Chaired by Anita Hill, an attorney who in 1991 infamously accused Supreme Court judge Clarence Thomas of harassment, "Time's Up" is a fund supported by many prominent women within and adjacent to the film industry who want to provide legal support for victims, particularly victims who lack resources. Their fund is administered by the National Women's Law Center, an organization founded in 1972 that focuses on a range of policy and court decisions that affect women's access to civil and human rights. "Time's Up" brought the movement to the Golden Globes in January 2018; a huge number of women from the film industry wore black to the awards, and a number of them brought longtime activists and organizers from outside the film industry. Tarana Burke herself attended with the actress Michelle Williams. All of these actions brought more attention to the pervasive problem of sexual assault and harassment across many industries and continues to inform the national conversation about the social and legal treatment of gendered imbalances in all levels of society.

The next chapter discusses gendered hate crime, including theories, crimes against LGBTQ people, legal issues, and the effects of hate crime.

> **#METOO**
> Reference to sexual harassment and assault used to highlight the depth and pervasiveness of the problem.
>
> **TIME'S UP**
> Movement against sexual harassment founded by Hollywood celebrities to provide legal support for victims, particularly victims who lack resources.

REVIEW AND STUDY QUESTIONS

1. Explain why sexual assault on campus is such an important, yet such a controversial, subject.

2. What are some of the ways in which being a victim of sexual assault impacts a person's health, well-being, and life choices?

3. How would you explain the rapid and widespread movement known as #MeToo in 2017 after lying dormant for over a decade?

GOING FURTHER

Readings:

Finkelhor, David, and Kersti Yllo. *License to Rape*. New York: Henry Holt, 1985.

Herman, Judith Lewis. *Trauma and Recovery: The Aftermath of Violence—from Domestic Abuse to Political Terror*. New York: Basic Books, 1992.

Krakauer, Jon. *Missoula*. New York: Anchor, 2015.

Websites:

Rape, Abuse, and Incest National Network (RAINN), https://www.rainn.org/about-rainn.

Videos/Movies:

Dick, Kirby. *The Invisible War*. Produced by Amy Ziering, Tanner King Barklow, and Chain Camera Pictures, 2012.

KEY TERMS

adversarial system A system, as the U.S. legal system, where the judge acts as a referee between the prosecution and the defense, who zealously represent their party's case.

chattel slavery System where people are treated as the owner's chattel, or personal property, and are bought and sold as possessions.

clear and convincing evidence Standard of proof that is more stringent than the preponderance of the evidence but not as high as beyond a reasonable doubt.

incest The crime of having sexual intercourse with a parent, child, sibling, or grandchild.

marital rape Sexual intercourse with one's spouse without the spouse's consent.

marital rape exemption Recognizes the "conjugal right" of the husband, or his absolute right to sexual relations with his wife.

#MeToo Reference to sexual harassment and assault used to highlight the depth and pervasiveness of the problem.

National Incident-Based Reporting System (NIBRS) FBI statistics that go into much greater detail that the UCR.

neurobiology of trauma Scientific study of how stress changes a person's neurobiology, including the brain.

preponderance of the evidence Standard of legal proof used in noncriminal cases, where the evidence indicates that the fact is more likely than not (more than 50 percent likely) to be true.

Time's Up Movement against sexual harassment founded by Hollywood celebrities to provide legal support for victims, particularly victims who lack resources.

Title IX Law that states that no person can be discriminated against by a federally funded education program on the basis of sex.

Uniform Crime Reporting (UCR) Summary-based reporting of crimes to the FBI from law enforcement agencies that voluntarily participate.

NOTES

[1] Juliet Macur and Nate Schweber, "Rape Case Unfolds on Web and Splits City," *New York Times*, December 16, 2012, https://www.youtube.com/watch?v=1wfuy-vnpWY.

[2] Macur and Schweber, "Rape Case Unfolds on Web."

[3] Macur and Schweber, "Rape Case Unfolds on Web."

[4] Macur and Schweber, "Rape Case Unfolds on Web."

[5] Connor Simpson, "The Steubenville Victim Tells Her Story," *The Atlantic*, March 16, 2013.

[6] FBI.gov, "Frequently Asked Questions about the Change in the UCR Definition of Rape," December 11, 2014, https://ucr.fbi.gov/recent-program-updates/new-rape-definition-frequently-asked-questions.

[7] FBI.gov, "Frequently Asked Questions."

[8] *Eisenstadt v. Baird*, 405 U.S. 438 (1972).

[9] *People v. Liberta*, 64 N.Y.2d 152 (New York State Court of Appeals 1984).

[10] Rebecca M. Ryan, "The Sex Right: A Legal History of the Marital Rape Exemption," *Law and Social Inquiry* 20, no. 4 (1995): 941–1001.

[11] David Lisak, Lori Gardinier, Sarah C. Nicksa, and Ashley M. Cote, "False Allegations of Sexual Assault: An Analysis of Ten Years of Reported Cases," *Violence against Women* 16, no. 12 (2010): 1318–34.

[12] Kimberly A. Lonsway and Joanne Archambault, "The 'Justice Gap' for Sexual Assault Cases: Future Directions for Research and Reform," *Violence against Women* 18, no. 2 (February 2012): 145–68.

[13] Eugene J. Kanin, "False Rape Allegations," *Archives of Sexual Behavior* 23, no. 1 (1994): 81–92.

[14] David Lisak and Paul M. Miller, "Repeat Rape and Multiple Offending among Undetected Rapists," *Violence and Victims* 17, no. 1 (2002): 73–84.

[15] Stephanie K. McWhorter, Valerie A. Stander, Lex L. Merrill, Cynthia J. Thomsen, and Joel S. Milner, "Reports of Rape Reperpetration by Newly Enlisted Male Navy Personnel," *Violence and Victims* 24, no. 2 (2009): 204–18.

[16] Russlyn Ali, "'Dear Colleague' Notice from the U.S. Department of Education Office for Civil Rights," U.S. Department of Education Office for Civil Rights, Washington, DC, April 4, 2011, https://www2.ed.gov/about/offices/list/ocr/letters/colleague-201104.pdf.

[17] U.S. Department of Defense, "Annual Report on Sexual Assault in the Military," 2017, http://www.sapr.mil/public/docs/reports/FY17_Annual/DoD_FY17_Annual_Report_on_Sexual_Assault_in_the_Military.pdf.

[18] Kirby Dick, *The Invisible War*, produced by Amy Ziering, Tanner King Barklow, and Chain Camera Pictures (2012).

[19] *Feres v. United States*, 340 U.S. 135 (1950).

[20] *Cioca v. Rumsfeld*, No. 12-1065 (4th Cir. 2013).

[21] Judith Lewis Herman, *Trauma and Recovery: The Aftermath of Violence—from Domestic Abuse to Political Terror* (New York: Basic Books, 1992).

[22] Centers for Disease Control and Prevention, "Youth Risk Behavior Survey: Data Summary and Trends Report, 2007–2017," https://www.cdc.gov/healthyyouth/data/yrbs/pdf/trendsreport.pdf.

[23] Alianza Nacional de Campesinas, "Dear Sisters," *Time*, November 10, 2017, http://time.com/5018813/farmworkers-solidarity-hollywood-sexual-assault.

[24] "Letter of Solidarity," Time's Up, January 1, 2018, https://www.timesupnow.com.

CHAPTER 5

Gendered Hate Crime

In this chapter you will read about crimes committed against people because of who they are or what they represent. You will begin by reading the case of a young man whose profound hatred of women led to a series of killings. The chapter proceeds to cover hate crimes based on sexual representation as well as race and concludes with a discussion of legal defenses and the impact on the victim.

LEARNING OBJECTIVES

After reading this chapter, you should be able to do the following:

- Explain what makes a crime a hate crime.
- Articulate the reasons someone might commit a hate crime.
- Identify recent defenses to hate crimes.
- Describe the impact hate crime has on victims.

Case #5: Elliot Rodger

On April 30, 2014, the parents of Elliot Rodger contacted police after becoming alarmed by his curious behavior and a series of videos he had uploaded to YouTube. The videos were particularly alarming—Rodger discussed both suicide and homicidal intentions toward others. Several officers responded to Rodger's parents' concerns, but after arriving at his apartment near the Santa Barbara campus of the University of California, their concerns were, for the most part, alleviated; Rodger explained to them that it must have been some sort of misunderstanding with his parents. The Santa Barbara county sheriff's office later reported that the deputies who had visited Rodger's apartment had seen no reason to pursue further action. They did not detect the homicidal rage that had built up inside Rodger over the previous several years, nor did they detect any possibility that within a month Rodger would end up at the center of a public discussion about murder, misogyny, and gendered hate crimes.

Less than a month later, on May 23, 2014, Rodger sent a manifesto of approximately 140 pages titled "My Twisted World: The Story of Elliot Rodger" to more than two dozen friends and family members. The manifesto was primarily a memoir, in which he details his life until that point: his childhood and family conflicts; his history of being bullied; his hatred of women; his hatred of men who were, in his eyes, undeservingly successful in romantic and sexual relationships with women; his desire for wealth; his contempt for racial minorities and happy couples, particularly interracial couples; and, crucially, his plans and preparations for what he saw as righteous retribution. Through the manifesto, it is possible to see what led to the tragedy that would unfold. That night, he murdered six people, injured many more, and fatally shot himself.

BACKGROUND

Elliot Oliver Robertson Rodger was born July 24, 1991, in London, England, to a father in the film industry and a mother who was a trained nurse. When Rodger was five, his family relocated from England to Los Angeles. His parents remember him as a cheerful and sweet boy, but by the time they divorced in 1998, he was becoming increasingly withdrawn. He showed signs of compulsive behavior and began to suffer from severe social anxiety. By his early teens, he had all but withdrawn from social life, turning instead to computer gaming. Though he was never officially diagnosed with any kind of neurodivergence, he was given prescriptions for antianxiety medications in the middle of his teenage years; he took them only sporadically, if at all. Rodger's high school years were marked by bullying; he found himself the victim of teasing and occasional physical harassment and even changed schools in order to escape the bullying. He writes of his high school years in his manifesto:

> They teased me because I was scared of girls, calling me names like "faggot." People also liked to steal my belongings and run away in an attempt to get me to chase after them. And I did chase after them in a furious rage, but I was so little and weak that they thought it was comical. I hated everyone at that school so much.

Despite his difficulties at school and his reclusive behavior, Rodger's parents saw him as simply shy and nervous. He was diffident and seemingly never displayed a violent streak. Rodger's father noticed that his son had trouble talking to girls, inhibited as he was by anxiety, but thought nothing of it—it was, he thought, typical teenage nerves. By the time Rodger had finished high school, however, his anxiety had transformed into resentment and was well on its way to becoming anger. By the time he arrived at college, his anger had deepened. It was not an abstract anger; instead, it manifested as a deep and unshakeable hatred for sex and women. In his manifesto, he writes,

> My hatred and rage towards all women festered inside me like a plague. Their very existence is the cause of all of my torture, pain and suffering throughout my life. My life turned into a living hell after I started desiring them when I hit puberty.... Women deemed me unworthy of having them, and so they deprived me of an enjoyable youth, while giving their love and sex to other boys. . . . My life has been wasted, all because women hate me so much.

Rodger refused therapy and medication and became increasingly isolated. Though he seemed to find solace in online gaming, where he could escape his hatred of women in general and women that were sexually active in particular, he also found corners of the internet that only stoked his anger. In a handful of online communities, he could openly share his desire to hurt women and to make them fear him. At one point, he showed some of the websites to his father, who was both confused and alarmed by these virtual spaces; his father, however, could not fathom that Rodger would actually act on any of these impulses.

Many people in Rodger's life now wonder what sorts of signs they missed, what kinds of alarms might have gone off in their heads in response to some of Rodger's behaviors and sentiments if they had known what to look for. Dale Launer, a family friend, received Rodger's manifesto via email shortly before his rampage began, and like the others, he looked back to search retroactively for warning signs, for anything that he could have seen or acted on.

Launer had known Rodger since adolescence and recalls that he had tried to give Rodger tips on how to relax and talk to people. In retrospect, he surmised that some of Rodger's responses to these tips had given him pause. For instance, after telling Rodger to try something simple, such as just giving people compliments, Launer checked back in to see if Rodger had been able to muster the courage to do so; he recalls that Rodger responded, "Why do I have to compliment them? Why don't they compliment me?" Launer also recalls that Rodger had once said to him, "I have to blame someone for my troubles, and I don't blame myself." In the moment, these sentiments seemed innocuous, if curious; in hindsight, they take on much more weight. Rodger's penchant for playing online war games fits into this framework as well; though he played the games, none suspected that he would attempt to get his hands on guns in real life, let alone use them. And everyone wonders how things might have turned out differently if that visit from law enforcement in April 2014 had resulted in a search of Rodger's apartment.

LIFE AND DEATH IN ISLA VISTA

Rodger's time at UC Santa Barbara was marked by rising anger and an increasing willingness to act on that anger. The manifesto details many scattered incidents that Rodger acknowledges as precursors to his final act. At one point, he writes of feeling jealous of a couple that he saw in a café, and he describes following them out of the café in order to throw his coffee on them. In a later incident, he threw a latte on two girls sitting at a bus stop in Isla Vista; he was enraged at them for not smiling at him.

On July 20, 2013, Rodger attended a party in Isla Vista where he hoped to finally meet a girl; as he wrote in his manifesto, "I was giving the female gender one last chance to provide me with the pleasures I deserved from them." Instead, he attempted to push several women off a ten-foot ledge. Accounts of the night are contradictory, so it is not clear what actually transpired. Rodger ended up at the hospital the next day for a broken ankle, but an accurate account of the events surrounding the broken ankle is difficult to piece together. Others said he was trying to physically force women off the ledge and that he then fell off the ledge himself; then, after disappearing for a short time, he tried to pick a fight with several men at the party. Rodger reported that a physical altercation was instigated by other men at the party and that he had been pushed off the ledge in a vicious act of bullying. Muddying the story even more is the fact that his telling of the story in the manifesto contradicts the story he told officers when they came to question him at the hospital where his ankle was being treated, and both of Rodger's versions of the events contradict accounts of other partygoers that were collected by officers. Officers ultimately determined that it was likely that Rodger had been the one who had instigated any

altercation. Despite the hazy story, one thing is clear: this incident was the final catalyst for Rodger's eventual actions. He writes in his manifesto, "The highly unjust experience of being beaten and humiliated in front of everyone in Isla Vista, and their subsequent lack of concern for my well-being, was the last and final straw."

By the start of 2014, Rodger was beginning to more actively take out his anger on others. On January 15, 2014, he accused his roommate Cheng Yuan Hong of stealing his candles; he performed a citizen's arrest and called 911. Hong was charged with petty theft. Rodger also began to be more active on YouTube, broadcasting his anger into the digital world in videos titled, among other things, "Why do girls hate me so much?" and "Life is so unfair because girls don't want me." In the videos, he indicated that he wanted to punish women for rejecting him and that he also wanted vengeance against sexually active males for living a more enjoyable life than his own. It was these videos that caused his parents to contact police. We now know that Rodger's videos were indeed cause for concern; we also know from his manifesto that by the time the police visited him in April, he had already planned the killings, and that if the officers who interviewed him at his apartment had conducted a search, they would have found his plans, his manifesto, and three legally purchased semiautomatic handguns and more than four hundred rounds of ammunition. In his manifesto, Rodger recalls his relief at the officers' departure:

> The police would have searched my room, found all of my guns and weapons, along with my writings about what I plan to do with them. I would have been thrown in jail, denied of the chance to exact revenge on my enemies. I can't imagine a hell darker than that. Thankfully, that wasn't the case, but it was so close.

Just after 9 p.m. on May 23, 2014, Rodger sent his manifesto, "My Twisted World: The Story of Elliot Rodger," to around two dozen friends and family members, including his therapist, who immediately called Rodger's mother. In a panic, his mother checked his YouTube channel to find that he had quite recently uploaded a video titled "Elliot Rodger's Retribution," in which he clearly detailed his plans: "Well, this is my last video, it all has come to this. . . . Tomorrow is the day of retribution, the day in which I will have my revenge against humanity, against all of you. . . . On the day of retribution I am going to enter the hottest sorority house of UCSB and I will slaughter every single spoiled, stuck-up blond slut I see inside there." His mother now understood: this plan was not hypothetical, and his anger had real targets.

> Vengeance is the only path; all other paths had been closed shut. I thought it to be such a tragedy that I was actually going to wage war against women and

all of humanity. But then again, women's rejection of me was a declaration of war. They insulted me by deeming me inferior of their love and sex. They hate me, and I will return that hatred one-thousand fold. I will inflict suffering on everyone in Isla Vista, just like they have made me suffer.

His mother frantically called his father, and the two of them raced to Isla Vista, hoping that they could reach their son before his "day of retribution." It was, however, too late—they were still on the road when they got news of the rampage.

Rodger began by murdering his two roommates, Cheng Yuan Hong (twenty) and Weihan Wang (twenty), as well as George Chen (nineteen), a friend of theirs who had stopped by; each of them was stabbed many times and had injuries indicating that they had tried to fend Rodger off. Police reports of the stabbings suggest that they had each come into the apartment alone and that Rodger had dragged each successive body out of sight so as to take each new entrant into the apartment by surprise. From there, he headed toward campus in his car. He tried unsuccessfully to enter the Alpha Phi sorority house, and when he found that he was unable to get in, he began shooting at people on the street. Katherine Cooper (twenty-two) and Veronika Weiss (nineteen) were fatally shot in this stage of the attack. Rodger then moved on to a section of Isla Vista where several restaurants and shops are located where he shot wildly at several more people and killed Christopher Michael Martinez (twenty). Over the eight minutes of this public attack, several more people were injured, both by gunfire and by his vehicle, which he was also using as a weapon. Police responded quickly, briefly exchanging fire with Rodger. Rodger eventually crashed his car, and when officers approached the vehicle, they found that he had a fatal gunshot wound to the head that was apparently self-inflicted.

A search of his apartment would later reveal several knives of various sizes, a hard copy of his manifesto, bloody clothes, and slashed-up pillows and sheets. An examination of his internet search history revealed searches for knife attacks, Adolf Hitler, and pornography, as well as very specific search terms, such as "roommate takes very long showers."[1] His browser history also included visits to body-building sites and various sites centered around the "pickup artist" (PUA) and men's rights communities, including the now-defunct site puahate.com, where men would share frustrations about their unsuccessful attempts to learn pickup artistry and seduction from sites and gurus that claimed to offer such guidance. These were the same sites that Rodger had shown his father, to his father's consternation.

AFTERMATH

After Rodger's rampage, users of the pickup artist and men's rights sites responded in many ways. One user said,

"Many people commented that it was inevitable something like this would happen. . . . Maybe people thought it was humor, maybe no one thought someone would actually do it. But you have a site that cultivates these type of thoughts, and men who have this type of rage." Another agreed: "The site was a ticking time bomb." Another commented on the way that the sites could turn into a dangerous echo chamber: "There's an amplification effect. . . . It spurs people on, and people who come in with disagreements tend to be chased out. It's made clear that dissenting opinions aren't welcome, especially ones that go against the dominant narrative." Several commenters note that some users expressed open admiration for Rodger's actions. There were others, however, who defended the sites, arguing that they were not dangerous but were rather "more light-hearted than violent."[2]

While the nation debated the issues that arose in this case—gun rights, mental illness and depression, and misogyny—UC Santa Barbara reeled from the loss of their students and from the shock of such violence. The families of those who had been killed, along with the campus community, raged and mourned. Police cleared Cheng Yuan Hong posthumously of the charge of petty theft of the candles.

THINKING CRITICALLY ABOUT THE CASE

1. Were Elliot Rodger's case to go to court, is it likely that he would have been charged with a hate crime? Why or why not?

2. What, if any, responsibility for Rodger's actions should be assigned to the law enforcement officers who initially determined that he was not a threat?

3. What, if any, responsibility for Rodger's actions should be assigned to the online communities that fostered his anger?

REFERENCES

This case is adapted from the following sources:

Brugger, Kelsey. "Elliot Rodger Report Details Long Struggle with Mental Illness." *Santa Barbara Independent*, February 20, 2015. https://www.independent.com/2015/02/20/elliot-rodger-report-details-long-struggle-mental-illness.

Launer, Dale. "How I Tried to Help Elliot Rodger." BBC.com, July 9, 2014. https://www.bbc.com/news/magazine-28197785.

"The Manifesto of Elliot Rodger." *New York Times*, May 25, 2014. https://www.nytimes.com/interactive/2014/05/25/us/shooting-document.html?_r=0.

Mozingo, Joe. "Frantic Parents of Shooting Suspect Raced to Isla Vista during Rampage." *Los Angeles Times*, May 25, 2014. https://www.latimes.com/local/lanow/la-me-ln-frantic-parents-isla-vista-shootings-20140525-story.html.

Penny, Laurie. "Laurie Penny on Misogynist Extremism: Let's Call the Isla Vista Killings What They Were." *New Statesman*, May 25,

2014. https://www.newstatesman.com/lifestyle/2014/05/lets-call -isla-vista-killings-what-they-were-misogynist-extremism.

"The Secret Life of Elliot Rodger." ABC News. Accessed June 1, 2019. https://abcnews.go.com/US/fullpage/secret-life-elliot-rodger -24322227.

Woolf, Nicky. "'PUAhate' and 'ForeverAlone': Inside Elliot Rodger's Online Life." *Guardian*, May 30, 2014. https:// www.theguardian.com/world/2014/may/30/elliot-rodger-puahate -forever-alone-reddit-forums.

CONTEXT AND ANALYSIS

The actions of Elliot Rodger ignited a public discussion that veered in many directions. As often happens in cases of mass shootings, much of the discussion focused on the questions of gun control and mental illness. As contentious as those topics are, much of the public discourse surrounding the event centered on a perhaps even more contentious issue: Rodger's hatred of women and the larger discussion of **misogyny** that his actions evoked. Some commentators reject the notion that Rodger's actions were a hate crime driven by misogyny. Others argued that misogyny was at the core of his anger, pointing to his manifesto, titled "My Twisted World: The Story of Elliot Rodger,"[3] as evidence:

> Females truly have something mentally wrong with them. Their minds are flawed, and at this point in my life I was beginning to see it. The more I explored my college town of Isla Vista, the more ridiculousness I witnessed. All of the hot, beautiful girls walked around with obnoxious, tough jock-type men who partied all the time and acted crazy. They should be going for intelligent gentlemen such as myself. Women are sexually attracted to the wrong type of man. This is a major flaw in the very foundation of humanity . . .
>
> Women should not have the right to choose who to mate and breed with. That decision should be made for them by rational men of intelligence. If women continue to have rights, they will only hinder the advancement of the human race by breeding with degenerate men and creating stupid, degenerate offspring . . .
>
> Women are like a plague. They don't deserve to have any rights. Their wickedness must be contained in order to prevent future generations from falling to degeneracy. Women are vicious, evil, barbaric animals, and they need to be treated as such.

Focusing on not only Rodger's hatred for women, but also the online spaces that stoked his anger, feminist commentator Laurie Penny writes,

> We have allowed ourselves to believe, for a long time, that the misogynist subcultures flourishing on- and offline in the past half-decade, the vengeful sexism seeding in resentment in a time of rage and austerity, is best ignored. We have allowed ourselves to believe that those fetid currents aren't really real, that they don't matter, that they have no relation to "real-world" violence. But if the Isla Vista massacre is the first confirmed incident of an incident of gross and bloody violence directly linked to the culture of "Men's Rights" activism and Pickup Artist (PUA) ideology, an ideology that preys on lost, angry men, then it cannot be ignored or dismissed any more.[4]

Penny and others pointed to those sections of the internet where "men's rights" and "pickup artist" ideologies grew, where social media sites and other online platforms allow men to gather and discuss, among other things, tactics for picking up women, hatred for women, and their own frustrations and resentment.

So, the question is, was this a hate crime?

HATE CRIME IN THEORY

A hate crime arises from a strong bias against a group that then manifests as the targeting of a person, persons, or property that represent said group. The bias itself may have social, historical, cultural, psychological, economic, or interrelational underpinnings that give rise to deep hostility and, in some cases, violence.

The legal understanding of hate crime has changed over the years. According to the FBI, hate crimes have generally been understood as crimes against groups and individuals in which the ethnicity, race, religion, or nationality of the victim is the major driver of the crime. Since 2009, this definition has been expanded to include crimes that are driven by bias, discrimination, or hatred of particular genders, gender identities, sexual

MISOGYNY
Refers to prejudice, anger, hatred of, or contempt for women and girls.

orientations, and disabilities. The FBI currently defines hate crime as a "criminal offense against a person or property motivated in whole or in part by an offender's bias against a race, religion, disability, sexual orientation, ethnicity, gender, or gender identity."[5]

A hate crime may involve physical violence against individuals or groups, as well as physical destruction or vandalism of property. Historic and high-profile hate crimes in the United States include such acts as lynchings, mass shootings, arson and bombings of churches and other public spaces, and graffiti (for instance, spray-painted swastikas, racial slurs, or other messages meant to scare or intimidate).

There is much debate about what may be classified as a hate crime, and much of this debate hangs on the perceived intent of the offender. There is also debate about whether speech itself may be considered a hate crime, or a crime at all. Free speech is protected by the First Amendment of the U.S. Constitution, which reads, "Congress shall make no law respecting an establishment of religion, or prohibiting the free exercise thereof; or abridging the freedom of speech, or of the press; or the right of the people peaceably to assemble, and to petition the Government for a redress of grievances." Free speech, however, does have its limits. In the landmark 1969 Supreme Court case *Brandenburg v. Ohio*,[6] Ku Klux Klan member Clarence Brandenburg was convicted for advocating violence through speech, specifically in a speech he gave that called for violence against Jews and African Americans. This, the court argued, was criminal syndicalism, or direct advocacy of criminal acts for the purpose of political and social change. The decision of the Court in *Brandenburg v. Ohio* said in part that "the constitutional guarantees of free speech and free press do not permit a State to forbid or proscribe advocacy of the use of force or of law violation except where such advocacy is directed to inciting or producing imminent lawless action and is likely to incite or produce such action." In other words, speech that abstractly discusses a particular act or ideology is protected, even if such an act relates to violence or criminal behavior, but speech that directly incites violent or criminal behavior is not protected, as it is then an active participant in any ensuing act of violent or criminal behavior.

However, while Brandenburg's speech was meant to incite violent acts toward individuals based on those individuals' race or religion, the decision of the Court was in response to the incitement of a criminal act rather than to the bias against particular groups. In the United States, hate speech is not recognized as a criminal act in itself and is protected under the First Amendment. This stance was reaffirmed in the 2017 Supreme Court case of *Matal v. Tam*,[7] in which the Supreme Court decided that a U.S. Patent and Trademark Office provision prohibiting the trademark or patenting of disparaging or discriminatory names was in violation of the First Amendment. This, again, is due to the fact that speech that abstractly discusses a particular act or ideology is protected.

Misogyny

In the case of Elliot Rodger, his manifesto makes it clear that his anger was directed at particular populations—in particular, he had an extreme prejudice against women. This is what is known as misogyny.

Misogyny takes many forms. In the case of Rodger, it manifested as prejudice, anger, a sense of privilege or entitlement to women, a belief that women and girls are less intelligent and capable than men, and violence against and objectification of women. In other cases, it may take the form of discrimination by employers, legislation that does not protect equal rights, and sexual assault or harassment.

As we see above, while Rodger and others in online forums express hatred for and violent tendencies toward women, their discussions are seen as abstract rather than as direct incitement toward violence; hence, the forums and their participants are fully within their rights. These communities have bred what is now known as the **incel community**. "Incel" stands for "involuntary celibate" and is shorthand for a man who wishes to have a sexual partner but does not have one, and who is not only extremely unhappy about it but transforms that unhappiness into hatred for women. The **Southern Poverty Law Center (SPLC)** has included the incel ideology of male supremacy and violence against

INCEL COMMUNITY
Men called "involuntary celibates" who are an online subculture that define themselves as unable to find a romantic or sexual partner. They have increasingly become more extremist, often focusing on violence in recent years.

SOUTHERN POVERTY LAW CENTER (SPLC)
An organization that monitors hate groups and other extremists throughout the United States, exposing their activities.

women in their map of hate groups in the United States due to not only the violent comments and ideologies originating from this online subculture but for their elevation of Elliot Rodger to the status of hero and their advocacy for further violence against women. However, while the SPLC highlights two particular groups as propagating this ideology and essentially encouraging hate crimes, it is unusual for crimes against women, such as sexual assault or domestic abuse, to be prosecuted as hate crimes.

According to the FBI's 2017 hate crime statistics, collected from the Uniform Crime Reporting (UCR) Program, hate crimes resulting from gender bias were less than 1 percent of all hate crimes during the year in question. However, the UCR statistics suggest that these incidences of gender-based hate crimes were approximately evenly split between anti-female incidents (twenty-eight) and anti-male incidents (twenty-five).[8] This raises the question of whether forms of violence in which women are much more likely to be victims, such as sexual assault and domestic abuse, arise from misogynistic ideologies and are, as a result, hate crimes, and what the legal ramifications of classifying it as such might be. Second-wave feminist theorists such as Susan Brownmiller, Catharine MacKinnon, and Kate Millett have argued that the histories and prevalence of men sexually abusing and assaulting women are histories of gendered bias, intimidation, and domination and that these histories arise from misogynistic ideologies. Attorney Marguerite Angelari, drawing from these arguments, has demonstrated that acts of domestic and sexual violence often bear the same features as hate crimes: objectification and depersonalization of the victim by the attacker, lack of other forms of criminal motive, and a desire to control and terrorize. While it may be difficult to prove intent in such cases, it is difficult to prove intent in any instance of a hate crime. Angelari has argued that hate crime statutes should include acts of domestic and sexual violence and that "by focusing attention on the general hatred of women that violent acts motivated by gender bias demonstrate, these statutes could help overcome the two major barriers to prosecuting hate-motivated violence against women by de-emphasizing the significance of the relationship between the victim and her assailant and directing attention away from the sexual nature of so many violent crimes against women."[9]

Hate Crimes against LGBTQ Populations

Bias against gender identity and sexual orientation are a significant percentage of hate crimes in the Uniform Crime Reports and the Bureau of Justice Statistics National Crime Victimization Survey (NCVS). For this reason, in 2009, Congress passed the Matthew Shepard and James Byrd Jr. Hate Crimes Prevention Act, which was responsible for expanding the definition of a hate crime to include crimes that arise from bias based on gender, gender identity, sexual orientation, or disability. The act was named after two men who were killed in 1998: Matthew Shepard, a gay college student who was brutally beaten, burned, and tortured, dying from his wounds and from severe brain trauma, and James Byrd Jr., a middle-aged Black man who was tied to a pickup truck and dragged for several miles before being killed. Shepard's killers targeted him because he was gay; Byrd's killers were white supremacists. The act was put in place not only to expand the definition of hate crimes but to ensure that the FBI tracks hate crimes based on gender and gender identity, to provide further funding to state and local agencies for the investigation and prosecution of hate crimes, and to allow federal agencies to investigate potential hate crimes when state and local agencies choose not to pursue such crimes. Additionally, prior to the 2009 act, a hate crime was only recognized as such when the victim was engaged in a federally protected activity, such as going to school. That provision was removed to recognize that individuals should be protected from hate crime in any setting.

The 2009 act was deemed necessary because lesbian, gay, bisexual, queer, transgender, nonbinary, gender nonconforming, and intersex individuals are disproportionately likely to be victims of hate crimes. According to the FBI's UCR program, approximately 16 percent of all hate crimes are committed because of the victim's sexual orientation; the

NCVS places this number at approximately 25 percent. Of these, the majority of attacks and hate crimes are against gay men.

While the 2013–2017 UCR program reports that hate crimes based on gender bias are extremely rare and that hate crimes motivated by **gender identity** bias—in other words, hate crimes against those who are trans, nonbinary, gender nonconforming, or intersex—are less than 2 percent of all hate crimes, the NCVS during the same period places these figures much higher, reporting that gender-based hate crimes, both reported and unreported, comprise nearly 30 percent of all hate crimes. The NCVS does not differentiate between hate crimes motivated by gender bias and hate crimes motivated by gender identity bias, but even given this difference, it is clear that the rate of hate crimes based on gender and gender identity is much higher in the NCVS. The difference between the two is attributable to several factors; primary among them is the fact that the NCVS relies on the perception of victims to determine whether an incident was motivated by bias. Additionally, the UCR tends to classify hate crimes in terms of a single bias and only includes crimes that have been reported to law enforcement, while the NCVS data allows for multiple biases to be at play in a single incident and includes unreported incidents as well as incidents that law enforcement may not have attributed to bias.

Transgender individuals are at an even higher risk of being victims of hate crimes, particularly if they are nonwhite, and particularly if they are Black. The UCR and the NCVS both place racially motivated hate crimes at around 60 percent of all hate crimes. While the UCR tends to attribute hate crimes to a single bias, it is clear that forms of bias and discrimination intersect, and the prevalence of hate crimes against Black trans women highlights this deadly intersection. The **Transgender Law Center (TLC)** and **Southerners on New Ground (SONG)** collaborated on a survey of trans, nonbinary, and gender nonconforming individuals in the U.S. South that found that 42 percent of respondents of color experienced high levels of violence originating from strangers, while 58 percent of trans women and those who present as femme experienced high levels of violence originating from strangers. Significantly, more than 40 percent of the respondents in general, and more than 50 percent of respondents of color, also reported experiencing high levels of violence originating from law enforcement, meaning that they may not be likely to go to law enforcement to report harassment and violence, for fear that they will only encounter more harassment and violence.[10] This reluctance to report may be a large factor in the discrepancy between gender-based hate crimes in the UCR and the NCVS. In chapter 13, we discuss further obstacles that transgender, nonbinary, and gender nonconforming individuals and communities face within the criminal/legal system, particularly in prisons and jails.

Explaining Hate Crimes?

As in the Elliot Rodger case, mental illness has, both in the media and in the courts, been vilified for its supposed connection to violent criminal behavior. Rodger's history with depression and anxiety was as much a part of the national discussion surrounding his rampage as his misogynistic ideologies and his access to guns. A 2008 Supreme Court decision in *District of Columbia et al. v. Heller*[11] upheld "longstanding prohibitions on the possession of firearms by felons and the mentally ill," suggesting that mental illness and felonious behavior go hand in hand. However, multiple studies have shown that less than 5 percent of violent crimes in the United States are committed by those with mental illness, and those who have been diagnosed with mental illnesses are less likely to commit violent crimes involving guns than those who are considered neurotypical.[12]

Further, studies have shown that mental illness and other disabilities make an individual much more likely to be the victim rather than the perpetrator of a hate crime. While the UCR recognized bias against those with disabilities as responsible for less than 2 percent of hate crimes, the NCVS reports that bias against those with disabilities appears in approximately 15 percent of hate crimes. This discrepancy may once again be attributable to minimal reporting or social and legal misunderstandings of acts of **ableism**. The Arc, a national organization that focuses on policy and advocacy for those with intellectual

GENDER IDENTITY
Personal sense of one's own gender; can be the same or different from their sex assigned at birth.

TRANSGENDER LAW CENTER (TLC)
Largest national trans-led organization advocating self-determination for transgender and gender nonconforming people; grounded in legal expertise and committed to racial justice.

SOUTHERNERS ON NEW GROUND (SONG)
Social justice advocacy organization supporting LGBTQ people, primarily in the South.

ABLEISM
Discrimination against people with physical, intellectual, or psychiatric disabilities.

or developmental disabilities (I/DD), states that "individuals with I/DD are significantly more likely to be victimized (at least two times more likely for violent crimes and four to ten times for abuse and other crimes), yet their cases are rarely investigated or prosecuted because of discrimination, devaluation, prejudice that they are not worthy of protection, and mistaken stereotypes that none can be competent witnesses."[13]

GAY PANIC DEFENSE AND TRANS PANIC DEFENSE

What has become known as the **gay panic defense** and the **trans panic defense** similarly ascribe hate crimes to a momentary mental illness instead of an inherent bias. From the mid-twentieth century to the current day, defense attorneys have invoked the "gay panic defense" in an attempt to explain violence against primarily gay men. The argument is that the offender has no inherent bias against gay men but experiences fear or panic upon realizing that a person with whom they are interacting is gay, thus responding with violence. In many of the cases in which this defense tactic has been used, defendants have claimed that they were acting in, essentially, self-defense in response to unwanted sexual advances. Studies have shown that this "gay panic defense" is particularly effective with juries that have conservative values, where "jurors might rely on their subjective ideological biases when deciding whether the defendant's reactions were reasonable."[14] Moreover, such juries are more likely to recommend a reduction of the charges against the defendant.

More recently, a version of this tactic has been used with the "trans panic defense." The premise is essentially the same as that in the "gay panic defense." It specifically involves an offender who ostensibly possesses no inherent transphobia but nevertheless responds with violence upon finding out that the person with whom they are interacting is transgender.

In 2014, California became the first state to ban the "gay panic defense" when California governor Jerry Brown signed into law an amendment to the California Penal Code 192, which defines the three recognized kinds of manslaughter in the state. In California, manslaughter is "the unlawful killing of a human being without malice," and voluntary manslaughter is seen to occur "upon a sudden quarrel or heat of passion." The amendment recognizes that "gay panic" is not a reasonable defense or a cause for the reduction of a charge from homicide to manslaughter:

> For purposes of determining sudden quarrel or heat of passion . . . the provocation was not objectively reasonable if it resulted from the discovery of, knowledge about, or potential disclosure of the victim's actual or perceived gender, gender identity, gender expression, or sexual orientation, including under circumstances in which the victim made an unwanted nonforcible romantic or sexual advance towards the defendant, or if the defendant and victim dated or had a romantic or sexual relationship.[15]

The law further states that "'gender' includes a person's gender identity and gender-related appearance and behavior regardless of whether that appearance or behavior is associated with the person's gender as determined at birth.

In other words, "gay panic" is no longer acknowledged as an objectively acceptable reason for an offender to act in the heat of the moment. Since California banned this defense tactic, several other states have followed suit. As of 2019, the "gay panic defense" has also been banned in Connecticut, Hawaii, Illinois, Nevada, New York, and Rhode Island.

INDIVIDUAL AND SOCIAL EFFECTS OF HATE CRIMES

According to the American Psychological Association, the effects of hate crime extend far beyond momentary victimization and injury. Whether the hate crime is directed toward people or property, the emotional and psychological distress that victims of hate crime experience may include posttraumatic stress disorder, anxiety, depression, anger, and

GAY PANIC AND TRANS PANIC DEFENSES
Legal strategy used to bolster other defenses that argues that a defendant's violence is due to the victim's sexual orientation or gender identity/expression.

heightened concern for personal and community safety.[16] In addition to discussing many of the symptoms and effects of posttraumatic stress disorder in chapters 3 and 4, we must widen our understanding of what may lead to posttraumatic stress and who may experience it. When it involves hate crimes, trauma may extend beyond the individual(s) who experience hate crimes to the larger community of which they are a part. Due to the fact that a hate crime arises from bias against an entire group that manifests in the targeting of a particular person, persons, or property, even those who are not directly affected by a particular instance of crime may feel the effects of that crime. Clinical psychologist Monnica Williams, for example, has worked with colleagues to develop the UConn Racial/Ethnic Stress & Trauma Survey (UnRESTS), which aims to assist in diagnosing individuals who suffer from PTSD arising from direct experience with racialized violence or exposure to racialized violence in news and social media.[17] This form of traumatic stress may also be referred to as cultural trauma. In 2016, the Association of Black Psychologists and the Community Healing Network, in recognition of the growing awareness of this form of trauma, published the "FamilyCare, CommunityCare and SelfCare Tool Kit." Subtitled "Healing in the Face of Cultural Trauma," the tool kit assists individuals and communities with self-assessing emotional, psychological, and behavioral signs of racial stress and trauma and also offers tools and tactics for addressing that trauma.

Fear of racialized, gendered, homophobic, and other forms of hate crime may have social and behavioral, as well as psychological and emotional, effects. While we have seen that violence against women is rarely prosecuted as a hate crime, it is clear that many women have developed particular behaviors that are meant to act as deterrents against the possibility of being targeted because of their gender. For example, Jackson Katz, an educator who has long been involved in gender violence prevention, describes the usual outcome when first asking men and then women to describe their strategies for protecting themselves from sexual violence. The men, Katz reports, have no strategies to share, while the women often have countless responses:

> Hold my keys as a potential weapon. Look in the back seat of the car before getting in. Carry a cell phone. Don't go jogging at night. Lock all the windows when I go to sleep, even on hot summer nights. Be careful not to drink too much. Don't put my drink down and come back to it; make sure I see it being poured. Own a big dog. Carry mace or pepper spray. Have an unlisted phone number. Have a man's voice on my answering machine. Park in well-lit areas. Don't use parking garages. Don't get on elevators with only one man, or with a group of men. Vary my route home from work. Watch what I wear. Don't use highway rest areas. Use a home alarm system. Don't wear headphones when jogging. Avoid forests or wooded areas, even in the daytime. Don't take a first-floor apartment. Go out in groups. Own a firearm. Meet men on first dates in public places. Make sure to have a car or cab fare. Don't make eye contact with men on the street. Make assertive eye contact with men on the street.[18]

While it is true that most acts of violence committed against women are carried out by acquaintances, friends, and family members, the vastly different responses that men and women give to this inquiry are indicative of a social norm in which gender is clearly understood as a factor in particular forms of criminal violence.

We return, then, to our original question. Did Elliot Rodger commit a hate crime? He was not charged with anything, as he himself did not survive his rampage. However, given the fact that the FBI defines a hate crime as an act "motivated in whole or in part by an offender's bias against a race, religion, disability, sexual orientation, ethnicity, gender, or gender identity," it is unlikely that he would have been charged with a hate crime, especially since four of his six victims were men. The legal answer, then, may be clear, but the dynamic of any hate crime involves a relationship between ideology and action that may be difficult to impossible to prove beyond a reasonable doubt.

In the next chapter, we discuss the juvenile justice system, including its history and detention policies. The school-to-prison pipeline, the criminalization of young people of color, and gangs are also covered.

1. What is a hate crime and how would you distinguish it from other crimes?

2. In 1984, Bernard Goetz shot four African American men on the subway in Manhattan. He pleaded self-defense, contending that he had an implicit fear of men of color. In what ways is this similar to the gay and trans panic defenses? In what ways is it different?

3. Describe the impacts that being the victim of a hate crime can have on an individual.

GOING FURTHER

Readings:

Brownmiller, Susan. *Against Our Will: Men, Women, and Rape.* New York: Simon & Schuster, 1975.

MacKinnon, Catharine. *Toward a Feminist Theory of the State.* Cambridge, MA: Harvard University Press, 1989.

Millett, Kate. *Sexual Politics.* New York: Doubleday, 1970.

Websites:

Learn about Hate Crimes. https://www.justice.gov/hatecrimes/learn-about-hate-crimes.

Videos/Movies:

Kaye, Tony. *American History X.* New Line Cinema, 1998.

Ramsay, Lynne. *We Need to Talk about Kevin.* BBC Films, 2011.

KEY TERMS

ableism Discrimination against people with physical, intellectual, or psychiatric disabilities.

gay panic and trans panic defenses Legal strategy used to bolster other defenses that argues that a defendant's violence is due to the victim's sexual orientation or gender identity/expression.

gender identity Personal sense of one's own gender; can be the same or different from their sex assigned at birth.

incel community Men called "involuntary celibates" who are an online subculture that define themselves as unable to find a romantic or sexual partner. They have increasingly become more extremist, often focusing on violence in recent years.

misogyny Refers to prejudice, anger, hatred of, or contempt for women and girls.

Southern Poverty Law Center (SPLC) An organization that monitors hate groups and other extremists throughout the United States, exposing their activities.

Southerners on New Ground (SONG) Social justice advocacy organization supporting LGBTQ people, primarily in the South.

Transgender Law Center (TLC) Largest national trans-led organization advocating self-determination for transgender and gender nonconforming people; grounded in legal expertise and committed to racial justice.

NOTES

[1] Kelsey Brugger, "Elliot Rodger Report Details Long Struggle with Mental Illness," *Santa Barbara Independent*, February 20, 2015, https://www.independent.com/2015/02/20/elliot-rodger-report-details-long-struggle-mental-illness.

[2] Nicky Woolf, "'PUAhate' and 'ForeverAlone': Inside Elliot Rodger's Online Life," *Guardian*, May 30, 2014, https://www.theguardian.com/world/2014/may/30/elliot-rodger-puahate-forever-alone-reddit-forums.

[3] All quotations from Rodger's manifesto taken from "The Manifesto of Elliot Rodger," *New York Times*, May 25, 2014, accessed June 1, 2019, https://www.nytimes.com/interactive/2014/05/25/us/shooting-document.html?_r=0.

[4] Laurie Penny, "Laurie Penny on Misogynist Extremism: Let's Call the Isla Vista Killings What They Were," *New Statesman*, May 25, 2014, accessed June 1, 2019, https://www.newstatesman.com/lifestyle/2014/05/lets-call-isla-vista-killings-what-they-were-misogynist-extremism.%20Accessed%2006/01/19.

[5] "Hate Crimes," FBI.gov, accessed June 1, 2019, https://www.fbi.gov/investigate/civil-rights/hate-crimes.

[6] *Brandenburg v. Ohio*, 395 U.S. 444 (1969).

[7] *Matal v. Tam*, 582 U.S. ___ (2017).

[8] Barbara Oudekerk, "Hate Crime Statistics: Briefing Prepared for the Virginia Advisory Committee," U.S. Commission on Civil Rights, Panel 1: Hate Crime History in VA, Current Legal Framework, Enforcement and Data, 2017 Hate Crime Statistics, FBI, March 29, 2019, https://www.bjs.gov/content/pub/pdf/hcs1317pp.pdf.

[9] Marguerite Angelari, "Hate Crime Statutes: A Promising Tool for Fighting Violence against Women," *American University Journal of Gender, Social Policy & the Law* 2, no. 1 (1993): 105.

[10] "The Grapevine: A Southern Trans Report," Southerners on New Ground and the Transgender Law Center, 2019, http://transgenderlawcenter.org/wpcontent/uploads/2019/05/grapevine_report_eng-FINAL.pdf.

[11] *District of Columbia v. Heller*, 554 U.S. 570 (2008).

[12] Jonathan M. Metzl and Kenneth T. MacLeish, "Mental Illness, Mass Shootings, and the Politics of American Firearms," *American Journal of Public Health* 105, no. 2 (2015), http://doi.org/10.2105/AJPH.2014.302242.

[13] "Position Statement: Criminal Justice System," TheArc.org, accessed June 1, 2019, https://www.thearc.org/who-we-are/position-statements/rights/criminal-justice.

[14] Jessica M. Salerno et al., "Excusing Murder? Conservative Jurors' Acceptance of the Gay-Panic Defense," *Psychology, Public Policy, and Law* 21, no. 1 (2015), https://doi.org/10.1037/law0000024.

[15] California Penal Code § 192, accessed June 1, 2019, https://leginfo.legislature.ca.gov/faces/printCodeSectionWindow.xhtml?lawCode=PEN&sectionNum=192.&op_statues=2014&op_chapter=684&op_section=1.

[16] "The Psychology of Hate Crimes," APA.org, accessed June 1, 2019, https://www.apa.org/advocacy/civil-rights/hate-crimes.pdf.

[17] Monnica T. Williams, Isha W. Metzger, Chris Leins, and Celenia DeLapp, "Assessing Racial Trauma within a DSM-5 Framework: The UConn Racial/Ethnic Stress & Trauma Survey," *Practice Innovations* 3, no. 4 (2018), https://doi.org/10.1037/pri0000076.

[18] Jonathan Katz, *The Macho Paradox: Why Some Men Hurt Women and How All Men Can Help* (Naperville, IL: Sourcebooks, 2006), 2.

At Risk: Youth, Race, and Gender

In this chapter you will read about youth as victims of crime as well as those who commit crime. We begin with a case of a boy, yet another instance of a Black person being shot and killed by police, and his community.

LEARNING OBJECTIVES

After reading this chapter, you should be able to do the following:

- Explain the history of the juvenile "justice" system.
- Articulate connections between victimization and offending.
- Identify the differential impacts on girls, youth of color, and LGBTQ youth.
- Describe the changes throughout time in the punishment of youth.

Case #6: Tamir Rice

Twelve-year-old Tamir Rice lived with his family just a step away from Cudell Recreation Center in Cleveland, Ohio. His mother, Samaria, had decided to move her small family to that location because of the rec center and the adjoining park; it seemed like a safe place to raise her children. The park, the rec center, and the nearby school kept Tamir and his older sister Tajai within walking distance of their home and gave them space and activities to keep them busy during the weekend. On Saturday, November 22, 2014, Tamir volleyed between the rec center and the park, excited to have a chance to play with an airsoft gun a friend had traded him for the day in return for an old cell phone that had games on it. The toy gun was meant to look like a Colt 1911—his friend had, at some point, even removed the small orange tip at the end of the barrel when he had dismantled and fixed the gun when it had stopped shooting correctly. Tamir's mother was not a fan of guns, so it was a treat for him that day. Tamir and his sister played outside all morning until it was time to go home for lunch, and after a quick meal, Tamir and Tajai went back out to continue on with their lazy fall Saturday.

People around the rec center and the park saw Tamir playing with the airsoft gun that day and thought nothing of it; he was a kid, after all, just playing around with a bunch of other kids on a Saturday. Sometime after three o'clock, however, a man sitting in the park, drinking a beer and waiting for the bus, saw Tamir with his airsoft gun and decided to call 911.

The recording of the call indicates that the man who phoned for emergency services was calling primarily as a precaution; he was uncertain about the authenticity of the gun and seemed to suspect that the person holding the gun was indeed a child. "There's a guy in here with a pistol . . . and, you know, it's probably fake, but he's, like, pointing it at everybody. . . . The guy keeps pulling it in and out of his pants—it's probably fake, but you know what? He's scaring the shit out of me. . . . Probably a juvenile, you know? . . . He's right nearby the, you know, the youth center or whatever, and he keeps pulling it in and out of his pants. I don't know if it's real or not." He reported that Tamir was sitting on the swings.[1] Like a bad game of telephone, when the police dispatcher got notes from the 911 operator and passed them along to a squad car, Tamir had transformed into a Black male who was pulling a handgun from his pants to point at people; he became an active shooter. The fact that the gun was very likely a fake—a point the caller had made several times—and the suspicion of the caller that Tamir was a child did not make it to the dispatcher or to the officers on call. This call was a Code 1: high priority.

Frank Garmback and Timothy Loehmann were the officers on duty nearby, and they were the ones who got the call. Loehmann was new to the force; he had only been a patrol officer in Cleveland for three months, and Garmback was meant to be training him. This was a complicated job, as Loehmann had previously worked for the police department in Independence, Ohio, before resigning for, among other things, lying and emotional instability. In a report that had been written about him by Jim Polak, deputy chief of the department from which Loehmann had resigned, it was noted that his emotional behavior "leads one to believe that he would not be able to substantially cope, or make good decisions, during or resulting from any other stressful situation." Polak also stated, "I do not believe time, nor training, will be able to change or correct these deficiencies."[2] The report also noted that he had poor coordination, difficulty following directions, and handled service weapons poorly. A series of unsuccessful attempts to get hired at other police and sheriff's departments eventually resulted in one successful application: the Cleveland Division of Police hired him in March 2014.

The two officers arrived at the park, driving off the street and straight onto the grass up to a gazebo where they could see Tamir sitting on a table, nothing in his hands. Tamir stood up and took a few slow steps as the cruiser pulled up to less than ten feet away from him. Before the car had even come to a full halt, Loehmann jumped out of the car, drew his gun, and shot twice; one of the bullets hit Tamir in the abdomen and traveled through his intestines. Tamir fell, his hands empty.

Garmback called it in, reporting that a Black male presumed to be approximately twenty years old was down. For four long minutes, neither he nor Loehmann made any effort to help Tamir as Tamir lay bleeding. They stood and watched. Tajai, Tamir's sister, had been in the bathroom, and though she was close enough to hear the pop of the gunshot, it took her a moment to piece together that it may have been her brother on the receiving end of a bullet. About two minutes after the shooting, Tajai ran across the park to her brother; it was reported that she was screaming. As she got closer, Garmback pushed her to the ground, put her in handcuffs, and then sat her in the backseat of the police cruiser; she could not help, touch, or comfort her brother. It was not until an FBI agent arrived four minutes after the shooting that anyone began to administer aid to Tamir.

The entire series of events was caught on video surveillance. It was plainly visible that Tamir had no gun in his hands, and video evidence does not suggest that he began to reach for the toy gun as the cruiser sped up to him. He did nothing to provoke them; he simply stood up from his seat and was shot. An attorney for Tamir's family, Jonathan S. Abady, said, "What we have is objective evidence that they summarily executed this child as fast as humanly possible. . . . There is nothing Tamir could have done to not get shot that day."[3]

Two neighborhood boys ran to Tamir's mother at home to tell her what happened. As it turned out, the lunchtime pause in between playing with friends was the last time she saw Tamir truly alive. By the time she saw him at the hospital, he was only barely holding on to life, and he passed away without regaining consciousness. She was not allowed to touch or hug him; his body was now evidence.

Tamir's killing polarized the public. The surveillance footage, available on the internet, led many to shock, anger, and disbelief. The city and the police were not acting fast enough to address it, they felt. The police union took a defensive stance. Steve Loomis, the president of the Cleveland Police Patrolman's Association, felt that the public outcry was misled and that the officers had done nothing irresponsible at all. In fact, they argued, it was Tamir who was at fault. In a scattered statement, Loomis said,

Tamir Rice is in the wrong. . . . He's menacing. He's 5-feet-7, 191 pounds. He wasn't that little kid you're seeing in pictures. He's a 12-year-old in an adult body. Tamir looks to his left and sees a police car. He puts his gun in his waistband. Those people—99 percent of the time those people run away from us. We don't want him running into the rec center. That could be a whole other set of really bad events. They're trying to flush him into the field. Frank [the driver] is expecting the kid to run. The circumstances are so fluid and unique. . . . The guy with the gun is not running. He's walking toward us. He's squaring off with Cleveland police and he has a gun. Loehmann is thinking, "Oh my God, he's pulling it out of his waistband."[4]

To the officers and their defenders, Tamir was not at all a twelve-year-old boy with a toy; he was an active threat, and he brought his death upon himself.

As time dragged on, the public became increasingly impatient. For several months, there was little public acknowledgment from the city or the police department of an investigation into the deadly use of force or any concrete discussion of the steps being taken. The officers were on restricted duty but had faced no other fallout from their actions. Tamir's family and a group of supporters had begun the slow process of filing a civil suit against the officers, and in February 2015, the city of Cleveland responded: it was Tamir's actions and his failure to exercise due care that had resulted in his death. In May 2015, the county prosecutor's office issued their first public statements, though they were undetailed and inconclusive; they had been putting together evidence, and they were almost done. The officers, however, had still not been formally interviewed. Finally, in June, more than half a year after Tamir's death, there were some developments: the county sheriff's office produced a report based on their investigation of the incident and delivered it to the county prosecutor, and a Cleveland municipal court judge, Ronald Adrine, offered the opinion that there was certainly enough evidence to suggest that the officers should be charged. Both officers, he said, could be charged with negligent homicide and dereliction of duty, and Loehmann could be additionally charged with murder, reckless homicide, and manslaughter. The video, Adrine argued, indicated that Tamir had no time to respond to the officers in any way or any chance to show defiance or cooperation, indicating that the actions of the officers had been rash and had not followed proper protocols. Adrine also stated that his statement had arisen in response to a weighty affidavit from local activists, organizers, and clergy; a quirk in Ohio law allows criminal charges to be brought by citizen petition. Adrine, however, had no legal ability to push the case to trial or to issue warrants himself. Instead, he could only make recommendations for the county prosecutor. All legal roads seemed to lead to Cuyahoga County prosecutor Timothy J. McGinty, and he ultimately decided that the case should go to a grand jury.

McGinty, in his time in the role, has claimed that he is interested in making the investigation of police shootings more public and more transparent, and to this end, he argues, convening a grand jury is preferable to a private police investigation of fatal use of force. However, grand juries themselves are by law private. The decisions made by a grand jury are released to the public, but the way that those decisions are made is not. Prosecutors, presenting their case without the opposition of a defense, are able to use their full sway to swing the grand jury in their preferred direction, and the specifics of the process are not a matter of public record. Instead, the decision from the grand jury emerges; the public assumes that their decision was built on reasoned and balanced evidence, testimony, and discussion; and the case disappears into the past. The decision of whether or not to indict the officers for the death of Tamir Rice would happen behind closed doors in the final month of 2015.

The experts and prosecutors that McGinty began to call on had worked previously on matters related to the deadly use of force on the part of law enforcement and had generally fallen on the side of defending the use of force. The team that was convened was ostensibly meant to argue for indictment of the officers; they were, after all, the prosecution team, and their influence would determine the decision of the grand jury. All of those convened by McGinty released their initial statements: each of them believed that the shooting was justified. Neither Tamir's family nor their legal team were notified of these statements before they were released to the public, and they were dismayed—but perhaps not surprised—that the experts and opinions that had been brought together by McGinty seemed immediately to be so heavily weighted against indictment. McGinty did, however, allow Tamir's family's attorneys to add their own experts to the docket. This was an unorthodox move, and it suggested that it was going to have to be the family's attorneys, rather than the prosecution team, that would advocate for Tamir. The experts brought in by the family's attorneys noted the fact that this was not standard practice, and it is mostly their reports that have demystified at least a small part of what occurred during the grand jury process.

Roger Clark, a retired police officer, was brought on by Tamir's family's attorneys, and he recalls that the behavior of the prosecution was strange. Clark had testified in dozens of courtrooms across the country in investigations of fatal use-of-force events by police officers. It had been a special area of training and focus for him in his almost thirty years in the Los Angeles County Sheriff's Department, and since his retirement in the early 1990s, he had been acting as an expert witness in court cases. To Clark, something seemed amiss about this particular grand jury investigation. According to Clark, Matthew Meyer, a prosecutor in the grand jury case, showed to the grand jury a gun that was identical to the toy gun that Tamir had been holding on the Saturday of his death, and he did it with a flourish. Clark was unsure why the prosecutor even had the gun in the first place. The grand jury, after all, was there only to decide if they should call to indict the police officers who had arrived on the scene and shot Tamir, and this wielding of a very realistic-looking toy gun seemed designed to convince the jury that it was perfectly reasonable to argue that the rookie cop had fired in self-defense. All this from the prosecutor, the person who was supposed to be arguing for an indictment. Clark had studied the video, the forensic findings, witness statements, and more, and he was fully prepared to say that, no, the use of force in this case was in no way reasonable. To him, it seemed to be an easy open-and-shut discussion. However, what he encountered was two prosecutors attempting to discredit his testimony. They repeated that what the officers had done had required great courage and that they had been heroically confronting an active shooter. What Clark was ready to call recklessness was instead being called bravery. Clark argued that the event had to be seen in its full context and that it was necessary to question how the behavior of the officers as they pulled up to the boy may have exacerbated the situation enough to lead to immediate gunfire, not in self-defense but in a chaotic moment of already rash decision making. Meyer at this point turned the toy gun on Clark and asked him whether or not being faced with such a sight, or even something like it, would have prompted him, as an officer, to shoot at the person holding the gun. This, however, was beside the point, a scare tactic unrelated to what had transpired when Garmback and Loehmann had pulled onto the grass at Cudell Park. Tamir had not pointed his toy gun at them, nor had he even reached for it, as video evidence made clear. It seemed to Clark that the prosecutors were attempting to dissuade the grand jury from issuing an indictment.

Jeffrey J. Noble, another expert brought in by Tamir's family's attorney and, like Clark, a veteran officer, also saw the shooting as unreasonable. The officers, he argued, even in pulling up so close to Tamir in the first place, had breached norms of conduct: "Reasonable police officers responding to a man-with-a-gun call . . . would have stopped their vehicle prior to entering the park to visually survey the area to avoid driving upon a subject who may be armed. This serves not only to protect the officers, but also serves to protect others who may be in the area and provides both time and distance for the officers to evaluate the situation and develop a plan." And, again like Clark, Noble also felt that the prosecution immediately attempted to discredit his opinions and his qualifications as an expert. He recalls, "I've definitely never seen two prosecutors play defense attorney so well." He also noted that the prosecution consistently referred to Tamir as an "active shooter" and that by the end of the process, the jury seemed to forget that Tamir had been, in actuality, a child with a toy gun.

Loehmann and Garmback both produced written testimonies for the grand jury. This was unnecessary and unusual. In a grand jury setting, where the only decision to be made is whether to issue an indictment or not, there is no reason for the defense to offer testimony because, generally, they do not have legal representation of their own; it is only the prosecution that presents the case. The decision to include statements from Loehmann and Garmback once again blurs the line between defense and prosecution. In both of their statements, they claimed that they had not seen Tamir until they were within just a few yards of him, and both were afraid that he was going to try to flee. Loehmann claimed that though he was new to the force, he had already dealt with "active shooter" situations, a claim that police records in Cuyahoga County would contradict. He also claimed that he had been yelling to Tamir to show them his hands and that Tamir had been reaching for his waistband where, presumably, there was a gun. "With his hands pulling the gun out and his elbow coming up, I knew it was a gun and it was coming out. I saw the weapon in his hands coming out of his waistband and the threat to my partner and myself was real and active," Loehmann reported.[5] He also claims that he got out of the car and tried to take cover behind it. Video evidence does not align with Loehmann's testimony, nor does the very short timeline between their arrival at the park and the shooting of Tamir; they would have had little to no time to ask that Tamir show them his hands, nor to give him a chance to do it, and Loehmann, contrary to his report, fired his shots nearly as soon as his passenger-side door was opened. Neither officer was questioned on any point of their written statements, and both relied on the Fifth Amendment to avoid saying anything more.

The video surveillance footage was also called into question. McGinty's experts claimed that it revealed that Tamir had indeed been reaching for his waistband. Opposing experts argue that he was doing no such thing and that his hands were in fact in his pockets. In their reading of the video, the motion of pulling his hand upward, which the prosecution argued was a threatening reach for a gun, was actually a physical response to getting shot in the abdomen. McGinty's experts do not comment on the fact that there would be no reason for Tamir to be reaching for a gun, for the simple fact that he did not really have one. They also estimate that it was less than two seconds from Loehmann's car door opening to shots being fired; the expert brought in by Tamir's family's legal team, Jesse Wobrock, argues that it was less than one second. Wobrock's experience testifying in front of the grand jury was similar to Clark's and Noble's; Wobrock reports that the prosecutors "were acting in a way like they were defense attorneys for the cops."[6] And, as with Noble and Clark, Wobrock felt that the prosecutors attempted to discredit his qualifications as an expert witness.

Samaria, Tamir's mother, was also brought in to testify. She recalls that she was being portrayed as a selfish, self-serving, and irresponsible mother; she was said to be just looking for money from her civil suit against the city, and her son was characterized as a thug and a threat. She had always refused to let Tamir play with toy guns of any kind, but her character as a mother seemed to be on trial. Remembering her time testifying, she recalled, "The look he had on his face, it was almost like they were trying to blame me. . . . I'm saying in my head, *Why are they talking to me like that?* They were talking to me like I was a bad mother, like I gave him that BB gun."[7] Tajai also testified; little is known about what was asked or what she said. Samaria only reported that it had been traumatizing for her. The family felt that they knew where this process was headed.

Late in December 2015, the grand jury returned its decision: no indictment. The grand jury was praised and thanked for their diligence.

Tamir's death, the grand jury said, was a mistake. McGinty said it was a "perfect storm of human error, mistakes, and miscommunications by all involved."[8] Tamir's team felt that McGinty, his prosecutors, and the experts they brought in had essentially sabotaged the case, putting Tamir and his family on trial rather than the officers themselves.

In April 2016, the city of Cleveland, while continuing to deny that there had been wrongdoing, paid out $6 million to Samaria and Tajai.

The Critical Incident Review Committee, a committee of city officials, began to independently review the events around Tamir's death in February 2016, and in April 2017, they released their final report, concluding that neither Loehmann nor Garmback had violated any departmental policies. However, they advised that Garmback should be suspended for ten days, and Constance Hollinger, the 911 operator who had failed to tell the dispatcher that the caller had suspected Tamir of being a child, was suspended without pay for one week.

In May 2017, Loehmann was fired from the Cleveland Police Department. It was not the killing of Tamir but dishonesty in his application for the job that ultimately led to his dismissal. He had not disclosed the circumstances of his resignation from the Independence Police Department and had not been forthright about a written examination that he had failed when applying for yet another police department. In 2021, the Ohio appeals court upheld Loehmann's firing.

THINKING CRITICALLY ABOUT THE CASE

1. What aspects of Tamir Rice's person seemed to indicate to either onlookers or law enforcement that he was a potential threat?

2. What purpose did the grand jury serve in the case against Loehmann and Garmback?

3. Why was the video evidence and expert testimony ultimately unsuccessful in regard to calling for the officers' indictment?

REFERENCES

This case is adapted from the following sources:

Capehart, Jonathan. "It's Tamir Rice's Fault." *Washington Post*, March 2, 2015. http://www.washingtonpost.com/blogs/post-partisan/wp/2015/03/02/its-tamir-rices-fault.

Elizabeth Goodwin, Administrator of *Estate of Tamir Rice Plaintiff v. Timothy Loehmann et al., Defendants*. Case No. 1:14-CV-2670. *Time*, February 27, 2015. http://www.time.com/wp-content/uploads/2015/03/rice-answer.pdf.

Ferrise, Adam. "Cleveland Officer Timothy Loehmann Fired in Wake of Tamir Rice Shooting." Cleveland.com, May 30, 2017. http://www.cleveland.com/metro/2017/05/cleveland_officer_timothy_loeh_1.html.

———. "Cleveland's Critical Incident Review Committee Found No Violations in Officers' Response to Tamir Rice Shooting." Cleveland.com, April 28, 2017. http://www.cleveland.com/metro/2017/04/clevelands_critical_incident_r.html.

———. "Fired Cleveland Cop Timothy Loehmann, Who Shot Tamir Rice, Set for Arbitration." Cleveland.com, January 9, 2018. https://www.cleveland.com/metro/2018/01/fired_cleveland_cop_timothy_lo.html.

———. "Tamir Rice's Sister: Cleveland Police Officer 'Attacked Me.'" Cleveland.com, December 14, 2014. http://www.cleveland.com/metro/2014/12/tamir_rices_sister_cleveland_p.html.

Flynn, Sean. "The Tamir Rice Story: How to Make a Police Shooting Disappear." *Gentlemen's Quarterly*, July 14, 2016. https://www.gq.com/story/tamir-rice-story.

Frantz, Ashley, Steve Almasy, and Catherine E. Shoichet. "Tamir Rice Shooting: No Charges for Officers." CNN, December 28, 2015. http://www.cnn.com/2015/12/28/us/tamir-rice-shooting/index.html.

Graham, David A. "'Probable Cause' in the Killing of Tamir Rice." *The Atlantic*, June 11, 2015. http://www.theatlantic.com/politics/archive/2015/06/tamir-rice-case-cleveland/395420.

Lee, Jaeah. "It's Been 6 Months since Tamir Rice Died, and the Cop Who Killed Him Still Hasn't Been Questioned." *Mother Jones*,

May 15, 2015. http://www.motherjones.com/politics/2015/05 /tamir-rice-investigation-cleveland-police.

Schultz, Connie. "A City of Two Tales." *Politico*, February 23, 2015. https://www.politico.com/magazine/story/2015/02/tamir-rice -cleveland-police-115401.

Swaine, Jon, and Daniel McGraw. "Tamir Rice: Judge Finds Cause for Murder Charge over Police Killing of 12-Year-Old." *The Guardian*, June 11, 2015. http://www.theguardian.com/us-news/2015 /jun/11/tamir-rice-police-officer-murder-charge.

CONTEXT AND ANALYSIS

Brief History of Juvenile Justice

The original purpose of the juvenile justice system was to hold young people accountable for delinquent behavior by providing treatment and rehabilitation programs. In response to the harsh treatment of children in the criminal/legal system, the first juvenile court in the United States was established in Illinois in 1899, which was quickly followed by a majority of the states. The early juvenile courts were built on the doctrine of ***parens patriae***, which provides that the state has the responsibility and authority to protect young people. As such, the juvenile justice system focused on rehabilitation rather than punishment. Emphasizing the best interests of the child, the courts stressed a nonadversarial, informal approach to cases. That treatment model continued until the early 1960s, when profound changes were triggered by several U.S. Supreme Court decisions establishing due process rights for juveniles who were involved in juvenile court proceedings.

In the 1960s, the modern juvenile court was born, and the juvenile rights period began. The 1967 Supreme Court decision in ***In re Gault***[9] declared that juvenile proceedings must comply with the Fourteenth Amendment's due process rights, including notice of the charges against the young person, the right to legal counsel, the right against self-incrimination, and the right to confront and cross-examine witnesses. Three years later in ***In re Winship***,[10] the Supreme Court extended the standard of proof for a juvenile accused of a crime to beyond a reasonable doubt instead of a preponderance of the evidence. At the same time, major cultural changes were influencing delinquency theory and practices.

While each state sets its own age jurisdictional requirements and procedures, modern juvenile courts continued to focus on rehabilitation and nonadversarial proceedings. In 1974, the Juvenile Justice Delinquency Prevention Act[11] established that children, young people, and families involved with the juvenile justice courts must be protected by federal standards of care and custody, while at the same time upholding community safety and preventing victimization. The law, which was reauthorized in 2018, encourages states to develop diversion programs for minor delinquency and **status offenders**, to remove juveniles from adult carceral facilities, and to focus on lowering recidivism through rehabilitation efforts.

The juvenile rights period continued through the early 1980s, when the law-and-order crime control period began. Juveniles were no longer viewed as young people who needed to be protected, but as adults, no matter what their age. The mantra "If you do the crime, you do the time" became the focus of the juvenile justice system. Despite the belief that juvenile criminal offending would be deterred with harsher treatment, juvenile offending began to increase in the 1980s.

Although the crime control period continues today, there is a growing awareness that young people are different from adults. Scientific research shows that the young brain is not fully developed until the early to mid-twenties. Prior to that time, teens can be impulsive, irrational, and even dangerous. Nevertheless, rehabilitation is promising since the teenage brain can change, adapt, and respond to its environment. Some states still focus on punishment, while others emphasize both punishment and treatment. Most, however, are seeking a balanced approach that includes restorative justice practices, emphasizing offender accountability, public safety, and competency development. For an understanding of restorative and transformative justice, see chapter 14.

Criminalization of Young People

The criminalization of young people in the United States begins with the assumptions and stereotypes that many young people are potentially dangerous, would-be "thugs" who must be controlled and punished. These young people are criminalized not just because of their young age, but also because of the color of their skin, their gender, poverty, and mental health challenges. Although it is often explained as an effort to make schools and streets safer, this criminalization actually victimizes young people who have experienced

PARENS PATRIAE
The principle that the government or other political authority has the responsibility to protect those who are unable to protect themselves, including children.

IN RE GAULT
U.S. Supreme Court decision granting juvenile defendants due process rights, including notice of the charges against the young person, the right to legal counsel, the right against self-incrimination, and the right to confront and cross-examine witnesses.

IN RE WINSHIP
U.S. Supreme Court decision extending the standard of proof for a juvenile accused of a crime to beyond a reasonable doubt instead of a preponderance of the evidence.

STATUS OFFENDER
A young person who is under court jurisdiction for noncriminal behavior that is considered a law violation because of the youth's age, such as truancy, running away, violating curfew, underage use of alcohol, or general ungovernability.

early life traumas. The tough-on-crime platforms of the political system exploit the public's fear of a dangerous and violent criminal class that needs to be controlled and punished. That punitive culture extends to schools where harmful disciplinary practices begin as early as preschool.

Criminalization of Young People of Color

Evidence shows that perceptions of the age of a child can be affected by race. Viewing children as older than they actually are can have serious implications about how they are viewed by the criminal/legal system. According to a recent American Psychological Association study,[12] Black boys as young as ten years old are often perceived as older than their years, triggering a perception that they are guilty and potentially dangerous. On the other hand, white boys the same age are assumed to possess the innocence of childhood. In addition, adults view Black girls as young as five years old as older than white girls of the same age. Such stereotypes can lead to young Black girls and boys being criminalized and labeled as "bad kids" when their white counterparts are viewed as innocent children. Such labeling leads to children being treated in school as if they are potential criminals and troublemakers. That treatment leads to a pathway into the criminal/legal system that is called the **school-to-prison pipeline**.

School-to-Prison Pipeline

The school-to-prison pipeline is the pathway through which overzealous disciplinary practices lead to a student's later involvement in the criminal/legal system. As is further explained in chapter 8, children who experience early life traumas often respond to neglect, abuse, and emotional abandonment with anger, aggression, and even violence. When these children begin school, their behavior is often treated as criminal behavior instead of recognizing the victimization that led to the behavior. In addition, for students of color, immigrant children, students living in poverty, and students with a learning or developmental disability, the challenges they experience in school can lead to a lack of confidence and self-esteem, which can result in adverse behavior. How that behavior is treated depends on the person who responds to the behavior and how they view a student who is "acting out." Knowledge of youth development converges with their personal biases, including racial, gender, and cultural ones, to determine the response. As a result, an aggressive child is often inappropriately disciplined, sometimes with corporal punishment, which is legal in almost half of all states, or by being referred to law enforcement.

Zero-tolerance policies and the subsequent establishment of law enforcement in the form of **school resource officers (SROs)** became popular starting in the 1980s. Those developments transformed schools from learning centers into authoritarian spaces. With interactions with students based on preserving authority and regulating punishment, the relationships between teachers and students shifted from one of instruction to one of power and control. Harsh punishments for both minor and major behavioral infractions have led to significant increases in suspensions and expulsions, starting as early as preschool and particularly for students of color, both boys and girls.

Research shows that contact with law enforcement in school increases the possibility of suspension, expulsion, dropping out of school, and involvement with the juvenile justice and criminal/legal systems. While all students are impacted, students of color are particularly affected, especially Black boys. According to the U.S. Department of Education Office for Civil Rights,[13] during the 2015–2016 school year, about 2.7 million (5 to 6 percent) of K–12 students received one or more out-of-school suspensions. Black male students represented 8 percent of all students but 15 percent of suspended students and 23 percent of expelled students. Black female students were 8 percent of enrolled students but 14 percent of suspended students and 10 percent of expelled students. Overall, Black students represented 31 percent of students who were referred to law enforcement or

SCHOOL-TO-PRISON PIPELINE
The process of criminalizing students through overzealous disciplinary practices that push students out of schools and put them in contact with law enforcement, thus leading to later involvement in the criminal/legal system.

ZERO-TOLERANCE POLICIES
School policies that mandate expulsion or referral to juvenile or criminal court regardless of the circumstances or nature of the offense.

SCHOOL RESOURCE OFFICER (SRO)
A law enforcement officer with sworn authority who is stationed in a school.

arrested, often for the exact same offenses committed by other students, who received less or no discipline. Latinx, Asian, and white students were not referred to law enforcement or arrested at a percentage higher than their overall student enrollment during the 2015–2016 school year.

Further, male students were referred to law enforcement or arrested more often than female students. Males, who represented 51 percent of all enrolled students, were 69 percent of those who were referred to law enforcement or arrested. Students with disabilities are also referred to law enforcement or arrested at higher rates than other students.[14]

Girls' Entry

Girls have been the fastest-growing segment of the population in the juvenile justice system over the past three decades, yet they account for less than half of all juvenile arrests and only about 15 percent of juvenile offenders in residential placements.[15] A 2012 report describes girls in the system this way: "The typical girl in the system is a non-violent offender, who is very often low-risk, but high-need, meaning the girl poses little risk to the public but she enters the system with significant and pressing personal needs."[16] When girls do enter the criminal/legal system, it is more likely to be for nonserious offenses, technical probation violations such as missing a meeting with a probation officer, or status offenses such as truancy or running away.

Girls often enter the system from violent and chaotic family situations. Studies indicate that nearly 75 percent of girls entering the system report being victims of physical and/or sexual violence,[17] 29 percent have been pregnant at some point,[18] and 30 percent report moving at least ten times in their lives.[19] Due to the high rates of abuse, many girls' first experience with government control occurs in the social service system, where they may be in foster care or in a residential facility. One study in Great Britain found that 61 percent of the girls in the custody of the criminal/legal system had previously been in the care of social services.[20] While not specifically reflective of the U.S. system, it is consistent with studies in the United States, which indicate that youth (not broken out by gender) in group homes are 2.5 times as likely to end up in the criminal/legal system.[21] Especially impacted are youth of color, who are already at substantially higher risk of criminalization, and LGBTQ youth, who have increased risk of placement into and movement between foster care and group homes.[22]

Girls and Violence

Beginning in the early 2000s, mainstream media and popular culture came together to present an image of ever-increasing violence among girls. Some suggested that girls were, and are, taking increasing risks, possibly as the result of "women's liberation," and that these risks put them into positions for which they are not adequately prepared, thus posing a danger to themselves and others. Most researchers in the field disagree; Mike Males and Meda Chesney-Lind call this the "myth of mean girls."[23] They contend that even statistics fail to support this increase. Indeed, the only available statistics that support the contention that girls are increasingly violent are arrest rates, where we saw a more than 200 percent increase of girls arrested for assault between 1981 and 2000.[24] But arrest rates measure enforcement to a greater extent than they measure actual behavior.

How, then, do we explain the focus on girls and violence? First, referring back to the discussion of media and crime in chapter 2, we must recall that violence "sells" and sex and violence sell the most. Another explanation is that we are simply witnessing a redefinition of girls' behavior so that what was once viewed as minor (truancy) or seen as victimization (fighting off sexual threats) is now being classified as an act of aggression or violence. This redefinition of criminal behavior comes at a time when social expectations for both girls and boys are changing rapidly, and though we expect girls to "stand up" for themselves, we continue to penalize them when they don't behave in ways that are considered "feminine."

Yet another explanation provides that as interest in, and enforcement of, intimate partner violence has increased, more girls are getting caught up in the net. Giordano and Copp remind us that "where self-reports of perpetration [of intimate partner violence] have been found to be similar across gender . . . research has consistently shown that the consequences are generally more serious for female victims."[25] Related to this is the theory that girls experience significantly more violence while growing up, in their most interpersonal relationships of family, peers, and community. As one researcher states, "girls' heightened fears of victimization, concerns about the capacity for self-defense, and concerns about the potential for sexual victimization may result in particularly acute reactions when confronting extreme forms of community violence."[26]

GANGS AND YOUTH

A Brief History of Gangs in the United States

Broadly defined, a gang is an organized group of individuals who adopt a group identity and often pose a security threat. Gangs have existed in the United States since the nineteenth century, when New York City gangs were organized by ethnic minorities, including Irish Americans, Polish Americans, and Italian Americans. As cities grew in the 1950s and 1960s, street gangs continued to develop, later expanding to smaller cities and some suburbs. Eventually, Black and Latinx gangs were organized in response to racialized violence from bordering white neighborhoods, as well as to protect their turf or the drug trade.

Gangs are not all alike. Some are large organizations with a strong hierarchical structure, while others are small neighborhood groups. Turf gangs are organized by neighborhood young people who are defending their territorial turfs, by organized crime gangs defending their drug trade, and by ethnic gangs that are defined either by the ethnicity of their members or the ethnicity of their enemies. Today there are street gangs, motorcycle gangs, prison gangs, hate groups, and terrorist organizations, among others. Some are organized in distinct geographical areas, while others are organized on the internet in online communities, such as white supremacists or jihadists.

Nevertheless, it is important to understand that gang structures, dynamics, activities, and alliances change over time. Recently, the traditional vertically organized hierarchy of "supergangs" has been fragmenting due to the arrest and imprisonment of their leaders, as well as the dislocation of gang members from housing developments. In its place, horizontally organized, neighborhood gangs and **cliques or sets** with little or no formal leadership structure have emerged. In addition to structural changes that have occurred over time, alliances between and among gangs change as circumstances fluctuate.

Street Gang Life

The reasons for a young person joining a gang are personal and complex. Chronic poverty, troubled schools, and aggressive policing can exacerbate the effects of early life traumas in the home to render the young person vulnerable to negative societal institutions to which they are exposed. Sometimes a young person joins a gang because family members are involved or the gang is the culture of the neighborhood. In those cases, the young person may begin their association by hanging around gang members, whether they are family members or neighborhood friends. During that process, the young person finds out who is important and learns what the gang does. Other times, the young person joins a gang that is part of the drug culture in order to escape poverty. Often those gangs recruit children to carry weapons or drugs because they are less likely to be arrested.

CLIQUES OR SETS
Smaller street gangs, usually in one neighborhood, that operate independently.

The early life traumas experienced by Stanley Tookie Williams, as you will read about in detail in the chapter 8 case study, and the culture of his neighborhood laid the groundwork for cofounding the Los Angeles Crips street gang. Williams, who was exposed to community violence and drug addiction, began to engage in street fights to prove his hypermasculinity. He wanted to distinguish himself from other boys not only to survive but also to become dominant. In that quest, he joined with other neighborhood leaders to organize a street gang that would control the neighborhoods, recruiting new members and absorbing smaller gangs.

Like Tookie Williams, male gang members adhere to a code of hypermasculinity, which results in being hypersensitive to insults and responding to conflict in an aggressive or violent manner. Those responses can be large-scale territory disputes authorized by gang leaders or interpersonal conflict and retaliatory shootings by young men who are organized in block-to-block cliques.

Female Gangs

Although much smaller than male gang membership, female gang membership is rising. Most gang research focuses on male gangs and hypermasculine acts of aggression, violence, and other serious threats.[27] Until recently, research stereotyped female gang members as peripheral members of the gang, either sex objects of male gang members or tomboys. As attention is paid to female gang members, the variations become more apparent. Today we believe that girl gangs may be autonomous or allied with a male gang, or female gang members may be part of a fully gender-integrated gang.

In many ways, the experiences of males and females in gangs are similar, but girls' experiences can also be shaped by gender roles and expectations. While most females join gangs for friendship and self-affirmation, recent research has begun to shed some light on economic and family pressures motivating many young women to join gangs. Female gang members tend to be considerably younger than their male counterparts, and they are much less likely to engage in serious criminal behavior. Moreover, females are significantly more likely to be victims of sexual assault or exploitation.

LGBTQ YOUTH

Youth surveys inform us that between 7 and 9 percent of young people identify as lesbian, gay, bisexual, transgender, or queer, yet they represent almost 15 percent of those in the juvenile justice system. According to a 2016 report by the Center for American Progress and the Movement Advancement Project,[28] LGBTQ youth are much more likely—depending on the study, between 25 percent and 300 percent more likely—than their peers to be formally sanctioned, whether that is being expelled from school or stopped by police. They are also vastly overrepresented in juvenile detention facilities. According to one survey of juvenile facilities, of those being held, "20% identified as LGBT or gender non-conforming. Forty percent of girls . . . identified as LGBT or gender non-conforming, and 85% of LGBT and gender non-conforming youth were youth of color."[29]

LGBTQ youth face numerous obstacles that lead them into the system, or perhaps lead the system to them. Gender nonconforming youth are more likely to face family rejection. A California study reported that 42 percent of those in out-of-home placements related that they left their home because their family rejected them.[30] The result of this rejection is sometimes homelessness and sometimes placement in the foster care system, where they are also overrepresented. One study of LGBTQ youth in Los Angeles found that 19 percent of youth in out-of-home care identified as LGBTQ.[31] Once on the streets, LGBTQ youth face overpolicing and are more susceptible to the enforcement of drug laws and antiprostitution laws. For LGBTQ youth, especially LGBTQ youth of color, they are often the target of harassment and violence at the hands of police. A study in New Orleans found that 59 percent of transgender youth reported being asked for sexual favors by police, compared with 12 percent of nontransgender youth.[32] And finally, while statistics are difficult to collect on immigrants at the border, the expectation is that LGBTQ people, including youth, constitute a disproportionate number of those fleeing persecution at home in other countries.

You will read more, especially about transgender people in prison, in chapter 13.

CRIMINALIZATION OF IMMIGRANT YOUTH

The criminalization of immigrants and immigrant youth we are experiencing in 2021 is part of a long history of criminalization of young people and people of color in the United States. Many of today's immigrant youth arrive in the United States as children and adolescents, not of their own volition but brought here by their parents or adult relatives trying to protect the child—and themselves—and hoping to build a better life. But the arrest, incarceration, or deportation of youth and their families has a lasting impact on their physical health, their mental health, and their educational success.

Two stories are presently being told in the United States. The first is that of the Dreamers. Named for the legislation more formally titled the Development, Relief, and Education for Alien Minors Act, or **DREAM Act**, the legislation was first introduced in Congress for a vote in 2001. Numerous versions of the bill, which have been introduced but not passed by the Senate, would grant temporary residency to young people who were sixteen or younger when they arrived in the United States, who have been residents for at least five consecutive years, and who have graduated from high school (or obtained an alternative degree). In 2012, the Obama administration used an executive order to create the **Deferred Action for Childhood Arrivals** program, or DACA, designed to have much the same effect as the DREAM Act. In 2017, the Trump administration reversed the executive order, thereby ending the program. This action was challenged in the courts, and in the case of *Department of Homeland Security et al. v. Regents of the University of California et al.* (2020), the Supreme Court reversed the Trump administration's action. Without congressional action, the future for the so-called Dreamers is still uncertain.

At the same time, immigration enforcement on the border between Mexico and the United States, and elsewhere around the country, has been increasing. Children are being separated from their families, family members are being deported or locked up, and the children, sometimes infants, are being imprisoned in brutal conditions. Regardless of who is to blame, the future for these young people is bleak. They are experiencing fear, uncertainty, and chronic stress and are not getting proper medical care or education. Anecdotally (as data is only now being collected), these immigrant youth are suffering from posttraumatic stress disorder and other mental health afflictions in numbers that reflect those of other communities with high rates of incarceration and uncertain futures.

YOUTH DETENTION

Prior to the 1980s, the juvenile justice system provided rehabilitation and education services for young people who were adjudicated as delinquent. This was followed by the law-and-order policies that routinely held juveniles in detention centers or adult prisons if convicted of crimes. Beginning in the 2000s, when the number of young people incarcerated peaked, a debate has been growing about the culpability of young people and the subsequent sanctions for criminal behavior.

DREAM ACT
Proposed legislation that would grant temporary residency to young people who were sixteen or younger when they arrived in the United States without documents, have been residents for at least five consecutive years, and have completed a high school education.

DEFERRED ACTION FOR CHILDHOOD ARRIVALS
An immigration policy that allows some individuals who were brought to the United States without documentation as children to receive deferred action from deportation for a two-year period.

However, according to the Prison Policy Initiative,[33] over 50,000 young people are still incarcerated in juvenile detention centers and 4,500 in adult prisons and jails. Black and Native American young people continue to be overrepresented in juvenile facilities. While just 14 percent of all youth are Black, 43 percent of boys and 34 percent of girls in juvenile facilities are Black.[34]

Many youth of color are held before they are found to be delinquent, often for non-violent behavior. Others are held for years following adjudication as a delinquent. Such incarceration can increase the possibility of future involvement in the criminal/legal system. Detained young people are more likely to be rearrested, adjudicated, convicted, and incarcerated for new crimes than young people who stay at home awaiting the court proceedings.

The national consensus against subjecting juveniles to the death penalty began in the 1980s. It is based on new neuroscientific research that shows that the brain of a young person is not fully formed until the early to mid-twenties. As a result, juveniles are more susceptible to peer pressure, are less able to understand the consequences of their behavior, and are less able to control their impulses. Considering this research, the U.S. Supreme Court ruled in *Thompson v. Oklahoma* (1988)[35] and *Stanford v. Kentucky* (1989)[36] that the minimum age for the death penalty was sixteen. Later, in 2005, the Supreme Court ruled in **Roper v. Simmons** (2005)[37] that the U.S. Constitution protects people from the death penalty for crimes committed before they were eighteen years old. Subsequent U.S. Supreme Court decisions ruled against mandatory sentencing of juveniles to life in prison. In **Graham v. Florida** (2010),[38] the Supreme Court ruled that juvenile offenders cannot be sentenced to life imprisonment without parole for nonhomicide offenses, and in 2012, in **Miller v. Alabama**,[39] the Court ruled that mandatory sentences for life without parole, even in cases of murder, are unconstitutional for juvenile offenders. Federal and state courts are required to consider unique circumstances when determining individualized sentences for juvenile defendants. In **Montgomery v. Louisiana** (2016),[40] the Supreme Court held that *Miller v. Alabama* must be applied retroactively. It gave states the option of either resentencing affected juveniles or offering parole. Over two thousand individuals' cases have been affected by the ruling.

The next chapter covers nonviolent street crime. Among the topics discussed are the war on drugs, offending by women, and the movement to decriminalize and legalize marijuana.

ROPER V. SIMMONS
U.S. Supreme Court decision that the death penalty cannot be used against someone who committed murder before they were eighteen years old.

GRAHAM V. FLORIDA
U.S. Supreme Court decision that juvenile offenders cannot be sentenced to life imprisonment without parole for nonhomicide offenses.

MILLER V. ALABAMA
U.S. Supreme Court ruling that mandatory sentences for life without parole, even in cases of murder, are unconstitutional for juvenile offenders. Federal and state courts are required to consider unique circumstances when determining individualized sentences for juvenile defendants.

MONTGOMERY V. LOUISIANA
The Supreme Court held that *Miller v. Alabama* must be applied retroactively.

REVIEW AND STUDY QUESTIONS

1. The juvenile court system was founded on the belief that society should try to rehabilitate, not punish, juvenile offenders. In the due process cases of the 1960s and 1970s, the Supreme Court often questioned whether the juvenile courts had been successful in their efforts to address the problems of young offenders. Should rehabilitation of juvenile offenders still be considered an important goal of the juvenile justice system? Why or why not?

2. If the goal of the juvenile justice system is rehabilitation, should juvenile court judges be limited by due process rights to try different approaches and apply different standards to individual juveniles? Why or why not?

3. If you, as a juvenile, were accused of committing a criminal offense, would you rather be tried by a jury of adults from your community or have your case heard by a judge? Would your answer differ if you were tried by a jury of young people? Why or why not?

4. Given that early life traumas are important factors for someone to join a gang, what policies and programs can be initiated to prevent the growth of gangs?

GOING FURTHER

Readings:

"The Fracturing of Gangs and Violence in Chicago: A Research-Based Reorientation of Violence Prevention and Intervention Policy." Great Cities Institute, University of Chicago, January 2019. https://great cities.uic.edu/wp-content/uploads/2019/01/The_Fract uring_of_Gangs_and_Violence_in_Chicago.pdf.

Miller, Jody. *One of the Guys: Girls, Gangs, and Gender.* New York: Oxford University Press, 2000.

Pollack, William, and Mary Pipher. *Real Boys: Rescuing Our Sons from the Myths of Boyhood.* New York: Henry Holt, 1999.

Rios, Victor M. *Punished: Policing the Lives of Black and Latino Boys.* New York: New York University Press, 2011.

Websites:

National Center for Victims of Crime. https://victims ofcrime.org/help-for-crime-victims/get-help-bulletins -for-crime-victims/bulletins-for-teens/crime-teens -and-trauma.

Videos/Movies:

Jury of Their Peers. Youth court aims to keep students out of criminal legal system. https://www.youtube .com/watch?v=LGLhGDNLusA.

Youth Justice in Canada. Building Safe Streets and Communities video series. https://www.justice.gc.ca /eng/cj-jp/yj-jj/video/ycja-lsjpa.html.

KEY TERMS

cliques or sets Smaller street gangs, usually in one neighborhood, that operate independently.

Deferred Action for Childhood Arrivals An immigration policy that allows some individuals who were brought to the United States without documentation as children to receive deferred action from deportation for a two-year period.

DREAM Act Proposed legislation that would grant temporary residency to young people who were sixteen or younger when they arrived in the United States without documents, have been residents for at least five consecutive years, and have completed a high school education.

Graham v. Florida U.S. Supreme Court decision that juvenile offenders cannot be sentenced to life imprisonment without parole for nonhomicide offenses.

In re Gault U.S. Supreme Court decision granting juvenile defendants due process rights, including notice of the charges against the young person, the right to legal counsel, the right against self-incrimination, and the right to confront and cross-examine witnesses.

In re Winship U.S. Supreme Court decision extending the standard of proof for a juvenile accused of a crime to beyond a reasonable doubt instead of a preponderance of the evidence.

Miller v. Alabama U.S. Supreme Court ruling that mandatory sentences for life without parole, even in cases of murder, are unconstitutional for juvenile offenders. Federal and state courts are required to consider unique circumstances when determining individualized sentences for juvenile defendants.

Montgomery v. Louisiana The Supreme Court held that *Miller v. Alabama* must be applied retroactively.

parens patriae The principle that the government or other political authority has the responsibility to protect those who are unable to protect themselves, including children.

Roper v. Simmons U.S. Supreme Court decision that the death penalty cannot be used against someone who committed murder before they were eighteen years old.

school resource officer (SRO) A law enforcement officer with sworn authority who is stationed in a school.

school-to-prison pipeline The process of criminalizing students through overzealous disciplinary practices that push students out of schools and put them in contact with law enforcement, thus leading to later involvement in the criminal/legal system.

status offender A young person who is under court jurisdiction for noncriminal behavior that is considered a law violation because of the youth's age, such as truancy, running away, violating curfew, underage use of alcohol, or general ungovernability.

zero-tolerance policies School policies that mandate expulsion or referral to juvenile or criminal court regardless of the circumstances or nature of the offense.

NOTES

1 Sean Flynn, "The Tamir Rice Story: How to Make a Police Shooting Disappear," *Gentlemen's Quarterly*, July 14, 2016, https://www.gq.com/story/tamir-rice-story.

2 Flynn, "The Tamir Rice Story."

3 Flynn, "The Tamir Rice Story."

4 Connie Schultz, "A City of Two Tales," *Politico*, February 23, 2015, https://www.politico.com/magazine/story/2015/02 /tamir-rice-cleveland-police-115401.

5 Schultz, "A City of Two Tales."

6 Schultz, "A City of Two Tales."

7 Schultz, "A City of Two Tales."

8 Schultz, "A City of Two Tales."

9 In re Gault, 387 U.S. 1 (1967).

10 In re Winship, 397 U.S. 358 (1970).

11 Juvenile Justice Delinquency Prevention Act, Pub. L. No. 93-415, § 5601, 42 U.S.C. (1974), https://ojjdp.ojp.gov /about/legislation.

12 "Black Boys Viewed as Older, Less Innocent than Whites, Research Finds," American Psychological Association, 2014, https://www.apa.org/news/press/releases/2014/03/black-boys -older.

13 "School Climate and Safety," 2015–16 Civil Rights Data Collection, U.S. Department of Education Office for Civil Rights, April 2018, https://www2.ed.gov/about/offices/list /ocr/docs/school-climate-and-safety.pdf.

14 "School Climate and Safety."

15 "Getting the Facts Straight about Girls in the Juvenile Justice System," National Council on Crime & Delinquency, 2009, https://www.nccdglobal.org/node/440.

16 Liz Watson and Peter Edelman, "Improving the Juvenile Justice System for Girls: Lessons from the States," Georgetown Center on Poverty, Inequality and Public Policy, October 2012, https://nationalcrittenton.org/wp-content /uploads/2015/03/1-Improving-the-Juvenile-Justice-System -for-Girls.pdf.

17 Elizabeth Cauffman, Shirley Feldman, Jaime Watherman, and Hans Steiner, "Posttraumatic Stress Disorder among Female Juvenile Offenders," Journal of the American Academy of Child & Adolescent Psychiatry 37, no. 11 (November 1998): 1209–16, https://doi.org/10.1097/00004583-199811000 -00022.

18 Leslie Acoca, "Are Those Cookies for Me or My Baby? Understanding Detained and Incarcerated Teen Mothers and Their Children," Juvenile and Family Court Journal, Spring 2004.

19 Vanessa Patino, Lawanda Ravoira, and Angela Wolf, "A Rallying Cry for Change," 2006, https://www.nccdglobal.org /sites/default/files/publication_pdf/cry-for-change.pdf.

20 Katie Ellis, "Contested Vulnerability: A Case Study of Girls in Secure Care," Children and Youth Services Review 88 (May 2018): 156–63, https://doi.org/10.1016/j .childyouth.2018.02.047.

21 J. J. Cutuli et al., "From Foster Care to Juvenile Justice: Exploring Characteristics of Youth in Three Cities," Children and Youth Services Review 68 (August 2016): 84–94, https:// doi.org/10.1016/j.childyouth.2016.06.001.

22 "LGBTQ Youth in the Foster Care System," Human Rights Campaign, accessed September 12, 2019, https://assets2 .hrc.org/files/assets/resources/HRC-YouthFosterCare-Issue Brief-FINAL.pdf.

23 Mike Males and Meda-Chesney Lind, "The Myth of Mean Girls," New York Times, April 2, 2010, http://www.nytimes .com/2010/04/02/opinion/02males.html.

24 "Are U.S. Girls Becoming More Violent?," Population Reference Bureau, accessed September 12, 2017, https://www .prb.org/areusgirlsbecomingmoreviolent.

25 Peggy C. Giordano and Jennifer E. Copp, "Girls' and Women's Violence: The Question of General versus Uniquely Gendered Causes," Annual Review of Criminology 2 (January 2019): 167–89, https://doi.org/10.1146/annu rev-criminol-011518-024517.

26 Christopher R. Browning, Margo Gardner, David Maimon, and Jeanne Brooks-Gunn, "Collective Efficacy and the Contingent Consequences of Exposure to Life-Threatening Violence," Developmental Psychology 50, no. 7 (2014): 1878–90, https://doi.org/10.1037/a0036767.

27 Alan Lizotte and David Sheppard, "Gun Use by Male Juveniles: Research and Prevention," Office of Juvenile Justice and Delinquency Prevention, July 2001, https://ojjdp.ojp .gov/library/publications/gun-use-male-juveniles-research-and -prevention.

28 "Unjust: How the Broken Juvenile and Criminal Justice Systems Fail LGBTQ Youth," Center for American Progress and MAP, August 2016, http://www.lgbtmap.org/file/lgbt-crimi nal-justice-youth.pdf.

29 Angela Irvine, "Dispelling Myths: Understanding the Incarceration of Lesbian, Gay, Bisexual, and Gender Nonconforming Youth" (unpublished paper, National Council on Crime and Delinquency, Oakland, CA, 2014), as cited in Center for American Progress and MAP.

30 Caitlin Ryan and Rafael Diaz, "Family Responses as a Source of Risk & Resiliency for LGBT Youth," Child Welfare League of America Preconference Institute, Washington, DC, February 2005, http://www.cwla.org.

31 Bianca D. M. Wilson et al., "Sexual and Gender Minority Youth in Foster Care: Assessing Disproportionality and Disparities in Los Angeles," Social Services & Child Welfare, Williams Institute, UCLA School of Law, August 2014, https:// williamsinstitute.law.ucla.edu/publications/sgm-youth-la-foster -care.

32 BreakOUT!, "We Deserve Better: A Report on Policing in New Orleans by and for Queer and Trans Youth of Color," National Council on Crime & Delinquency, October 24, 2014.

33 "Prison Policy Initiative," accessed September 12, 2017, https://www.prisonpolicy.org/research/youth.

34 "Black Disparities in Youth Incarceration," Sentencing Project, accessed September 12, 2017, https://www.senten cingproject.org/publications/black-disparities-youth-incarcer ation.

35 Thompson v. Oklahoma, 487 U.S. 815 (1988).

36 Stanford v. Kentucky, 492 U.S. 361 (1989).

37 Roper v. Simmons, 543 U.S. 551 (2005).

38 Graham v. Florida, 560 U.S. 48 (2010).

39 Miller v. Alabama, 567 U.S. 460 (2012).

40 Montgomery v. Louisiana, 577 U.S. ___ (2016).

CHAPTER —— 7

Traditional Street Crime

Nonviolent

In this chapter you will meet Alva Mae Groves and Dorothy Gaines, two women who were caught up in the nation's aggressive war on drugs and spent time in prison on drug conspiracy convictions despite little or no evidence that they possessed or sold drugs. Then we look at the trends in nonviolent crimes, including property and drug crimes, and review theories explaining women's involvement.

LEARNING OBJECTIVES

After reading this chapter, you should be able to do the following:

- Evaluate the nature and extent of women's involvement with nonviolent crimes.
- Explain the tools employed by the criminal/legal system.
- Describe the impact the "war on drugs" has had on women's lives.
- Compare the consequences of the "war on drugs" on women from different social, ethnic, and racial backgrounds.

Case #7: Alva Mae Groves and Dorothy Gaines

Alva Mae Groves and Dorothy Gaines never should have met. One was from small-town North Carolina and in her early seventies; the other was from Mobile, Alabama, and in her early forties. One sold eggs for small change; the other had a nursing background and described herself as a "PTA mom." But in the mid-1990s, they both found themselves in a federal women's prison in Tallahassee, Florida.

On the morning of June 22, 1994, both federal and county law enforcement agents converged around the trailer of seventy-two-year-old Alva Mae Groves in Clayton, North Carolina. Clayton, though only twenty or so miles from Raleigh, the state capital, was only just beginning to bounce back from a decades-long postdepression slump. Alva Mae was out tending her garden when the investigators arrived. They had a warrant; they wanted her to go with them.

Alva Mae lived in a double-wide mobile home on a lot belonging to her son, William Robert. Two of her granddaughters—Fontara, who was eleven, and Jasmine, who was only nine—lived with her. Her daughter Margaret, also known as Monk, lived in the trailer next door. Both trailers were searched, and Alva Mae and Margaret were taken into custody.

Neighbors recall that the middle generation of the family were into petty crimes—selling bootlegged liquor and drugs here and there. But when the crack boom happened, it seemed that their business ramped up. They had runners that would meet the cars that came along the dirt road, selling them rocks of crack cocaine. They accepted various forms of payment: cash, food stamps, and sometimes bartered items if they had any value. The money, several members of the family reported later, was good.

Federal prosecutors agreed that the money had indeed been significant, to the tune of approximately $1.7 million in profits. Over the period that their operation was in effect, federal agents and informants had reportedly completed approximately twenty-six controlled buys from the Groves family, and they estimated that there were at least sixteen people involved in the business. Alva Mae and Margaret were key players, prosecutors argued, along with a handful of Alva Mae's nine children and other family members across three generations. Alva Mae's double-wide, they claimed, was the central distribution point; a gun found in her home was used as further evidence. The raid was referred to as Operation Wipeout by officials, who also claimed that the Groves family was perhaps one of the largest distributors of crack cocaine in the nation. Despite this claim, and despite federal estimates of the Groves family's profits, only about $3,000 was found.

Though her children argued that Alva Mae was not involved in the business and was instead an innocent bystander who simply chose to ignore their dealings, she was arrested alongside them and faced charges of conspiracy to possess with intent to distribute and distributing cocaine base.

Fontelle, Alva Mae's youngest son, got twelve years. Charlie, her eldest, got seventeen. Margaret got thirty years, and Margaret's daughter Pam got thirteen, down from seventeen and a half because of information she provided about her mother's brother, Ricky.

Ricky got life. Ricky was thought to be the kingpin, and when he heard that his mother had been arrested and that her home was being searched, he immediately fled, only to be picked up by U.S. marshals three months later. Ricky could see himself having sold two or three kilos of crack cocaine at most, not nearly eighty as law enforcement said. Either way, however, because of federal sentencing guidelines that had been put in place in the mid-1980s at the height of the drug war, only a kilo and a half would have been enough to send him to prison for life. Ricky was on-and-off living with Alva Mae; this is perhaps what brought the chaos to her door.

It was in part the fact that some members of the Groves family informed on each other that caused Alva Mae to get such a harsh sentence. Margaret's son, with whom she had an ongoing feud, gave up information about his family members; in return for his assistance, he faced no conviction. Pam, too, offered up information, though she later claimed she regretted it. Alva Mae, on the other hand, refused to implicate any members of her family, and her children would later argue that her refusal to cooperate with investigators and prosecutors made her sentence disproportionately severe. Alva Mae herself agreed with this assessment and also suspected that her lack of knowledge of the law and unfamiliarity with legal jargon was also used against her; though she pleaded guilty, she was not given a reduced sentence for accepting responsibility, and she was coerced into giving up her right to appeal her sentence. Although she was already in her mid-seventies, Alva Mae was sentenced to twenty-four years in federal prison. Serving the entire term would mean that she would not be released until she was nearly one hundred years old.

Despite her harsh sentence, there was never any evidence that Alva Mae—or Margaret, for that matter—had any money, or anything to show for a supposedly booming business. Alva Mae lived on the cheap, selling eggs from her chickens and soda pop to kids passing by, and primarily subsisted on Social Security, food stamps, and public assistance. She had no assets to speak of, and yet she was sentenced to twenty-four years' imprisonment with no chance of appeal and, realistically, no chance of parole. In 2001, at eighty years old, Alva Mae wrote from prison to the November Coalition, a nonprofit organization working to free those imprisoned on nonviolent drug convictions, and reflected on what she considered to be the multiple injustices she faced:

My real crime, according to today's laws of betrayal, was refusing to testify against my sons, children of my womb, that were conceived, birthed and raised with love, of which there were fourteen children in all—nine girls and six boys. The government said I could have received a reduction in my sentence if I would have testified, but since I couldn't do such a thing, prosecutors then said I was a manager/supervisor in this offense, thereby raising my offense level by three points and increasing my sentence substantially. Of course I didn't really understand all this talk about enhancements, acceptance of responsibility, and so on, that had to do with my sentencing. But I did understand that since I wouldn't turn against my own family that I was going to receive a very lengthy prison term. Never did I dream it would be twenty-five years. . . . I still don't understand how one can sign their right to appeal away when one hasn't even received their sentence. It's all beyond me. I know I sat there and watched while my whole family was buried by sentences of thirty years (my daughter Margaret), seventeen-and-a-half years (my granddaughter Pam) and my other sons, one who received natural life. I still don't understand all of it.[1]

Approximately 70 percent of the women incarcerated at the prison in Florida were there for similar offenses, and often with very similar circumstances to Alva Mae. Many of them had been only minorly involved with drugs but had been connected to men with more major involvement. Dorothy Gaines was one of these women.

Dorothy had also been convicted of conspiracy to distribute crack cocaine. A mother of three, Dorothy had been mixed up with a man who allegedly sold crack cocaine, and despite the fact that a raid on Dorothy's home in 1993 yielded no drugs or other evidence, federal prosecutors upheld the charges against her. Her boyfriend and his associates pointed fingers at Dorothy; she pointed fingers at no one. The men got sentences of five years; in March 1995, Dorothy got a sentence of nearly twenty. Like Alva Mae, she had refused to offer testimony, and like Alva Mae, she was confounded by her sentence.

Dorothy knew Alva Mae at the penitentiary; she remembers that Alva Mae had been treated like an elder and called "Granny" by some of the other prisoners, who made sure to look out for her and help her navigate her wheelchair through the facility.

One crucial difference between Alva Mae and Dorothy, however, was that Dorothy had advocates on the outside that were tirelessly advocating for her release. Her advocates focused not just on Dorothy's case but on the disproportionately long sentences handed to those who had been convicted of nonviolent offenses, particularly those who had been found in possession of crack cocaine. Dorothy's friends and family, particularly her children, kept up their sustained campaign until finally, in December 2000,

in the twilight of his presidency, President Clinton commuted her sentence, and she was released after six years of imprisonment.

Alva Mae remained in prison, despite failing health. In early 2000, she was transferred to Carswell Federal Medical Center, outside Fort Worth, Texas. An application to have her sentence commuted had failed, and she was sent back to the prison in Tallahassee. Prison was undoubtedly a health hazard; the food was a particular sticking point for Alva Mae, who continued to dream about the garden she would plant when she was released and the great-grandchildren she would finally get to meet. She also continued to appeal to those on the outside who might advocate for her. In the same letter to the November Coalition, she wrote,

I realize everyone has a day to die; death is a fate that will not be cheated. But I don't want to die in prison. I want to die at home surrounded by the love of what's left of my family. I do not have enough years left of my life to finish serving this twenty-four-year sentence as I am already 80 years old. I'm appealing to anyone to write letters for me to the Pardon Attorney's Office in Washington while my application is still pending.[2]

Her appeals continued to be denied, and in early 2007, after being transferred back to Carswell for further kidney- and diabetes-related health complications, Alva Mae passed away, at the age of eighty-six, in a prison hospital bed. Her daughter, Everline Johnson, was there with her when she passed, relieved that her mother had not seen the most recent letter denying the family's petition for compassionate release. Officials felt that the charges against Alva Mae were simply too serious and that she had to remain under prison supervision.

Dorothy Gaines, upon her release, continues to advocate for prisoners and their families. She speaks at schools and reflects on the fact that it was not until she went to prison that she understood the processes of institutional racism and the disparities of incarceration. Despite her activism, returning to life after prison continues to be littered with obstacles. Both she and her children, who are now grown, continue to suffer from the long-term effects of her sentence.

THINKING CRITICALLY ABOUT THE CASE

1. Why were Alva Mae Groves and Dorothy Gaines given longer sentences than those that were associated with them?

2. What risk would it have posed to society to grant Alva Mae compassionate release in the years leading up to her death?

3. Aside from the food, in what other ways might prison have been a health hazard for Alva Mae?

REFERENCES

This case is adapted from the following sources:

Burroughs, Gaylynn. "Carswell Prison Blues." *Huffington Post*, November 29, 2008. http://www.huffingtonpost.com/entry/carswell-prison-blues_b_138999.html.

"Dorothy Gaines." Sentencing Project, 2020. http://www.sentencingproject.org/stories/dorothy-gaines.

Hallinan, Joseph T. *Going Up the River: Travels in a Prison Nation.* New York: Random House, 2003.

Locke, Mandy. "Tight-Lipped 'Granny' Dies in Prison." November Coalition, August 17, 2007. http://www.november.org/stayinfo/breaking07/GrannyAlvaMae.html.

"November Coalition Letter on the Passing of Alva Mae Groves." November Coalition, July 30, 2008. http://www.november.org/thewall/cases/groves-a/groves-a.html.

Pupovac, Jessica. "Crack Users Do More Time than People Convicted of Manslaughter." *AlterNet*, October 16, 2007. http://www.alternet.org/story/65406/crack_users_do_more_time_than_people_convicted_of_manslaughter.

Saunders, Debra J. "Why Clinton Should Pardon Dorothy Gaines." *SFGate*, September 26, 2000. http://www.sfgate.com/opinion/saunders/article/Why-Clinton-Should-Pardon-Dorothy-Gaines-3316047.php.

Smith, P. "Drug War Prisoners: 86-Year-Old Alva Mae Groves Dies behind Bars." Stop the Drug War, August 23, 2007. http://www.stopthedrugwar.org/chronicle/2007/aug/23/drug_war_prisoners_86yearold_alv.

United States v. Ricky Lee Groves, 89 F.3d 830 (Court of Appeals, 4th Circuit 1996). http://www.law.resource.org/pub/us/case/reporter/F3/089/89.F3d.830.95-5173.95-5172.html.

United States v. Willie Lee Strickland, 89 F.3d 830 (Court of Appeals, 4th Circuit 1996). http://www.law.resource.org/pub/us/case/reporter/F3/089/89.F3d.830.95-5173.95-5172.html.

CONTEXT AND ANALYSIS

In this chapter we examine the gendered nature of nonviolent street crime. Street crime acquired its name because it is often committed out of doors, but in fact it doesn't only refer to outside crimes. Street crime is a loosely organized amalgam of acts defined as criminal that are not conducted in the course of business, private or public. The latter are addressed, as crimes of power, at length in chapter 10. Street crime is generally considered to include both violent and nonviolent crimes. We have made the decision to divide our exploration of violent and nonviolent crimes, as the extent and nature of these crimes varies greatly by gender. Chapter 8 looks at street crimes that are considered violent and explores, in particular, theories of masculinity that help explain the vastly disproportionate amount of violent crimes committed by men.

While women in general engage in less criminal behavior than men at a rate of approximately 3:1, they are represented in greater numbers in nonviolent crimes, such as **larceny**, **fraud**, **embezzlement**, prostitution or other sex crimes, and an array of drug-related crimes. As prostitution and sex crimes are discussed at length in chapter 9, this chapter focuses on property crimes and drug crimes, as well as the added burden placed on women of color.

Extent and Nature of Women's Crime

Approximately 28 percent of crimes committed by females are property crimes, with another 24 percent labeled as drug crimes. Less than one-third are violent offenses,[3] and when women do commit violent offenses, it is most often targeting a close relative or intimate partner and is frequently in self-defense.[4] The most recent data available about the number of arrests is for 2017 and is derived from the Uniform Crime Reports (UCR). According to the UCR, when considering nonviolent offenses, the percentages of women among persons arrested are as follows: for larceny theft (larceny, though the UCR uses the term larceny theft to distinguish it from motor vehicle larceny, which they record separately), 43.1 percent; for arson as property crime (rather than arson as violent—again, the UCR separates these), 37.4 percent; for forgery and counterfeiting, 37.2 percent; for fraud, 40.5 percent; for embezzlement, 48.4 percent; and for prostitution, 67.7 percent. For all other UCR crimes, females account for about a third of those charged.[5] Somewhat consistent with the state data reported by the UCR, federal data finds that women account for 13 percent of those receiving federal sentences in 2018, with the principal charged offenses being drug trafficking, fraud, and immigration-related offenses. The vast majority (68.4 percent) had little or no prior criminal history.[6] When considering drug-related crimes in particular, it is important to look not simply at crimes such as use, possession, and distribution of drugs, but also to understand that many other crimes are secondarily related to drug use and addiction. Data from one large-scale sample reveals, for example, that 76 percent of women arrested for robbery tested positive for drugs, as well as 74 percent of women arrested for stolen property and 85 percent of those arrested for prostitution.[7] This suggests that the impact of drugs on women's involvement with the criminal/legal system extends far beyond what are called drug crimes.

In 2013, 1.2 million women were under the authority of the criminal/legal system in some manner, from arrest to probation to incarceration.[8] The impact of this involvement varies by race and ethnicity. For example, in 2014, the rate of imprisonment for African American women was more than twice the rate of imprisonment for white women; for Hispanic women, the incarceration rate was 1.2 times that of white women.[9] We discuss women's incarceration, the trends and the inequities, further in chapter 13.

During the late twentieth and the first two decades of the twenty-first centuries, the rate of women being arrested for crimes increased at a rate about twice that for men. Despite this statistic, it is important to remember that women began at a much lower base line number and continue to be arrested for approximately 20 percent of property crimes and 11 percent of violent crimes overall.[10] Over the past decade, the trend for both women and men has been toward lower arrest rates, reflecting lower rates of crime in

LARCENY
Theft of personal property.

FRAUD
Wrongful deception intended for financial or personal gain.

EMBEZZLEMENT
Taking assets, money, or property that belongs to another but over which one has control and using it for personal gain.

general. One interesting anomaly concerns motor vehicle theft, where the rate of arrests for females increased by 25.9 percent between 2006 and 2015.[11]

Larceny, Fraud, and Embezzlement

When women commit crimes, it is often a response to their life circumstances. As you read about elsewhere in this text, a large percentage of women who are drawn into the criminal/legal system have experienced multiple traumas. When we consider larceny, fraud, and embezzlement, crimes usually characterized as minor property crimes, the causes are often economic marginalization and limited economic opportunities.

The Brookings Institute conducted research on women and economic mobility. They had several relevant findings. For instance, "forty percent of women are the primary or sole provider for their families."[12] They also found that women who work today earn more than their mothers but less than their fathers, while men have higher wages than both. More significant in understanding the limited mobility that women, especially poor women, face is the finding that, of women born into the bottom fifth of the economic ladder, 47 percent stay in the bottom fifth throughout their adult lives.[13] For men that number is 35 percent,[14] still all too many to be lacking in mobility. In fact, appreciably fewer men are held back compared to women. While women have made considerable progress toward economic equality to men, that has not been true for the poorest among us, where both men and women suffer from limited opportunity.

The larceny/theft and fraud that women commit typically involve shoplifting, writing bad checks, and welfare fraud. These are crimes of necessity and crimes of opportunity—necessity because, as the sole provider for a family, not being able to adequately provide for them brings shame and desperation, and opportunity because it is often women dealing with welfare, where it might be easier to lie about the boyfriend staying in the apartment than to risk losing benefits that help feed and clothe the children.

Embezzlement typically involves taking money or property from one's employer or a business entity. It is also known as "employee theft" and is a type of fraud. As it involves taking something that you have been given control over, embezzlement is seen as a crime of opportunity, and because women in general have less access, what they embezzle is usually modest. Embezzlement can be as small as using your employer's stamps for personal mail or as large as the $50 billion scam, discovered in 2008, perpetrated by Bernie Madoff.

THE "WAR ON DRUGS" AS A WAR ON US

As we saw in the case studies of Groves and Gaines, large numbers of women, old and young, Black and white, are being dragged into the criminal/legal system for relatively minor drug offenses. Indeed, more than 60 percent of women incarcerated in federal prisons are there for nonviolent drug offenses. Between 1986 and 1999, years that saw the "**war on drugs**" reach its peak, the number of women held in state jails and prisons for drug-related offenses increased by 888 percent, compared to an increase of 129 percent for all other offenses.[15]

Drugs, including many that are currently illegal in the United States, have been used for centuries for a variety of medical, religious, or spiritual practices. Drug use first became apparent in the United States in the 1800s. Opiates, including heroin, and cocaine were used in medicines to treat pain and respiratory illnesses, as well as in Coca-Cola, named for the coca leaf. Indeed, the Sears and Roebuck catalog, a mainstay of American culture, in the 1890s sold "a syringe and a small amount of cocaine for $1.50."[16]

From the beginning, U.S. drug policy, while claiming to be based on moral imperative, has been used as a tool to punish or disadvantage people who were deemed different based on race, ethnicity, or gender. The first drug laws were passed in the 1870s, criminalizing opium and targeting the Chinese immigrants who had recently arrived to build the

WAR ON DRUGS
Government-led campaign to stop illegal drug use and distribution by enforcing and increasing penalties.

national railroads. In the early 1900s, the first anti-cocaine laws targeted Black men in the South, and a decade later the first anti-marijuana laws were aimed at Mexican migrants. And, of course, the early 1900s saw alcohol prohibition, with the 1919 passage of the Eighteenth Amendment banning the "manufacture, sale, or transportation of intoxicating liquors." **Prohibition** ended in 1933 when the Twenty-First Amendment was passed, overturning the Eighteenth.

Throughout the 1930s, 1940s, and 1950s, the federal government, with the aid and support of private industries, launched a propaganda campaign designed to associate marijuana with murder, temporary insanity, and sexual permissiveness. Associations with jazz musicians, largely Black and Latino men, abounded. The 1960s saw a growth in the use of drugs, from the counterculture that popularized marijuana and hallucinogens to Vietnam veterans who used drugs to deal with the realities of war, and who too often returned home addicted to heroin. In 1971, President Nixon formally declared a "war on drugs." John Ehrlichman, a top Nixon aide, later admitted that the motivation for this "war" was purely political, saying,

> The Nixon campaign in 1968, and the Nixon White House after that, had two enemies: the antiwar left and black people. You understand what I'm saying? We knew we couldn't make it illegal to be either against the war or black, but by getting the public to associate the hippies with marijuana and blacks with heroin, and then criminalizing both heavily, we could disrupt those communities. We could arrest their leaders, raid their homes, break up their meetings, and vilify them night after night on the evening news. . . . Did we know we were lying about the drugs? Of course we did.[17]

Nixon remained committed, and it was during his administration that the Drug Enforcement Administration (DEA) was established.

There was a brief pause in this "war" during the Carter administration, but President Reagan restarted and expanded the battle. Between 1980 when he was elected (the Reagan presidency officially began in January 1981) and 1997, the number of people incarcerated for drug-related offenses rose from approximately fifty thousand to four hundred thousand.[18] The mid-1980s was known especially for the introduction of **crack cocaine**. Crack is a smokable form of cocaine, marketable in smaller, less expensive quantities than powder cocaine. It effectively moved cocaine use from inside one's home onto the streets, from the white suburbs to poorer urban communities. Once again, propaganda and racism combined to create a panic by associating Black women and men with a new "epidemic." The campaign was successful. Studies show that in 1985 roughly 4 percent of the public considered drug abuse to be the country's number-one problem. By 1989, 64 percent of the American public identified drugs as the most important issue facing the nation. This shift in public attitudes allowed for stricter laws and even more enforcement.

Thus was passed the **Anti–Drug Abuse Act of 1986**, a bill that followed Reagan's zero-tolerance agenda, moving from earlier ideas of rehabilitation to a strictly punitive system of incarceration, prosecuting and penalizing with a specific focus on the *users* of drugs. The act also included mandatory minimum sentences. In a manner that was clearly racist, it created federal regulations that mandated a minimum sentence of five years without parole for possession of five grams of crack cocaine; the same sentence was mandated for five hundred grams of powder cocaine, a 100:1 disparity between crack cocaine and powder cocaine.

Although President Clinton advocated for drug law reform and a return to treatment, he was not very successful and ultimately did not follow through with any significant changes. It was not until the Obama administration that the law was moderated somewhat by the **Fair Sentencing Act**, passed in 2010. This act changed the sentencing ratio from a 100:1 disparity to 18:1, altering the measurement of crack from grams to ounces, with one ounce equaling twenty-eight grams. The new law also eliminated the five-year mandatory sentence for possession.

PROHIBITION
The Eighteenth Amendment banned the "manufacture, sale, or transportation of intoxicating liquors"; ended in 1933 when the Twenty-First Amendment was passed.

CRACK COCAINE
Smokable form of cocaine, marketable in smaller, less expensive quantities than powder cocaine.

ANTI-DRUG ABUSE ACT OF 1986
Created strict punishment in the form of prosecution, sentencing, and incarceration, including mandatory minimum sentences, for drug use.

FAIR SENTENCING ACT
2010 act that changed the sentencing ratio of crack and powder cocaine from a 100:1 to an 18:1 disparity.

Impact on Women

During the past century, the "war on drugs" has not just targeted people based on race and ethnicity, but also gender. Several factors have come together to greatly increase the impact this "war" has had on women. As with other property crimes, women's limited economic and social mobility increases financial incentives to become involved in the sale and distribution of small amounts of illegal substances. But just as importantly, the shame and desperation noted above make the self-medicating aspects of drug use immediate and appealing.

For those women suffering with addiction, many have coexisting mental health problems that are not being addressed. According to the United Nations, women who inject drugs are more vulnerable to diseases such as HIV and hepatitis C than are men.[19] Very few addiction services exist that are gender specific, designed to address the range of issues women face.

Conspiracy is among the ways the law is used against women. As defined by law, conspiracy occurs when two or more people reach an agreement to commit a crime. In theory there has to be an agreement, though an act in furtherance of the crime can be considered an agreement. Once there is such an agreement, it doesn't matter if the crime is actually committed; all parties can be charged with conspiracy. You can be sentenced for the mere conspiracy, or for the underlying crime that is committed. For women, they are often charged with conspiracy for living with a drug dealer or for not being willing to inform on their partner or another family member. We saw this firsthand in the Groves and Gaines cases (case study 7).

Civil asset forfeiture allows police to seize property believed to be associated with a crime, whether or not a crime has actually been committed. Police may take, and sell, homes, cars, cash, and any other items deemed related to the crime. Reports of seizures include kitchen utensils, baby strollers, and phones. For a woman to fall victim to forfeiture, she does not need any criminal culpability; she merely has to share access to those items with someone who is a suspect. A family can lose their home if it can be shown to have been purchased with money acquired from drug sales. A car that was borrowed from a sister and then used to deliver drugs can be confiscated. It is possible that a woman can recover her family's forfeited possessions by employing an innocent owners exception to the law, but it is costly to fight and narrowly defined. Further, she would be battling stereotypes that assume that intimate partners are fully aware of the other's activities, something we know is not always the case, especially where abuse is present. And finally, the fact that police are able to sell forfeited property and retain the proceeds promotes and rewards police abuse.

Finally, not all women are victims of intimate partners. In some instances, their economic situation, and the lack of access to legitimate markets, leads them to enter the illegal marketplace and engage in the sale of drugs. Ironically, and in sharp contrast to what the media would have us believe with such shows as *Queen of the South*, the drug economy, like other economies, is **gender stratified**. Women are unlikely to be granted access to this economy in any but the most low-level and fringe positions.[20]

Drug Courts

Drug courts are recent innovations, with the first drug court appearing thirty years ago in Miami, Florida. Since that time, there has been a trend toward guiding nonviolent drug offenders into treatment rather than incarceration. Drug courts are designed to provide treatment to participants who admit having an addiction. By using their **coercive authority** to mandate treatment, the courts promise that charges will be dropped upon successful completion. Failure results in sentencing. The hope of those who support drug courts is that they will increase access to treatment and decrease recidivism.

Drug courts have seen rapid expansion and are considered "one of the fastest growing programs designed to reduce drug abuse and criminality in nonviolent offenders in

CONSPIRACY
Occurs when two or more people reach an agreement to commit a crime.

CIVIL ASSET FORFEITURE
Allows police to seize property believed to be associated with a crime, whether or not a crime has actually been committed.

GENDER STRATIFIED
Refers to inequalities between women and men regarding wealth, power, and privilege.

COERCIVE AUTHORITY
Refers to motivation by threat of punishment to mandate treatment.

the nation."[21] According to the National Institute of Justice (NIJ), there were 3,100 drug courts throughout the United States in 2018.[22] The rapid rise in drug courts has been attributed to four converging problems within the justice system: (1) the growth of drug cases coming before the courts as a result of the escalating "war on drugs," (2) the public perception that punishment for drug crimes amounts to no more than a revolving door between incarceration and free society, (3) growing judicial resentment of the restrictive nature of mandatory sentencing laws, and (4) increasing reliance on the courts to solve social problems.[23]

Research suggests that few drug court participants graduate in the prescribed year.[24] Extending the duration of contact with the court and with the treatment provider results in an increase in services and can be expected to increase the cost per participant. It remains uncertain whether the longer-than-anticipated court involvement plays a role in the rate of subsequent offending.

In 2014, women made up 32 percent of drug court participants.[25] Research suggests that they graduate in lower numbers than men. Understanding why requires that we reflect on the general challenges faced by women in seeking treatment and managing their lives, including lack of financial resources, fear of losing their children, lack of available services, lack of suitable and affordable child care, lack of transportation, homelessness, mental health needs, and, again, the shame and stigma associated with addiction and not being a "good" mother.

Decriminalization

The "war on drugs" has waned in the past decade. As of October 2019, marijuana is fully legal in ten states and fully illegal in only nine; the others have a range of laws that **decriminalize** marijuana or provide for its medical use.[26] The public has generally grown weary of large numbers of people imprisoned for drug offenses. With the recent publicity about opiate addiction, which strikes white individuals at twice the rate of nonwhite individuals,[27] the public and the medical community are more likely to view the problem as medical and treatable.

The United Nations issued a report in 2019 advocating **harm reduction**, decriminalization, and no discrimination against people who use drugs, and suggesting that people who use drugs need support, not incarceration.[28] An example of this type of policy is Portugal, which decriminalized all drugs in 2001 and is now relying on a harm reduction and treatment policy. There has been a significant increase in the number of people seeking treatment, with overdose deaths decreasing by over 80 percent. In comparison, "in 2017, there were more than 72,000 overdose deaths in the U.S. If the U.S. overdose death rate were on par with Portugal's, there would have been fewer than 800 overdose deaths that year."[29] Portugal has also witnessed a reduction in HIV/AIDS cases and a sharp decrease in incarceration.

By changing our laws and policies regarding illegal drugs from an enforcement to a harm reduction perspective, removing drug enforcement from the criminal/legal system and moving it to a support and treatment model, women would be less subject to the ways in which our criminal/legal system disadvantages them.

THE OVERCRIMINALIZATION OF WOMEN OF COLOR

The "war on drugs" was only part of the so-called tough-on-crime movement that began in the 1980s. Many of the policies that emerged from that movement involved regulating **quality-of-life offenses**, which are acts normally considered not to be criminal, such as loitering, graffiti, public drinking, and panhandling. Quality-of-life policing requires aggressive enforcement of these violations, giving police license to stop, harass, and criminalize people for going about their daily lives, opening the door to racism and bias in enforcement. In New York City, police were arresting people for trespassing on the

DECRIMINALIZE
To eliminate penalties for the use and possession of drugs for personal use, as well as penalties for possession of equipment used to transfer drugs into the body.

HARM REDUCTION
Practical strategies aimed at reducing the negative consequences of drug use.

QUALITY-OF-LIFE OFFENSES
Acts such as loitering, graffiti, public drinking, and panhandling.

premises of public housing projects. That practice has been stopped, but not before many people pleaded guilty.[30]

In addition, a Maryland court put a stop to the police practice of arresting people for loitering if they failed to move along when officers told them to do so. The courts said that merely standing on the street does not constitute loitering, but not until many were charged and jailed.

Women and girls of color, especially Black women and girls, as well as LGBTQ people of color, like their male counterparts, are racially profiled, stopped by police for no reason other than driving while female, and singled out at airports and schools. When they experience IPV, they may not be able to seek police assistance without being put at risk of excessive force themselves. They also experience an increased risk of sexual assault. And, as you will see in chapter 11, even their pregnancies and parenting are policed in ways not experienced by white women.

What is the result of all this racism? Women of color, especially Black and Native women, are disproportionately arrested, prosecuted, and imprisoned. According to a 2003 Bureau of Justice Statistics special report, 1 in every 18 African American women will go to prison during their lifetime if incarceration rates continue at their current level. This is far greater than the rates for white women and Latinas—1 in 111 women and 1 in 45 women, respectively.[31] For indigenous women, the rate is 1 in 17.[32] While women of color comprise 36 percent of women in the United States, they are 50 percent of the female population in prison and 66 percent of the population in local jails.[33]

Throughout this text you will read about the ways in which the most vulnerable among us—women, women of color, LGBTQ people, men of color, and girls—are revictimized by the criminal legal system. The next chapter explores violent crimes and theories of early life trauma, masculinity, and racism that contribute to that violence.

REVIEW AND STUDY QUESTIONS

1. Why are women involved in such a relatively high percentage of property crimes, as compared to violent crimes?

2. Why has the "war on drugs" had such a disproportionate impact on women? Can you think of any explanations not offered in the text?

3. What would be the best societal response to drugs? The safest? The most humane? If these are not the same, how would you reconcile your response?

GOING FURTHER

Websites:

Drug Policy Alliance's video chronicling its Portugal visit: http://www.drugpolicy.org/portugal.

Thirty Years of American Drug Wars, Frontline, PBS. https://www.pbs.org/wgbh/pages/frontline/shows/drugs/cron.

KEY TERMS

Anti–Drug Abuse Act of 1986 Created strict punishment in the form of prosecution, sentencing, and incarceration, including mandatory minimum sentences, for drug use.

civil asset forfeiture Allows police to seize property believed to be associated with a crime, whether or not a crime has actually been committed.

coercive authority Refers to motivation by threat of punishment to mandate treatment.

conspiracy Occurs when two or more people reach an agreement to commit a crime.

crack cocaine Smokable form of cocaine, marketable in smaller, less expensive quantities than powder cocaine.

decriminalize To eliminate penalties for the use and possession of drugs for personal use, as well as penalties for possession of equipment used to transfer drugs into the body.

embezzlement Taking assets, money, or property that belongs to another but over which one has control and is using it for personal gain.

Fair Sentencing Act 2010 act that changed the sentencing ratio of crack and powder cocaine from a 100:1 to an 18:1 disparity.

fraud Wrongful deception intended for financial or personal gain.

gender stratified Refers to inequalities between women and men regarding wealth, power, and privilege.

harm reduction Practical strategies aimed at reducing the negative consequences of drug use.

larceny Theft of personal property.

Prohibition The Eighteenth Amendment banned the "manufacture, sale, or transportation of intoxicating liquors"; ended in 1933 when the Twenty-First Amendment was passed.

quality-of-life offenses Acts such as loitering, graffiti, public drinking, and panhandling.

war on drugs Government-led campaign to stop illegal drug use and distribution by enforcing and increasing penalties.

NOTES

1 "Letter from Alva Mae Groves," November Coalition, August 10, 2007, http://www.november.org/thewall/cases/groves-a/groves-a.html.

2 "Letter from Alva Mae Groves."

3 E. Ann Carson, "Prisoners in 2014," Department of Justice, Bureau of Justice Statistics, September 2015, http://www.bjs.gov/index.cfm?ty=pbdetail&iid=5387, as cited by https://cjinvolvedwomen.org/wp-content/uploads/2016/06/Fact-Sheet.pdf.

4 Marilyn Van Dieten, Natalie J. Jones, and Monica Rondon, "Working with Women Who Perpetrate Violence: A Practice Guide," National Resource Center on Justice Involved Women, April 2014, http://cjinvolvedwomen.org/wp-content/uploads/2015/09/Working-With-Women-Who-Perpetrate-Violence-A-Practice-Guide6-23.pdf, as cited by https://cjinvolvedwomen.org/wp-content/uploads/2016/06/Fact-Sheet.pdf.

5 "Arrests by Sex, 2017," FBI, Uniform Crime Reporting, Crime in the United States, table 42, 2017, accessed October 16, 2019, https://ucr.fbi.gov/crime-in-the-u.s/2017/crime-in-the-u.s.-2017/topic-pages/tables/table-42.

6 "Quick Facts: Women in the Federal Offender Population," U.S. Sentencing Commission, accessed October 16, 2019, https://www.ussc.gov/sites/default/files/pdf/research-and-publications/quick-facts/Female_Offenders_FY18.pdf.

7 "Fact Sheet: Drug-Related Crime," Drugs and Crime, Bureau of Justice Statistics, accessed February 16, 2016, https://www.bjs.gov/content/pub/pdf/DRRC.PDF.

8 Lauren Glaze and Danielle Kaeble, "Correctional Populations in the United States, 2013," Bureau of Justice Statistics, December 2014, https://www.bjs.gov/content/pub/pdf/cpus13.pdf, as cited by https://cjinvolvedwomen.org/wp-content/uploads/2016/06/Fact-Sheet.pdf.

9 "Incarcerated Women and Girls," Sentencing Project, 2015, accessed August 23, 2019, http://www.sentencingproject.org/doc/publications/Incarcerated-Women-and-Girls.pdf.

10 "Arrests by Sex, 2017."

11 "Crime in the United States, 2017," FBI, Uniform Crime Reporting, https://ucr.fbi.gov/crime-in-the-u.s/2017/crime-in-the-u.s.-2017, as cited in Stacey Mallicoat, *Women, Gender and Crime: Core Concepts*, 3rd ed. (Los Angeles: Sage, 2019).

12 Richard V. Reeves and Joanna Venator, "Gender Gaps in Relative Mobility," Brookings Institute, Washington, DC, November 13, 2013, https://www.brookings.edu/blog/social-mobility-memos/2013/11/12/gender-gaps-in-relative-mobility.

13 Reeves and Venator, "Gender Gaps in Relative Mobility."

14 Reeves and Venator, "Gender Gaps in Relative Mobility."

15 Lenora Lapidus et al., "Caught in the Net: The Impact of Drug Policies on Women and Families," ACLU, 2004, http://www.aclu.org/files/images/asset_upload_file431_23513.pdf.

16 "War on Drugs," History.com, accessed October 19, 2019, https://www.history.com/topics/crime/the-war-on-drugs.

17 Dan Baum, "Legalize It All: How to Win the War on Drugs," *Harper's Magazine*, April 2016, accessed October 17, 2019, https://harpers.org/archive/2016/04/legalize-it-all.

18 "A Brief History of the Drug War," Drug Policy Alliance, accessed October 19, 2019, http://www.drugpolicy.org/issues/brief-history-drug-war.

19 "Health, Rights and Drugs: Harm Reduction, Decriminalization and Zero Discrimination for People Who Use Drugs," UNAIDS, 2019, https://www.unaids.org/sites/default/files/media_asset/JC2954_UNAIDS_drugs_report_2019_en.pdf.

20 Lisa Maher and Suzie Hudson, "Women in the Drug Economy: A Metasynthesis of the Qualitative Literature," *Journal of Drug Issues* 37 (2007): 805–26, http://doi.org/10.1177/002204260703700404.

21 Shannon M. Carey et al., "Drug Courts and State Mandated Drug Treatment Programs: Outcomes, Costs, and Consequences," National Criminal Justice References Service, March 2008, https://www.ncjrs.gov/pdffiles1/nij/grants/223975.pdf.

22 "Drug Courts," NCJ 238527, National Institute of Justice, U.S. Department of Justice, May 2018, https://www.ncjrs.gov/pdffiles1/nij/238527.pdf.

23 Michael C. Dorf and Jeffrey Fagan, "Problem-Solving Courts: From Innovation to Institutionalization—Forward," *American Criminal Justice Review* 40, no. 40 (2003): 1501–12.

24 James L. Nolan, "Redefining Criminal Courts: Problem-Solving and the Meaning of Justice," *American Criminal Justice Review* 40, no. 14 (2003): 1541–65.

25 "Painting the Current Picture: A National Report on Drug Courts and Other Problem-Solving Courts in the US," National Drug Court Institute, June 2016, https://www.ndci.org/wp-content/uploads/2016/05/Painting-the-Current-Picture-2016.pdf.

[26] "Map of Marijuana Legality by State," DISA, accessed October 20, 2019, https://disa.com/map-of-marijuana-legality-by-state.

[27] Taylor N. Santoro and Jonathan D. Santoro, "Racial Bias in the US Opioid Epidemic: A Review of the History of Systemic Bias and Implications for Care," *Cureus* 10, no. 12 (2018): e3733, http://doi.org/10.7759/cureus.3733.

[28] "Health, Rights and Drugs."

[29] "Drug Decriminalization in Portugal: Learning from a Health and Human-Centered Approach," Drug Policy Alliance, accessed October 20, 2019, http://www.drugpolicy.org/sites/default/files/dpa-drug-decriminalization-portugal-health-human-centered-approach_0.pdf.

[30] Alexandra Natapoff, "The Cost of 'Quality of Life' Policing: Thousands of Young Black Men Coerced to Plead Guilty to Crimes They Didn't Commit," *Washington Post*, November 11, 2015, https://www.washingtonpost.com/news/the-watch/wp/2015/11/11/the-cost-of-quality-of-life-policing-thousands-of-young-black-men-coerced-to-plead-guilty-to-crimes-they-didnt-commit.

[31] Jamal Hagler, "6 Things You Should Know about Women of Color and the Criminal Justice System," Center for American Progress, March 16, 2016, accessed October 16, 2019, https://www.americanprogress.org/issues/criminal-justice/news/2016/03/16/133438/6-things-you-should-know-about-women-of-color-and-the-criminal-justice-system.

[32] "Native Lives Matter," LakotaLaw.org, accessed October 20, 2019, https://www.lakotalaw.org/resources/native-lives-matter.

[33] Eleanor Brock, "The Truth about Women of Color behind Bars," September 25, 2018, https://www.logikcull.com/blog/women-color-behind-bars.

CHAPTER 8

Traditional Street Crime

Violent

In this chapter you will read about violent crime and about the gendered nature of violence. You will read theories of masculinity and violence and about men who are breaking the patterns and redefining manhood.

LEARNING OBJECTIVES

After reading this chapter, you should be able to do the following:

- Explain trends in violent offending.
- Differentiate between violent offenses committed by men and women.
- Describe theories of masculinity.
- Identify programs created to address men and violence.

Case #8: Stanley Tookie Williams

On the night of December 12, 2005, thousands of people gathered outside San Quentin State Prison in California. They were there to protest and to mourn. Stanley Tookie Williams III, former figurehead of the sprawling and infamous gang known as the Crips, was to be executed by the state of California in the first minutes of December 13 after twenty-six years on death row. His supporters had come to the prison hoping for last-minute clemency.

While it may seem strange that thousands of protestors turned out to call for clemency for a gang leader, Williams had spent his final decade in prison calling for an end to gang violence. He wrote books, fostered antiviolence movements, and in 2000 was nominated for a Nobel Peace Prize. His work, however, was not enough to convince then-governor Arnold Schwarzenegger to grant him clemency, and at 12:35 a.m. on December 13, 2005, Williams was pronounced dead from lethal injection.

BACKGROUND

Stanley Tookie Williams III was born in 1953 in Louisiana to a teenage mother and a father who left the family very soon after Williams's birth. When Williams was still a young boy, his mother relocated the family to Southern California, to an area known as South Central Los Angeles. It was not long before Williams started to get into trouble.

South Central L.A. has become synonymous with gang violence over the last several decades. Histories of first legal and then economic segregation meant that the neighborhoods comprising South Central L.A. became predominantly Black, and deindustrialization and a host of other factors meant that it also became predominantly impoverished. By the time Williams and his family moved to South Central in the late 1950s, racial violence carried out against residents of South Central, as well as the loss of employment opportunities stemming from the closure of manufacturing businesses, had left the area economically and socially unstable. Williams's mother, in search of economic stability for at least herself and her family, juggled several jobs, leaving Williams to have to learn to occupy himself.

The landscape of South Central in those years was perilous. Moving through his boyhood and teenage years, Williams was witness to violence, drug use, dogfighting, and consistent tension between residents of South Central and law enforcement. In order to prove himself, Williams began to engage in street fights and other activities common to those teenage boys struggling to become the kind of men that could not only survive but become dominant in such a world. Williams began to distinguish himself from the others because of his strength, skill, and pure viciousness as a fighter, and by his mid-teens, he was beginning to be welcomed into circles that would soon transform into gangs.

Williams had trouble staying in school, both because of his own antipathy toward school and because his reputation as a fighter and a troublemaker had made him unwelcome at the public schools in the area. He gravitated toward other pastimes, and in the late 1960s, at the age of sixteen, he found himself in trouble with the law, spending approximately two years in a juvenile detention facility for car theft. His time inside was occupied with weightlifting and generally dreaming of rising through the unofficial ranks of the street.

By the time Williams was released in 1971, the lay of the land was evolving. Street coalitions had been forming since the 1950s, initially to protect the neighborhoods from racialized violence originating in bordering white neighborhoods, and through the 1950s and 1960s, they began to consolidate into gangs. While some left to join more organized and ideological Black Power groups and movements, others chose to build and strengthen their small circles to become powerful in small territories throughout South Central. Williams was not interested in these small circles—he wanted to build a larger group, a larger gang, that would cover all of the neighborhoods of the area and eliminate the smaller gangs that were locked in a constant battle for survival, creating consistent and pervasive collateral damage. When Williams met Raymond Lee Washington, the pieces for this larger gang began to come together.

Speaking from death row in 2005, Williams would describe their initial intentions with the clarity of hindsight: "We started out—at least my intent was to, in a sense, address all of the so-called neighboring gangs in the area and to put, in a sense—I thought I can cleanse the neighborhood of all these, you know, marauding gangs. But I was totally wrong. And eventually, we morphed into the monster we were addressing." Williams and Washington wanted to stem the violence by essentially monopolizing it, and, still in his late teens, Williams began to work with Washington to join their respective gangs together. Williams came from the West Side Crips, Washington came from the East Side Crips, and they soon joined forces with a Crips gang from the neighboring city of Compton, led by a young man named Mac Thomas. Together, the three of them, along with close allies and their growing circles, began to recruit new members and absorb smaller gangs in their entirety. The Crips became unified, a network of smaller sets that worked in unison to dominate not just South Central and Compton but widening areas across Los Angeles and neighboring cities. In time, Crips sets would be formed in other cities and states across the United States, primarily west of the Mississippi River, as well as in a small handful of other countries.

Williams's reputation grew over the following years, and he became recognized as a prominent leader, not just by Crips sets and other gangs but by local and federal law enforcement as well. He was pursued and targeted by rival gang leaders and members and by police forces alike, but he was able to dodge both death and capture for several years. Other leaders did not fare as well throughout the 1970s—Thomas was killed in the mid-1970s, and Washington was imprisoned. And while Williams survived the 1970s, he did not do so unscathed. He was shot in a drive-by shooting in 1976, nearly losing his ability to walk, and the deaths of several people who were close to him and an increasing reliance on a variety of substances led to both mental and physical breakdowns and trauma. Washington's imprisonment meant that Williams was alone at the top, and in-fighting between different Crips sets, rivalries with other gangs, and increased targeting by law enforcement ramped up by the end of the 1970s.

DEATH ROW

In 1979, Washington was released from prison, only to be murdered in a drive-by shooting, and Williams was arrested—this time for murder. It was alleged that Williams, along with accomplices, had been responsible for a murder and robbery on February 28, 1979, as well as a triple homicide and robbery on March 11. The charges went to trial by jury, and the jury found Williams guilty on all counts. The judge sentenced him to death.

Williams, up until the moment of his death, maintained that he was innocent of these crimes. He acknowledged his criminal past and the destructive brutality of violent street gangs in general and of the Crips in particular, but on these counts, he said, he was not guilty. He was convicted and sentenced, he argued, because of who he was and because of a string of injustices:

> It was a paradigm of racism. We are talking about prosecutorial misconduct. We are talking about exclusion of exculpatory evidence. We are talking about I.A.C., which is ineffective assistance of counsel. We are talking about biased jury selection, which results in an all-white jury. We're talking about involuntary psychotherapic druggings, the misuse of jailhouse and government informants. And last, but not least—no—not a shred of tangible evidence, no fingerprints, no crime scenes of bloody boot prints. They didn't match my boots, nor eyewitnesses. Even the shotgun shells found conveniently at each crime scene didn't match the shotgun shells that I owned. . . . Everything was predicated on hearsay and circumstantial evidence.

Much of the witness testimony that was used at the trial rested on individuals who claimed that they had heard Williams talking about the robberies and murders after the fact; Williams claimed that these witnesses were either groomed or coerced or had ulterior motives for testifying against him.

Williams was sent to San Quentin State Prison in the San Francisco Bay Area to live out his years on death row. His first several years at San Quentin were spent primarily in solitary confinement, as he was confrontational with both officers and other prisoners. It was during this time in solitary confinement that he began to experience what he would later call his redemption:

> I can easily demythologize the thought that, well, a person, when he goes to prison, of course, they'll change. They're locked up. That's not so, because I was incorrigible from the moment I got here all the way up to 1988, so that debunks that theory. And once I was in solitary confinement, it provided me with the isolated moments to reflect on my past and to dwell upon something greater, something better than involving myself in thuggery and criminality. It had to be more to life than that. It had to be more than the madness that was disseminating throughout this entire prison. . . . My redemptive transition began in solitary confinement, and unlike other people who express their experiences of an epiphany or a satori, I never experienced anything of that ilk. Mine—that wouldn't have been enough. I often tell people that I didn't have a 360-degree turnaround; I had a 720-degree turnaround. It took me twice as much. Just one spin around wouldn't have done it. I was that messed up, that lost, that mentacided, brainwashed. So, I was able to gradually in a piecemeal fashion change my life slowly but surely through education, through edification, through spiritual cultivation, battling my demons. And eventually, that led to me embracing redemption.

According to Williams, between 1988 and 1994, he began to deepen his study and to reflect on his life, and these years of reflection ultimately led him to begin, from inside San Quentin, a campaign calling for peace between the Crips and their major rivals, the Bloods. During this period, he began to work with activist and writer Barbara Becnel, who had contacted him in 1992, wondering if she could speak to him about a book she was writing about the Bloods and the Crips. As the two of them worked together, they began to envision a series of books for young readers about the risks and realities of gang life.

In 1993, Becnel assisted Williams in the creation of a video message. In the recording, Williams appeals directly to members of both the Crips and the Bloods, expressing his regret for the part he had played in building the Crips and in all the surrounding violence, and asking the gang members to recognize that they are the key to stopping gang violence. The video was eventually shown to members of both gangs, and it played a part in a short-lived but significant truce. The truce also stemmed from the citywide unrest following the beating of Rodney King and the subsequent lack of conviction of the law enforcement officers that beat him; both the Crips and the Bloods came together under what has become known as the Watts Peace Treaty, agreeing that they had enough to fear that they should not fear each other.

Williams then dedicated his life to the education of younger generations. Over the next several years, he and Becnel coauthored a series of nine children's books for readers between four and twelve years old, among them *Gangs and Your Friends*, *Gangs and Drugs*, *Gangs and Wanting to Belong*, and *Gangs and Self-Esteem*. Each was meant to educate young readers about the dangers of and alternatives to gang life. Alongside the books, he started work on the Internet Project for Street Peace, a digital and international mentoring program for at-risk youth. His commitment to this work was what eventually earned him a Nobel Peace Prize nomination, as well as national and international recognition as a prominent antiviolence crusader.

Williams also wrote two autobiographies: *Redemption: From Original Gangster to Nobel Prize Nominee; The Extraordinary Life Story of Stanley Tookie Williams* and *Blue Rage, Black Redemption: A Memoir*. In 2004, the actor Jamie Foxx played Williams in a television movie titled *Redemption: The Stan Tookie Williams Story*. That same year, Williams created the Tookie Protocol for Peace, a peace accord meant to facilitate a permanent cease-fire between the Crips and the Bloods, as well as to lay out the foundation for social transformation: basic, vocational, and political education; employment; and a commitment to community safety.

These acts were all acts that, to Williams, represented his redemption. The state of California, however, did not agree. Throughout the early 2000s, Williams's challenges to his conviction were repeatedly denied. The final several years of his life were marked by profound ironies: courts continued to reaffirm his conviction while he received acknowledgment from the Nobel Peace Prize committee; prison officials argued that execution was the only way forward even as San Quentin State Prison's Institutional Classification Committee praised his behavior and his antiviolence work; then-governor Schwarzenegger denied Williams clemency even as President George W. Bush presented him with the President's Call to Service Award, which was accompanied by the message, "Through service to others, you demonstrate the outstanding character of America and help strengthen our country."

Supporters of Williams were many and varied, from the ACLU to the rapper Snoop Dogg to former gang members to the NAACP to spiritual and religious groups. Attorneys and supporters worked on his case and called for clemency until the very last moment, but to no avail. Schwarzenegger denied the request for clemency, arguing that the sum of evidence still tipped the balance toward execution. Very late on December 12, 2005, with a quiet, solemn crowd of protestors outside the prison, and with Becnel and two of his lawyers present, along with family members of those he had allegedly murdered, Williams was executed by lethal injection. As Becnel and the others left the witness room, they turned back to the others and shouted, "The state of California just killed an innocent man!"

Williams's death was not the end of his story. Instead, he is still at the center of a long discussion about the death penalty, incarceration, rehabilitation and redemption, gang violence, and the relationship between state violence and street violence. The call that ends the Tookie Protocol for Peace is the call that still reverberates:

> Finally, I call upon the pure energy of human beings and institutions—gangs, ex-cons, parents, churches and mosques, schools and universities, youth centers, think tanks, university professors and other educators, entrepreneurs, entertainers, human rights agencies, social organizations, politicians, rappers, newspapers, media broadcast outlets, the employed and unemployed, the wealthy and the poor, the young and the elderly, and anyone else who is interested in promoting street peace—to help create a new community of safety and well-being. This peace protocol is not the solution. Look in the mirror. There is the solution.

THINKING CRITICALLY ABOUT THE CASE

1. What specific gender norms seemed to stoke Williams's early entrance into gang life?

2. In what ways do poverty and institutionalized racism contribute to the growth of gangs and gang violence?

3. What sorts of arguments support the rejection of Williams's appeals for clemency? What sorts of arguments would support his appeals for clemency?

REFERENCES

This case is adapted from the following sources:

Fagan, Kevin. "The Execution of Stanley Tookie Williams/ Eyewitness: Prisoner Did Not Die Meekly, Quietly." *San Francisco Chronicle*, December 14, 2005. http://www.sfgate.com /news/article/THE-EXECUTION-OF-STANLEY-TOOKIE-WIL LIAMS-2588632.php.

Goodman, Amy. "A Conversation with Death Row Prisoner Stanley Tookie Williams from His San Quentin Cell." *Democracy Now!*, November 30, 2005. http://www.democracynow .org/2005/11/30/a_conversation_with_death_row_prisoner.

Wagner, Venise. "Tookie Williams." *Mother Jones*, May 5, 2001. http://www.motherjones.com/politics/2001/03/tookie-williams.

Williams, Stanley Tookie. *Blue Rage, Black Redemption*. New York: Touchstone, 2004.

———. *The Tookie Protocol for Peace: A Local Street Peace Initiative*. N.d. http://undergroundguerrilla.tripod.com/sitebuildercontent /sitebuilderfiles/tookie_peace_protocol.pdf.

CONTEXT AND ANALYSIS

Violent crime, including a broad range of individual, community, and family violence, takes a substantial emotional, physical, and economic toll on the community as well as on the direct victims. Indirect effects of violence include mental health problems, chronic disease, lower quality of life, and an increased risk of committing violence.

This chapter focuses on violent street crime, or the use or threat of use of force against a victim, which includes criminal homicide, sexual assault, robbery, and aggravated assault. **Aggravated assault**, which is the largest category of violent crime, is the use of physical force or the threatened use of physical force against another person; **robbery** is defined as the taking of property from another person by force or threat of force; and **criminal homicide** includes unjustified murder and nonnegligent homicide. Sexual assault and intimate partner violence are discussed in chapters 3 and 4.

The roots of violence are varied, including individual, relationship, community, and societal factors. Individual roots include being a victim of child maltreatment, psychological/personality disorders, alcohol/substance abuse, and a history of prior violent behavior. Relationship roots are child abuse or neglect, family chaos, and poverty. Community roots include poverty, high crime levels, high residential mobility, high unemployment, and local drug trade. Societal factors include gender, race, and class inequality; rapid social change; poverty; weak economic safety nets; and cultural norms that support violence.

TRENDS OF VIOLENT OFFENDING

Although most Americans regularly think that violent crime is increasing, it has actually declined significantly since it peaked in the early 1990s. According to the FBI Uniform Crime Reports (UCR),[1] which count crimes reported to the police in eighteen thousand jurisdictions, the violent crime rate declined 49 percent between 1993 and 2017. The Bureau of Justice Statistics (BJS) National Crime Victims Survey (NCVS), which surveys crime victims, reports that the violent crime rate fell 74 percent during that same time.[2] The discrepancy can be explained because only 47 percent of violent crimes tracked by the BJS were reported to police.

According to the FBI's UCR Crime in the United States, an estimated 1,247,321 violent crimes occurred nationwide in 2017, which represents a rate of 382.9 violent crimes per 100,000 people, as compared to 680 violent crimes per 100,000 people in 1998. Aggravated assault accounted for 65 percent of violent crime. In 2017 there were 810,825 aggravated assaults, which was 248.9 per 100,000 people, as compared to 361.4 per 100,000 people in 1998. Further, there were an estimated 319,356 robberies (98 per 100,000 people), which accounted for 25.6 percent of violent crime offenses. That compared to 165.5 per 100,000 people in 1998.[3]

The most serious violent crime is homicide, the killing of one human being by another, which includes both murder and manslaughter. Homicide was the fifteenth-leading cause of death overall in the United States in 2017. According to the FBI's UCR Supplemental Homicide Reports, the estimated number of murders in the nation in 2017 was 16,617 (5.3 murders per 100,000 people), as compared to 18,208 murders in 1997 (6.8 per 100,000). The overwhelming majority, almost three-quarters, of homicides in the United States involve a male killing another male, usually between the ages of nineteen and thirty-four.[4]

The risk of being a homicide victim varies across the population. Gender, race, and age greatly influence the chance of being a victim or an offender. As discussed in chapter 3, between three and four thousand women and girls are murdered each year in the United States. Although it occurs among women of all ages and among all races and ethnicities, young women of color are disproportionately affected. According to the Centers for Disease Control and Prevention, it is the second-leading cause of death for African American women between the ages of fifteen and twenty-four, the fourth-leading cause of death

AGGRAVATED ASSAULT
Use of physical force or threatened use of physical force against another person.

ROBBERY
Taking of property from another person by force or threat of force.

CRIMINAL HOMICIDE
Killing that includes unjustified murder and nonnegligent homicide.

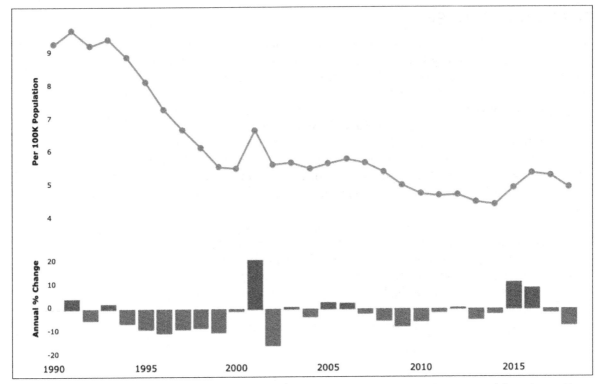

Figure 8.1.   Trends in homicide rates in the United States, 1990 to 2018. *Retrieved from https://www.macrotrends.net/countries/USA/united-states/murder-homicide-rate*

TOXIC MASCULINITY
Traditional and stereotypical patriarchal masculinity norms that emphasize strength, power, control, and aggression.

PATRIARCHY
System that perpetuates oppressive and limiting gender roles.

MALE CODE
Related to toxic masculinity, its expectations are strength, control, power, and the silencing of emotion, as well as fearlessness through risk-taking behavior and dominance through aggressive and violent behavior.

for white women between those ages, and the leading cause of on-the-job deaths for all women.[5] The CDC reports that while homicide is the third-leading cause of death for all males aged one to nineteen and the fourth for all males aged twenty to forty-four, it is the second-leading cause of death for Hispanic males aged one to nineteen, and the leading cause of death for Black males aged one to forty-four.[6]

Of the estimated number of murders in the United States, 45.9 percent were reported in the South, 22.6 percent were reported in the Midwest, 20.2 percent were reported in the West, and 11.3 percent were reported in the Northeast.[7]

THE GENDERED NATURE OF VIOLENCE

There is a strong association between masculinity and violence, as not only victims of violence as discussed in the previous section, but also perpetrators. The vast majority (90 percent) of homicide offenders are male, primarily between the ages of eighteen and thirty-four. To understand the pathways to violence, we must consider **toxic masculinity**, which is linked to aggression and violence.

Toxic Masculinity

Although **patriarchy** is organized to benefit men, it can hurt men by holding them to a patriarchal ideal that limits how men express emotion and ultimately encouraging violence. Boys experience societal and cultural pressure to uphold gender-appropriate behaviors according to the ideal **male code**, the expectations of which are strength, control, power, and the silencing of emotion, as well as fearlessness through risk-taking behavior and dominance through aggressive and violent behavior. Negative effects of harmful masculinity, also called toxic masculinity, can occur when destructive masculine ideals are upheld.[8] For a discussion of masculinity theory, see chapter 2.

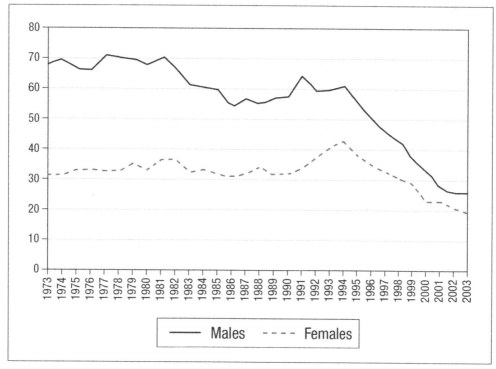

Figure 8.2. Violent crime rates by gender, 1973–2003, per 1,000 people.
Data: Bureau of Justice Statistics

The roots of toxic masculinity lie in a boy's early childhood experiences. The more trauma a boy experiences, the more he will conform to toxic masculinity. Violence can occur when a boy becomes depressed after his experiences of early abuse (physical and sexual), neglect, abandonment (physical and emotional) by a parent, disrupted relationships at home and in the community, exposure to violence and drugs, drug use/abuse, poverty, or residential mobility. These traumas combined with cultural messages about masculinity lead to a pathway toward violent behavior.

Constant reinforcement of masculine gender stereotypes contributes to a culture of toxic masculinity by restricting men's emotional expression and pressuring them to conform to expectations of dominance and aggression, thus increasing the potential for boys to engage in acts of violence.

In early childhood, aggression and violence are used to express emotions and distress. During adolescence and beyond, male aggression shifts to asserting power over another person, especially when masculinity is threatened. This chapter discusses the most common traumas that boys experience during their early childhood that may affect the development of violent behavior.

Early Trauma and Parental Abandonment

Young boys tend to develop violent behavior after experiencing certain traumas during their early childhood, especially when they suppress their emotions. According to Garbarino, the major risk factors that lead to violent offending are attachment disorder, which is the failure of the parent and child to connect, as well as neglect, abuse, and poverty, among others.[9]

Bowlby's **attachment theory** explains that in the first year of life, human beings develop and maintain close relationships and emotional bonds with significant others who provide comfort and safety.[10] Babies who do not attain a healthy attachment with a primary caregiver are often defensive, suspicious, and withdrawn. As a result, the child experiences intense anxiety or fear, learning to disconnect from their feelings. Further, physical or emotional abandonment by either parent can cause the child to feel rejected,

ATTACHMENT THEORY
Infants need to develop a relationship with at least one parent for successful social and emotional development.

which enhances the child's negative feelings about themselves. For example, emotional abandonment can result from the unavailability of the parent due to drug use/abuse or being emotionally absent.

Child maltreatment, specifically childhood abuse (physical and sexual), and neglect are common traumas that lead to the development of violent behavior in a boy's experience. When abuse and neglect occur, the boy learns that the world is an unpredictable place. He becomes hypersensitive to negative cues in the environment. In response, he develops aggressive behaviors to be ready to confront perceived danger. Ultimately, he concludes that aggression gains you attention, respect, and power. Boys learn that, to be a real man, the proper response to a threat is to fight back and not back down.

Toxic Shame

These dehumanizing traumas and humiliating abandonments can lead to emotional numbing, dissociation, and depression, labeled **toxic shame**.

Boys are taught to hide their emotions, which may cause depression and a feeling of internal rotting. "Boys are routinely taught to ignore or deny their feelings by parents and others who are training them to be men in a culture that demands male stoicism."[11] Instead, they place their emotions in boxes, hiding them away, even regarding feelings of pain and sorrow as dangerous to their masculinity. By feeling that emotions like pain, fear, and sorrow are less masculine, they learn that they should never show or speak of these emotions. Eventually, they begin to internally rot with depression, expressing their emotions in other ways, such as using or abusing drugs and alcohol, engaging in deviant or criminal behavior, and acting excessively hostile toward their peers. Eventually they will do whatever it takes to help them get attention.

Garbarino states that "people who live with toxic shame feel fundamentally disgraced, intrinsically worthless, and profoundly humiliated in their own skin, just for being themselves."[12] In other words, toxic shame is when someone hates themselves for who they are. He also discusses how toxic shame appears "when an individual's inner core is tormented through rejection."[13] He believes that the person's soul is hurt and destroyed through the process of rejection, and therefore it causes them to hate themselves.

These toxic shame feelings of rejection, loneliness, and worthlessness can lead to a lack of developing empathy. Boys particularly respond to feelings of toxic shame by committing acts of violence. Shame at being abused, neglected, or abandoned causes depression, which leads to rage, which causes violence.

When a boy experiences early trauma, he is vulnerable to the aspects of popular culture, including music, movies, video games, and social media that emphasize the negative gender stereotypes for men. Those stereotypical male gender role expectations emphasize fearlessness through risk-taking behavior and dominance through aggressive and violent behavior. Aggression and violence are heralded as the epitome of masculinity.

Residential mobility can be detrimental for young people because it disrupts social ties and damages the relationships between parents and their children as well as between children and their peers and community members. Moreover, residential mobility may increase the risk of an adolescent associating with delinquent peers and can be a disorderly experience for the lives of adolescents. Current literature suggests that repeatedly moving may lead to detrimental psychological outcomes, increased likelihood of dropping out of school, declining academic performance, and elevated levels of delinquency. Other traumas caused by significant residential mobility are poverty and homelessness, which also affect the development of violent behavior in boys.

Lastly, exposure to violence, whether violence in the home, community, media, or violent video games, has a detrimental effect on the development of violent behavior in young boys.[14] The growth of video games, especially violent video games such as *Call of Duty* and *Grand Theft Auto*, has raised new questions about the potential impact of media violence, since the video game player is an active participant rather than merely a viewer. Recent research reported by the American Psychological Association has shown

TOXIC SHAME
Feeling of worthlessness, humiliation, and self-loathing emanating from trauma.

that playing violent video games can increase a person's aggressive thoughts and feelings, leading to increased aggressive behavior and cognition as well as decreased empathy and prosocial behavior. Adolescents who are directly or indirectly exposed to violence report significantly higher levels of depressive symptoms, along with other negative emotions.[15]

Nevertheless, there is research that refutes these findings. Despite the links between media violence and aggression, media violence is only one of many risk factors for aggressive and violent behavior. Extremely violent behavior occurs when there are multiple risk factors present, not just one. It is theorized that these other risk factors, rather than video games, cause aggressive and violent behavior. Finally, researchers theorize that children who are already at risk may be more likely to choose to play violent video games.

Reducing the Effects of Early Trauma

To reduce the effects of toxic shame, including aggression and toxic masculinity, interventions to address the exposure to trauma and stress are necessary. These different methods include therapy, intervention programs, proper education programs, creating more positive family environments, strong positive community environments, restorative justice, and transformative justice programs (discussed in chapter 14). Therapy can assist boys by allowing them to discuss their lives, their own victimization, and their personal experiences in a safe environment, which can promote healing from trauma and proper emotional health development. A positive education program can assist boys with their mental development, promote learning, and create a safe space away from dysfunctional homes. Further, teaching parents how to create positive family environments, even if a parent is absent, promotes stability and benefits emotional development. Finally, a strong, positive community assists families, builds a sense of community, and creates safe spaces.

Gangs

The early life traumas experienced by Stanley Tookie Williams laid the groundwork for cofounding the Los Angeles Crips street gang. As described in chapter 6, there are many different reasons to join a gang. For Williams, who was exposed to violence in his home as well as poverty, drug addiction, and violence in his community, he began to engage in street fights in order to prove his hypermasculinity. He wanted to distinguish himself from other boys to not only survive but also to become dominant. Because of his antipathy toward school and his reputation as a fighter and a troublemaker, he was suspended numerous times. Eventually his path led to becoming a leader of a major street gang.

WOMEN AS PRIMARY OFFENDERS OR COCONSPIRATORS

Although the number of violent crimes in the United States has been decreasing, the number of women arrested for committing violent crimes has increased over the last couple of decades. Similar to males, abuse and other childhood maltreatment are the strongest risk factors for female violent behavior. Research has shown that women who are arrested for violence are more likely to be younger, African American, and unemployed, and to have an extensive criminal history, as well as dysfunctional families and to have experienced childhood abuse. Women with a history of childhood maltreatment, physical abuse, sexual abuse, and neglect are at significantly increased risk of being arrested for violence. Research also highlights the important role of posttraumatic stress disorder as a risk factor for female violent offending, rather than an outcome. For a discussion of feminist pathways perspectives, see chapter 2.

Nevertheless, there is a continuing debate about whether the increase in female arrests for violence is due to girls and women becoming more violent or to changes in arrest policies.[16] This is discussed further in chapter 14.

MASS KILLINGS AND DOMESTIC TERRORISM

Although **mass killings** are relatively rare in the United States, they are much more frequent in the United States than in other countries. Moreover, they receive much attention from the public, sometimes even being exaggerated in how often they occur. Statistics vary about the number of mass killings and shootings depending on the definition used by the researchers. A common definition of mass killings is the killing of four or more victims in one location at the same time. They occur at schools, workplaces, houses of worship, malls, community events, and music concerts, among other venues. Regardless of the exact number of mass shootings and killings, it is undisputable that they are increasing.

The overwhelming majority of mass murderers are young white men,[17] many of whom exhibit toxic masculinity, discussed earlier in this chapter. Although fewer than one in ten mass murderers is a woman, typical news accounts and commentaries about school shootings and rampage killings rarely mention gender.

Most mass murders are planned in advance, usually as an act of revenge or retribution for perceived slights or wrongs. Anger, not mental illness, more commonly fuels mass murder. When a socially and emotionally isolated male does not receive societal confirmation of his masculinity, he may develop feelings of **aggrieved entitlement**. Aggrieved entitlement combines a humiliating loss of manhood, overwhelming hopelessness, and a sense of moral obligation and entitlement to get it back. Anger develops, and a violent masculinity can be adopted.[18] In addition to these emotional responses, easy access to firearms (especially assault-style weapons) adds to the possibility of a mass murder. While mental illness has been blamed for mass murders, there is no research that backs up that assertion. In fact, multiple studies have shown that less than 5 percent of violent crimes in the United States are committed by those with mental illness. Moreover, those who have been diagnosed with mental illness are less likely to commit violent crimes involving guns than those who do not have a mental illness.[19]

MASS KILLING
Killing of at least four people in a single event.

AGGRIEVED ENTITLEMENT
Term coined by Michael Kimmel to describe white male resistance to perceived challenges against masculinity and historical experiences of privilege.

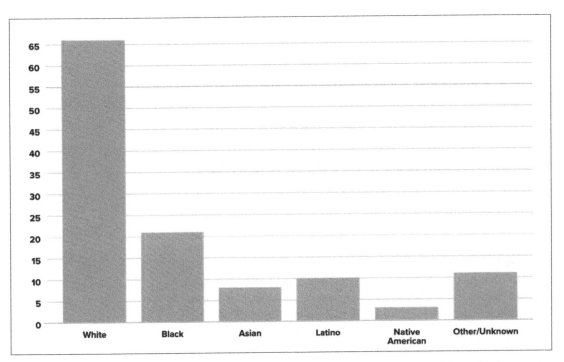

Figure 8.3. Mass shooting perpetrators by race. *Based on data obtained from Mark Follman, Gavin Aronsen, and Deanna Pan, "A Guide to Mass Shootings in America," Mother Jones, last updated February 26, 2020, retrieved February 29, 2021, https:// www.motherjones.com/politics/2012/07/mass-shootings-map*

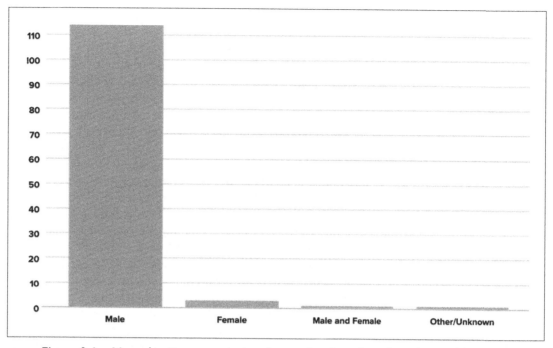

Figure 8.4.   Mass shooting perpetrators by gender. *Based on data obtained from Mark Follman, Gavin Aronsen, and Deanna Pan, "A Guide to Mass Shootings in America," Mother Jones, last updated February 26, 2020, retrieved February 29, 2021, https://www.motherjones.com/politics/2012/07/mass-shootings-map*

The increase in mass shootings has brought attention to the public's fear of being victimized. According to the Pew Research Center,[20] in the aftermath of the deadly February 14, 2018, shooting at Parkland, Florida's Marjory Stoneman Douglas High School, one of the deadliest mass school shootings in U.S. history, a majority of American teens were worried about the possibility of a shooting at their school. Overall, 57 percent of teens say they are worried about the possibility of a shooting at their school, with one in four saying they are very worried. Teens of color are more concerned than their white peers. Roughly two-thirds (64 percent) of teens of color, including 73 percent of Latinx teens, say they are at least somewhat worried, compared with 51 percent of white teens. School shooting fears differ by gender as well: 64 percent of girls say they are very or somewhat worried about a shooting happening at their school, compared with 51 percent of boys.[21]

After the Parkland shooting, teens all over the country organized school walkouts and marches demanding legislation to address gun violence. They put forward various proposals, including a ban on assault-style weapons, background checks, and **red flag laws**, which are state laws that authorize courts to issue a protective order that allows a temporary confiscation of firearms from people who are adjudicated to be a danger to themselves or to others. By contrast, only 39 percent of teens say that allowing teachers to carry guns in school would be very or somewhat effective at preventing school shootings; 35 percent of teens say this would be not at all effective.

Many mass killings are acts of **domestic terrorism**, which is defined by the FBI as violence that is "perpetrated by individuals and/or groups inspired by or associated with primarily U.S.-based movements that espouse extremist ideologies of a political, religious, social, racial, or environmental nature."[22] Although domestic terrorism is not a new concept in the United States, the threat is growing, including terrorism inspired by white supremacy, misogyny and rage against women, and anti-immigrant sentiment, among other hate-filled motivations. The FBI has said that more Americans have died in domestic terrorist attacks than international ones since September 11 and that domestic

RED FLAG LAW
A gun control law that permits police or family members to petition a court to order temporary confiscation of firearms from a person who allegedly presents a danger to others or themselves.

DOMESTIC TERRORISM
Violence committed by those in the United States who espouse extremist ideologies of a political, religious, social, racial, or environmental nature.

terrorism is increasingly motivated by white supremacist ideology. Common targets are Muslim mosques, African American churches, Jewish American synagogues, women, and left-wing politicians and activists.

The number of white supremacist domestic terrorist attacks has been growing. While there are many massacres that have taken place, a few typical examples are presented here. In 2015, Dylann Roof, a self-described white supremacist, killed nine African American worshippers in their Charleston, South Carolina, church. Roof confessed to committing the Charleston attack with the intention of starting a race war. The October 2018 Pittsburgh Tree of Life Synagogue massacre during religious services was motivated by the gunman's animus toward Jewish people, whom he considered the enemy of white people, and immigrants, whom he called invaders.

On August 3, 2019, a young self-proclaimed white supremacist, Patrick Wood Crusius, killed twenty-two people in an El Paso, Texas, Walmart with an AK-47-style assault weapon. Minutes before the shooting, he published a hate-filled, anti-immigrant racist screed on an online message board where domestic terror manifestos are judged and given low or high scores. Complaining of a "Hispanic invasion of Texas," it warned that white people were being replaced by foreigners, which described the "great replacement" conspiracy theory that has become popular with white nationalists and their allies. Proclaiming his intent to target Latinx people, he hoped his attack and words would inspire wider racial violence in pursuit of a white ethnostate.

Six days before the El Paso massacre, nineteen-year-old Santino William Legan killed three people and injured thirteen in a mass shooting at the Gilroy, California, Garlic Festival. Although he did not post a manifesto, his Instagram postings prior to the massacre promoted a white supremacist text that is often shared online by neo-Nazis.

Just as white supremacist domestic terrorism is increasing, so are misogynist domestic terrorism attacks. For that reason, gun reform advocates urge that the role of misogyny in these attacks should be recognized. From 2009 to 2017, the majority of mass shootings were related to domestic violence or family violence. Many of the shooters had a history of hating women, assaulting intimate partners or female family members, or sharing misogynistic views online. These cases included the large-scale massacres at the Orlando Pulse nightclub in 2016; at the First Baptist Church in Sutherland Springs, Texas, in 2017; and in Dayton, Ohio, in 2019.

Elliot Rodger Redux

One of those rampage murderers motivated by misogyny was Elliot Rodger, highlighted in the chapter 5 case study. On May 23, 2014, Rodger went on a killing spree in Santa Barbara, California. After fatally stabbing three of his roommates, he shot and killed two women in front of a University of California, Santa Barbara, sorority house. He continued his killing spree, eventually killing six people and wounding thirteen others before committing suicide. He wrote a manifesto, which was a misogynist rant against college women. His life story indicates that he suffered early childhood traumas, including a lack of parental or peer attachment, as well as bullying. His history indicates that he suffered from toxic shame, which occurs when a person's inner core being is tormented through rejection. Moreover, he identified as part of a subculture of virulent misogynists who self-identify as "involuntarily celibate" and voice their rage and revenge fantasies against women online.

GUN RIGHTS VERSUS GUN REFORM

These recent white supremacist mass shootings and the shooting at Marjory Stoneman Douglas High School in Parkland, Florida, have reignited a national debate about guns in the United States. Where the UCR program received weapon information in 2017, firearms were used in 72.6 percent of the nation's murders, 40.6 percent of robberies, and 26.3 percent of aggravated assaults. Counting murders and suicides, nearly forty thousand people died of gun-related violence in the United States in 2017.

Guns are deeply ingrained in American society. The Second Amendment to the U.S. Constitution gives Americans the right to bear arms. According to a Pew Research Center survey in 2017, 30 percent of American adults say they own a gun, and an additional 11 percent say they live with someone who does. Most of these gun owners say the right to own firearms is essential to their sense of freedom. Nevertheless, gun owners are more likely than non–gun owners to know someone who has been shot (51 percent versus 40 percent).[23]

Despite disagreement about gun reform versus gun rights, there are several proposals that have support from both groups. A majority of Americans say gun laws should be stricter. According to a 2018 survey, 57 percent of U.S. adults say gun laws should be stricter. In addition, a 2017 Gallup poll found that about 60 percent of women consistently support tougher gun restrictions, compared with approximately 40 percent of men. Some of those proposals include universal background checks, banning assault weapons and bump stocks, and a government-backed national gun registry. Sixty percent of Republican women gun owners favor banning assault-style weapons, and nearly as many favor a national gun registry.

There is also debate about the efficacy of having teachers carry guns in school. Fifty-five percent of U.S. adults oppose allowing teachers and officials to carry guns in K–12 schools.[24]

Marketing Guns to Women

In an effort to increase gun ownership among women, the gun lobby, including the National Rifle Association, is increasingly targeting women, trying to convince them that buying a firearm is an empowering, personal choice. An NRA online forum for women about gun culture called the Well Armed Woman began in 2012. A year later, a chapter program aimed at recruiting new women to gun ranges was created. Further, other female gun enthusiasts established other online groups such as Girl's Guide to Guns and A Girl & a Gun.[25]

Death Penalty

The ultimate punishment for taking the life of another person is the death penalty. As of 2021, twenty-seven states have the death penalty, though three of those states have issued a moratorium on its use.

The death penalty shows a difference in gender. Since 1976, when the Supreme Court lifted the moratorium on capital punishment in *Gregg v. Georgia*, 1,476 men and 16 women have been executed in the United States. The number of people being held on death row has been declining, as public opinion supporting the death penalty is at historic lows.

One reason the death penalty has lost support is the growing number of people on death row being exonerated. According to the Death Penalty Information Center, 166 innocent people on death row were exonerated, twenty through postconviction DNA testing, between 1973 and 2019.

Moreover, research shows that race is a significant factor in death penalty cases. The race of the defendant and victim plays a crucial role in deciding who receives the death penalty in the United States. People of color have accounted for a disproportionate 43 percent of total executions since 1976, while more than half the people on death row are people of color.

COMMUNITY GROUPS ORGANIZING AGAINST VIOLENCE

There are a growing number of community organizations that are organizing against violence, many organized by women. Among those groups are Chicago Mothers against Senseless Killings,[26] who are peacekeepers on Chicago's South Side; Moms Demand Action for Gun Sense in America,[27] which is a grassroots movement of Americans demanding public safety measures to protect people from guns; Boston's Operation LIPSTICK (Ladies Involved in Putting a Stop to Inner-City Killing),[28] which attempts to disrupt the flow of guns by appealing to the women who help buy, hold, or hide guns for their partners whose criminal pasts prevent them from legally obtaining or holding guns themselves; and the Louis D. Brown Peace Institute, which is a center of healing, teaching, and learning for families and communities impacted by murder, trauma, and loss. The Brown Peace Institute works with families impacted by murder on both sides. It organizes an annual Mother's Day Walk for Peace and Survivors of Homicide Victims Awareness Month, which educates the public and policy makers about the impact of murder on families and communities in an effort to increase the peace-building efforts of survivors.

Alternatives to Violence Project

The **Alternatives to Violence Project (AVP)** is a worldwide grassroots movement dedicated to creative conflict resolution built on respect for all, community, cooperation, and trust. It has helped thousands of incarcerated people to deal with their anger in a prosocial manner. Since its beginning in 1975 at Green Haven Prison in Upstate New York, it has expanded to over sixteen thousand workshops in the United States involving a quarter of a million people, mostly in prisons and jails but also in a variety of community settings (community centers, churches, schools, and halfway houses). AVP workshops have been held in thirty-three states and forty-five countries.[29]

The core concept of AVP is **transforming power**, which is centered on the belief that behavior cannot be effectively altered unless emotions are changed. Its vision is to build a nonviolent society where we all live in peace and dignity, and its aim is to liberate everyone's innate power to positively transform themselves, resulting in transforming the world.

AVP involves active participation of all participants and facilitators and is not a group therapy, mediation, crisis intervention, lecture, or "how-to" class. Interpersonal experiences with peer feedback in group settings have a greater chance of being successful and of countering other, more negative peer norms, since peer feedback encourages prosocial skills and supportive norms through group skill building. The strength of AVP lies in conflict resolution skill training, value clarification, self-discipline, and personal empowerment. Participants' lives are changed through increased self-awareness, practical skills, and community living tools. Participants are exposed to a variety of nonviolent alternatives of behavior and practice in role-play scenarios with conflicts from their personal experience. Role-plays and subsequent discussions are important parts of experiential learning, allowing participants to try out new roles in a safe, supportive environment. Exercises examine how injustice, prejudice, frustration, and anger lead to aggressive and violent behavior.

Research shows that participation in AVP workshops leads to a reduction of violence within jails and prisons as well as a reduction of recidivism after incarceration. Studies suggest that improved anger (self) management and personal decision-making skills can mediate many difficulties of individuals with psychosocial problems.[30] Many incarcerated individuals did not survive socially in the world of academics, work, or even their own families. Aggression and acting-out behaviors often lead to social rejection by normative peers and acceptance by deviant peer groups, aggravating the problems that individuals face.

A 2002 Delaware study found that there was a 60 percent reduction in disciplinary write-ups according to Department of Correction records. A 2005 Delaware recidivism

ALTERNATIVES TO VIOLENCE PROJECT (AVP)
Anticonflict program in prisons and the community that builds on respect for all, community, cooperation, and trust, leading to transformation.

TRANSFORMING POWER
AVP core, which is centered on the belief that behavior cannot be effectively altered unless emotions are changed.

study found a reduction in overall recidivism of 46 percent over a comparison group of incarcerated men for three years post-release. Only 13.5 percent of the AVP graduates were convicted of another felony in those three years.[31] A 2004 California study, a 2010 Minnesota study, and a 2001 Maryland study found that AVP had a significant impact on changing attitudes away from violence toward others.[32] In addition to showing a 40 percent reduction in overall post-release recidivism, the Maryland study found that after a six-month follow-up, incarcerated men who participated in AVP had significantly lower anger levels. In addition, those who had taken the AVP workshops had significantly fewer incidents of confrontations within the facility.

A 2018 Massachusetts study examined whether the AVP workshops are effective in changing attitudes so that participants' behavior would become more nonviolent. The study consisted of all incarcerated men at a state prison who expressed interest in participating in AVP workshops. It measured both state anger and trait anger. State anger is an emotional-physiological condition occurring in response to an immediate situation. Irritation, annoyance, frustration, and stronger feelings of fury and rage fluctuate and vary in intensity over short periods. It varies physiologically from little or no change in physiological arousal to pronounced sympathetic arousal, demonstrated by increased tension in facial and skeletal muscles and release of adrenal hormones. On the other hand, trait anger is a stable personality dimension of anger, which is thought to be the propensity to experience state anger. It is a relatively stable individual difference in frequency, intensity, and duration of state anger. Individuals with high trait anger experience more frequent and intense state anger.[33]

In the next chapter, we discuss sex work and trafficking. It raises the issue of decriminalizing or legalizing prostitution and the difference between voluntary sex work and sexual exploitation.

REVIEW AND STUDY QUESTIONS

1. What is the difference between traditional masculinity and toxic masculinity, and how is toxic masculinity manifested in the larger society?

2. Because domestic terrorism is increasing in the United States, what can be done to prevent those attacks besides increased law enforcement?

3. What are red flag laws? Do you think they will be successful in decreasing the level of violence, including both individual and mass killings? What provisions of such laws are important and which can be improved?

4. What is aggrieved entitlement? What policies and programs can be developed to counteract its effects?

GOING FURTHER

Readings:

Garbarino, James. *Lost Boys: Why Our Sons Turn Violent and How We Can Save Them.* New York: Anchor, 2000.

Kimmel, Michael S. *Angry White Men: American Masculinity at the End of an Era.* New York: Nation Books, 2017.

Krajicek, David J. *Mass Killers: Inside the Minds of Men Who Murder.* London: Arcturus, 2019.

Messerschmidt, James W. *Nine Lives: Adolescent Masculinities, the Body, and Violence.* New York: Basic Books, 1999.

Williams, Stanley Tookie. *Blue Rage, Black Redemption.* New York: Touchstone, 2004.

Websites:

"The Terrible Numbers That Grow with Each Mass Shooting." *Washington Post*, last updated March 15, 2020. https://www.washingtonpost.com/graphics/2018/national/mass-shootings-in-america.

The Tookie Protocol for Peace. 2004. http://underground guerrilla.tripod.com/sitebuildercontent/sitebuilderfiles/tookie_peace_protocol.pdf.

Videos/Movies:

Katz, Jonathan. *Tough Guise* and *Tough Guise 2.* 1999, 2013. Available from Media Education Foundation, https://shop.mediaed.org/tough-guise-p163.aspx and https://shop.mediaed.org/tough-guise-2-p45.aspx.

KEY TERMS

aggravated assault Use of physical force or threatened use of physical force against another person.

aggrieved entitlement Term coined by Michael Kimmel to describe white male resistance to perceived challenges against masculinity and historical experiences of privilege.

Alternatives to Violence Project (AVP) Anticonflict program in prisons and the community that builds on respect for all, community, cooperation, and trust, leading to transformation.

attachment theory Infants need to develop a relationship with at least one parent for successful social and emotional development.

criminal homicide Killing that includes unjustified murder and nonnegligent homicide.

domestic terrorism Violence committed by those in the United States who espouse extremist ideologies of a political, religious, social, racial, or environmental nature.

male code Related to toxic masculinity, its expectations are strength, control, power, and the silencing of emotion, as well as fearlessness through risk-taking behavior and dominance through aggressive and violent behavior.

mass killing Killing of at least four people in a single event.

patriarchy System that perpetuates oppressive and limiting gender roles.

red flag law A gun control law that permits police or family members to petition a court to order temporary confiscation of firearms from a person who allegedly presents a danger to others or themselves.

robbery Taking of property from another person by force or threat of force.

toxic masculinity Traditional and stereotypical patriarchal masculinity norms that emphasize strength, power, control, and aggression.

toxic shame Feeling of worthlessness, humiliation, and self-loathing emanating from trauma.

transforming power AVP core, which is centered on the belief that behavior cannot be effectively altered unless emotions are changed.

NOTES

1 "Crime in the United States, 2017," FBI, Uniform Crime Reporting, https://ucr.fbi.gov/crime-in-the-u.s/2017/crime-in-the-u.s.-2017/topic-pages/violent-crime.

2 "Crime Victimization 2018," NCJ 253043, Bureau of Justice Statistics, September 2019, https://www.bjs.gov/content/pub/pdf/cv18.pdf.

3 "Crime Trends: 1990–2016," Brennan Center for Justice, https://www.brennancenter.org/publication/crime-trends1990-2016.

4 "Crime Trends: 1990–2016."

5 Melonie Heron, "Deaths: Leading Causes for 2017," National Vital Statistics Reports 68, no. 6. (June 24, 2019), https://www.cdc.gov/nchs/data/nvsr/nvsr68/nvsr68_06-508.pdf.

6 "Leading Causes of Death in Males, United States," Centers for Disease Control and Prevention, https://www.cdc.gov/healthequity/lcod/index.htm.

7 Heron, "Deaths: Leading Causes for 2017."

8 "Harmful Masculinity and Violence," In the Public Interest, American Psychological Association, accessed September 10, 2018, https://www.apa.org/pi/about/newsletter/2018/09/harmful-masculinity.

9 James Garbarino, Lost Boys: Why Our Sons Turn Violent and How We Can Save Them (New York: Anchor, 2000).

10 John Bowlby, "Attachment and Loss," in Attachment, vol. 1 (New York: Basic Books, 1969).

11 Garbarino, Lost Boys, 86.

12 Garbarino, Lost Boys, 58.

13 Garbarino, Lost Boys, 59.

14 Craig Anderson et al., "Violent Video Game Effects on Aggression, Empathy, and Prosocial Behavior in Eastern and Western Countries: A Meta-analytic Review," Psychological Bulletin 136, no. 2 (2010): 151–73, http://doi.org/10.1037/a0018251.

15 "APA Review Confirms Link between Playing Violent Video Games and Aggression," American Psychological Association, August 13, 2015, https://www.apa.org/news/press/releases/2015/08/violent-video-games.

16 Joanne Belknap and Kristi Holsinger, "The Gendered Nature of Risk Factors for Delinquency," Feminist Criminology 1 (2006): 48–71.

17 "Number of Mass Shootings in the United States between 1982 and August 2019, by Mass Shooter's Race and Ethnicity," Statista, accessed October 31, 2019, https://www.statista.com/statistics/476456/mass-shootings-in-the-us-by-shooter-s-race.

18 Rachel Kalish and Michael Kimmel, "Suicide by Mass Murder: Masculinity, Aggrieved Entitlement, and Rampage School Shootings," Health Sociology Review 19, no. 4 (2014): 451–64, http://doi.org/10.5172/hesr.2010.19.4.451.

19 Jonathan Katz, "Memo to Media: Manhood, Not Guns or Mental Illness, Should Be Central in Newton Shooting," Huff-Post, December 18, 2012, https://www.huffpost.com/entry/men-gender-gun-violence_b_2308522.

20 John Gramlich and Katherine Schaeffer, "7 Facts about Guns in the U.S.," Pew Research Center, October 22, 2019, https://www.pewresearch.org/fact-tank/2018/12/27/facts-about-guns-in-united-states.

21 Juliana Menasce Horowitz, "Americans Narrowly Opposed Allowing Teachers and School Officials to Carry Guns," Pew Research Center, February 23, 2018, https://www.pewresearch

.org/fact-tank/2018/02/23/in-2017-americans-narrowly-op posed-allowing-teachers-and-school-officials-to-carry-guns.

22 "Terrorism," FBI, accessed November 1, 2019, https://www .fbi.gov/investigate/terrorism.

23 Gramlich and Schaeffer, "7 Facts about Guns in the U.S."

24 Horowitz, "Americans Narrowly Opposed."

25 Ben Woffard, "The NRA's Most Wanted Customer: Women," *Glamour*, June 28, 2018, https://www.glamour.com/story /how-the-nra-is-trying-to-reach-women.

26 "Mothers against Senseless Killing," accessed October 25, 2019, http://ontheblock.org.

27 "Mothers Demand Action," accessed October 25, 2019, https://momsdemandaction.org.

28 "Operation Lipstick," accessed October 25, 2019, https:// www.operationlipstick.org.

29 Kathryn Tomlinson, "A Review of Literature concerning the Alternatives to Violence Project," Alternatives to Violence Project, Britain, 2007, http://www.avpav.org/files/2007-Tom linson_AVPBritain_Lit_Review.pdf.

30 Christine Walrath, "Evaluation of an Inmate-Run Alterna tives to Violence Project: The Impact of Inmate-to-Inmate Intervention," *Journal of Interpersonal Violence* 16, no. 7 (2001): 697–711.

31 Marsha L. Miller and John A. Shuford, *The Alternatives to Violence Project in Delaware: A Three-Year Cumulative Recidivism Study* (Alternatives to Violence Project, 2005), http://www.avpav.org/files/res-avp-rpteval-delaware-2005 .pdf.

32 Terry Kayser, Laura Roberts, John Shuford, and John Michaelis, "Minnesota AVP Anger Study," *International Journal of Trauma Research and Practice* 1, no. 1 (2014): 2–13.

33 Jo-Ann Della Giustina and Jennifer Hartsfield, "Evaluation of the Alternatives to Violence Project in Massachusetts" (unpublished paper, 2019).

Sex Work and Trafficking

In this chapter you will read about sex work, about those forced into it and those who enter it by choice. You will read about the potential effects sex work has on those who participate in it and about the controversy surrounding decriminalizing prostitution.

LEARNING OBJECTIVES

After reading this chapter, you should be able to do the following:

- Explain commercial sexual exploitation.
- Identify laws in place to protect children from sex trafficking.
- Articulate the arguments for and against decriminalization.
- Describe the intersections of immigration and trafficking.

Case #9: Rachel Lloyd and GEMS

Rachel Lloyd was born in England in the mid-1970s, and even her earliest memories were marked by violence, fear, instability, and abuse—a shadowy recollection of a traumatic experience as a toddler at the hands of some teenage boys, the return of a stepfather while she was in adolescence, and the increasing physical abuse that he directed toward her and her mother, and her mother's coping mechanism of drinking. When Lloyd was only thirteen, she was raped but found that police would not take her seriously and instead assumed that she had somehow brought it on herself. That same year, she attempted suicide. During her hospitalization, she attempted suicide several more times but was soon released back to her mother, into the traumatizing conditions that had led her to the suicide attempts in the first place. By fourteen, she had dropped out of school and was working in factories full time, soon vacating her mother's house and care entirely and turning to substances, petty stealing, more suicide attempts, and relationships with older and often physically and sexually abusive men. Still in her mid-teens, she found herself with the opportunity to do a bit of modeling work; it was only print ads here and there, but nevertheless it made her feel special. When she was asked to do some modeling sessions that included nudity, she accepted, as it felt like an opportunity to experience some glitz and glamour outside of the dreary norms.

At seventeen, having difficulties at home and with a boyfriend, Lloyd bought a one-way ticket to Munich, where she found that the haphazard whim that had taken her abroad brought her to new lows of poverty and desperation. After looking for work in all the local restaurants, bars, and cafés, coming up short and down to nothing but change, she tried her luck at a strip club, convincing herself that, should she get a job there, it would only be temporary. This was the result of a narrowing road with very few options at the end of it, coercion by extreme circumstance rather than a full and informed choice. At the club, she became a "hostess," which meant an entertainer, a temporary date for strangers, and a stripper. The temporary job developed into a central feature of her life, and a string of abusive men accompanied her through her late teens. She found herself entangled with a would-be pimp, much younger and slicker than her normal strip club clientele, who raped her and proceeded to stalk her for a few weeks before giving up. She moved on to an abusive boyfriend who battered her psychologically and physically; when she found the wherewithal to go to the police about the abuse, she found herself discredited when he told the police that she was nothing but a stripper and a whore. It was, however, JP—an American that Rachel fell in love with for his smooth southern accent and his initial air of chivalry—that brought her closer to the brink of death than she had ever been. It was only later that she would be able to recognize that their relationship was that of a pimp and a commercially sexually exploited young girl

rather than a union based on love. At the time, however, with no one close and no prospects, she felt that she was truly in love with him, despite the fact that she worked but he kept all the money, and despite the fact that he beat her and spent all of her earnings on crack cocaine. She began to smoke crack cocaine, too, to dull the panic and pain of the abuse she experienced. She endured abuse from JP that was so extreme, and faced death threats from him so regularly, that she even made arrangements for her body to be sent home in the event of her death and left information about his identity at a local kebab shop so that he could be identified if she turned up dead. She had her nineteenth birthday with JP; she did not know how she had fallen so far.

Finally, after a beating so extreme that she was sure she would finally be killed, followed by a failed suicide attempt, Rachel found herself in a moment of awakening. She had faced death so many times, but somehow she was still alive, and she decided that there was a reason she had not died yet; she vowed to find out what that reason was. She found herself in a church; there, a new community began to surround her, and she began to develop the will to move forward, not just from the years of commercial sexual exploitation and abuse, but from all the trauma that led to it. The posttraumatic stress disorder would not be so easy to walk away from, and yet she would find that she was one of the "lucky ones."

Three years later, in 1997, after flourishing with community support, Rachel arrived in New York City at the age of twenty-two. She had a job with the Little Sister Project, a service for women trying to get out of commercial sexual exploitation, many of whom had had run-ins with law enforcement; they had not been the "lucky ones." Adult women on "the track" often pointed her to the younger girls—the girls needed more help than they did, they told her. These young girls were, too often, also not the "lucky ones." It was this work—and the realities of her own life—that led Rachel to create Girls Educational and Mentoring Services, or GEMS, which provides support services for minors who are being commercially sexually exploited. She wanted to build a program and services that were not offered by the state in order to give young girls choices that she felt she had not had. She wanted to help them avoid simply being arrested, criminalized, and destined to be tangled up in exploitation or the criminal/legal system, or both. In 1998, GEMS became the only nonprofit agency in New York State that offered alternatives to incarceration for girls who would otherwise be sent to prison for falling, as Rachel had, into a life of abuse and human trafficking. In order to help girls permanently escape "the life," GEMS has to compete with the things that pimps can offer, which might only be occasional gifts and words of love, but which are still powerful for girls who have a history of trauma. As Rachel herself knows all too well, girls who have not experienced love, safety, and security are vulnerable to the shrewd manipulations of older men; even small hints of love and romance can stoke a hope in girls that leads them into "the life" and wraps them up until they see no way out.

Of course, there are also girls who enter "the life" through kidnaping and violence, and their stories are easier for the American public to understand—they are more readily identified as victims. For girls who get into it, as Rachel did, because of abuse and trauma and a desperate lack of other options, the American public tends to see them as complicit in their own undoing, and the legal system may offer only punishment, rather than support and assistance. For those girls who are not the "lucky ones," Rachel and GEMS offer help and a chance to turn their luck around. In the twenty years she has been running the service, Rachel has encountered thousands of girls with stories like her own or worse, some of them as young as eleven years old.

Before the passage of New York State's safe harbor legislation in 2008, the transactional quality of commercial sexual exploitation classified minors as prostitutes rather than victims. This meant that many victims of trafficking would end up with punishment rather than support. For this reason, Rachel's work takes place not just in the streets or at GEMS, but in prisons and juvenile detention centers. At Horizon Juvenile Center, a facility in the Bronx for kids who are under sixteen, Rachel met Keisha, who was thirteen years old and had already been arrested for prostitution. One night while on the track, Keisha had gotten into a car with a man she presumed to be a John. She asked him if he was a cop, and he said no; it is widely believed by girls who are being commercially sexually exploited that police officers are not allowed to lie when asked plainly if they are cops. Keisha had not done a hotel job before, so she used the John's cell phone to call her pimp to ask how much it should cost. As soon as she relayed the cost to the John, $150, the John revealed himself to be a police officer, pulled out handcuffs, and told Keisha that she was under arrest. Keisha's pimp, who had been standing quite near the car, was also arrested. Though her pimp was soon released on bail, Keisha's prostitution charges remained, and she had already been in detention for several months awaiting trial by the time Rachel came to talk to her.

Keisha had not been cooperative with police during the arrest and interrogation—unsurprising, given that her dealings with men were primarily exploitative and abusive, and one of the police officers who arrested her had been, up until the moment of the arrest, one of these exploiters and abusers. Add to this the fact that she was being treated like a criminal rather than a victim, and the fact that her pimp was intimidating her and her family in order to convince Keisha to stay silent, and it is easy to see that for Keisha, at only thirteen years of age, there were no choices that were not dangerous or dead ends. Rachel recounts that, as with other girls, law enforcement and correctional officers believed that Keisha simply did not want help, but

in reality, for Keisha, it was difficult to see anything they could offer as help; incarceration does not seem like help, particularly when counseling and support for trauma are not part of the program. Keisha was, at least, a different version of "lucky"—she was not yet sixteen, so she was not sent to Rikers Island, a more dangerous facility with even less possibility for counseling, where girls who are sixteen (or at least claim to be sixteen) are sent. Either way, however, detention and incarceration do not prevent girls from going back out onto the streets and back to their pimps; nothing fundamental changes during detention, no traumas are usefully addressed and no new choices established, so release from incarceration often means release back to pimps, back into a different sort of captivity.

GEMS is meant to offer the opposite of all this. It is meant to nurture and amplify the voices of the girls and to help them carve out new paths that do not lead to prison or the streets. At GEMS, they are able to access all kinds of practical support services, from help finding jobs and new apartments of their own to assistance when they decide to go back to school or work toward their GED. They can also participate in different types of programming, such as leadership training, discussion groups, peer support and counseling, and education about national and global structures of power that create the conditions for the kinds of exploitation they have experienced. But to Rachel and others, these kinds of services can only partially offset the pain and trauma of criminalization and incarceration, and she and other activists, in 2004, began a years-long fight to ensure that minors who were being commercially sexually exploited would no longer face criminalization. In 2008, the Safe Harbour for Exploited Children Act finally passed into New York State law. Finally, minors are not to be criminalized for their own exploitation.

Despite these laws, however, Rachel notes that the public consciousness continues to blame young women who are commercially sexually exploited for their own victimization. Lloyd recounts the experience she has had, over and over, of telling people what she does for a living—she explains that she works with trafficked girls and that her agency serves hundreds of girls every year, and the response to this is one of compassion, horror, and disbelief. But then when she clarifies that the girls she works with are more often seen as "teen prostitutes" rather than "victims of human trafficking," the response from the listener invariably changes. "'Oh, that . . . but that's different. Teen prostitutes choose to be doing that; aren't they normally on drugs or something?' In under three minutes, they've gone from sympathy to confusion to blame."[1] As this mindset persists despite the passage of the Safe Harbour Act, Rachel continues to emphasize the importance of empowering victims and survivors and giving them the tools to support each other and themselves so that they can escape from "the life," forge a path through adversity and misunderstanding, and find new roads and new options.

THINKING CRITICALLY ABOUT THE CASE

1. What are the specific risk factors that might increase the likelihood of a minor being caught up in commercial sexual exploitation?

2. What are the barriers that may prevent an individual from escaping commercial sexual exploitation?

3. How do courts that are not bound by safe harbor legislation justify the criminalization of minors that are caught up in commercial sexual exploitation?

REFERENCES

This case is adapted from the following sources:

"Assembly Speaker Sheldon Silver Press Release: Assembly Passes 'Safe Harbour' Legislation." New York State Assembly. Accessed July 1, 2019. https://assembly.state.ny.us/Press/20080619.

Lloyd, Rachel. *Girls like Us: Fighting for a World Where Girls Are Not for Sale; An Activist Finds Her Calling and Heals Herself.* New York: HarperCollins, 2011.

Mullen, Katherine, and Rachael Lloyd. "The Passage of the Safe Harbor Act and the Voices of Sexually Exploited Youth." In *Lawyer's Manual on Human Trafficking: Pursuing Justice for Victims*, edited by Jill Laurie Goodman and Dorchen A. Leidholdt, 129–40. Supreme Court of the State of New York, Appellate Division, First Department, and New York State Judicial Committee on Women in the Courts, 2011.

Schisgall, David, and Nina Alvarez, dirs. *Very Young Girls.* Showtime and Swinging T Productions, 2007.

CONTEXT AND ANALYSIS

Rachel Lloyd's story and work exposes the tension between our understanding of what constitutes prostitution and what constitutes commercial sexual exploitation and trafficking. Treatments of these categories by the criminal/legal system, by feminist theorists, and by mainstream perceptions are highly dependent on the interplay of questions of gender, race, age, nationality, economic class, legality, and morality.

Commercial Sexual Exploitation

In 1977, social psychologist Lee Ross coined the concept of the fundamental attribution error. Ross describes this as the "general tendency to overestimate the importance of personal or dispositional factors relative to environmental influences" and surmises that this causes people to overlook "the potency of situational pressures and constraints."[2] This fundamental attribution error in terms of the treatment of those who are commercially sexually exploited may result in victims being treated as criminals, as if they are driven more by their own desires to sell sex than by the external factors of vulnerability, threats, and having nowhere else to turn.

Part of the reason for this misreading of their situations has to do with societal views on prostitution and trafficking, as well as intersecting forms of oppression (to draw on Kimberlé Crenshaw's definition of intersectional forms of oppression, in which "the experiences of women of color are frequently the product of intersecting patterns of racism and sexism").[3] Concepts of who is likely to be a criminal and who is likely to be a victim inform the ways in which the criminal/legal system determines who should be convicted and who should be protected.

Concepts of minors caught up in commercial exploitation are highly skewed by these patterns of oppression. A 2003 *Newsweek* article, "This Could Be Your Kid," turns commercial sexual exploitation into a suburban horror spectacle, where malls are a place for teenage girls to decide to "sell themselves as a way to make quick, easy money." The article gives a quick nod to the fact that "many kids come from troubled homes," but it also suggests that this is a rising problem primarily in middle- to upper-middle-class families, where ashamed parents feel the need to say, "We're not from the ghetto."[4] Lloyd argues that this article, in line with images in the popular imagination, "dismissed the real issues of commercial sexual exploitation, such as race, poverty, homelessness, abuse, ineffective city systems, and a public policy that blames the victims."[5] To be sure, the distancing of oneself from "the ghetto" suggests that prostitution and trafficking are supposed to happen in "the ghetto," which then continues to normalize commercial sexual exploitation among particularly vulnerable populations.

An oft-cited 2001 study by Richard Estes and Neil Weiner, *The Commercial Sexual Exploitation of Children in the U.S., Mexico, and Canada*, highlights the interplay of several factors that may increase the likelihood that minors will get caught up in commercial sexual exploitation. Estes and Weiner write,

> For many older children, the response to sexual victimization at home is to flee their local communities in an effort to build new lives for themselves elsewhere. Sadly, the majority of these runaways become victimized again when they reach the streets and, often, are recruited into commercial sexual activities—including pornography, prostitution, and trafficking for sexual purposes—that not only compound their original abusive situation but also exposes them, among other things, to homelessness, malnutrition, street violence, sexually transmitted diseases.[6]

To be sure, Estes and Weiner are attentive to the multiple pressures that may result in a child being vulnerable to commercial sexual exploitation. However, Lloyd notes that while family histories of abuse and trauma are certainly a part of the story, the study does not comprehensively address the intersections of socioeconomic status, race, and other large external factors that may make certain populations more likely to exhibit these patterns. As we have seen, traffickers take advantage of these multiple vulnerabilities.

Legal scholar Cheryl Nelson Butler applies theories of **critical race feminism** to argue that "race intersects with other forms of subordination including gender, class, and age to push kids of color into prostitution and keep them there."[7] She goes on to argue that "racial constructs of Blacks and Native Americans were used to justify slavery and colonization," that in the contemporary era, these constructs "were perpetuated in order to justify targeting people of color for sexual exploitation in America's modern-day commercial sex industry," and that "the modern antitrafficking movement continues to marginalize African Americans and other people of color."[8] In chapter 6, we examined ways in which youth of color are routinely viewed as older and therefore more culpable than they are. Statistics show that this is reflected in the arrest rates of minors: while nationwide arrests of minors on prostitution charges have fallen over the last several years (from nearly 1,500 in 2008 to 280 in 2019, representing a decrease of more than 80 percent), Black minors are disproportionately likely to be arrested for prostitution, making up more than half of those arrested.[9]

Intersecting factors of race, gender, and socioeconomic status clearly affect the likelihood that a minor will be caught up in commercial sexual exploitation, as well as the likelihood that they will be criminalized. These intersecting factors also impact adults involved in prostitution or in commercial sexual exploitation. There are additional complications for adults, given that they are above the age of consent and are therefore more likely to be seen as legally culpable for their actions. Clear and dependable data about adults who are sex trafficked is difficult to obtain, partially because victims are reluctant to draw attention to themselves out of fear of being criminalized, and partially because of the ways in which they are silenced and manipulated by sex traffickers.[10] For this reason, data on prostitution charges among adults is marginally more available and is discussed in further detail below.

Safe Harbor

The Victims of Trafficking and Violence Protection Act of 2000 (reauthorized in 2003, 2005, 2008, and 2013) states,

> For the knowing commission of any act of sex trafficking involving force, fraud, coercion, or in which the victim of sex trafficking is a child incapable of giving meaningful consent, or of trafficking which includes rape or kidnapping or which causes a death, the government of the country should prescribe punishment commensurate with that for grave crimes, such as forcible sexual assault.[11]

This implies that if a person is under the **age of consent**, it is not necessary for "force, fraud, or coercion" to be present for the person to be considered a victim rather than a criminal in cases of prostitution or commercial exploitation. However, it is clear that many minors have continued to be criminalized rather than offered the necessary treatment and support to escape their predicament. For this reason, Rachel Lloyd and a group of lawyers, advocates, and survivors of sex trafficking worked toward the creation of new laws in the state of New York that would more effectively address the needs of survivors of commercial sexual exploitation.

It was the 2004 case around a twelve-year-old girl, Nicolette R., that led Rachel, Legal Aid attorney Katherine Mullen, and others to begin working toward what became known as **safe harbor laws**. Nicolette had been arrested in June 2003 for prostitution in the Bronx; though she was twelve, it was not the first time she had been arrested. The debate about whether or not she should be seen as a criminal or a victim continued for nearly a year. Nicolette's case was unusual in that she and her lawyers fought hard and insisted that she not be criminalized, but everything else about her story was, sadly, quite typical.

CRITICAL RACE FEMINISM
Legal theory that recognizes the intersection of race, gender, class, and age when analyzing oppression.

AGE OF CONSENT
Age when a person is considered to be legally competent to consent to sexual acts.

SAFE HARBOR LAWS
Laws that prevent a minor from being prosecuted for prostitution.

Nicolette's journey can be explained by feminist pathways theory, discussed in chapter 2. Her childhood was marked by trauma, abuse, and abandonment, so at ten years old, she began running away from home. At age eleven, at a group home for runaways, she was approached and then recruited by the man who would become her pimp. Prosecutors would, of course, argue that she was a hardened criminal who should be incarcerated; the psychologist they called in to be an expert agreed. Her defense made the case that she was simply too young to consent to sexual acts and should therefore be treated not as a criminal but as a victim of sexual exploitation; the child psychiatrist that they called as a witness agreed. Nicolette's presence in the courtroom only hurt her case, as many were unable to see her as a traumatized child. Instead, they saw only an angry and dangerous young woman. The judge ultimately agreed with the prosecution, but when Nicolette's defense appealed the conviction, it was mandated that Nicolette be placed in a treatment center instead of a juvenile detention facility. Part of the reason for this adjustment was that a representative of the detention facility to which she had been sentenced argued that they did not, in fact, have the necessary treatment services for her. Nicolette was sent, finally, to a residential treatment program outside of the city.[12] The various issues exposed at her trial compelled many advocates for commercially sexually exploited children to come together, finally, to try to change the laws.

Lloyd, Mullen, and other advocates of the **Safe Harbour for Exploited Children Act** argued that preexisting trauma is what leads girls to end up on the streets, where they are commercially sexually exploited, which adds to the trauma they have experienced. Incarceration, they argued, provides neither safety nor opportunity to access the services that may help girls actually heal from the trauma, as correctional officers and penal institutions have neither the resources nor the training to deal with the long-term effects of posttraumatic stress disorder. Given this reality, girls who are commercially sexually exploited should be entered into social service programs that recognize them as victims and survivors and attend to them as such. Girls from **Girls Educational and Mentoring Services (GEMS)** were among those who worked to ensure that the laws passed, presenting to legislators in Albany year after year, arguing for the relevance of the laws and sharing their stories of early trauma, exploitation and abuse, rape by law enforcement officers, and incarceration and detention as young teenagers.

After more than four years of outreach, attending and presenting at hearings, writing reports, and advocating for exploited youth, in 2008 the Safe Harbour for Exploited Children Act finally passed into New York State law, becoming effective in April 2010. When the New York State Assembly passed the act into law, they acknowledged clearly that, "since the overwhelming majority of these youths have a history of psychological, physical or sexual abuse as younger children and many have been raised in poverty, simply arresting, prosecuting and incarcerating them as criminals did little more than re-traumatize survivors of sexual exploitation."[13] The act focuses on three specific areas: diversion (or the handling of such cases by family court, rather than criminal court), services (such as treatment and support through GEMS, rather than conviction and incarceration), and protection (or placement in a safe house, rather than incarceration). While the act may still have shortcomings with respect to funding and the treatment of those between sixteen and eighteen years of age, who are still able to be prosecuted as adults within the New York penal code,[14] it represents a massive shift in the legal treatment of commercially sexually exploited minors.

For Rachel, other advocates of the act, and the girls who worked for more than four years to bring attention to the need for such an act, the passing of these safe harbor laws was much more than an act of legislation. It was an incredibly emotional triumph that allowed some of their trauma to transform into a feeling of victory and a sense of finally being seen and supported. Currently, more than half the states in the country now have some form of safe harbor laws.[15]

SAFE HARBOUR FOR EXPLOITED CHILDREN ACT
Law that defines a sexually exploited child as someone under eighteen years old who has been subjected to sexual exploitation.

GIRLS EDUCATIONAL AND MENTORING SERVICES (GEMS)
Nonprofit organization that provides services to sexually exploited and domestically trafficked girls and young women.

Trauma and Treatment

Angelina came to GEMS when she was sixteen years old and had already served one year in juvenile detention for prostitution. She had run away from home at twelve and had almost immediately gotten targeted and recruited by a pimp. Despite Rachel's support, however, and the abuse that Angelina had suffered at the hands of her pimp and those to whom he sold her, she still missed him and felt that she loved him. When Rachel suggested to Angelina that it might be helpful to make a list of why she loved him, alongside another list of how he hurt her or made her angry, the list skewed heavily to the latter. In the column headed "Things That Made Me Feel Sad/Cry," she wrote, "He hit me," "He makes me have sex with other men," "He gave me an STD," "He beat me with an extension cord," "He said I was a dumb bitch," "Set me up to get raped," "Left me in jail"; and more. In the column headed "Things He Did That Made Me Feel Happy/Loved," she wrote, "He told me he was my daddy," "He takes me on trips," "He told me he loved me," and "Cheetos." Rachel inquired about the last point on the list and discovered that one day, after delivering a beating that made her cry, Angelina's pimp went to the store and bought her Cheetos and a Yoo-Hoo, her favorites; the fact that he knew they were her favorites touched her.[16] In a life marked by continual trauma and abuse, even this small act represented something better than everything else. These are not the experiences of a criminal but of a victim. Nevertheless, Angelina had been arrested, criminalized, and marked as deviant, a harsh punctuation at the end of an already traumatic story of abuse and victimization.

Trauma plays multiple roles in commercial sexual exploitation. Albert Biderman's chart of coercion,[17] originally developed in the 1970s for Amnesty International to examine the coercion experienced by political prisoners and prisoners of war, has been utilized by such organizations as the National Center on Domestic and Sexual Violence (NCDSV) to highlight the ways in which interpersonal and sexual violence mirrors forms of coercion used in wartime and political settings. Among the tactics used against prisoners are isolation, monopolization of perception (or controlling any stimuli that prisoners receive), induced debility and exhaustion (including withholding food and physical restraint), threats (of violence or death, for example), occasional indulgences (to placate or reward the prisoner for cooperation), demonstrating omnipotence (or power), degradation (or attempting to dehumanize the prisoner), and enforcing trivial demands.[18] We see many of these tactics in Angelina's story. Advocates for survivors of commercial sexual exploitation, such as Lloyd, argue that these tactics also mirror those used by pimps and sex traffickers to control those they are exploiting.[19] Not only are these forms of violence and coercion key factors in sex traffickers' control over those they are exploiting, but they also take advantage of the likelihood that their targets are already accustomed to such forms of violence, coercion, and trauma.

Approximately 60 to 90 percent of those being commercially sexually exploited experienced some form of abuse or extreme neglect in their early lives, very often involving family members and those close to them.[20] This, perhaps, contributes to their vulnerability in the face of the forms of coercion described above. As Lloyd writes, "The pimp, the trafficker, doesn't need to do much training. It's already been done—by her father, her uncle, her mother's boyfriend, her teacher. She's well prepared for what's to come."[21]

Trauma, however, does not only precede one's entrance into commercial sexual exploitation; it also follows it. One-half to three-quarters of those who have experienced sexual violence and physical injury within their history of sex trafficking are likely to exhibit ongoing posttraumatic stress disorder, depression, and anxiety.[22] Given what we know of trauma and its effect on one's behavior and psychological state (see chapters 3, 4, and 8), we see that the trauma itself may severely impede the ability of those who are being commercially sexually exploited to advocate for themselves or escape from situations that seem, for so many reasons, inescapable.

Prostitution: To Criminalize or Decriminalize?

Prostitution was not criminalized in the United States until the end of World War I as a result of a decades-long campaign originating from many different sectors of society. It represented, opponents of prostitution said, family and moral decay, a threat to public health, and unacceptable sexual deviancy, among other things.[23] It has been only a little more than a century since the criminalization of prostitution in the United States, and debates about decriminalization are bringing the social, moral, economic, racialized, and gendered dimensions of prostitution back into mainstream discourse.

There were, legal studies scholar Ann M. Lucas argues, racialized and classist dimensions of the initial criminalization of prostitution: "Prostitution policy was part of a larger effort to defuse the threat to dominant values posed by working-class and immigrant communities, waged work, industrialization, urbanization, and anonymity."[24] This association of moral decay with immigrant communities, poor communities, and communities of color continues to pervade contemporary conceptions of prostitution and continues to influence who is criminalized.

Even before the criminalization of prostitution, Black and indigenous women were characterized as sexually deviant and lascivious; these racialized gender constructs acted as a justification for violence against Black and indigenous women.[25] These characterizations and stereotypes persist and are visible in the popular image of prostitution and "streetwalkers" as well as in the treatment of those who are arrested and charged for prostitution. For example, while the vast majority of prostitutes do not walk the streets but instead work in establishments such as brothels or massage parlors or arrange private escort services, those who work on the street are the most likely to be profiled, policed, and criminalized. As Lucas writes, the result of this is that "street prostitutes—predominantly poor women and women of color—disproportionately suffer police harassment and arrest, while their sisters who are often white, more financially stable, less publicly visible, and less 'offensive' to the public, are treated more leniently."[26] Despite the fact that those who work on the street make up only 10 to 20 percent of sex workers, they are the majority of those arrested and charged for prostitution. Additionally, sex workers of any race, ethnicity, or gender, particularly those who work on the street, are also very vulnerable to violence, both at the hands of the public and of law enforcement, and are much more likely to contract HIV and other sexually transmitted diseases.[27] Problematically, the fact that many are afraid of both arrest and violence originating from law enforcement means that they may be reluctant to report instances of violence.

It is not only women, of course, that are involved in prostitution. Cis men, trans, gender nonconforming, and intersex individuals also work as prostitutes. Perceptions of them are highly informed by similarly dynamic factors and are threaded through their treatment by the criminal/legal system. Moreover, trans women, particularly Black trans women, are disproportionately likely to experience violence and persecution.[28]

For these and other reasons, one argument for decriminalization is that those doing sex work will be safer. Without the fear of being arrested or stigmatized, they will be better able to advocate for themselves and seek the health care they need. Further, it will be easier for them to escape situations of coercion or trafficking.[29] There are many who advocate for the Nordic model, based on legislation originating in Nordic countries, in which sex work is decriminalized, but buying sex is a criminal offense. Nevertheless, there are counterarguments to this model that point to uneven implementation, continued vulnerability to sex trafficking, and perhaps an increased risk of violence to sex workers when buyers situate the sex trade even further underground in order to avoid arrest.[30]

In 2018, two bills regarding the use of online platforms for the advertisement of sex work were signed into federal law: the Stop Enabling Sex Traffickers Act (SESTA) and the Allow States and Victims to Fight Online Sex Trafficking Act (FOSTA). SESTA determines that those who support or facilitate sex trafficking—in this case, online platforms—are participating in the criminal act and therefore punishable, while FOSTA determines that websites and online platforms are not protected by section 230 of the

Communications Act of 1934, which protects online platforms from being held liable for content generated by its users.[31] Proponents of these bills argued that they were crucial in restricting the online sale of those being commercially sexually exploited. Opposing voices argued that the criminalization of available online platforms and their users made it impossible for sex workers to make a living and to share necessary information with one another, sometimes relating to safety and security, while including no penalties for sex traffickers themselves.[32]

Further debates about decriminalization have reached legislative halls. In several states, including Maine, Massachusetts, and New York, bills to decriminalize were introduced. In New York, these opposing viewpoints faced off again, this time in response to a proposal to decriminalize sex work in New York State. First, a rally was held by Decrim NY, a coalition aiming to "decriminalize, decarcerate, and destigmatize the sex trade."[33] A mere two weeks later, a coalition calling itself the New York Alliance against the Legalization of Prostitution, with participation from the National Organization for Women's New York chapter and the New York City Faith-Based Coalition against Human Trafficking and Domestic Violence, held their own rally. Both coalitions argue that they have the best interests of the most vulnerable populations in mind,[34] but their proposed routes to protecting these interests vary greatly. Kaitlyn Bailey, a former sex worker speaking on behalf of the organization Decriminalize Sex Work, said, "We've learned this lesson many times with the prohibition of alcohol, or criminalization of abortion, or even the criminalization of marijuana: The black market creates dark circumstances and provides cover for a lot of violence and exploitation." On the other hand, Ane Matheison of the organization Sanctuary for Families, opposing decriminalization, said, "Prostitution is inherently violent. . . . Sex buying promotes sex trafficking, promotes pimping and organized crime, and sexual exploitation of children." Others in opposition argue that the Nordic model and other attempts to decriminalize sex work have not shown decreases in the numbers of either adults or children in the sex trade, and that the most vulnerable populations will remain vulnerable or perhaps even find themselves worse off.[35] Arguments on any side of this debate must include considerations of how any legislation—either continued criminalization or decriminalization—may continue to produce inequitable outcomes for individuals based on age, race, ethnicity, economic status, and other factors.

Sex Work as Self-Determination

Swirling alongside debates about criminalization and decriminalization, feminist theorists have long debated the position of prostitution and sex work in terms of exploitation and self-determination. Over time, there have been many theorists who have argued that, given the patriarchal nature of society at large, sex work is inherently exploitative because it relies on the limitation of choice for those who enter into the profession, while others have defended the position of consensual, willing sex work as an act of self-determination and self-empowerment.

Well-known feminists such as Kathleen Barry and Catherine MacKinnon have argued that prostitution is inherently reflective of patriarchal social structures and power dynamics and that, given the imbalance of power, there is no way for female prostitutes to truly give consent, as they are coerced by these patriarchal social structures into selling sex.[36] Alongside these theorists, there are those who themselves have been in the industry of selling sex, such as Rachel Lloyd and Rachel Moran, who detail the ways in which the lack of choice and agency led them into prostitution and exploitation, which in turn whittled down their choices still further. Moran, in her memoir *Paid For: My Journey through Prostitution*, is clear about the fact that all the men who paid for sex with her "are abusive on some level, whether they know it or not."[37] Clearly, she agrees with the premise put forth by Barry and MacKinnon that the dynamics of exploitation and abuse are ever present.

Those who defend the position of sex work argue that individuals who choose to enter the profession are activated by their own agency, which can function as an empowering and feminist act.[38] Some of these advocates are, like those who oppose sex work, formerly or currently in the profession. Clearly, there is no consensus about the causes, effects, or fundamental factors governing sex work, at either the societal or individual level. It should be noted, however, that the most prominent voices on both sides of this debate have historically been white. Even the term "sex work" was coined by white artist and activist Carol Leigh during the era when predominantly white second-wave feminists were engaged in debates about sex positivity versus antipornography,[39] so it has its roots in particular understandings of empowerment that may not acknowledge the lived realities of women of color, those who are poor, and those who do not have entry into certain spaces and discourses. We must return again to the stigmatization of the sexuality of women of color and question whether, in terms of a debate about empowerment, it is possible to include those who are consistently disempowered by racialized gender norms and economic inequality in any sector of the economy.

International Trafficking, Immigration, and Asylum

In 2003, the United Nations' Protocol to Prevent, Suppress and Punish Trafficking in Persons Especially Women and Children came into effect. The protocol made extensive recommendations to member nations, both in terms of domestic law and international cooperation.[40] While approximately four-fifths of the nations that had participated in the United Nations' Global Initiative to Fight Human Trafficking's data collection and reporting developed antitrafficking legislation, the UN acknowledges that there is still much work to be done. In 2009, the United Nations' Office on Drugs and Crime found that nearly 80 percent of global human trafficking involved commercial sexual exploitation, with women and girls being disproportionately represented among those trafficked, while nonsexual forced labor was the second most prevalent form of human trafficking, trailing far behind at under 20 percent. The report suggests, however, that these numbers may reflect the easier detectability of sexual forced labor as opposed to nonsexual forced labor.[41] In 2014, while data suggested that trafficking in women had decreased somewhat, trafficking in girls had risen, while global conviction rates were still very low.[42] The complicated global nature of international trafficking acts to obscure its contours, preventing a robust national and international response.

The Victims of Trafficking and Violence Protection Act, as well as other pieces of legislation, contain laws regarding the response to non-U.S. nationals who are being trafficked within the United States. Those who are found to be trafficked in the United States are eligible for T nonimmigrant status or U nonimmigrant status; the former specifically stipulates that some victims of human trafficking may reside in the United States for four years if they have been helpful with investigations or prosecutions of traffickers, while the latter stipulates that those who have suffered abuse or assault as victims of crime may reside in the United States for four years if they have been helpful with investigations or prosecutions.[43] One fundamental complication for those who are being trafficked or abused, however, is the fact that they are very likely to have little information about where to go for help and may feel that seeking help itself is dangerous because of the possible consequences if their traffickers find out. The International Marriage Broker Regulation Act (IMBRA) stipulates that "the U.S. Government provide foreign fiancé(e)s and spouses immigrating to the United States information about their legal rights as well as criminal or domestic violence histories of their U.S. citizen fiancé(e)s and spouses."[44] For a number of reasons, including language barriers, lack of information, lack of services in the relevant language, and fear of deportation, victims of trafficking and abuse may be prevented from coming forward and seeking help.[45]

Those who seek **asylum** or **refugee** status in the United States because of persecution in their home countries are able to apply for asylum once they have reached the United States, or refugee status from abroad; because of the backlog in immigration courts, this process can take anywhere from a few months to several years.[46] In July 2019, a new policy regarding asylum in the United States says that any person crossing the southern border seeking asylum from torture or other forms of persecution is ineligible for asylum if they

ASYLUM
Protection granted to someone who has left their native country because they suffered persecution due to violence, race, religion, or political opinion, among other reasons.

REFUGEE
A person who has been forced to leave their country in order to escape war, persecution, or natural disaster.

did not apply for asylum in a country that they passed through en route to the United States. The rule, however, is ostensibly meant to prioritize asylum requests from those who are trafficked; it "prioritizes individuals who are unable to obtain protection from persecution elsewhere and individuals who are victims of a 'severe form of trafficking in persons'" because the understanding is that these victims have not crossed these borders of their own free will.[47] Several groups, including the American Civil Liberties Union, are challenging this rule, calling it "patently unlawful."[48] The wider effects of such rules remain to be seen.

The next chapter discusses crimes of power, including abuse by police, corporate crimes, and white-collar crimes. Further, sexual harassment and discrimination are explored, as well as the gendered impact of immigration.

REVIEW AND STUDY QUESTIONS

1. What are safe harbor laws, and are they effective in addressing sex trafficking?
2. What are some of the unintended consequences of criminalizing sex work?
3. Do you believe that sex work is ever a matter of choice or self-determination? How would you support that belief with evidence?

GOING FURTHER

Readings:

Lloyd, Rachel. *Girls like Us: Fighting for a World Where Girls Are Not for Sale; An Activist Finds Her Calling and Heals Herself*. New York: HarperCollins, 2011.

Mapp, Susan C. *Domestic Minor Sex Trafficking*. Oxford: Oxford University Press, 2016.

Moran, Rachel. *Paid For: My Journey through Prostitution*. New York: Norton, 2013.

Videos/Movies:

Victim of Sex Traffickers Speaks Out. FBI, 2013. https://www.fbi.gov/video-repository/victim-of-sex-trafficking-speaks-out.mp4/view.

KEY TERMS

age of consent Age when a person is considered to be legally competent to consent to sexual acts.

asylum Protection granted to someone who has left their native country because they suffered persecution due to violence, race, religion, or political opinion, among other reasons.

critical race feminism Legal theory that recognizes the intersection of race, gender, class, and age when analyzing oppression.

Girls Educational and Mentoring Services (GEMS) Nonprofit organization that provides services to sexually exploited and domestically trafficked girls and young women.

refugee A person who has been forced to leave their country in order to escape war, persecution, or natural disaster.

safe harbor laws Laws that prevent a minor from being prosecuted for prostitution.

Safe Harbour for Exploited Children Act Law that defines a sexually exploited child as someone under eighteen years old who has been subjected to sexual exploitation.

NOTES

[1] Rachel Lloyd, *Girls like Us: Fighting for a World Where Girls Are Not for Sale; An Activist Finds Her Calling and Heals Herself* (New York: HarperCollins, 2011), 11.

[2] Lee Ross, "The Intuitive Psychologist and His Shortcomings: Distortions in the Attribution Process," *Advances in Experimental Social Psychology* 10 (1977): 184.

[3] Kimberlé Williams Crenshaw, "Mapping the Margins: Intersectionality, Identity Politics, and Violence against Women of Color," *Stanford Law Review* 43, no. 6 (July 1991): 1243, https://doi.org/10.2307/1229039.

[4] Suzanne Smalley, "This Could Be Your Kid," *Newsweek*, August 17, 2003, accessed July 1, 2019, https://www.newsweek.com/could-be-your-kid-135949.

[5] Lloyd, *Girls like Us*, 44.

[6] Richard J. Estes and Neil Alan Weiner, "The Commercial Sexual Exploitation of Children in the U. S., Canada and Mexico," National Institute of Justice, September 18, 2001, 60, https://abolitionistmom.org/wp-content/uploads/2014/05/Complete_CSEC_0estes-weiner.pdf.

[7] Cheryl Nelson Butler, "The Racial Roots of Human Trafficking," *UCLA Law Review* 62 (2015): 1468, https://www.uclalawreview.org/racial-roots-human-trafficking.

8 Butler, "The Racial Roots of Human Trafficking," 1469.

9 "Crime in the United States, 2016," FBI, Uniform Crime Reporting, table 21B, https://ucr.fbi.gov/crime-in-the-u.s /2016/crime-in-the-u.s.-2016/topic-pages/tables/table-21.

10 Priscilla Alvarez, "When Sex Trafficking Goes Unnoticed in America," *The Atlantic*, February 23, 2016, https://www .theatlantic.com/politics/archive/2016/02/how-sex-trafficking -goes-unnoticed-in-america/470166.

11 Victims of Trafficking and Violence Protection Act, Pub. L. No. 106-386 (2000), 106th Congress, accessed June 15, 2019, https://www.govinfo.gov/content/pkg/PLAW-106publ386 /pdf/PLAW-106publ386.pdf.

12 Leslie Kaufman, "Determining the Future of a Girl with a Past: Is the Answer to Child Prostitution Counseling, or Incarceration?," *New York Times*, September 15, 2004.

13 "Assembly Speaker Sheldon Silver Press Release: Assembly Passes 'Safe Harbour' Legislation," New York State Assembly, accessed July 1, 2019, https://assembly.state.ny.us /Press/20080619.

14 Karen Wigle Weiss, "A Review of the New York State Safe Harbor Law," End Child Prostitution and Trafficking (ECPAT), April 2013, accessed July 1, 2019, https://d2jug8yyubo3yl.cloud front.net/26999B2F-7C10-4962-918C-E964709E745D/8d5cf ab4-a75e-4dd6-97c8-2f9752d16b5d.pdf.

15 "Toolkit 2017," Protected Innocence Challenge, accessed July 1, 2019, https://sharedhope.org/wp-content /uploads/2017/11/2017-PIC-Fact-Sheet_2.pdf.

16 Lloyd, *Girls like Us*, 161–62.

17 Rus Ervin Funk, "Biderman's Chart of Coercion," National Center on Domestic and Sexual Violence, accessed July 1, 2019, http://www.ncdsv.org/images/Chart%20of%20Coer cion1.pdf.

18 "Report on Torture," Duckworth and Amnesty International Publications, 1973.

19 Lloyd, *Girls like Us*, 95.

20 Mimi H. Silbert and Ayala M. Pines, "Sexual Child Abuse as an Antecedent to Prostitution," *Child Abuse & Neglect* 5, no. 4 (1981): 407–11, https://doi.org/10.1016/0145-2134 (81)90050-8.

21 Lloyd, *Girls like Us*, 65.

22 Mazeda Hossain et al., "The Relationship of Trauma to Mental Disorders among Trafficked and Sexually Exploited Girls and Women," *American Journal of Public Health* 100, no. 12 (2010): 2442–49, http://doi.org/10.2105/AJPH.2009.173229.

23 Ann M. Lucas, "Race, Class, Gender, and Deviancy: The Criminalization of Prostitution," *Berkeley Journal of Gender, Law & Justice* 10, no. 1 (September 1995): 47–60, https:// scholarship.law.berkeley.edu/cgi/viewcontent.cgi?article=10 96&context=bglj.

24 Lucas, "Race, Class, Gender, and Deviancy," 47.

25 Butler, "The Racial Roots of Human Trafficking."

26 Lucas, "Race, Class, Gender, and Deviancy," 49.

27 "Addressing Violence against Sex Workers," World Health Organization, 2012, https://www.who.int/hiv/pub/sti/sex _worker_implementation/swit_chpt2.pdf.

28 Erin Fitzgerald et al., "Meaningful Work: Transgender Experiences in the Sex Trade," National Transgender Dis-

crimination Survey, Red Umbrella Project, Best Practices Policy Project, and National Center for Transgender Equality, December 2015, https://www.transequality.org/sites/default /files/Meaningful%20Work-Full%20Report_FINAL_3.pdf.

29 Fitzgerald, "Meaningful Work."

30 Sarah Kingston and Terry Thomas, "No Model in Practice: A 'Nordic Model' to Respond to Prostitution?," *Crime, Law, and Social Change* 71, no. 4 (May 2019), 423–39, https://link .springer.com/article/10.1007/s10611-018-9795-6.

31 "Protection for Private Blocking and Screening of Offensive Material," 47 U.S. Code § 230 of the Communications Act of 1934, accessed July 1, 2019.

32 "U.S.A. FOSTA Legislation," Briefing Note, Global Network of Sex Work Projects (NSWP), 2018, https://www.nswp.org /sites/nswp.org/files/fosta_briefing_note_2018.pdf.

33 Decrim NY, "Our Goals," accessed July 1, 2019, https:// www.decrimny.org.

34 Marie Solis, "The Feminist Divide over Decriminalizing Sex Work," *Vice*, March 12, 2019, https://www.vice.com/en_us /article/vbwjp4/sex-work-decriminalization-new-york-feminist -movement.

35 Jesse McKinley, "Could Prostitution Be Next to Be Decriminalized?," *New York Times*, May 31, 2019, https://www .nytimes.com/2019/05/31/nyregion/presidential-candidates -prostitution.html.

36 Kathleen Barry, *Female Sexual Slavery* (New York: New York University Press, 1979).

37 Rachel Moran, *Paid For: My Journey through Prostitution* (New York: Norton, 2013), 5.

38 Carol Queen, *Real Live Nude Girl: Chronicles of Sex-Positive Culture* (Jersey City, NJ: Cleis Press, 1997).

39 Carol Leigh, "Inventing Sex Work," in *Whores and Other Feminists*, ed. Jill Nagle (New York: Routledge, 1997), 226–31.

40 "Protocol to Prevent, Suppress and Punish Trafficking in Persons Especially Women and Children, supplementing the United Nations Convention against Transnational Organized Crime," United Nations Human Rights Office of the High Commissioner, 2000, https://www.ohchr.org/Documents/Pro fessionalInterest/ProtocolonTrafficking.pdf.

41 "Global Report on Trafficking in Persons Executive Summary," United Nations Office on Drugs and Crime, 2009, https://www.unodc.org/documents/human-trafficking/Execu tive_summary_english.pdf.

42 "Global Report on Trafficking in Persons," United Nations Office on Drugs and Crime, 2014, https://www.unodc.org /res/cld/bibliography/global-report-on-trafficking-in-persons _html/GLOTIP_2014_full_report.pdf.

43 "Victims of Human Trafficking: T Nonimmigrant Status," U.S. Citizenship and Immigration Services, accessed July 1, 2019, https://www.uscis.gov/humanitarian/victims -human-trafficking-other-crimes/victims-human-trafficking-t -nonimmigrant-status; "Victims of Criminal Activity: U Nonimmigrant Status," U.S. Citizenship and Immigration Services, accessed July 1, 2019, https://www.uscis.gov/humanitarian /victims-human-trafficking-other-crimes/victims-criminal-activity -u-nonimmigrant-status/victims-criminal-activity-u-nonimmi grant-status.

[44] "Information on the Legal Rights Available to Immigrant Victims of Domestic Violence in the United States and Facts about Immigrating on a Marriage-Based Visa," U.S. Citizenship and Immigration Services, accessed July 1, 2019, https://www.uscis.gov/sites/default/files/document/brochures/IMBRA%20Pamphlet%20Final%2001-07-2011%20for%20Web%20Posting.pdf.

[45] Crenshaw, "Mapping the Margins," 1248–49.

[46] Zuzana Cepla, "Fact Sheet: U.S. Asylum Process," National Immigration Forum, January 10, 2019, https://immigrationforum.org/article/fact-sheet-u-s-asylum-process.

[47] "Asylum Eligibility and Procedural Modifications," U.S. Homeland Security Department and the Executive Office for Immigration Review, accessed July 17, 2019, https://www.federalregister.gov/documents/2019/07/16/2019-15246/asylum-eligibility-and-procedural-modifications.

[48] "ACLU Comment on New Trump Asylum Restrictions," American Civil Liberties Union, July 15, 2019, https://www.aclu.org/press-releases/aclu-comment-new-trump-asylum-restrictions.

Crimes of Power

State and Corporate

In this chapter you will be introduced to the concept of crime and power. You will read about crimes from police abuse of power to corporate crimes and the disproportionate impact they have on women, children, immigrants, and the LGBTQ community. The chapter includes a discussion of sexual harassment in the workplace.

LEARNING OBJECTIVES

After reading this chapter, you should be able to do the following:

- Explain the source of police authority and the ways in which this authority is abused.
- Distinguish between types of corporate crime.
- Identify the impact of crimes of power on various populations.
- Describe community responses to crimes of power.

Case #10: Stonewall

The police raid on the Stonewall Inn in the Greenwich Village area of Manhattan occurred in the wee hours of Saturday, June 28, 1969. It was not the first time this kind of sudden raid had happened, at Stonewall or anywhere else— gay bars across the country were regularly raided. Although the premise for the raids was often ostensibly to check if the bars were compliant with alcohol regulations, and then to confiscate any illegal liquor in the event that the venue indeed had no valid liquor license, it was clear to patrons, workers, and the larger gay community that it was a way to target establishments that had gay clientele. The raid at Stonewall on that June night was notable not because of the raid itself, but because of the response of the clientele, who decided that night that they were done accepting such harassment. There had been angry responses at other bars and in other cities, but what made Stonewall significant was the degree to which the LGBTQ community fought back, as well as the actual changes in laws and recognition of the LGBTQ community that eventually resulted from the days-long skirmish between law enforcement and the citizenry.

The response at Stonewall and the LGBTQ community's refusal to continue to put up with discrimination and harassment was likely a result of the political and social climate of the late 1960s. The year before the events at Stonewall, Martin Luther King Jr. and Robert Kennedy had been assassinated, and the United States was quickly recognizing that the Vietnam War was a disaster. An increasingly radical antiwar movement, along with the civil rights movement, Black Power movements, the free speech movement, and feminist movements, created a citizenry that was increasingly skeptical of the structures of law and order and were much more likely to fight back.

The growing LGBTQ movement—in those days often referred to as the "homophile" movement in activist circles—had been encouraging people to come out of the closet, to band together and resist social and institutional discrimination, and to work for rights and for recognition. Some LGBTQ activists advocated for openly confrontational and militant action. However, the LGBTQ community was still marginalized in such a way that it was often difficult to find places to convene, whether for political activities or for simple socializing. In most major cities, there were bars in which they could congregate, but these bars, though open to serving an LGBTQ clientele, were often not actually gay friendly. Many of the bars were Mafia-owned and focused on potential profits, not on civil rights. They were sometimes openly hostile to their customers, and they made a practice of overcharging people because they knew that, given the circumstances, they essentially had the market cornered.

The Stonewall Inn was not much better than these other bars. One particularly egregious and unsanitary problem was that the bar at Stonewall lacked running water—this meant that used glasses were not cleaned but were merely dunked in tepid and dirty water before being used again for the next customer. There were other complaints, as well: occasional accusations of exploitation of the small percentage of Stonewall's clientele that was underage, the sometimes disruptive presence of organized crime, and a general sentiment that Stonewall was too seedy. For the most part, however, it was a dependable gathering place for those who simply wanted to be able to go out with their friends and be themselves. It became the most popular venue in the area, thanks in no small part to the fact that the crowd was very racially, economically, and socially diverse, which brought an air of fun and dynamism. In addition, unlike at other bars, Stonewall actually permitted patrons to dance.

Tony Lauria, aka "Fat Tony," was the owner of the Stonewall Inn, and his Mafia connections allowed him to open the bar and actually stay open despite general antipathy to the LGBTQ community; Lauria paid the Sixth Precinct of the New York Police Department approximately $2,000 a week to turn a (mostly) blind eye to the bar's operation and clientele. This was affordable because Stonewall, with its growing reputation as a place that was generally welcoming and secure, turned a sizable profit. The cast of characters—from quietly wealthy businesspeople to ostentatiously wealthy mobsters to drag queens to conservative-looking types to hippies to all-night partiers—drew crowds to the lively bar and enticed them to return. In particular, Stonewall was a favorite of drag queens; many other bars did not welcome them, and as a group, they were particularly vulnerable to the ire of the public and the attention of law enforcement. Customers were also appreciative of the selective entry to the bar, designed to keep out undercover police officers and other perhaps homophobic aggressors, and they were willing to pay a cover charge and sign a guest book that gave the bar the cover it needed to stay open. Stonewall was, after all, officially a "bottle club," which ostensibly meant that customers brought their own liquor, and the bar itself needed no liquor license. Inside, there were go-go dancers and strobing multicolored lights that would be switched off whenever workers suspected that law enforcement was entering the bar; at the first sign of a potential police officer, workers would quickly turn off the dance floor lights and turn on regular white lights, which would then send the signal to patrons to stop any dancing and revelry, particularly of a physical nature.

When the police raided the Stonewall Inn at around 1:30 in the morning on June 28, 1969, they arrested both workers and customers, and they did it with violence and homophobic slurs. Though the white lights on the dance floor had gone on, many of the patrons had not taken notice quickly enough and did not expect the rush of police. Central targets for arrest were bartenders, any customers lacking identification, and transvestites, but no one was safe during a raid. The raid was unexpectedly harsh. The Stonewall owners had been warned about the raid a day earlier and expected it to be quick and routine, but this raid was different: the Sixth Precinct, who collected bribes from Stonewall, were only assisting rather than leading the raid. It had been discovered that Stonewall was selling smuggled, stolen, or bootlegged liquor, so the Sixth Precinct was supporting federal agents and the Bureau of Alcohol, Tobacco and Firearms. They had calculated the timing of the raid to coincide with the peak of large crowds and merriment.

Generally, raids on gay bars were predictable affairs—some slurs, some arrests, some words exchanged, but they were often over relatively quickly. Raids would send the clientele of the bars running, eager to avoid arrest and potentially hazardous interactions, but business at the bars would often get back to normal even on the same night. This time, however, was different. Patrons of the bar, gathering outside as the raid and arrests intensified, felt that there was a new energy in the air, that something felt different. Gay men, drag queens, lesbians, and others began drowning out the homophobic slurs of the law enforcement officers with "gay power" chants of their own, and several people who were being arrested and loaded into police vans began to struggle to get free and even escaped. The patrons of the bar lashed out, kicking and punching, shouting support to one another, and creating multiple skirmishes among the chaotic crowd. Those who were not physically fighting began to pick up things to throw—bottles, bricks, and even trash cans, one of which smashed Stonewall's front window. The police, taken by surprise by this sudden revolt, were ordered to gather inside the bar to take shelter.

There were many activists in the crowd at Stonewall that night, and it is believed that one of the first people to start the physical rebellion against the police was Marsha P. Johnson. Johnson would say that the "P" stood for "pay it no mind," and while she is now recognized as a Black trans woman, she described herself at the time as a transvestite or a gay drag queen. Johnson was known in the community as a captivating performer, as a recognizable and loved figure in the community who always had a way about her and put people at ease with her generosity and kindness, and as a fierce believer in and fighter for human rights and gay liberation. She particularly cared about rights for the LGBTQ community, most especially those who were poor and particularly vulnerable. According to accounts, Johnson threw a shot glass against a mirror during the raid, sparking the crowd into physical resistance. Alongside Johnson was Sylvia Rivera, also a trans woman and namesake of the Sylvia Rivera Law Project, an organization that began in 2002 and provides legal and practical support for particularly marginalized communities, with the basic belief that "gender self-determination is inextricably intertwined with racial, social and economic justice." It is possible that Johnson and Rivera were so willing to engage in militant resistance because the trans community was so marginalized and

endangered in general that they felt that they had less to lose and more to gain through open rebellion. They were both known as active revolutionaries who tirelessly fought for their community's rights, and it is likely that it was not just their physical actions but their general energy that emboldened the crowds at Stonewall to start fighting back with such determination.

As the clash intensified, one patron, Craig Rodwell, an active LGBTQ rights organizer, thought to call local media to alert them to the raid, the riot, and the continued conflict, while others were able to pull a parking meter from the sidewalk and began to use it as a ramrod against the door of the Stonewall Inn, inside which the officers were sheltered. Others were throwing things against the plywood that had been put in place of the smashed plate-glass window, and both the door and the plywood began to give way. The crowd outside was noisy and angry. Some officers tried to make their way out of the bar to get clear of the melee but found themselves pushed back in by the advancing crowd. Officers tried to direct the spray of a fire hose toward the crowd outside, but it succeeded only in drenching the inside of the bar. As the door broke in, a member of the crowd sprayed lighter fluid through the front window, and the match that followed it created a quick ball of flame. Just at this moment, as the police were considering drawing their weapons, the sirens of a riot control unit could be heard approaching.

Riot control, it turned out, was not to be achieved. Instead, the police found themselves outnumbered as the crowd refused to disperse and instead strengthened. Members of the crowd ran around the block in order to approach the riot police from behind, and the line of officers that had arrived in formation became scattered throughout the crowd. Some officers, separated from their colleagues, had to simply run as the crowd realized that they vastly outnumbered the officers. Others found themselves covered in trash and debris thrown by the crowd, and still others endured a shock as a cinder block was dropped with a bang onto their car. It was a full two hours before law enforcement finally succeeded in clearing and securing the area, but not before a number of injuries had been visited on the erstwhile revelers of the Stonewall Inn. The streets were once again quiet.

They would not, however, stay quiet. Intermittent violent clashes between law enforcement and the LGBTQ community would continue for the next few days. The raid and riot had made the front page of local papers, and by the next day, thousands of people had gathered to see the damage, or perhaps to bear witness to another phase of confrontation. And more damage and confrontation did indeed materialize. Though there is some disagreement in retrospect about which night resulted in more chaos and violence, the second night at least rivaled the first. The next few days were relatively quiet, perhaps due to poor weather, but on July 3, the crowds returned, along with the police. More people were arrested or beaten and bloody, more bricks and bottles were thrown at police officers, and more homophobic taunts were met with more declarations of gay power. This, however, was the last of this particular series of conflicts. The battle was now no longer just outside the Stonewall Inn—it had reached the front page of national newspapers and had sparked conversation and further activism across the nation.

Stonewall was not the first place that a clash between law enforcement and the LGBTQ community had occurred, but it continues to be understood as a primary catalyst for the growth of the gay rights movement in the United States—the duration of the conflict between police and the LGBTQ community and the growing national attention to it meant that in other cities, those who attended gay bars were increasingly emboldened to fight back against discriminatory treatment by law enforcement. The events at Stonewall spurred on a new and productive phase of LGBTQ activism across the country. Rivera and Johnson started the group STAR—Street Transvestite Action Rev-olutionaries—and they worked together to find housing for trans youth who were homeless because they had been thrown out of their family homes, one of the first projects of its kind. Simultaneously, a group coalesced in New York; they became known as the Gay Liberation Front, and chapters were formed not only across the country but in other countries where similar types of anti-LGBTQ discrimination were taking place. Craig Rodwell and others, having watched the events at Stonewall evolve and the divisions it had revealed even in the gay rights movements, went on to create what they would call Christopher Street Liberation Day, which was to be a large march and demonstration for LGBTQ rights; this march would eventually evolve into the gay pride parade, which is held annually in different cities all around the world. Rather than making the LGBTQ community retreat as planned, the events at Stonewell catalyzed a movement that still continues.

Thirty years later, in June 1999, the Stonewall Inn, along with the blocks around it where the clash played out, was placed on the National Register of Historic Places in recognition of its significance in the movement for LGBTQ rights in the United States. Marsha P. Johnson did not live to witness this recognition. In the summer of 1992, her body was found in the Hudson River. Her death was ruled a suicide, despite the fact that witnesses claim to have seen someone harassing her and later bragging about killing her. Hundreds of people attended her memorial. The case was reopened in 2012.

THINKING CRITICALLY ABOUT THE CASE

1. Was the Bureau of Alcohol, Tobacco and Firearms within their rights in their storming of the bar? Were bar-goers within their rights to fight back?

2. In retrospect, does the violence at Stonewall seem to have accelerated or slowed down advancement toward LGBTQ rights?

3. To what degree does the history of the Stonewall riots appear in contemporary manifestations of pride parades?

REFERENCES

This case is adapted from the following sources:

"About SRLP." Sylvia Rivera Law Project. https://srlp.org/about.

Bronski, Michael. "Stonewall Was a Riot." *ZNet*, June 10, 2009. https://zcomm.org/znetarticle/stonewall-was-a-riot-by-michael-bronski.

Duberman, Martin. *Stonewall*. New York: Penguin, 1993.

Dunlap, David. "Stonewall, Gay Bar That Made History, Is Made a Landmark." *New York Times*, June 26, 1999. https://www.nytimes.com/1999/06/26/nyregion/stonewall-gay-bar-that-made-history-is-made-a-landmark.html.

Kasino, Michael. "Pay It No Mind: The Life and Times of Marsha P. Johnson." 2012. https://www.youtube.com/watch?v=rjN9W2KstqE.

Mogul, Joey L., Andrea J. Ritchie, and Kay Whitlock. *Queer (In)justice: The Criminalization of LGBT People in the United States*. Boston: Beacon, 2011.

CONTEXT AND ANALYSIS

Policing as State Power

The Tenth Amendment of the U.S. Constitution gives to the states the authority to control and regulate all powers that are not otherwise granted to the federal government, including the ability to regulate the "health, safety and morality of its citizens." These powers are known as the **policing powers** of the state. These powers are manifested, and abused, by the police.

Overpolicing in communities of color all too often results in the killing of citizens by police. The *Washington Post* has kept a tally of fatal shootings by police since 2015; they report a steady average of nearly one thousand fatal shootings a year since their project began.[1] These are conservative numbers, and there is little agreement about the actual number of people killed by police each year. What we do know is that Black people are three times as likely as white people to be killed by police; Black women are 1.4 times as likely as white women.[2] And further, 21 percent of Black victims were unarmed compared to 14 percent of white victims.[3] Outrage over police killings, along with other injustices, brought hundreds of thousands of people worldwide into the streets in 2020. Though activists have long called for reform and a response to excessive use of force, extrajudicial killing, and abuse of power by police, there have been more widespread and worldwide demonstrations and concrete efforts to enact systemic change and to demand accountability as regards state violence.

Police violence against women of color often does not receive mainstream attention. Though some cases do receive some notice, such as the death of Sandra Bland in police custody or the killings of Atatiana Jefferson and Breonna Taylor, both of whom were killed in their homes, state violence against women of color often remains invisible or disappears quickly from public view.

Though the Department of Justice website[4] indicates that they pursue and prosecute cases of police violating the constitutional rights of citizens, recent history displays a minimal response from both local and federal officials to police violence. On the local level, police are rarely held accountable for their abuse of power and authority. This is not to suggest that there is no accountability—when police violate departmental rules, officers may face discipline that ranges from being placed on desk duty to removal from the force. But when use of force is involved, the matter is less often pursued. The problem arises when there is no clear understanding, either by the police themselves or by the community, of what constitutes excessive force and what is "necessary" to perform the job of maintaining public safety. Even when the violation of a department's excessive force standards appears clear, prosecutors are hesitant to pursue such cases, perhaps because juries so rarely convict. For example, according to research conducted by Philip Matthew Stinson, who maintains the largest database on police crimes,[5] including data from 2005 to 2014, he found that during that period, eighty officers, or on average 6.6 officers per year, were arrested for on-duty homicides, but only 35 percent of those arrests resulted in conviction.[6] And even when convicted, sentencing is often minimal. This was clearly evidenced in the recent conviction of an off-duty Dallas police officer charged with shooting and killing her neighbor in his own apartment. The same jury that found her guilty imposed a sentence of ten years, a small fraction of the possible ninety-nine-year sentence that could have resulted from her actions.[7]

An interesting—and terrifying—connection between police abuse of power and women is the extreme presence of intimate violence, and the unique vulnerability of women, in relationships with police. Two recent studies have concluded that 40 percent of police families experience intimate violence, compared with 10 percent of families that don't include police officers.[8] In addition to the increased occurrence, the circumstances and the danger also increase where police are the abusers. Police carry guns, they know where confidential shelters are located, and they are able to manipulate the system, other officers, and the courts. And, not surprisingly, when penalized, the penalties are exceedingly minimal. A panel found that New York City officers found guilty of IPV were typically punished by losing thirty vacation days. Another study found that of the ninety-eight officers arrested

POLICING POWER
Absent a federal law, the fundamental authority of a state government to make laws to control and regulate behavior and enforce order; often manifested and abused by the police.

for IPV in Puerto Rico over a three-year period, including three who had shot and killed their spouses, only eight officers lost their jobs.[9] Despite the fact that multiple studies have found a correlation between domestic abuse and the use of excessive force on the job, few officers are removed as a result of IPV claims.

Policing of LGBTQ People

Historically, the very existence of LGBTQ people was considered to be illegal. Legal prohibitions against cross-dressing, entrapment for same-sex solicitation, and violation of sodomy laws were grounds for harassment and arrest. Sodomy laws, originally designed to prohibit certain sexual acts, were most frequently used against men who engaged in consensual sexual behaviors with other adult men. These laws were found to be constitutional as recently as 1986 in the case of *Bowers v. Hardwick* (478 U.S. 186). That precedent was reversed by the Supreme Court in 2003 in *Lawrence v. Texas* (539 U.S. 558). In the *Lawrence* case, the Court found that intimate sexual conduct between consenting adults, no matter what gender, was an exercise of liberty pursuant to the due process clause of the Constitution, and, absent any legitimate state interest, it could not be prohibited. Yet, as of 2019, sixteen states still had not repealed laws criminalizing private consensual sexual behavior between adults of the same sex.[10]

Tension exists today between the expectation of protection from hate crimes and police targeting of marginalized communities, especially communities of color, low-income people, and the homeless. So-called **quality-of-life policing** especially targets these communities for public behaviors such as making noise or drinking in public. For example, groups of LGBTQ youth gathering outside LGBTQ centers or meeting spaces have been targeted for loitering. Moreover, the criminalization and policing of people living with HIV enhances the vulnerability of LGBTQ people, even resulting in requirements that they be entered into the sex offender registries in some states. Further, police often scapegoat gender nonconforming people simply because of their nonconformity. Latina lesbians in Los Angeles were labeled as gang members simply based on their appearance. And transgender women, especially trans women of color, are often assumed by police to be sex workers.

A number of studies today indicate that members of the LGBTQ community continue to experience harassment from the police. And though sexual orientation is not noted in arrest reports, self-reporting studies make clear that LGBTQ people experience verbal assaults, sexual harassment, and even physical assault at the hands of law enforcement at rates substantially higher than those experienced by the general population.

Finally, when LGBTQ people seek assistance from the police, they often become targets themselves. In some instances, the person who was victimized is subsequently defined as the perpetrator, simply for defending themselves. This is especially true in SSIPV (same sex IPV) cases, where police frequently arrest both parties rather than make a determination of who is the aggressor, and they often mistreat both parties.

Though direct attacks by police, as those witnessed in the Stonewall case study, may have subsided, police continue to use the power given them by the state in ways that injure, discriminate, and even kill citizens.

In recent years there has been conflict within the LGBTQ community over commodification and merchandizing. This has become especially poignant for pride parades. Some people object to the notion that parades, or floats and banners, have been sold to sponsors or that cultural icons have been miniaturized and sold as souvenirs. Some parades have requested police escorts, and as more police "come out," there are police contingents marching in the parades. This has left some community members in fear, and organizers have been accused of forgetting that some people participating in the parade, especially trans people and people of color, continue to be at risk of police violence.

QUALITY-OF-LIFE POLICING
Heavily policing normally noncriminal activities and minor offenses (congregating, drinking in public spaces, graffiti, public urination, panhandling, littering, and unlicensed street vending), theorizing that those behaviors will lead to serious crime.

Responding to Police Abuses of Power

There is a growing movement against police abuses of power. In addition to Black Lives Matter, which is discussed in chapter 14, local communities organize around individual cases of police abuse. People gather together to protest or to worship, and to show their support for victims and their families. Efforts abound to bring accountability and transparency to policing. Some stress more education and training for police, noting that studies show that college-educated officers are less authoritarian, have better communication skills, are less likely to use excessive force, and receive fewer complaints.[11] Some community members ask for a stronger role for civilian oversight and review boards. Several NGOs have begun funding projects to look at how best to alter police departments in regard to their roles and relationships within their communities.[12] Others believe that as long as some members of society are given the extensive authority and power that is given to police, incidents of abuse are inevitable.

The Power of Corporate Crime

Corporate crime and white-collar crime are often used interchangeably, and while they may overlap and have many similar features, corporate crime is inherently distinct. **Corporate crime** refers to crimes committed by a corporation or other business entity, or by individuals acting on behalf of a corporation or business. It is a crime involving power and influence. A corporation may be created for the intended purpose of committing crime, but that is not what we are referring to here. Corporate crime includes a range of environmentally damaging behaviors, exploitation of workers, violating antitrust laws, bribery, tax evasion, negligence, and a variety of types of fraud. **White-collar crime** is more broadly defined and typically refers to any crime that is not a "street crime." White-collar crime is as likely to describe an act of an individual employee stealing money from a business account (embezzlement, and, as described, an act of opportunity rather than power) as a company selling a knowingly dangerous product.

Examples of corporate crime abound. The *Exxon Valdez* oil tanker ran aground in Prince William Sound in Alaska in 1989 and spilled eleven million gallons of crude oil that spread over 1,300 miles of coastline. The tanker's captain was fined $50,000 and sentenced to perform one thousand hours of community service. Exxon paid about $4.8 billion in cleanup and restoration costs in the two decades following the spill—less than one year's profit. Another example is Countrywide, a real estate sales and lending company bought by Bank of America in 2009, which was found guilty of fraud in connection to the sale of subprime mortgages before, during, and after the financial crisis of 2008; they eventually settled with the government for $8.5 billion.[13] In 2015, Citibank was fined $700 million for deceptive credit card marketing, and Bumble Bee tuna settled a suit where it was accused of violating worker safety rules related to the death of an employee "trapped in an industrial oven."[14] And in 2016, Freedom Industries Inc. was given a fine of $900,000 for environmental damage related to a January 2014 chemical spill into the Elk River in Charleston, West Virginia.

> Thousands of gallons of a chemical used for cleaning coal (MCHM) leaked from the company's tank farm into the Elk River, flowed into a water treatment plant, and contaminated the water supply. As a result of the spill, the local economy nearly ground to a halt. Schools shut down, hospitals had to cancel non-essential surgeries, and restaurants were forced to close, leaving many people out of work.[15]

These cases represent only a small percentage of corporate violations of local, state, and federal laws and demonstrate punishments (generally fines) that rarely have an effect on corporate profitability. Such crimes are difficult to prosecute for a variety of reasons. For example, the crime may not be immediately apparent; the chemicals dumped in the 1980s may not appear in the cow that produces milk for a decade or more. The victims may not be one or two individuals but a neighborhood or a community. Or only scattered members

CORPORATE CRIME
Refers to crimes committed by a corporation or other business entity, or by individuals acting on behalf of a corporation or business.

WHITE-COLLAR CRIME
A broad term that typically refers to any crime associated with work or the workplace.

of a community may suffer, as is the case with cancer-causing agents, making the legal matter of **causation** difficult to prove. If you prosecute a "corporation" as an individual, who do you hold accountable? The individuals behind the corporation may have protected their assets or may attempt to separate them from the business, as we have seen with the Sackler family in the shadow of lawsuits against drug companies for falsely advertising their drugs and allegedly helping to create the "opioid crisis." It may be against the political interests of the state when the perceived choice is between protecting citizens from harm and ensuring a healthy economy. Money for the "best" lawyers often means more justice.

Society is increasingly aware of the ways in which these crimes disproportionately impact poor communities, communities of color, and immigrant communities. Hazardous waste leaked into the rivers of West Virginia. Contaminants and excessive lead are found in the water system of Flint, Michigan. The stories of environmental racism incorporate the experiences of Latinx farmworkers, indigenous people, urban African Americans, and others lacking the power and resources to assert control themselves.

Deceptive lending practices involving **subprime mortgages** profited off the backs of people in markets traditionally underserved by banks—communities of color, in particular—who were given loans with higher fees or loans they were incapable of paying, which often ended up being foreclosed. A researcher who analyzed home mortgage loans between 2006 and 2012 found that

> relative to comparable white applicants, and controlling for geographic factors, blacks were 2.8 times more likely to be denied for a loan, and Latinos were two times more likely. When they *were* approved, blacks and Latinos were 2.4 times more likely to receive a subprime loan than white applicants. The higher up the income ladder you compare white applicants and minorities, the wider this subprime disparity grows.[16]

The manner by which corporate crime specifically impacts women and LGBTQ people is often ignored. For example, criminologist Michael Lynch notes that **green criminology** has largely disregarded the victimization of women. Indeed, harm to both women and the environment is "accepted as routine outcomes associated with capitalist production,"[17] and a review of the literature indicates a lack of attention to these uneven outcomes. Patriarchy, by historically centering cisgender white males, has led to a structural absence of studies about the impact environmental pollutants have on women and LGBTQ people. Medical studies are scarce, and there is a general lack of interest in the results of those studies that do exist. When medical studies do include women, they often fail to analyze gender-specific differences. In fact, it was not until 1990 that the National Institutes of Health established an Office of Research on Women's Health, and not until 1994, when required by a congressional mandate, that the Food and Drug Administration created an Office of Women's Health.[18]

The inattention to gender and the consequences of that inattention are clear in clinical trials of pharmaceuticals. Bodies react differently to drugs based on a range of factors, including weight, muscle mass, body fat, hormone levels, and metabolic enzymes that regulate the breakdown of glucose and amino acids, as well as other essential bodily functions. In our present structural environment, it is not surprising that pharmaceuticals specifically created for women fail to be fully vetted. And when studies fail to consider the impact of gender, the outcomes can be deadly. The examples of diethylstibestrol (DES) and the Dalkon Shield are illustrative.

DES is a form of synthetic estrogen that was given to women who were considered to be at high risk of miscarriage. The drug was in use from 1938 to 1971. Pregnant women who were given this medication were told it was safe. In 1953, research found that the drug was not effective for its intended use, yet it continued to be prescribed until a study was published in 1971 that found it caused a rare form of vaginal cancer in daughters who had been exposed to DES in utero. This group of unwilling victims became known as DES daughters. Over time, other risks emerged, including reproductive tract deformities, pregnancy complications, and infertility. (Men exposed—DES sons—were also found to

CAUSATION
Legal concept that requires a direct link from the act committed to the harm caused.

SUBPRIME MORTGAGES
Deceptive lending practices, including loans with higher fees or loans incapable of being repaid, which end in foreclosure.

GREEN CRIMINOLOGY
Synergy between criminological theory and environment harms.

be at risk for noncancerous cysts.) According to the CDC, "researchers are still following the health of persons exposed to DES to determine whether other health problems occur as they grow older."[19]

The Dalkon Shield was an IUD (intrauterine contraception device) sold to an estimated 2.5 million women in the 1970s and 1980s. Many users described experiencing a pelvic infection known as pelvic inflammatory disease, or PID. The Dalkon Shield, while not the only cause of PID, was shown to cause the disease at a rate seven times that of women using no contraception.[20] In addition to PID, researchers discovered that the Dalkon Shield posed risks of infertility, unintended pregnancy, miscarriage, and even death. Though concerns began to be raised in the early 1970s, the Dalkon Shield remained on the market for another decade. Eventually over three hundred thousand women filed lawsuits against the shield's manufacturer, the A. H. Robins Company, and the company paid approximately $860 million before declaring bankruptcy in 1985.

Sexual Harassment and Gender Discrimination

Since the Industrial Revolution in the late 1700s, the workplace has been a male-dominated environment. For the better part of two hundred years, this order was maintained in a variety of ways. Enforcing the ideology of the "good home" left women who had no choice but to work—often immigrants, African Americans, and their children—feeling diminished and alienated. Moreover, employers were able to oppress working-class men by using the threat of female labor. However, perhaps the most effective tool for keeping many women out of the workplace was the notion that, away from the protection of the home, women's goodness was threatened. This was accomplished by men who "deployed sexual innuendo, demanded sexual quid pro quos, and intimidated women with aggressive sexual commentary about looks, dress, and body language."[21] The strategy was effective.

In 1964, the Civil Rights Act was passed by Congress, including Title VII, which prohibits discrimination in employment on the basis of sex, as well as race, religion, and national origin. It took a series of court cases to define sexual harassment. In the first case, *Williams v. Saxbe*,[22] the federal court recognized **quid pro quo harassment** requests as a form of gender-based discrimination. In *Bundy v. Jackson*,[23] Sandra Bundy described a workplace replete with supervisors making sexually suggestive comments and solicitations. When she refused advances, her work was criticized. While the lower court held that Title VII only applied to salary and other terms of employment, the D.C. Circuit Court reversed that decision and found that Bundy's rights were violated. The first sexual harassment case to reach the Supreme Court was *Meritor Savings Bank v. Vinson* in 1986.[24] Citing the sexual harassment guidelines issued by the U.S. Equal Employment Opportunity Commission (EEOC) in 1980, the court unanimously agreed that sexual harassment violates Title VII of the Civil Rights Act. And in the case of *Faragher v. City of Boca Raton*,[25] the Supreme Court held that the employer could be held liable for the harassing actions of its employees.

It is particularly notable that Black women were, and are, at the forefront of this challenge to sexual power. Williams, Bundy, Barnes, and Vinson were all Black, as were the

The Equal Employment Opportunity Commission (EEOC) defines sexual harassment as unwelcome sexual advances, requests for sexual favors, and other verbal or physical conduct of a sexual nature, when

(1) submission to such conduct is made either explicitly or implicitly a term or condition of an individual's employment;

(2) submission to or rejection of such conduct by an individual is used as the basis for employment decisions affecting such individual; or

(3) such conduct has the purpose or effect of unreasonably interfering with an individual's work performance or creating an intimidating, hostile, or offensive working environment.

QUID PRO QUO HARASSMENT
When an employer requires an employee to submit to unwelcome sexual advances, requests for sexual favors, or other verbal or physical conduct of a sexual nature as a condition of employment, either implicitly or explicitly.

women whose faces represent the two most socially solidifying acts of the past three decades. The term "sexual harassment" didn't gain general social recognition until 1991. That year, Clarence Thomas was nominated for a lifetime seat on the Supreme Court. Anita Hill was a young attorney who had served as an assistant to Thomas. His confirmation hearing had concluded when word of Hill's allegations emerged, forcing the hearings to reopen. Hill testified for days before the Senate Judiciary Committee. She described Thomas making inappropriate sexual references and clear sexual advances, all of which Hill alleged rose to the level of illegal sexual harassment. The hearing was televised, and the nation was enthralled. Thomas was narrowly confirmed despite the allegations.

In 2006, Tarana Burke, a civil rights activist, forged the #MeToo campaign, which would become a worldwide movement a decade later. Although others might have more name recognition, Burke was there first. She started the movement to provide support and solidarity for women of color, who are particularly targeted as victims of sexual harassment. In 2017, Burke's idea became popularized as #MeToo. Beginning in Hollywood, but extending around the world, women (and others) have been sharing stories of sexual harassment and sexual violence. The widespread and profound impact of sexual violence—in the workplace and in society—is evidenced by the continuing #MeToo postings.

Protections for discrimination based on sexual orientation and gender identity vary widely by state, with twenty-one states prohibiting discrimination in both public and private employment, fourteen states offering no protection, and the remaining states offering a limited range of protections. Federal protections are also uncertain and apparently easily reversed. President Obama signed multiple executive orders creating employment protection for LGBTQ people in federal employment and contracts. Those were all reversed by the subsequent administration. The EEOC has ruled that discrimination based on gender identity and sexual orientation are both forms of sex discrimination and therefore are prohibited by Title VII. A U.S. District Court ruling[26] concurred in a case that found that failure to promote based on nonconformity to gender expectations is at least sufficient to withstand a motion to dismiss. None of these were definitive until the Supreme Court ruled, and in a landmark ruling during the 2019–2020 session, *Bostock v. Clayton County*, the Court ruled that discrimination based on sexual orientation or gender identity is in violation of Title VII.[27]

The legal remedies for sexual harassment and discrimination (sexual violence is addressed in chapter 4 and throughout this text) may include job reinstatement or financial rewards for lost wages and other employment-related damages, as well as any demonstrable related expenses. Compensation for emotional harm or **punitive damages** is available under most laws but is much less common, especially against a corporate offender. In recent cases, courts have reduced jury verdicts for punitive damages from $1.3 million to $750,000[28] and from $1.7 million to $299,999.[29]

THE GENDERED IMPACT OF IMMIGRATION POLICY AND ENFORCEMENT

Immigration policy and immigration enforcement are prime examples of state power, and at no time in this country's history, since the abolition of chattel slavery, has the use and abuse of that power been more impactful than at the present moment. There are multiple ways that immigration enforcement under our current federal administration has aggravated women's vulnerability during the immigration encounter, as there are ways that women and those who are gender nonconforming have always been particularly at risk as migrants.

PUNITIVE DAMAGES
Legal damages that punish the litigant for bad behavior.

The first of the present vulnerabilities is the widespread policy of separating young children from their mothers. In the last two years, approximately 3,700 families have experienced separation when migrating into the United States, and roughly 500,000 children have had at least one parent apprehended or deported.[30] Not only do these separations have a profound effect on the children, but the parents, especially the mothers, who are often the primary caretaker, suffer great and often irreparable harm. There is evidence of ICE (Immigration and Customs Enforcement) agents using children, or the threat of permanent separation, as a tool to manipulate mothers to their own advantage.

Second is the lack of access to medical attention and feminine hygiene needs. For example, observers found evidence of increasing numbers of miscarriages in places of migrant detention on the U.S. border. Not only are there severe shortages of medical care available to women during migration and subsequent detention, but once settled, immigrant women are less likely to have access to health insurance and reproductive care than are U.S.-born women.

Third is the changing policies around granting asylum to victims of domestic violence. Historically, domestic violence was not considered grounds for granting asylum, but in 2014 the Board of Immigration Appeals granted asylum to a survivor, formally recognizing domestic violence as a form of persecution. However, in June 2018, then–attorney general Jeff Sessions imposed a ban on domestic violence claims (along with gang activity) as grounds for asylum. Six months later, a U.S. district judge ruled that the ban was illegal, but that only applies to the first phase of screening. Evidence suggests that the Sessions ban is having an impact on immigration courts' rulings.

Fourth, women have fewer legal or legitimate options for migration, as they are less likely to be educated in desirable STEM fields and often have fewer sophisticated market skills to offer. As a result, they arrive as dependents and must rely on their husbands for support.

And fifth is the constant risk of sexual assault and sex trafficking—risks posed by other migrants as well as staff and ICE officers. "ICE has reported 1,310 claims of sexual abuse against detainees from fiscal years 2013 to 2017. . . . Watchdog organizations estimate the occurrence of sexual abuse to be significantly higher."[31] According to the Women's Legal Defense and Education Fund, screening of girls for sexual abuse or trafficking, as policy requires, is not being conducted.

This risk of sexual assault is particularly acute for gender nonconforming people, whose very existence may be seen as a threat to those in power or those seeking power. During detention, transgender women are disproportionately detained, often with men, leaving them at increased risk of sexual assault, or placed in solitary confinement so that ICE doesn't have to take other steps to protect them. Additional evidence shows that trans women may not be provided with necessary life-saving medical interventions and are statistically less likely to be granted asylum.[32]

While many of the challenges facing women also impact LGBTQ people, there are unique impacts as well. The Williams Institute at the UCLA School of Law estimated in 2013 that there were at least 267,000 undocumented people in the United States who identified as LGBTQ.[33] Despite recent changes in marriage laws, undocumented people are unable to marry, even when their partner is documented. And the lack of protection for LGBTQ people in employment, housing, and health care is exaggerated for those without documentation.

In the next chapter, we look more closely at the criminalization of parenting and reproduction.

1. Explain "quality-of-life" policing. How and why does this model of policing create communities that are particularly vulnerable to police abuse?

2. Why are women and people of color historically ignored when it comes to medical testing and pharmaceutical trials?

3. How could we design an immigration policy to minimize the negative impacts on the most vulnerable populations?

GOING FURTHER

Readings:

Dodge, Mary. "Women: White-Collar Offending and Victimization," Oxford Handbooks Online, May 2016, https://www.oxfordhandbooks.com/view/10.1093/ox fordhb/9780199935383.001.0001/oxfordhb-978019 9935383-e-108.

Gross, Kali Nicole. "Policing Black Women's and Black Girls' Bodies in the Carceral United States." *Souls* 20, no. 1 (2018): 1–13, http://doi.org/10.1080/10999949 .2018.1520058.

Websites:

Gender Inequality and Women in the Workplace. https://www.summer.harvard.edu/inside-summer /gender-inequality-women-workplace.

Videos/Movies:

Heilbroner, David, and Kate Davis. *Stonewall Uprising*. First Run Features, 2010. https://www.pbs.org /wgbh/americanexperience/films/stonewall.

KEY TERMS

causation Legal concept that requires a direct link from the act committed to the harm caused.

corporate crime Refers to crimes committed by a corporation or other business entity, or by individuals acting on behalf of a corporation or business.

green criminology Synergy between criminological theory and environment harms.

policing power Absent a federal law, the fundamental authority of a state government to make laws to control and regulate behavior and enforce order; often manifested and abused by the police.

punitive damages Legal damages that punish the litigant for bad behavior.

quality-of-life policing Heavily policing normally noncriminal activities and minor offenses (congregating, drinking in public spaces, graffiti, public urination, panhandling, littering, and unlicensed street vending), theorizing that those behaviors will lead to serious crime.

quid pro quo harassment When an employer requires an employee to submit to unwelcome sexual advances, requests for sexual favors, or other verbal or physical conduct of a sexual nature as a condition of employment, either implicitly or explicitly.

subprime mortgages Deceptive lending practices, including loans with higher fees or loans incapable of being repaid, which end in foreclosure.

white-collar crime A broad term that typically refers to any crime associated with work or the workplace.

NOTES

[1] "Fatal Force," *Washington Post*, last updated May 17, 2021, https://www.washingtonpost.com/graphics/investigations/po lice-shootings-database.

[2] Brentin Mock, "What New Research Says about Race and Police Shootings," City Lab, August 6, 2019, https://www .citylab.com/equity/2019/08/police-officer-shootings-gun-vio lence-racial-bias-crime-data/595528.

[3] "Mapping Police Violence," accessed October 7, 2019, https://mappingpoliceviolence.org.

[4] "Law Enforcement Misconduct," U.S. Department of Justice, accessed October 7, 2019, https://www.justice.gov/crt /law-enforcement-misconduct.

[5] Henry Wallace Police Crime Database, accessed October 7, 2019, https://policecrime.bgsu.edu.

[6] Philip M. Stinson, "Police Shootings Data: What We Know and What We Don't Know," *Criminal Justice Faculty Publications* 78 (2017), https://scholarworks.bgsu.edu/crim_just _pub/78.

[7] Bobby Allyn, "Amber Guyger, Ex-Officer Who Killed Man in His Apartment, Given 10 Years in Prison," NPR, October 2, 2019, https://www.npr.org/2019/10/02/766454839/amber -guyger-ex-officer-who-killed-man-in-his-apartment-given-10 -years-in-prison.

[8] Leanor Boulin Johnson, *On the Front Lines: Police Stress and Family Well-Being*, Hearing before the Select Committee on Children, Youth, and Families, House of Representatives, 102d Congress, 1st Sess. (May 20, 1991), 32–48, https://eric .ed.gov/?id=ED338997.

[9] Rachel Aviv, "What If Your Abusive Husband Is a Cop?," *New Yorker*, October 7, 2019.

10 Naomi G. Goldberg et al., "Police and the Criminalization of LGBT People," in *The Cambridge Handbook of Policing in the United States*, ed. Tamara Rice Lave and Eric J. Miller, 374–91 (Cambridge: Cambridge University Press, 2019).

11 Ben Stickle, "A National Examination of the Effect of Education, Training and Pre-Employment Screening on Law Enforcement Use of Force," *Justice Policy Journal* 13, no. 1 (Spring 2016): 1–15, http://www.cjcj.org/uploads/cjcj/documents/jpj_education_use_of_force.pdf.

12 See, for example, the Vera Institute for Justice, https://www.vera.org/centers/policing, and the Advancement Project, https://advancementproject.org/the-change-we-need-5-issues-that-should-be-part-of-efforts-to-reform-policing-in-local-communities.

13 Ben Lane, "Finally: $8.5B Countrywide Mortgage Bond Settlement Gets Green Light," *Housing Wire*, May 13, 2016, https://www.housingwire.com/articles/37033-finally-85b-countrywide-mortgage-bond-settlement-gets-green-light.

14 Phil Mattera, "17 of the Worst Corporate Crimes of 2015," *AlterNet*, December 18, 2015, https://www.alternet.org/2015/12/17-worst-corporate-crimes-2015.

15 "Major Criminal Cases," U.S. Environmental Protection Agency, accessed September 17, 2019, https://www.epa.gov/enforcement/2016-major-criminal-cases.

16 As cited in Emily Badger, "The Dramatic Racial Bias of Subprime Lending during the Housing Boom," *City Lab*, August 16, 2013, https://www.citylab.com/equity/2013/08/blacks-really-were-targeted-bogus-loans-during-housing-boom/6559.

17 Michael J. Lynch, "Acknowledging Female Victims of Green Crimes: Environmental Exposure of Women to Industrial Pollutants," *Feminist Criminology* 13, no. 4 (2018): 404–27, 409.

18 Katherine A. Liu and Natalie A. Dipietro Mager, "Women's Involvement in Clinical Trials: Historical Perspective and Future Implications," *Pharmacy Practice* 14, no. 1 (2016): 708, http://doi.org/10.18549/PharmPract.2016.01.708.

19 "About DES," U.S. Department of Health and Human Services, Centers for Disease Control and Prevention, accessed October 3, 2019, https://www.cdc.gov/des/consumers/about/index.html.

20 Gina Kolata, "The Sad Legacy of the Dalkon Shield," *New York Times Magazine*, December 12, 1987, https://www.nytimes.com/1987/12/06/magazine/the-sad-legacy-of-the-dalkon-shield.html.

21 Alice Kessler-Harris, "The Long History of Workplace Sexual Harassment," *Jacobin*, March 23, 2018, https://www.jacobinmag.com/2018/03/metoo-workplace-discrimination-sexual-harassment-feminism.

22 *Williams v. Saxbe*, 413 F.Supp. 654 (1976).

23 *Bundy v. Jackson*, 641 F.2d 934 (D.C. Cir. 1981).

24 *Meritor Savings Bank v. Vinson*, 477 U.S. 57, (1986).

25 *Faragher v. City of Boca Raton*, 524 U.S. 775 (1998).

26 *Terveer v. Billington*, Civil Action No. 2012-1290 (D.D.C. 2014).

27 *Gerald Lynn Bostock v. Clayton County*, Georgia, 590 U.S. ___ (2020).

28 *Quinby v. Westlb AG*, 245 F.R.D. 94 (S.D.N.Y. 2006).

29 *Mayo-Coleman v. American Sugars Holdings Inc.*, No. 1:2014cv00079—Document 195 (S.D.N.Y. 2018).

30 "Recent Immigration Policies Negatively Affect Women." Women's Legal Defense and Education Fund, July 17, 2018, https://www.legalmomentum.org/blog/recent-immigration-policies-negatively-affect-women.

31 Emily Kassle, "Sexual Assault inside ICE Detention: 2 Survivors Tell Their Stories," *New York Times*, July 17, 2018, https://www.nytimes.com/2018/07/17/us/sexual-assault-ice-detention-survivor-stories.html.

32 Janet Arelis Quezada, "Transgender Immigrants Not Safe in Detention Centers," September 22, 2015, https://www.glaad.org/blog/transgender-immigrants-not-safe-us-detention-centers.

33 Gary J. Gates, "LGBT Adult Immigrants in the United States," March 2013, https://williamsinstitute.law.ucla.edu/research/census-lgbt-demographics-studies/us-lgbt-immigrants-mar-2013.

Pregnancy, Birthing, and Rearing

"Damned If You Do, Damned If You Don't"

This chapter introduces you to a wide range of legal issues surrounding parenting, specifically focusing on the ways in which women are criminalized for their parenting choices. Topics include the proscription of ordinary acts of parenting and regulating pregnancy. The chapter concludes with a look at fathers.

LEARNING OBJECTIVES

After reading this chapter, you should be able to do the following:

- Articulate laws designed to regulate parenting.
- Describe the development of laws regarding pregnancy and abortion.
- Identify the various issues related to childbirth and their impact on different populations.
- Evaluate the impact of models of parental fitness.

Case #11: Regina McKnight

Until 1998, Regina McKnight and her three very young children lived with McKnight's mother in Horry County, South Carolina. Because of mental illness and some degree of impaired cognition, McKnight had never been able to live independently and relied on her mother to act as a caretaker for her and her children. When her mother passed away in 1998, though McKnight was a legal adult at twenty-one years old, it was clear to her that she was in no position to care for her children on her own. No longer able to live in her mother's house and lacking employment, McKnight sent her children to live with relatives so the children would not have to endure the instability she knew was coming.

Soon after her mother's death, homeless and jobless, McKnight began to use crack cocaine. The fact that she was living rough and lacked the capability to hold consistent employment and provide for herself financially made her vulnerable to predatory and abusive relationships, and from one of these relationships, she became pregnant.

On May 15, 1999, at twenty-two years of age, McKnight gave birth—the baby was stillborn. The pregnancy had not gone fully to term—it was estimated that she was at about thirty-four to thirty-seven weeks pregnant when she went into labor. South Carolina state law dictates that, in the case of a stillbirth, the mother must take a drug test, and an initial urine test showed that there was benzoylecgonine in her system, a by-product of cocaine use. As a result of the urine test, a nurse was required to secure McKnight's consent for a second test that was meant to definitively confirm the presence of cocaine in her system. Neither McKnight nor the nurse requesting consent were clear about the potential legal consequences if the test came back positive, so the nurse was not able to ensure that the terms of consent were clear to McKnight. Nevertheless, McKnight agreed to the test. She and the fetus were both tested, and in both cases, the tests came back positive for traces of cocaine use. The doctor that performed and interpreted the results of the autopsy on the fetus estimated that the fetus had likely died in the day or two before birth but did not indicate whether or not the fetus would have been otherwise "viable," or able to survive outside the womb. The positive results of the drug test on both mother and fetus meant that the hospital was obliged to notify Horry County police.

Police responding to the call charged McKnight with homicide by child abuse, on the grounds that, they stated, McKnight had murdered the fetus because of the use of crack cocaine during her pregnancy. Had McKnight miscarried due to drug use or terminated the pregnancy prior to viability, the charge would not have existed. Instead, it was the fact that she intended to carry the pregnancy to term that led to the charge, as the question of whether the fetus was "viable" and therefore potentially classified by the court as a "child" was now relevant. According to South Carolina law, the charge of homicide by child abuse applies to any person who "causes the death of a child under the age of eleven while committing child abuse or neglect and the death occurs under circumstances manifesting an extreme indifference to human life."[1] That McKnight faced this charge indicated that the fetus, despite having never lived outside the womb, was being classified as a child for the purpose of the charge and the forthcoming conviction.

South Carolina had a history of prosecuting mothers who were drug users, as well as recognizing unborn fetuses as people. Since the mid-1980s, unborn fetuses have been recognized as people in the case of murder, and since the late 1980s, state laws had begun to call for the arrest of any woman who gave birth but was found to have drugs in her system. In 1997, a precedent had been set for greater individual rights being granted to the fetus and for any fetus that was deemed viable to be treated by the court as a child. McKnight's case had the potential to set an even clearer precedent and potentially change the understanding of South Carolina state law, and her case went to the South Carolina Supreme Court. The common-law definition of "person" and "child" in South Carolina (and elsewhere), after all, does not automatically include viable fetuses, but it is clear in the words of the court that this was the use of "child" that was being employed in the McKnight case. Judge James Brogdon, who was presiding over the trial, told the jury clearly, "I tell you that under South Carolina law a viable fetus is a child."[2] The prosecutor also stated that he had decided to classify the viable fetus as a child. This indicates that both the judge and the prosecutor felt the need to clearly set the terms for the understanding of "child" during McKnight's trial, which would certainly affect the outcome of not only her trial but potentially subsequent similar trials as well.

Despite the fact that McKnight showed signs of mental illness and an inability to care for herself, the court decided that she was fit to stand trial. She reportedly had an IQ of only seventy-two, which indicates impaired cognition, and friends and acquaintances note that, based on their observations, she was perhaps even more impaired than this score might indicate. From the very beginning of the trial, it was clear that McKnight was facing a likely conviction. Testimonies came from the obstetrician that had delivered the baby, the pathologist who had performed the autopsy on the fetus as well as two other pathologists brought in as experts, a nurse who had tended to McKnight during and after the labor, and a social worker who had been assigned to McKnight's case and could testify to her use of crack cocaine.

The prosecutor argued that McKnight was neither capable of acting as a loving parent nor interested in caring for the child; otherwise, he argued, she would have stopped using drugs. This argument assumed that she was both capable of beating an addiction while having very few resources to do so and that she was consciously aware of and dismissive of the effects of drug use during a pregnancy. Despite the fact that South Carolina has a very poor record nationally for both drug rehabilitation and infant mortality, the fact that her options and resources were limited by homelessness and poverty was also not taken into consideration, nor did the court proceedings address the question of what the options may have been for education, treatment, and support for a woman in McKnight's position. Instead, she was characterized as malicious, uncaring, and pathetic; as an irresponsible absentee mother for the three children she already had; and as an immoral and promiscuous woman. This latter part of the argument was based on the fact that McKnight, at the time of the trial, was pregnant once again. The jury was susceptible to this narrative, as well as to the narrative that crack cocaine is especially and egregiously harmful to pregnancies—an argument about which there is still debate—and the proceedings did not engage with other salient questions surrounding McKnight's character, actions, and circumstances. The fact that she had been deemed essentially mentally disabled in school, that she was low functioning to the extent that she had never been able to hold a steady job, that her other three children were stable and healthy in the homes of McKnight's relatives, and that she had knowingly placed them there for their own well-being—none of this was part of the characterization of McKnight.

Also omitted from the trial was the fact that it had been a counselor at a drug treatment center that had impregnated McKnight this most recent time, a fact that attests to her social and mental vulnerability: she had gone to counseling after a first attempt to prosecute her had ended with a mistrial, and instead of finding the help she needed to address her trauma, she became pregnant. She had, in fact, tried to seek treatment a few times and had never successfully been able to access dependable counseling, for a number of bureaucratic and financial reasons. Even amid homelessness and abusive relationships, and even considering her disabilities, McKnight had tried to take proactive steps, only to be faced with obstacles that she was not able to navigate and a treatment counselor who had taken advantage of her vulnerable position.

The prosecution argued that McKnight was visibly disinterested in the trial proceedings, which, they said, indicated that she was remorseless. Testimony from hospital nurses, however, indicated that McKnight had mourned the loss of her baby as any mother would have; she held the baby and wanted photographs with which to remember her.

Meanwhile, McKnight's defense team focused on prior precedents to argue that the statutes and codes clearly indicated that a "child" does not include "viable" fetuses, and that though it had been interpreted as such in the past, the court had not actually changed the definition of "child,"

meaning that in this case, McKnight could not be convicted of homicide. The definition of "viability" had to be examined, as well, they argued—if "viable" means able to survive outside of the womb, this is an impossible conclusion to draw about a fetus that had not displayed its ability to do such a thing. They argued that since this homicide classification depended on an unwritten definition of "child," McKnight's rights to due process were being violated, as the severity of her actions were not known to her and she could not have displayed "an extreme indifference to human life" that would be necessary to call for a conviction for homicide. Finally, her team argued that "the application of the homicide by child abuse statute to pregnant women who give birth to still born fetuses violates the equal protection clause of the Fourteenth Amendment in three distinct ways—(1) it unlawfully distinguishes between pregnant and non-pregnant persons; (2) it discriminates based on gender by subjecting women to enhanced penalties; and most importantly, (3) it discriminates based on race, as Black women experience significantly more stillbirths each year than white women, making them significantly more vulnerable to prosecution."[3] For all of these reasons, they argued, the jury should recognize that McKnight was being unlawfully targeted.

It took the jury less than fifteen minutes to reach their verdict: guilty of homicide by child abuse. McKnight was sentenced to twenty years in prison, with Judge Brogdon reducing the sentence to twelve years with no chance of parole. McKnight was the first woman to be convicted of this particular crime for the death of an unborn fetus. The decision hinged primarily on the belief that she should have known of the potentially deleterious effects of crack cocaine and that she had behaved in a consciously reckless way, all of which added up to criminal intent. The decision did not take into account some of the potentially mitigating circumstances—McKnight's lack of prior convictions, her mental ability, or the state of mind she was in following the death of her mother. It also arguably overlooked McKnight's right to reproductive privacy and focused instead on her use of crack cocaine, which was clearly not a given or protected right.

After the conviction, the prosecutor used the fact that McKnight was once again pregnant to argue that he had saved a life through this verdict, when in actuality prison is not proven to be a healthy place for pregnancy. Judge James Brogdon told McKnight after the conviction, "At least with 12 years hopefully you can get beyond this substance problem that you have and no[t] be a threat to yourself or to any children that you might carry,"[4] similarly overlooking the fact that meaningful counseling and treatment may not be available in prison.

In 2002, McKnight and her legal team tried to revisit and appeal the verdict based once again on the use of "child" in the decision, but the court upheld the conviction, arguing that the interpretation of the word "child" could here include a viable fetus. An appeal to the U.S. Supreme Court to review the case was rejected.

A number of organizations continued to advocate for McKnight, including the Drug Policy Alliance, National Advocates for Pregnant Women, the American Civil Liberties Union, the South Carolina Medical Association, the South Carolina Nurses Association, the South Carolina Association of Alcohol and Drug Abuse Counselors, and the South Carolina Coalition for Healthy Families. Regionally and nationally, voices from the legal and medical professions protested the trial proceedings and results.

In 2008, McKnight's case was once again revisited. Susan Dunn, counsel on an *amicus* or "friend of the court" brief that was put together by various organizations advocating for McKnight, appealed to the South Carolina Supreme Court, arguing that the opinion of McKnight's advocates "acknowledges that current research simply does not support the assumption that prenatal exposure to cocaine results in harm to the fetus, and the opinion makes clear that it is certainly 'no more harmful to a fetus than nicotine use, poor nutrition, lack of prenatal care, or other conditions commonly associated with the urban poor.' . . . This decision puts solicitors [prosecutors] across the state on notice that they must actually prove that an illegal drug has risked or caused harm—not simply rely on prejudice and medical misinformation."[5] In addition to this factual error, they argued, there had been legal errors as well: the defense for McKnight had not presented expert testimony that might have remedied the overemphasis on McKnight's use of crack cocaine; they had not themselves investigated the veracity of the prosecution's evidence that argued with certainty that crack cocaine was the cause of the stillbirth; and they had not challenged the determination of the prosecution or the court that McKnight's intent was clear. Finally, in a general sense, those that appealed to the court argued that the South Carolina policies that lead to the arrest of pregnant women who are using drugs does more to dissuade women from seeking prenatal care than it does to deter them from using drugs in the first place.

In May 2008, the South Carolina Supreme Court determined finally that McKnight's trial had not been fair, and they overturned the conviction. Rather than go through yet another trial, McKnight pleaded guilty to involuntary manslaughter. This plea meant a shorter sentence, and given the time that she had already served, McKnight was released from prison in June 2008.

THINKING CRITICALLY ABOUT THE CASE

1. How might McKnight's impaired abilities have contributed to each step of her eventual case, from pregnancy to imprisonment?

2. Should the fact that McKnight's other children were well cared for have been used in her defense? Why or why not?

3. How do gender disparities come into play in cases such as these that involve drug use and pregnancy?

REFERENCES

This case is adapted from the following sources:

Bhargava, Shalini. "Challenging Punishment and Privatization: A Response to the Conviction of Regina McKnight." *Harvard Civil Rights–Civil Liberties Law Review* 39 (2004): 513–42.

Green, Sharon. "Regina McKnight Released from Prison." ABC 15 WPDE, June 19, 2008. http://wpde.com/news/videos /regina-mcknight-released-from-prison.

Page, Dana. "The Homicide by Child Abuse Conviction of Regina McKnight." *Howard Law Journal* 46 (2003): 363–403.

Paltrow, Lynn, and Tony Newman. "South Carolina Supreme Court Reverses 20-Year Homicide Conviction of Regina McKnight." Drug Policy Alliance Press Release, May 11, 2008. http://www .drugpolicy.org/news/2008/05/south-carolina-supreme-court-re verses-20-year-homicide-conviction-regina-mcknight.

South Carolina Code of Laws Title 16—Crimes and Offenses. Ch. 3: Offenses against the Person, Article 1: Homicide, § 16-3-85. https://www.scstatehouse.gov/code/t16c003.php.

CONTEXT AND ANALYSIS

As we saw in the Regina McKnight case, the behavior and choices that women make, before, during, and after pregnancy, have been subject to increasing surveillance, social and legal judgment, and sometimes—indeed all too often—even prosecution. And while men are occasionally caught in this web (as we later address in this chapter), they are often given a pass. This is true even where, as in some instances of intimate partner abuse, the victim—the woman—is charged with abuse, neglect, or worse. The case of Hedda Nussbaum in chapter 3 illustrates this point.

This chapter begins with a look at the many ways in which society criminalizes parenthood, especially the ways in which that criminalization is biased and racialized. Next, we explore the regulation of pregnancy, including conception, sterilization, and abortion, as well as surrogacy and reproductive technologies. Included in this discussion is the impact of parenthood for LGBTQ people. And finally, we consider the "father's rights movement" and the implications it has for both distributing and controlling parenting.

Criminalizing Parenthood

A woman is arrested for leaving her child at home alone so she can go to a job interview. Another mother is arrested for leaving her sleeping baby in a stroller outside a restaurant while she went inside, where, she says, she never lost sight of the stroller. A woman leaves her child in a locked car, on what she describes as a comfortably cool day, while she runs a quick errand. Someone takes a picture and sends it to the police, and she gets charged with "contributing to the delinquency of a minor." A woman who is eight months pregnant attempts suicide; she lives, but the fetus does not. She is charged with murder and attempted feticide (killing of a fetus). And yet another woman, not even aware she is pregnant, miscarries alone at home. Not knowing what to do, she puts the fetus in a bag in the trash. When it is discovered, it is turned over to the police who use the DNA of the fetus to track her. A 2013 study by Paltrow and Flavin found over 380 cases of women charged with crimes following a miscarriage between 1973 and 2005.[6] A pregnant woman, mother of two, falls down the stairs in her home. Upon visiting the emergency room, she is reported to the police and charged with "attempted feticide"; she spends two nights in jail. These are all real cases, and there are many more examples of the ways in which laws and local norms have made criminal these acts of coping, survival, struggle, or just choosing how to parent.

Cultural differences in child rearing could result in child services intervention, and ultimately even the loss of the child. When a social worker enters another's home, it is often a challenge to leave their personal judgments about dress, cleanliness, and discipline behind. Teachers, as well, often misjudge family behaviors. Culturally, differences that exist around discipline and medical interventions may cause the most problems for a parent. One medical practice that has had negative consequences for the family is cupping. Cupping is a practice where cups are placed on the skin to improve circulation. The cup leaves a temporary mark or scrape on the skin. Teachers not familiar with the treatment have mistaken the scars and reported the parents for child abuse.

Data indicates that about 15 percent of children may be "chronically absent" from school, meaning two or more days a month. And while there is general agreement that attending school is good for children, truancy occurs for a wide range of reasons, some beyond the control of the parent. The Marshall Project conducted a study of truancy and the U.S. criminal legal system.[7] While it is difficult to identify reliable national data, state and local data indicate the extent of the issue. In Berks County, Pennsylvania, more than 1,600 parents, mostly mothers, have been incarcerated for failing to pay fines related to truancy. One mother died while in jail. The city of Atlanta passed an ordinance that could result in parents paying a $1,000 fine or spending up to sixty days in jail when their child skips school.[8] Atlanta also refers parents directly to the courts if their child has ten absences. In one month during the fall of 2014, police in Jacksonville, Florida, issued

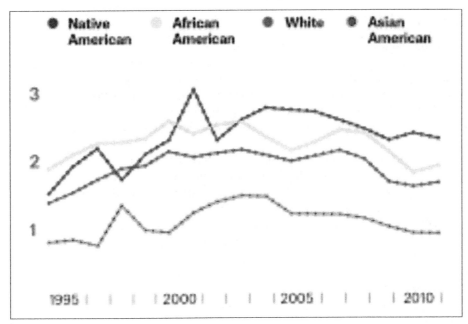

Figure 11.1.   Truancy rates by ethnicity per 1,000 people.
Dana Goldstein, "Inexcusable Absences," New Republic, March 6, 2015, retrieved September 10, 2019, https://newrepublic.com /article/121186/truancy-laws-unfairly-attack-poor-children-and -parents

forty-four arrest warrants related to truancy, charging parents with contributing to the delinquency of a minor. In one case in West Virginia, a child who had been suspended from school was accused of truancy. Enforcement of truancy laws has a discriminatory impact on poor families and families of color, where rates of absence and suspension are higher and fewer resources are available to prevent state intervention.

One of the most significant threats to women has come from those individuals and laws that assert personhood for an embryo or fetus. Fetal rights are based on the idea that the fetus, which is living inside a woman, receiving nourishment from her, is an independent entity with rights of its own, even when those rights are in conflict with the body housing it. Fetal protection statutes come in many forms. Thirty-eight states recognize the fetus or "unborn child" as a potential homicide victim; in at least twenty-nine of those states, the laws apply from conception.[9] In some instances, legislatures amend existing statutes to include the fetus; in others, entirely new statutes are created, for example penalizing injury to a pregnant woman. Whatever form the legislation takes, the result is to shift the balance of rights away from the woman. In 1987 Janet Gallagher wrote, "No state interest described by fetal rights advocates has enough force to override a woman's fundamental rights of privacy, bodily integrity, and self-determination. . . . Until the child is brought forth from the woman's body, our relationship with it must be mediated by her,"[10] warning us that a woman and her fetus cannot and should not be regarded as separate entities, lest the two become adversaries.

Not all criminal charges arise from affirmative acts on the part of the pregnant woman. In the case of Marshae Jones, for example, she was shot while she was pregnant, and she lost the fetus. She was charged with manslaughter; the person who actually pulled the trigger was not charged. The theory of the case, according to a police lieutenant from Pleasant Grove, Alabama, was that it is the mother's responsibility to protect the unborn fetus.[11]

The idea of fetal rights became popularized during what was considered the "crack epidemic" of the 1980s. Powder cocaine was a popular intoxicant in the 1970s. It was expensive in powder form; converting it to a solid form and breaking it into rocks allowed for smaller quantities to be sold at lower prices. Once prices were lowered, the drug, now called "crack," was heavily marketed in urban areas and became popular among those with less money. It was reportedly highly addictive. During the 1980s and 1990s, more babies were being born that tested positive for the presence of cocaine. They were referred to as "crack babies" and led to a national panic. There was a fear that "crack babies" would be permanently damaged and would need a lifetime of care. The realities were many and varied. It was often impossible to determine whether a newborn's maladies were caused by the drug rather than other maternal circumstances—poor diet, cigarette use, alcohol use, and most notably lack of prenatal care, which many avoided out of fear of being reported for their drug use. Perhaps more importantly, the damage caused by crack itself was vastly overblown. The myth of "crack babies" included an expectation of permanent brain damage. What some researchers knew at the time and as has been validated in recent studies is that many of the exposed children have grown into fully functioning adults.[12] Unfortunately, the same cannot be said for **fetal alcohol syndrome**, which has been proven to cause irreparable damage to the fetus.

Ignoring the realities, the national panic led to increased testing of pregnant women for drug use, especially at public hospitals that serve the poor. Testing led to stigmatization and all too often to criminal prosecution. And where the laws didn't exist to charge a woman with harming the body growing within her, new laws were proposed. While these laws and beliefs endanger the rights of all women—and men—the impact is disproportionately experienced by poor women and women of color. Black women comprise 52 percent of the cases reported in the Paltrow and Flavin study, while seven out of ten of the women charged could not afford attorneys.

Pitting the rights of the embryo against those of the woman carrying it has the potential to lead to policing of more mundane behaviors as well. Should a pregnant woman be arrested for having a cigarette, a drink, a hot bath? Can a woman be required to eat a healthy diet or drink a glass of milk? Suggesting any behaviors are the best option might be helpful or annoying, and they can vary. What constitutes proper nutrition and appropriate weight gain during pregnancy has changed over the years. Requiring that a pregnant woman follow rules that are not law, and do not apply to others, violates a woman's right to privacy, autonomy, and agency and assumes that she is not able to make wise and correct decisions for herself.

Luckily for Hedda Nussbaum (chapter 3 case study), New York State didn't have a **failure to protect** law. In some states, IPV is considered to be failure to protect, triggering child endangerment or neglect charges. While it is never good for children to place them in difficult or potentially dangerous situations, research suggests that the long-term impact of witnessing IPV varies greatly from child to child, and in the vast majority (78 percent) of children, the detriment may be considered within the range of normal stressors.[13] Despite this, and despite the fact that there is no evidence that punishing the parent or removing the child from the home aids the child, states use these laws to charge women with crimes. For the women, they are being punished for being victimized. The punishments have been severe, with sentences as long as thirty years for a mother in Oklahoma[14] to forty-five years for a mother in Texas.[15] In 2016, the National Council of Juvenile and Family Court Judges revised their recommendations[16] to advise judges that they should view victims of IPV as "partners" in protecting their children and that punishing the parent only serves to revictimize them.

Men are not able to escape the scrutiny of parenting either. Accusations of child abuse and homicide are aimed at both parents and are especially overblown if you are a racial or ethnic minority.[17] Children experience trauma during play and other routine activities. The results of that trauma are often not evident for a day or two, until a lump or bruise develops that the parent notices. For most parents, they can take their child to the emergency room or doctor's office and receive advice and sympathy. But if you are Black or Latino, there is a much greater risk that you will be interrogated about the cause of the injury and reported to children's services or charged with abuse.

At the extreme end of abuse is **shaken baby syndrome**, or SBS. SBS causes permanent brain damage and may result in death. These tragic results are sometimes the result of

FETAL ALCOHOL SYNDROME
A condition that results from alcohol exposure during a mother's pregnancy, which is believed to cause brain damage and other possible birth defects.

FAILURE TO PROTECT LAWS
Laws created to protect children from the influence of intimate violence by criminalizing those who fail to remove a child from any home where violence is occurring.

SHAKEN BABY SYNDROME
A brain injury diagnosed in infants and toddlers who are injured or die as a result of forceful shaking.

intentional action, sometimes of neglect. An example of the latter might be using an old baby car seat that doesn't offer proper support. Whether intentional or not, parents may be charged with abuse or homicide when a child is diagnosed with resulting injuries. Recent scientific research has shown that SBS is overdiagnosed, that many of the symptoms previously identified as SBS appear in cases where SBS is not present. Many, as it turns out, have been falsely accused and convicted. An investigation conducted by the *Washington Post* found 1,600 SBS cases since 2001 where parents or caregivers faced criminal charges, including three on death row. Sixteen of those cases have been overturned in the past few years. In 2017, a man in California had his 2001 conviction overturned. He had been an eighteen-year-old father at the time of the infant's death. He reports accidentally dropping the baby while taking a shower. Witnesses testified that he was a good father, but the three "expert" witnesses testified that the injury could only have been the result of repeated shaking, not a short fall. He was sentenced to twenty-five years to life until the court was asked to reconsider based on the changing views of the medical community.[18] The next year, a Montana man was released after serving years in prison for the 2008 death of his son after his attorneys showed the court that the autopsy found the cause of death to be "undetermined." That same year, a judge in Mississippi overturned the death sentence of a man convicted in 2002 after hearing evidence challenging the validity of SBS. Uncertain medical science should not be sufficient to sustain criminal prosecution.

From Regulating Conception to Forcing Pregnancy and Sterilization

In 1965, the Supreme Court ruled, in the case of *Griswold v. Connecticut*,[19] that states had no right to ban contraception. In so doing, they established a constitutional **right to privacy**. In 1973, in the case of *Roe v. Wade*,[20] the Court ruled that this right to privacy also protects a woman's right to choose to have an abortion, without excessive government regulation. Despite the Supreme Court cases that define reproduction as a matter of privacy and choice, every aspect of reproduction is regulated either by state laws designed to restrict access to birth control options, federal legislation that limits funding or allows insurance to exempt entire categories of women's health care, or the Supreme Court, which upholds a great many of these laws. This government regulation is especially impactful for women, and men, with limited resources.

Contraception, Abortion, and the Embryo

The Court's ruling that contraception could not be banned did not at the same time create a right for access to such services. However, the Affordable Care Act, passed in 2010, provides that preventative health care, including women's health care, will be covered by insurance without out-of-pocket costs, and since 2012, that has been considered to include all FDA-approved forms of contraception. What about those who are still without insurance or are covered by Medicaid? In 1970, Congress passed the Title X Family Planning Program, which provides grants to clinical sites, especially those serving low-income clients, including both public health departments and nonprofit health care providers.

Contraceptive coverage policies and legislation continue to fluctuate. Since 2017, there have been efforts made to allow for exceptions to providing insurance for contraception based on moral or religious grounds, and for those exceptions to be available to all but government employers. As of this writing, the courts have blocked these efforts, but there are ongoing attempts to reduce requirements for fair access to contraception. In 2019, for instance, the administration created what is being called the Title X gag order, which is meant to prohibit those receiving Title X funding from counseling patients regarding their medical reproduction-related needs and alternatives if one of those alternatives is abortion. As a result of this "gag order," Planned Parenthood, which serves 41 percent of all Title X recipients, elected to no longer receive federal funding. According to Planned Parenthood, the "gag order" was not the first attempt to weaken Title X; since 2018, the administration had been trying "to push people toward abstinence programs or fertility

RIGHT TO PRIVACY
The right to privacy, as defined by *Griswold v. Connecticut*, says that the state may not unreasonably interfere with an individual's right to make a choice about matters considered private, such as health care and sexuality.

awareness methods (like the 'rhythm method' or 'calendar method') instead of more effective forms of birth control like the pill, the birth control shot, or IUDs." As of 2021, the current administration has announced its intention to begin to dismantle the "gag order" and restore pre-2019 regulatory frameworks.[21]

Despite continuing attempts to defund Planned Parenthood, in 2019 they were scheduled to receive about $60 million in Title X funds, with about a third of their overall funding coming from Title X and Medicaid funds. They continued to serve as a primary source of contraception for large numbers of girls and women, especially those without primary care doctors and with limited resources. According to TalkPoverty.org, "85% of [Planned Parenthood's] clients have an income at or below 150% of the federal poverty level."[22] In response to the so-called gag rule, they say they will no longer accept Title X funds if it means not providing complete medical care without constraints between the provider and client. While much of this seems only indirectly related to the legal and criminal issues of gender, a continued reading illustrates how the provision of contraception services is part of the control and criminalization of women's behavior.

Prior to 1973, women in the United States got abortions. If you had money, you traveled; if you didn't, you might have tried self-abortive measures or gone to someone who may or may not have been trained to conduct medical procedures. Some died, some lived with physical scars, and many just continued on with their lives. Then came *Roe v. Wade*, and it settled the legal questions surrounding abortion, forbidding states from limiting women's legal access to abortions with unreasonable restrictions. What followed was a backlash that has lasted nearly four decades and continues to become increasingly virulent.[23] States have been trying to limit abortions in a variety of ways. Some states have created requirements that medical facilities providing abortion meet unique criteria, making it economically impossible for providers to continue services. These laws have been upheld by the Supreme Court. Alabama has gone so far as to ban all abortions unless needed to prevent the mother's death or risk of "substantial physical impairment." This law, which was meant to go into effect in November 2019, is in limbo following an injunction and may eventually be appealed to the Supreme Court. The outcome, given the current Court, is unclear.

The movement to enhance the personhood of embryos, as described above, poses a significant challenge to abortion rights as well. At least three states have passed some version of a "heartbeat bill," declaring personhood at the first instance of a heartbeat, thus prohibiting abortion from that moment on. Several other states are considering such legislation or have passed laws that have been blocked or struck down by the courts. Medical concerns about the concept of fetal personhood extend beyond abortions. Depending on the language of the individual laws, it could mean that treating an ectopic pregnancy would also be illegal, leaving the woman in a potentially critically dangerous state, or risk murder charges for the medical center staff.

Sterilization in Exchange for Reduced Time or Benefits

In 1907, the United States allowed for state-sanctioned sterilization "to prevent anyone with undesirable traits . . . from procreating."[24] Known as **eugenics**, this practice was broadly supported by academics, scientists, and reformers. Among supporters, it was stated that the practice would prevent those with mental illness, "feeblemindedness," and serious physical defects from passing on those conditions. Forced sterilization was also deemed appropriate for those with low IQ, those inclined toward criminal behavior, and those of "inferior stock" (i.e., nonwhite). It is generally documented that eighty thousand forced sterilizations occurred during the twentieth century. African American and Native American women were especially vulnerable. One report describes the "involuntary" sterilization of more than two thousand Black women on welfare in the South who were told they would lose their benefits unless they agreed to the procedure.[25] Another report puts the number of indigenous women who were sterilized at 3,406.[26] It is interesting to note that eugenics was also employed to deny middle-class white women access to birth control, on the grounds that they should reproduce to "help better the race."

EUGENICS
The belief that we can improve the genetic quality of the human race by controlling who is able to reproduce.

Lest we imagine that forced sterilization no longer exists in the United States, there is powerful evidence to prove otherwise, especially for those involved with the criminal/legal system. Examples of this practice are widely reported. For instance, between 2006 and 2010, at least 148 women incarcerated in California were sterilized without their consent; in 2009, a mother was required to have her tubes tied as part of the terms of her probation on a marijuana possession charge in West Virginia; and in 2017, a judge in Tennessee offered a thirty-day reduction in their sentence to any prisoner who agreed to a permanent birth control procedure: sterilization, a vasectomy, or Nexplanon, an implant that prevents pregnancy for four years. A federal court order determined that the terms of this reduction in sentence were unconstitutional,[27] but, as has been explained throughout this text, the criminal/legal system has a disproportionate impact in Black and other communities of color, among the poor, and on anyone else who is considered nonconforming.

Assisted Reproductive Technologies, Surrogacy, and Adoption

Assisted reproductive technology (ART) includes a number of interventions that are theoretically available to individuals who have infertility issues, the most familiar among these being in vitro fertilization, artificial insemination, ovulation induction, donor conception, and surrogacy. Though widely available to those with sufficient resources, the costs—from about $12,400 for in vitro fertilization to about $100,000 for surrogacy—make access impossible for a majority of the population. And the laws and regulations, or lack thereof, make it sometimes difficult to navigate. In the United States, state rather than federal laws govern reproduction. This has resulted in unique problems, especially around the notion of citizenship. In one rather remarkable case, a mother, single by choice, was impregnated with a donor egg. The mother, a U.S. citizen, resides in Israel. She now has two children, the first conceived with her own egg and sperm, the second with both donor egg and sperm, donated to and implanted by a New York fertility clinic. Her first child received U.S. citizenship, but when she tried to get citizenship for her second child, she was told she needed proof that one of the donors was a U.S. citizen. Apparently, a child created from a donor egg and sperm and born overseas to a U.S. citizen must have proof that at least one of the donors is a U.S. citizen.[28]

It has long been the case that foreign-born children adopted by U.S. citizens acquired citizenship. That is, until today. The Trump administration redefined "residence" in the law such that U.S. military service members and other government employees who adopt or give birth to children while residing outside the United States will no longer have those children considered residents for purposes of acquiring U.S. citizenship.

Surrogacy describes a circumstance where a woman agrees to carry and birth a child on behalf of another person or couple. Again, the wide variation by states in the laws governing surrogacy makes it a difficult option. Courts in both California[29] and New Jersey[30] have upheld the rights of the biological parents, while other states' laws discourage surrogacy on the grounds that a surrogacy contract is not unlike contracting for the sale of a child. What happens when an individual contracts for surrogacy services across state lines? Or when the developing fetus is discovered to have serious developmental issues? Or when there are multiple fetuses and the donor only wants one? Can one donor force the surrogate to abort—or to continue to carry the fetus(es)? Cases have emerged that indicate the need for clear national laws to govern surrogacy.

All of these legal impediments are particularly concerning for LGBTQ people who may desire to use alternatives to traditional modes of reproduction. Additionally, there are legal hurdles unique to the LGBTQ population. In 2017, the Supreme Court ruled in *Pavan v. Smith*[31] that states must extend equal treatment in issuing two-parent birth certificates for children born to same-sex spouses. This decision clarifies matters of rights, responsibilities, and custody. Yet several states continue to allow state-licensed welfare agencies to refuse to place children for adoption or foster care with LGBTQ individuals or same-sex couples, even when legally married, if it violates the agency's religious or moral beliefs. And even when LGBTQ people are able to adopt, only seventeen states allow two-parent adoption whereby the second parent gains parental rights without the first parent's rights being terminated.

Racialized Views of Parental "Fitness"

Ever since Daniel Moynihan, then an undersecretary in the Johnson administration, published the report *The Negro Family: The Case for National Action* in 1965, the nation's views of what constitutes a "good" parent have been contaminated by racism. This is not to suggest that such views didn't exist prior to the release of the report, but the report—seventy-eight pages full of footnotes, graphs, and charts—which referred to a "tangle of pathology," painted a picture of the Black family that resulted in a wave of victim blaming. Reacting to this negative portrayal of Black culture, the head of the Congress of Racial Equality said, "We are sick unto death of being analyzed, mesmerized, bought, sold, and slobbered over, while the same evils that are the ingredients of our oppression go unattended."[32]

No doubt the image of the ideal mother as white has long been a part of Western culture and is regularly reinforced. Author Raka Shome points to the "Diana phenomenon," referring to Britain's Princess Diana and popular culture's representations of motherhood, as being a recent example. Compare the image of Princess Diana to the shocking stereotypes produced and reinforced in the imagery of the welfare mother, employed in the mid-1970s as a rallying cry by then–presidential candidate Ronald Reagan. Labeling mothers as "welfare queens," the reference was intended to reinforce racist stereotypes of Black mothers as single and collecting public money that was spent on personal luxury while the children suffered.[33] In an effort to avoid holding society or ourselves accountable for the social circumstances that honor greed, create poverty, perpetuate poor schools, and tolerate institutional violence, we blame Black mothers for the environments some find themselves in, and for the barriers and opportunities their children experience. Dorothy Roberts describes the profound challenges of Black mothers raising their children in a racist society and shares this from Patricia Williams:

> Patricia Williams mused about a lawsuit brought by a white woman against a clinic that negligently sold her a Black man's sperm. "I ponder this case about the nightmare of giving birth to a black child who is tormented so that her mother gets to claim damages for emotional distress. I think about whether my mother shouldn't bring such a suit, both of us having endured at least the pain of my maturation in the racism of the Boston public school system. Do black mothers get to sue for such an outcome, or is it just white mothers?"[34]

Fathers' Rights from a Feminist Perspective

For centuries, children were viewed as an economic asset, as the more children a family had, the more work could be done on the farm or in the factory. During that time, children were considered the property of the father. As perceptions of childhood changed in the late nineteenth century, the concept of "tender years" appeared, suggesting that children were best served by staying with their mother in the event parents separated. This preference persisted through the twentieth century.

Divorce rates increased dramatically during the 1960s and 1970s, and for the first time in the history of the United States, many of those divorces were initiated by women, whose opportunities for self-support and increased autonomy were also improving. Custody of the children was generally given to the mother, unless the father was able to show that the mother was unfit. Along with custody came **child support** orders, requiring the father to contribute to the care and support of the children. These orders survived even after **alimony** orders expired, limited by either time or remarriage. It is unclear whether the loss of custody or the requirement of paying sometimes a significant percentage of their salary was more of a catalyst, but in the early 1980s, a movement emerged called the fathers' rights movement.

CHILD SUPPORT
Money paid by one parent to another for the care and support of their child or children.

ALIMONY
Also referred to as spousal support, payments ordered by a court in the aftermath of a divorce or separation; generally ordered when the parties have widely disparate income and earning potential, and typically time limited.

The movement has become very diverse. While some in the movement advocate for being more present in their children's lives, seeking, for example, more access to paternity leave, many others in the movement are openly hostile to women. Some of the more misogynistic elements of the movement allege false reporting of intimate violence and demand that they have a voice in the decision to abort, going so far as to say that if the pregnancy proceeds without their consent, they should not be financially responsible.

Sociologists suggest that there are three types of fathers: those committed to sharing the emotional, physical, and financial care of their children; those who are absent and find sustained involvement with family to be difficult; and those who wish to restore traditional notions of family and fatherhood and reject the idea of women as equals. "The fathers' rights movements are filled with men who feel pushed out, denied of ties to their children, leaving them estranged and angry. The underbelly of this is anger toward women."[35] As the twenty-first century progresses and more fathers are playing a more active role in their children's lives, the fathers' rights movement will either naturally expire or be increasingly exposed, not as a group fighting for the rights of fathers or children, but as a group fighting to contain women's autonomy.

In the next chapter, we cover incarceration as a reproduction of masculinity, including discussions of the prison male code, the code of the street, and the infantilization of men in prison.

REVIEW AND STUDY QUESTIONS

1. What are some of the ways we criminalize parental behavior that are imbedded with bias relating to race, gender, and sexual representation?

2. How would it be possible to protect the interests of children while avoiding problematizing and criminalizing parents?

3. Given that reproductive technologies are likely to expand in the future, what steps should society and the law take to help ensure that technology is used in fair and unbiased fashion?

GOING FURTHER

Readings:

Brooks, Kim. *Small Animals: Parenthood in the Age of Fear.* New York: Flatiron Books, 2019.

Roth, Rachel. *Making Women Pay: The Hidden Cost of Fetal Rights.* Ithaca, NY: Cornell University Press, 2000.

Websites:

Cauterucci, Christina, Briahna Joy Gray, and Rachelle Hampton. "The #SayHerName Edition." *Slate,* August 2, 2018. https://slate.com/human-interest/2018/08/the-waves-on-sorry-to-bother-you-the-criminalization-of-motherhood-and-the-killing-of-nia-wilson.html.

Lombrozo, Tania. "Why Do We Judge Parents for Putting Kids at Perceived—but Unreal—Risk?" NPR, August 22, 2016. https://www.npr.org/sections/13.7/2016/08/22/490847797/why-do-we-judge-parents-for-putting-kids-at-perceived-but-unreal-risk.

KEY TERMS

alimony Also referred to as spousal support, payments ordered by a court in the aftermath of a divorce or separation; generally ordered when the parties have widely disparate income and earning potential, and typically time limited.

child support Money paid by one parent to another for the care and support of their child or children.

eugenics The belief that we can improve the genetic quality of the human race by controlling who is able to reproduce.

failure to protect laws Laws created to protect children from the influence of intimate violence by criminalizing those who fail to remove a child from any home where violence is occurring.

fetal alcohol syndrome A condition that results from alcohol exposure during a mother's pregnancy, which is believed to cause brain damage and other possible birth defects.

right to privacy The right to privacy, as defined by *Griswold v. Connecticut*, says that the state may not unreasonably interfere with an individual's right to make a choice about matters considered private, such as health care and sexuality.

shaken baby syndrome A brain injury diagnosed in infants and toddlers who are injured or die as a result of forceful shaking.

NOTES

[1] South Carolina Code of Laws Title 16—Crimes and Offenses, Ch. 3: Offenses against the Person, Article 1: Homicide, § 16-3-85, https://www.scstatehouse.gov/code/t16c003.php.

[2] Dana Page, "The Homicide by Child Abuse Conviction of Regina McKnight," *Howard Law Journal* 46 (2003): 363–403, 392.

[3] Page, "Homicide by Child Abuse Conviction," 397–98.

[4] Page, "Homicide by Child Abuse Conviction," 402.

[5] Lynn Paltrow and Tony Newman, "South Carolina Supreme Court Reverses 20-Year Homicide Conviction of Regina McKnight" (press release, Drug Policy Alliance, May 11, 2008), http://www.drugpolicy.org/news/2008/05/south-carolina-supreme-court-reverses-20-year homicide-conviction-regina-mcknight.

[6] Lynn Paltrow and Jeanne Flavin, "Arrests of and Forced Interventions on Pregnant Women in the United States (1973–2005): The Implications for Women's Legal Status and Public Health," *Journal of Health Politics, Policy and Law* 38, no. 2 (2013): 299–343.

[7] Dana Goldstein, "Inexcusable Absences," *New Republic*, March 6, 2015, https://newrepublic.com/article/121186/truancy-laws-unfairly-attack-poor-children-and-parents.

[8] Jaime Sarrio, "Student Truancy Can Spell $1000 Fine, Jail for Parents," *Atlanta Journal-Constitution*, December 18, 2011, https://www.ajc.com/news/local/student-truancy-can-spell-000-fine-jail-for-parents/kqr39rlYWqELUedZmC4hll.

[9] "State Laws on Fetal Homicide and Penalty-Enhancement for Crimes against Pregnant Women," National Conference of State Legislatures, May 1, 2018, http://www.ncsl.org/research/health/fetal-homicide-state-laws.aspx.

[10] Janet Gallagher, "Prenatal Invasions & Interventions: What's Wrong with Fetal Rights," *Harvard Women's Law Journal* 10 (1987): 9–58, 9, 37, 57.

[11] Sarah Friedmann, "Why Marshae Jones Was Charged with Manslaughter after She Was Shot & Lost Her Pregnancy," *Bustle*, June 27, 2019, https://www.bustle.com/p/why-marshae-jones-was-charged-with-manslaughter-after-she-was-shot-lost-her-pregnancy-18151897.

[12] "Crack Babies: Twenty Years Later," NPR, May 3, 2010, https://www.npr.org/templates/story/story.php?storyId=126478643.

[13] B. M. Ewen, "Failure to Protect Laws: Protecting Children or Punishing Mothers?," *Journal of Forensic Nursing* 3, no. 2 (2007): 84–86.

[14] Tim Talley, "Group Takes Aim at Oklahoma Failure-to-Protect Law," AP News, September 29, 2018, https://www.apnews.com/45a6f24af72c4750ac141f3fe10b3bc9.

[15] Alex Campbell, "Woman Sent to Prison for Failing to Protect Toddler Is Up for Parole," *BuzzFeed*, December 30, 2015, https://www.buzzfeednews.com/article/alexcampbell/woman-sent-to-prison-for-failing-to-protect-toddler-is-up-fo #.ktj2V7q6n.

[16] "Enhanced Resource Guidelines," National Council of Juvenile and Family Court Judges, May 26, 2016, https://www.ncjfcj.org/enhancedresourceguidelines.

[17] Antonio Riera and David M. Walker, "The Impact of Race and Ethnicity on Care in the Pediatric Emergency Department," *Current Opinion in Pediatrics* 22, no. 3 (2010): 284–89.

[18] Matthew Clarke, "'Shaken Baby Syndrome' Diagnoses Discredited, Convictions Questioned," *Criminal Legal News*, May 15, 2018, https://www.criminallegalnews.org/news/2018/may/15/shaken-baby-syndrome-diagnoses-discredited-convictions-questioned.

[19] *Griswold v. Connecticut*, 381 U.S. 479 (S. Ct. 1965).

[20] *Roe v. Wade*, 410 U.S. 113 (S. Ct. 1973).

[21] Ruth Dawson, "Trump Administration's Domestic Gag Rule Has Slashed the Title X Network's Capacity by Half," Guttmacher Institute, updated April 15, 2021, https://www.guttmacher.org/article/2020/02/trump-administrations-domestic-gag-rule-has-slashed-title-x-networks-capacity-half.

[22] Lea Hunter, "The U.S. Is Still Forcibly Sterilizing Prisoners," Associated Press, August 23, 2017, https://talkpoverty.org/2017/08/23/u-s-still-forcibly-sterilizing-prisoners.

[23] Funding for abortions is another matter. In the immediate aftermath of *Roe v. Wade*, Congress passed the Hyde Amendment (1976) that barred federal funds from paying for abortions except in the case of rape, incest, or where the mother's life is in danger. This prohibition expands to federal workers who receive their health insurance through the government as well as women who rely on Medicaid.

[24] Hunter, "U.S. Is Still Forcibly Sterilizing Prisoners."

[25] Martha C. Ward, *Poor Women, Powerful Men: America's Great Experiment in Family Planning* (Boulder, CO: Westview Press, 1986).

[26] Bruce E. Johansen, "Americans and the 'Last Gasp of Eugenics,'" *Native Americas* 15, no. 4 (December 31, 1998): 45.

[27] Adam Tamburin, "Federal Court Order Officially Ends Tennessee 'Inmate Sterilization' Program," *The Tennessean*, May 20, 2019, https://www.tennessean.com/story/news/2019/05/20/tennessee-inmate-sterilization-program/3748232002.

[28] Anna Stolley Persky, "Reproductive Technology and the Law," *Washington Lawyer*, July/August 2012, https://www.dcbar.org/bar-resources/publications/washington-lawyer/articles/july-august-2012-reproductive-tech.cfm.

[29] *Johnson v. Calvert*, 5 CAL. 4th 84 (California Supreme Court 1993).

[30] *In re Baby M*, 537 A.2d 1227 (Supreme Court of New Jersey 1988).

[31] *Pavan v. Smith*, 137 S.Ct. 2075 (S.Ct. 2017).

[32] Quoted in Lee Rainwater and William L. Yancey, *The Moynihan Report and the Politics of Controversy* (Cambridge, MA: MIT Press, 1967), 409–10.

[33] According to the website Welfare Info (www.welfareinfo.org), the average family of four receives up to $900 a month in welfare benefits. There might be other benefits, such as food stamps, housing supplements, and disability coverage.

However one might combine these resources, there is not much money for more than the very occasional luxury.

[34] Patricia J. Williams, *The Alchemy of Race and Rights* (Cambridge, MA: Harvard University Press, 1991), 186–87, as cited in Dorothy E. Roberts, "Racism and Patriarchy in the Meaning of Motherhood," *Faculty Scholarship at Penn Law* 595 (1993), http://scholarship.law.upenn.edu/faculty_scholarship/595.

[35] Kathleen Gerson, *No Man's Land: Men's Changing Commitments to Family and Work* (New York: Basic Books, 1994), as cited in Sarah Werthan Buttenweiser, "Fathers' Fight: What Every Mother Should Know about the Fathers' Rights Movement," Mothers Movement, accessed September 5, 2020, http://www.mothersmovement.org/features/05/fathers_fight/buttenwieser_0605_1.htm.

Incarceration as a Reproduction of Masculinity

In this chapter you will revisit theories of masculinity and examine how they interact with the prison system. You will read the story of one young man beaten down by the system, and many others who are trying to counteract the damage done.

LEARNING OBJECTIVES

After reading this chapter, you should be able to do the following:

- Describe the prison-industrial complex.
- Articulate the "prison code" and understand how it emerged.
- Explain the importance of programming in prison.
- Evaluate the impact the reproduction of masculinity has on corrections officers and other staff.

Case #12: Kalief Browder

In the spring of 2015, as a student at Bronx Community College, Kalief Browder wrote a paper called "A Closer Look at Solitary Confinement in the United States." In his paper, Kalief explores some of the origins of the practice of solitary confinement of prisoners and points out that despite long-standing and overwhelming evidence that solitary confinement is harmful rather than rehabilitative, it continues to be used in prisons across the country. He goes on to detail some of the known and profoundly negative effects of solitary confinement: severe physical, mental, and emotional disturbances; suicide attempts; and difficulties reintegrating into society, which prisoners and their families may be unable to successfully navigate, particularly when they do not have access to quality or dependable health care. He explains that the justification for the use of solitary confinement is that it is primarily meant to prevent violence, either against prisoners or correctional officers, but he argues that, in reality, it is an overused practice that traumatizes prisoners to such a degree that even when they are released, they are unable to thrive and are likely to reoffend. Finally, he points out that despite the Eighth Amendment's prohibition of "cruel and unusual punishments," these practices not only continue but are hidden from public view, and he concludes with a recommendation that more awareness of the practices within prisons needs to be brought to the public so that prisoners will no longer be forced to endure these conditions and new forms of order can be found.

His paper drew largely from academic sources, but also from personal experience. Kalief himself had been imprisoned on Rikers Island in New York City for three years, spending the majority of that time in solitary confinement. Released after the case against him—theft of a backpack that was never found in his possession—was dismissed due to insufficient evidence, Kalief emerged back into the world, determined to bring to light these faults in the criminal/legal system, and soon enrolled in school. Two years later, he committed suicide. He was twenty-two years old.

Kalief grew up in the Bronx, in one of the country's poorest congressional districts. Though he was essentially estranged from his father, he was close to his mother, Venida, his four brothers—Kamal, Deion, Akeem, and Raheem—and his sister, Nicole. Growing up, Kalief enjoyed typical things—sports, video games, Pokémon, and hanging out with friends from the neighborhood.

In the very early morning on May 15, 2010, just over a week before his seventeenth birthday, Kalief was arrested while walking home from a party with a friend. Confused about why they were being stopped, Kalief and his friend were told by the arresting officers that they were being accused of stealing a backpack several days earlier and that they had been identified by a witness. They were told that the backpack had contained cash, a credit card, a camera,

and an iPod, and despite the fact that neither Kalief nor his friend were in possession of either the backpack or its contents, they were taken to the Bronx's Forty-Eighth Precinct to be charged.

The case was chaotic from the start. The witness, who was also the victim of the robbery, had told officers multiple versions of the story, and many of the details of the robbery recorded in police reports were vague and inconsistent. The date of the robbery, for instance, varied from report to report, and though there was a recording of the 911 call made by the victim's brother on the night of the robbery, there was no date attached to the call and no police report filed. Both on the night of the original call and after Kalief's arrest, the victim's brother suggested that law enforcement locate footage from a camera in the alley where the robbery was said to have taken place, but there was no attempt to retrieve video evidence. Because the original date of the robbery is unknown, it is difficult to say how much time elapsed between the robbery and Kalief's arrest, but within days or weeks of the robbery, the victim and his brother saw Kalief and his friend on the street and called the police once again. All the witness was able to say was that Kalief and his friend were wearing clothes resembling those of the robbers.

Upon arriving at the precinct, Kalief was told that he would likely be released quickly. He thought it was probably not much more than a routine stop-and-frisk event, a common practice of the New York City Police Department that involves officers stopping, questioning, and potentially frisking anyone who seems suspicious; it is a practice that has been criticized as a racial profiling tool. Hours passed, however, and Kalief was not released. His family went to the precinct, hoping to be able to take him home, but they were told he was being charged with second-degree robbery and that his bail was set at $3,000. The bail bond was 30 percent of the bail ($900), and though his family was able to secure the bond, they learned that because he was on probation for participating in the theft of a delivery truck several months earlier, his bail was denied. Kalief maintained that he had in fact only watched friends steal the truck, rather than participating himself, but he had pleaded guilty for his involvement, nonetheless. The five years' probation he was given prevented him from being eligible to post bail. He would have to wait for a trial.

In New York, the age of criminal responsibility is sixteen. This meant that while Kalief was waiting for trial, he would be sent to prison. He was sent to Rikers Island, a notoriously dangerous prison complex on an island in New York's East River, south of the Bronx and north of the borough of Queens. Rikers Island has an almost exclusively African American prisoner population; a majority of the prisoners, like Kalief, could not pay bail and would wait, sometimes for years, for trials. Though there is a clause in the Sixth Amendment of the Constitution guaranteeing the right to a speedy trial (often defined as a trial six months or less after arrest), New York has slightly different policies regarding the definition of a speedy trial—the district attorney must be ready to go to trial in a given amount of time, but the trial itself need not occur within that time frame if the court is delayed for any reason. The courts in the Bronx are often particularly backed up due to the volume of cases, and public defenders tend to be overloaded; Brendan O'Meara, Kalief's court-appointed public defender, was no different. Kalief and O'Meara saw each other only quickly and rarely.

Kalief was first sent to the facility for adolescents, the Robert N. Davoren Center. It was a facility known for extreme violence among both prisoners and correctional officers. The correctional officers referred to the prisoners as "animalescents" because of what they perceived to be unpredictable and dangerous behavior. In reality, the correctional officers often participated in the violence, either directly or by inducing or allowing it. Fights, fires, broken bones, and forced starvation of prisoners were regular occurrences. In such an environment, the young prisoners learn that they have to fight to survive, both literally and figuratively. Kalief had never been one for going to the gym or working out, but he felt that in this new environment, it would be a good use of his time to start bulking up. Kalief reflected on this change in him; before prison, he recalled, "every here and there I did a couple pullups or pushups. . . . I went in there, that's when I decided I wanted to get big."[1]

Before his arrest and his time at Rikers, in fact, Kalief had not been prone to masculine posturing or fighting. In his neighborhood in the Bronx, there had been gang activity, primarily between Bloods, Crips, and Latin Kings. Though Kalief did briefly join the Bloods, it had been an attempt to find security and community, and after getting to Rikers, he was not interested in gang allegiance. Being in a gang would have offered protection, but he did not want that protection if it meant participating in violent acts that did not sit well with his conscience. He wanted to remain neutral but soon found that this was fraught with difficulty.

In the adolescent facility, there was a social order known as the "Program." Gangs controlled certain spaces and protected each other, and when Kalief chose to be unaffiliated, he became a target, continuously forced to prove himself and fight, either one-on-one or with a crowd. Getting on the bad side of a gang would mean relentless attacks, and even simple things, like sitting at a table or a using a phone, were imminent dangers—being in the wrong place at the wrong time could mean getting jumped or even killed. Kalief refused to get with the "Program," and his continued refusal angered other prisoners and correctional officers alike. Correctional officers were essentially a part of the "Program," sometimes coercing prisoners to perform acts of violence against other prisoners, which allowed the

correctional officers to carry out vendettas against individuals while bearing no obvious responsibility for the violence. In this environment, Kalief, who was not particularly tall or muscular, was a likely target for attack by new members of the "Program," who were desperate to prove themselves by destroying someone else. Kalief had to learn to fight, to "be a man."

Kalief's refusal to participate in the "Program" made him an enemy of the prisoners, and his continued comments to correctional officers about their collaboration in this violence made him an enemy of the correctional officers as well. On the occasions when groups of up to thirty other prisoners came together to attack Kalief, it is difficult to say if the correctional officers were unable to stop the beatings or if they were simply uninterested in protecting him. Either way, Kalief kept getting moved from one facility to another because he was on the receiving end of such constant violence, and gang vendettas against him followed him to each new location. After one particularly brutal attack, Kalief was placed in solitary confinement, which on Rikers Island is referred to as "the Bing."

As Kalief would later write in his paper at Bronx Community College, solitary confinement is often said to be a method for protecting prisoners, segregating them when they are in danger among the general population, but solitary confinement was far from a relief for Kalief. He did read a lot in the early days of his stay in solitary, from sports magazines to books on international politics, and he took advantage of a program that offered prisoners a chance to work toward their GED. Because Kalief was in solitary, he was only able to do worksheets given to him in his cell and was unable to spend time with teachers. At first, Kalief was able to keep himself occupied with these activities, but as his time in solitary stretched on, he became increasingly unable to focus on reading. There is clear evidence that extended time in solitary confinement can lead to mental health disturbances even in people who have never experienced mental or emotional health problems in the past. Kalief was not able to escape these effects. With no entertainment, no conversation, and no human or physical contact aside from brief, often combative moments with correctional officers, Kalief was increasingly unable to cope with his surroundings. His deteriorating condition was exacerbated by minimal access to showers, excessive heat in the stuffy New York summers, unreliable access to food, rodent problems, and visible signs of the deterioration of prisoners who had been in the cell before him, such as blood or feces on the wall, which represented the danger he faced. In such conditions, paranoia, fear, anger, and panic increase as the brain loses its ability to regulate the nervous system, which can lead to long-term posttraumatic stress disorder. Even given these circumstances, Kalief thought to request psychiatric help as he felt his mental state becoming more and more unstable. His requests were ignored, and no help was forthcoming. In fact, Kalief's continued insistence that he was being treated unjustly simply extended his stay in the Bing.

Correctional officers are not trained or prepared to deal with mental illness. As Kalief lost more and more weight, partially from being refused food and partially from the increasing anxiety of never knowing how long his stay in solitary confinement would last, he began to talk to himself. Throughout this time, court dates came and went: December 10, 2010, no court available; January 28, 2011, the court was still not ready; March 9, 2011, the district attorney had a scheduling conflict; and on and on. His mother attended every failed court date and visited him nearly every week, but with no ability to hug or protect her son, or to secure help for his failing physical and mental health, she felt helpless as she watched Kalief grow more distant from her, and from himself. With each unsuccessful court date, Kalief felt more and more like a throwaway lost in the system. On June 23, 2011, he was offered a plea deal—he could plead guilty, be sentenced, and at least have a definite end to his stay on Rikers Island in sight. He refused. He was determined to go to trial, to prove his innocence, to get justice. What he did not know at the time was that less than 5 percent of cases in the Bronx that year made it to trial; the rest simply pleaded guilty rather than engage in the process of endless uncertain waiting. But Kalief chose to wait—the court may have treated him like a throwaway, but despite the trauma and torment of prison, he was unwilling to participate in the unjust process of pleading guilty when, he insisted, he was innocent.

The United Nations classifies more than fifteen consecutive days in solitary confinement as torture. At seventeen years old, Kalief's first stay in solitary confinement lasted for more than three hundred days.

When Kalief was finally released from solitary and sent back into the general prison population, his experience in the Bing made him even more erratic with others. Just as he would later write in his paper on solitary confinement, the trauma of his experience made it difficult for him to reintegrate: the lack of impulse control that arises from the conditions of solitary confinement manifested as panic, anxiety, and anger, and it turned into physical outbursts. A fight put him back in the Bing; this time his stay would last fourteen months.

And, just as Kalief would later write in his paper, the time in solitary led to suicidal thoughts. On March 11, 2012, he shredded his bedsheets and attempted to hang himself. Correctional officers found him as he choked and struggled, and for a few moments they just stood watching. When they cut him down, they immediately began to attack him. Even in that mental state, Kalief thought to drag the attack out of his cell and into the hallway, still thinking of building a video record of his long experience of injustice. His experience in prison, and in solitary confinement in particular, had made him mentally unstable, and the only treatment he got for this forced instability was

further punishment. Correctional officers did not report it as a suicide attempt but as an attempt to get out of the Bing, and no psychiatric treatment was provided. Kalief attempted suicide four more times while in solitary, and as each attempt failed, he was simply put back in solitary.

Unbeknownst to Kalief, a month before his initial suicide attempt and almost two years after his arrest, there were some developments in his case. In February 2012, the district attorney discovered that they had lost contact with the original witness who had accused Kalief of stealing the backpack. The witness had reportedly left the country entirely, and as a witness needed to be present for the case to be valid, no witness meant no case. The DA did not immediately alert Kalief's public defender of this new information. Meanwhile, Kalief remained in solitary confinement, with abusive, violent correctional officers as his only contact with other humans. He had been on Rikers for nearly two years when his case crumbled, but poor communication and lack of attention to the details of his case meant another year on Rikers, more failed court dates, and Kalief's continued refusal to plead guilty.

It was not until Judge Patricia DiMango came to the Bronx in March 2013 that the realities of Kalief's case began to come to light. DiMango was known as a particularly efficient judge, and she had been sent to the Bronx to work through their stifling backlog of cases. She offered Kalief a new deal: plead guilty to two misdemeanors rather than a felony, which would mean a shorter sentence and quicker—nearly immediate—release. Kalief still refused. Fellow prisoners could not believe that Kalief continued to refuse to plead guilty, especially with this new deal, but to Kalief, pleading guilty was simply not an option. After his release, speaking to Jennifer Gonnerman of the *New Yorker*, Kalief recalled, "I used to go to my cell and lie down and think, like, Maybe I am crazy; maybe I am going too far. . . . But I just did what I thought was right."[2]

Just a few weeks after Judge DiMango's arrival in the Bronx, in April 2013, considering the still-missing witness and despite the district attorney's insistence that they would soon be ready to finally bring Kalief's case to trial, Judge DiMango determined that the case was invalid. On May 29, 2013, after 1,126 days in prison, approximately 700 of which had been spent in solitary confinement, Kalief was released. After more than thirty failed court dates, the charges were simply withdrawn. Kalief had been imprisoned for three years with no formal conviction, and suddenly, with not even a cursory recognition of what Kalief had been through from the court, the city, and the district attorney, his time on Rikers came to an end.

A LOST CHILDHOOD

Arrested just before his seventeenth birthday and released just after his twentieth, Kalief felt that he had lost much more than three years. He felt that he had lost his childhood and that he had not only been prematurely aged by his time in prison but had turned into a different person, a harder person who had no more access to happiness, fun, or freedom. The one thing that remained of the person he had been was his focus on justice. Despite his trauma, he gathered the energy and the presence of mind to begin to address what had happened to him. In November 2013, with the help of attorney Paul Prestia, Kalief sued the city of New York, the New York Police Department, the Bronx district attorney, and the Department of Corrections. His refusal to plead guilty while in prison had been just the beginning of his efforts to address the injustices he had experienced. He wanted to expose the violence of Rikers and to ensure that others would not be failed as he had been.

Even as he began to take on this new phase of his struggle and to get his life back on track with school and work, Kalief was haunted by his time in prison. In moments alone, he returned to those traumatic experiences; his mind would wander back to them and make him distant even when surrounded by family and friends. He felt that he could no longer fit into regular society. He was quiet, subdued, and plagued by bouts of paranoia, and there were no tools to help him reintegrate into society or to process his experience. He had a hard time finding work and was self-conscious about his behavior; he talked to himself in public and felt that others perceived him to be strange. At home, he spent a lot of time simply pacing. He had been released from prison, but not from its effects.

His life after prison was chaotic and marked by the new behavioral patterns he had developed. In December 2013, he attempted suicide but failed; he had been trying to escape his stress, his anger, and his feeling that he was being followed by state actors who were angry about his attempts to expose the failures of the criminal/legal system. (In fact, others confirmed that on this point, at least, his paranoia was valid; unmarked cars parked outside his house did indeed appear to be watching him). Just as it had been in prison, Kalief's mental state was unstable, and just as he had in prison, he actively tried to find help. And, just as it had been in prison, help was not easy to access. There were triggers for anger and fear everywhere. Paranoid episodes led to brief psychiatric hospitalizations. Even in more stable moments, Kalief did not like how hard he had become, but he could not seem to shake it. Not a fighter before going to prison, Kalief after prison was prone to fighting. During one fight in his neighborhood, he was shot in the stomach; after another, he and his brother Kamal were arrested after Kamal was robbed, and Kalief was determined to find the robbers and exact revenge. The arrest after this fight was a significant trigger for Kalief; handcuffs and booking brought on waves of posttraumatic stress. His attorney negotiated their release, and a court date was scheduled: June 10, 2015.

Meanwhile, even amid the constant challenges of simply living, Kalief continued with his efforts to pursue an education and justice. He passed his GED in March 2014 and enrolled at Lehman College of the City University of New York, as well as at Bronx Community College; he intended to pursue business management, and he proved himself to be a good student. His lawsuit against the city of New York required a lengthy deposition; the first was on December 5, 2014, and the last on May 22, 2015. Though the deposition was meant to collect evidence about Kalief's case against the city, much of it was an attack on his character and an attempt to discredit him as a reliable witness. After all, if Kalief's case was sound, it meant that every level of the criminal/legal system he had come in contact with would have to be investigated. As the suit continued, Prestia took Kalief's story to the media. Videos of Kalief's time in prison appeared on the internet, showing clearly the violence and abuse he had endured, and Kalief began to appear on talk shows and news broadcasts. People from across the country began writing letters to him; journalists called constantly. Celebrities from Shawn "Jay-Z" Carter to Rosie O'Donnell became champions for Kalief, bringing his story to the nation's attention and offering him personal support. He had not been pursuing this fanfare; he simply saw connections between the injustices he had suffered and similar cases of abuse of power and was determined to continue his fight.

Kalief juggled school, his suit against the city, and his new position in the public eye, even as he suffered the continuing symptoms of trauma. Just two weeks after his last deposition and four days before he and his brother Kamal were scheduled to go to court, on June 6, 2015, Kalief took his own life. It is possible that the thought of another court date was too much; it is possible that his paranoia got the best of him. His final reasoning is unknown, but his actions up until that point rippled across society, from the Bronx to the news to Washington, DC.

People gathered after Kalief's death to protest and to bring attention to the abuses at Rikers, to the unwieldy bail system, and to the failures of the prison system overall. Investigations of conditions at Rikers had already been underway, but what happens behind prison walls is essentially invisible to the rest of the population unless something draws the public's attention, and Kalief's work—and then his death—brought these investigations and their findings to the public. Florence Finkle, an investigator with the Department of Corrections from 2010 to 2014, had already begun to make efforts to suspend and even convict correctional officers who were caught abusing inmates, and a number of abuses had been documented: correctional officers extorting inmates; bringing in and selling cigarettes, drugs, and weapons; poisoning prisoners' food; accepting bribes; and physically and sexually assaulting prisoners. In 2014, concurrent with Kalief's lawsuit, the U.S. Department of Justice joined a class-action lawsuit, *Nunez vs. City of New York*, which alleged that "the Department of Correction ('DOC') has engaged in a pattern and practice of using unnecessary and excessive force against inmates" (U.S. Department of Justice, "Department of Justice Takes Legal Action"), and in 2015, the city of New York settled, agreeing to increase oversight of correctional officers and to increase mechanisms to prevent abuses at Rikers Island; in addition, minors will no longer be subject to segregation or solitary confinement.

The effects of Kalief's work are reverberating through city, state, and federal laws. In the 2015–2016 legislative session, New York State Senate Bill S1998A, known as "Kalief's Law," was introduced; the bill seeks to ensure that time limits for a speedy trial are actually upheld and that court delays no longer lead to years-long imprisonment for people still awaiting trial. In January 2016, President Barack Obama wrote an editorial for the *Washington Post* in which he describes Kalief's experience, using his story as evidence that practices of solitary confinement in the United States need to be examined and improved. In many ways, President Obama's editorial mirrors Kalief's paper for his Bronx Community College course—both mention the indisputable evidence of the negative effects of solitary confinement, the likelihood of suicide attempts, and the difficulties adjusting to life after release. Both also recommend that solitary confinement be avoided whenever possible. The largest difference between President Obama's statement and Kalief's paper is that President Obama was able to work with the U.S. attorney general and the Justice Department to reform federal laws around solitary confinement, and he was able to adopt new recommendations from the Justice Department, which include "banning solitary confinement for juveniles and as a response to low-level infractions, expanding treatment for the mentally ill and increasing the amount of time inmates in solitary can spend outside of their cells." The Justice Department's "Report and Recommendations concerning the Use of Restrictive Housing," released in January 2016, details clear guidelines for the reformation of solitary confinement practices in federal prisons in the United States. And in March 2017, New York City mayor Bill de Blasio announced his intention to work toward shutting down Rikers Island completely; in June of the same year, his office released a detailed long-term plan addressing the steps toward this goal, covering a network of issues such as bail, sentencing and trial processes, mental health, and recidivism. And in October 2019, the City Council of New York voted to close Rikers Island.

Abusive prison practices, particularly solitary confinement, permanently changed Kalief Browder; the extent to which Kalief Browder will also change abusive prison practices remains to be seen. His work continues.

THINKING CRITICALLY ABOUT THE CASE

1. What specific failings of the justice system led to Browder's unjust imprisonment?

2. How did prison change Browder? Which aspects of imprisonment seem to have led to specific changes?

3. Why did Browder's story resonate with such a large audience?

REFERENCES

This case is adapted from the following sources:

"Department of Justice Takes Legal Action to Address Pattern and Practice of Excessive Force and Violence at NYC Jails on Rikers Island That Violates the Constitutional Rights of Young Male Inmates." U.S. Department of Justice, December 18, 2014.

Gonnerman, Jennifer. "Before the Law." *New Yorker*, October 6, 2014.
———. "Kalief Browder, 1993–2015." *New Yorker*, June 7, 2015.

Mathias, Christopher. "Here's Kalief Browder's Heartbreaking Research Paper on Solitary Confinement." *HuffPost*, June 23, 2015.

Obama, Barack. "Why We Must Rethink Solitary Confinement: Its Overuse Leads to Tragic Results." *Washington Post*, January 26, 2016.

"Report and Recommendations concerning the Use of Restrictive Housing." U.S. Department of Justice, January 2016.

Senate Bill S1998A. New York State Senate. Accessed October 15, 2019. https://www.nysenate.gov/legislation/bills/2017/S1998.

"Smaller, Safer, Fairer: A Roadmap to Closing Rikers Island." City of New York Office of the Mayor, June 22, 2017.

Weiser, Benjamin. "New York City Settles Suit over Abuses at Rikers Island." *New York Times*, June 22, 2015.

Willoughby-Nason, Julia. *Time: The Kalief Browder Story*. Roc Nation, the Weinstein Company, and Cinemart, 2017.

CONTEXT AND ANALYSIS

The United States has the highest incarceration rate in the world. While it has only 5 percent of the world's population, it has nearly 25 percent of its incarcerated people. There are over two million people in federal prisons, state prisons, local jails, juvenile correctional facilities, and Indian country jails, as well as in military prisons, immigration detention facilities, civil commitment centers, state psychiatric hospitals, and prisons in U.S. territories. Imprisonment has become the first response to social, economic, and political problems, including mental illness, drug addiction, homelessness, and unemployment.

Beginning with the war on crime in the 1970s and the war on drugs in the 1980s, the number of people incarcerated skyrocketed sevenfold by the 2010s. This led to overcrowding and fiscal burdens. Due to changes in charging and sentencing practices as well as changes in drug laws, the incarcerated population has stabilized. Nevertheless, overincarceration remains a significant problem.

While men make up the vast majority of people in prison in the United States, women are about 6.8 percent of the nation's incarcerated population. The experiences of women and TGNCI (trans, gender nonconforming, and intersex) prisoners are documented in chapter 13. This chapter focuses on how masculinity is experienced in prisons and jails.

More than 60 percent of the people in prison today are people of color. Overall, African Americans are more likely to be arrested for the same crime, more likely to be convicted, and more likely to be sentenced to high incarceration terms. Black men are six times as likely, and Latino men are 2.7 times as likely, to be incarcerated as white men. For Black men in their thirties, about one in every twelve is in prison or jail on any given day.

The Prison-Industrial Complex

The **prison-industrial complex** is the prison system structure that rapidly expanded incarceration following the wars on crime and drugs as well as the passing of harsher sentencing legislation. It connects economic and political interests that encourage increased spending on incarceration—from building more prisons to operating privately owned prisons to contracting with corporations for cheap prison labor. Due to the political influence of private prison corporations and businesses, private prisons and private prison services and goods began to emerge to keep pace with the rapidly expanding prison population. Corporations contract with the government for cheap prison labor, prison construction, surveillance technology, prison food services, medical facilities, and telephone calls, among other services. MCI and other telephone companies charge prisoners and their families extremely high prices for the precious telephone calls that are often the only contact prisoners have with the outside world.

A growing number of federal and state prisons have been, and are being, privatized. In 2016, 8.5 percent of the total state and federal prison population was incarcerated in private facilities in twenty-seven states and by the federal government that were managed by corporations, including Core Civic (formerly Corrections Corporation of America), the GEO Group, and the Management and Training Corporation. To ensure the continuation of privatization, these corporations are involved in political lobbying in order to influence increased legislation that favors conditions that ensure the continued profitability of private prisons. Politicians often use the fear of crime, regardless of actual crime levels, for their elections and reelections.

The prison-industrial complex maintains its power in many ways, including creating mass media images of stereotypes of poor people, people of color, immigrants, and other oppressed communities as criminal; funding tough-on-crime politicians; and increasing the influence of correctional officer unions. Moreover, it utilizes private for-profit prisons to ensure a steady stream of people, as contracts are based on the number of people who are incarcerated.

> **PRISON INDUSTRIAL COMPLEX**
> Prison system structure that connects economic and political interests, encouraging increased spending on incarceration.

The Masculine Nature of Incarceration

Prison is a gendered institution dominated by a sharp male hierarchy that exists not only between prisoners and the prison staff but also among prisoners. The prison culture of masculinity enforces the toxic masculinity (discussed in chapter 8) that is embedded in the structure of prison, primarily in the rules and policies, and the ways correctional officers make decisions about rule enforcement. Moreover, the gender code among male prisoners is merely an exaggeration of the "male code" on the outside.[3] As discussed in chapter 8, the patriarchal society insists that a "real" man does not show weakness of any kind, suppresses emotions other than anger and aggression, is never vulnerable, does not rely on anyone, and suffers pain in silence. Moreover, he is forced to act in a tough and dominating way in order to gain and maintain respect.

Power relations are consistently and continuously being mediated through relationships with other prisoners as well as with correctional officers and other prison staff. This is achieved more often through showing power and intimidation rather than actual violence. Moreover, social status becomes an important source of power for inmates, who experience limited access to other forms of capital. Masculinity is authority and dominance over others.

Kupers identifies four obvious structural elements of the **male prison code**:

1. There is an exaggerated dominance hierarchy wherein the toughest men dominate those who are less tough.

2. There is a sharp demarcation between those at the top of the dominance hierarchy and those at the bottom. At the top are the "real men," whereas weaklings and "punks" populate the bottom of the hierarchy.

3. The bottom is defined in terms of the feminine. Whether a man is known as a loser, a weakling, a snitch, or a punk, he is accused of being less than a man—in other words, a woman. . . . When one man beats up another and sodomizes him, the message is clear: "I, the dominant man, have the right and the power to use you, the loser, sexually, as if you were a woman and my slave."

4. There is a narrowing of personal possibilities, and men are forced to act in hypermasculine and dominating ways merely to prove they are not feminine, they are not anyone's "punk." This hypermasculinity reinforces the misogyny and toxic masculinity that are central to the male prison culture.[4]

Code of the Street

The male prison culture is an extension of the **code of the street**, which are informal rules that govern interpersonal behavior, including violence. Just as respect is central to the male prison code, it is the heart of the code of the street. According to Elijah Anderson, having a reputation for violent behavior earns respect on the street. As a result, the use of violence is supported as a way to gain respect and to keep respect.[5]

The Mask of Masculinity

Surviving in a culture that demands rigid adherence to this masculine code requires incarcerated men to consistently maintain the **mask of masculinity**. A man who does not act tough enough or shows any empathy is likely to be accused of not being a man. That fear motivates prisoners to buff up with weights, conquer the mean stare, and follow the strict rules of prison culture.

Infantilization of Men in Prison

Just as in women's prisons, patriarchy in men's prisons takes the form of infantilizing, demeaning, and disempowering men. Although the form of infantilization differs by gender, it is just as damaging for male prisoners as for women prisoners. In both cases, the most powerful people in the prison are the correctional officers. Assumptions about masculinity are deeply embedded in the structure of prison and are the basis for

MALE PRISON CODE
Hierarchy based on forcing men to act in hypermasculine and dominating ways inside prisons and jails.

CODE OF THE STREET
A set of informal rules governing interpersonal public behavior, including violence.

MASK OF MASCULINITY
Maintaining a persona of hypermasculinity where acting tough and not showing any empathy enforces manhood.

maintaining security. In an effort to maintain control, the prison administration, staff, and individual correctional officers focus on their belief that men in prison exhibit dangerous masculinity. Consequently, subservience is institutionalized to challenge masculinity through prison rules and rituals that are designed to control, disempower, and make those incarcerated subservient to the system. This is accomplished by teaching (or training) the prisoner to passively follow orders. Not only are incarcerated men compelled to obey authority, but also their agency, autonomy, and independence are suppressed. Being forced to suppress leads to frustration and humiliation. Any resistance is met with disciplinary write-ups and time in "the hole," or solitary confinement. The consequence of infantilizing those who are incarcerated is that they are not fully prepared when they reenter free society.

Sexual Assault

While unwanted sexual victimization in prisons and jails has been occurring throughout the history of incarceration in the United States, public awareness of it is only recent. Rape is not about sex. It is about power and domination. As discussed earlier, the male prison culture enforces the superiority of toxic masculinity and its power and control. As a result, those with more power objectify, abuse, and dominate those with less power. One of the methods is through sexual assault, sometimes through brute force and other times through coercion.

In 2003, Congress passed the Prison Rape Elimination Act (PREA), which was the first federal law intended to deter the sexual assault and rape of incarcerated persons. It has set standards to prevent, detect, reduce, and respond to sexual abuse in prisons, jails, and juvenile detention facilities. Research has shown that juveniles incarcerated with adults are five times more likely to report being victims of sexual assault than young people in juvenile facilities. There is further discussion about PREA in chapter 13.

Solitary Confinement

Solitary confinement, or the separation of prisoners from the general population, is used in federal prisons and every state to punish or prevent violence. Solitary confinement means that the incarcerated person is held in their cells for twenty-two to twenty-four hours a day, isolated from any contact with another person except an occasional correctional officer. It has severe psychological and physiological effects. In addition to triggering depression, panic attacks, paranoia, and sometimes hallucinations, solitary confinement can also cause hypertension, headaches, and dizziness, among other symptoms. Because of these detrimental effects, most states are now attempting to reform their solitary confinement policies. Nevertheless, tens of thousands of prisoners are held each day in solitary confinement.

As evidenced by Kalief Browder's experiences, solitary confinement is harmful rather than rehabilitative. Despite the justification of solitary confinement as a means to prevent violence, against either prisoners or correctional officers, it is actually an overused system that traumatizes prisoners to such a degree that even when they are released, they are unable to thrive and are likely to reoffend. Solitary confinement is correlated with a range of psychological problems, including depression, self-harm, and suicide, as well as physical, mental, and emotional disturbances. Moreover, being incarcerated in solitary confinement has also been related to difficulties reintegrating into society.

Fatherhood and Parenting

According to the Pew Center on the States, there are 2.7 million children with a parent in prison or jail in the United States. One in nine African American children (11.4 percent), one in twenty-eight Latinx children (3.5 percent), and one in fifty-seven white children (1.8 percent) have an incarcerated parent.[6] Moreover, over a million incarcerated men are fathers of minor children. Many of them are not connecting with their families from behind prison walls, and most do not have personal visits with their children. Moreover, many prisons are hundreds of miles from their families, which makes it difficult, if not impossible, for incarcerated parents to continue their parental responsibilities.

The impact of incarceration on families negatively affects both the children and the incarcerated fathers. For the children, having a father in prison can have a negative impact on a child's physical, psychological, and social well-being. The emotional trauma and practical difficulties of a disrupted family life are often compounded by the social stigma and feelings of shame that may result. Children who grow up with an absent father are more likely to live in poverty, have behavioral problems in school, live in foster care, and be incarcerated themselves. Moreover, the overwhelming majority of incarcerated fathers were raised in a household without a father present.

In addition to the effects on the children, incarcerated fathers who are not involved with their children are more depressed and anxious than fathers who continue to be involved in their children's lives. To counteract the negative effects of being isolated from their children, it is important to build stronger bonds and greater support for those children. If the incarcerated father understands that they have a unique and irreplaceable role in their child's life, he most likely will experience increased confidence and growth in attitudes and skills. Incarcerated fathers who are connected with their children are motivated to maintain good behavior to keep visiting rights, which is beneficial for both the facility and the correctional officers working with them. Those transformations are a powerful motivator for a successful reentry into society.

There is evidence that maintaining a positive relationship with their children can lead to a positive reentry for the men. Research has found that the strongest predictor of success upon reentry is family support. Fathers who are involved with their children and families while incarcerated are less likely to return to jail or prison after release. For incarcerated fathers, they are less likely to recidivate after release if they maintained a relationship with their children during incarceration.

Returning Community Members

For a successful reentry to free society, the **returning community member** needs access to housing, employment, education, and therapeutic resources. Recent policy trends focus on preparing the incarcerated person for a successful reentry starting on the first day of incarceration. Strong reentry programs, both inside prior to release and outside after release, have led to lower recidivism rates of returning community members. In some states, such as Massachusetts, there are specific reentry workshops and programs that help prisoners develop a reentry plan and basic skills.

In addition to these practical needs, there is a need for the transformation of men who have learned how to function within the code of toxic masculinity. The prison male dominance hierarchy that reinforced the hypermasculinity that led to incarceration shapes the success or failure of reentry. The man who has successfully proven his manliness can have trouble lowering the mask of masculinity, trusting, and opening up when he enters the community.

In 2018, the federal **First Step Act** (Formerly Incarcerated Reenter Society Transformed Safely Transitioning Every Person Act) was passed as a reform to the federal prison system in an effort to lower the number of people incarcerated in federal prisons and to reduce recidivism. The act, among many provisions, retroactively applies the Fair Sentencing Act of 2010, which modified mandatory minimum sentences for serious drug offenses, and establishes a risk and assessment system. It also expands compassionate release for terminally ill patients, places prisoners closer to their family, mandates deescalation training for correctional officers and prison employees, and increases the number of good conduct time credits prisoners can accumulate. For women, who are 6.8 percent of the nation's incarcerated, the use of restraints on pregnant women is restricted, and feminine hygiene in prison has been improved. While these are important reforms, they apply only to the Federal Bureau of Prisons and do not affect state or local carceral institutions. Moreover, there has been limited funding for implementation of the act.

RETURNING COMMUNITY MEMBER
Nonstigmatizing term used for formerly incarcerated people.

FIRST STEP ACT
Reform to the federal prison system in an effort to lower the number of people incarcerated in federal prisons and to reduce recidivism.

Prison and Jail Programs

Whether the goal is to maintain a safe environment within the prison or to support successful reentry to free society, prison programs are essential. The structure of prison programs varies by facility and purpose. Successful prison programs for incarcerated men focus on unlearning the toxic masculinity that led to their incarceration and teaching tools of success, including life skills. These programs include educational programs, fatherhood programs, conflict resolution programs, and programs that promote a successful reentry. This section focuses on fatherhood programs and conflict resolution programs.

Fatherhood Programs

The purpose of **fatherhood programs** is to connect fathers with their children and to improve the father-child relationship if there is already contact. The father develops and hones social interactional skills and socially responsible behaviors they can apply in all aspects of their lives. Not only are there positive results for the children, but the programs give the incarcerated men a voice and encourage good behavior, which helps maintain safety and order within the facility.

These fatherhood groups not only help the incarcerated men learn tools to use with their children, but also connect the men with themselves. Over time, as the group's bonds create an atmosphere that allows the men to be vulnerable, the men begin to confront their own childhood traumas. They learn how to overcome those traumas so that they do not continue them with their own children. Moreover, those bonds promote good morale and fewer disciplinary infractions, which is important for the safety of the men.

Moreover, recidivism is 37 percent lower for those formerly incarcerated men who have taken a fatherhood program while in prison or jail compared to those who have not been involved in a fatherhood program. For these reasons, prison programs that focus on the father-child relationship are important.

The National Fatherhood Initiative,[7] a nonprofit organization created in 1994, has had a major impact on the development of fatherhood programs in carceral institutions. Its goal is to promote responsible fatherhood throughout society, including among incarcerated fathers by partnering with corrections systems, facilities, and organizations to integrate fatherhood programming into rehabilitation and reentry efforts. In addition to providing resources and training, it offers an online community discussion group.

While there are many fatherhood programs throughout the United States, two fatherhood programs are discussed here—Parenting Inside Out and Father Read to Me. Parenting Inside Out (PIO)[8] is an evidence-based, cognitive-behavioral parent management skills training program that gives the parent a way of navigating life that uses healthy, prosocial skills to interact with children, partners, coparents, officials, friends, and family. At the core of Parenting Inside Out is Parent Management Training (PMT), which was developed in consultation with incarcerated parents and their families. The program is centered on communication, problem solving, positive reinforcement, and nonviolent discipline techniques.

The Father Read to Me program allows fathers an opportunity to read to their children. The incarcerated father selects the book and makes a video recording while reading the book to the child. Both the book, with a written message, and the recording are then sent to the child.

Anticonflict Programs

There are several types of programs to reduce violence. Although there are multiple anticonflict programs in prisons and jails, this section discusses two special units within the facility, Connecticut's T.R.U.E. unit and Washington, DC's Young Men Emerging Unit. In addition, three successful prison programs for men in the general population are discussed: Guiding Rage into Power (GRIP),[9] the Alternatives to Violence Project (AVP), and the Emotional Literacy Project for Prisoners, all of which focus on transformation.

FATHERHOOD PROGRAMS
Programs that connect fathers with their children and, if there is already contact, improve the father-child relationship.

T.R.U.E. Special Unit

One of the more radical attempts at prison reform is taking place in the Cheshire Correctional Institution, a maximum-security prison in central Connecticut. Created in 2017 as an alternative to the typical punitive and warehousing environment found in most jails and prisons, the special unit, called **T.R.U.E.**, which stands for truthful, respectful, understanding, and elevating to success, incorporates therapy for eighteen- to twenty-five-year-old prisoners, whose brains are still developing. The model is based on prisons in Germany, which are more relaxed than American prisons. Focusing on counseling and personal growth, the main objective of Germany's prisons is rehabilitation, which has led to their recidivism rate being about half that of the United States.

After initial resistance, a unit was opened for about fifty young prisoners, whose crimes range from drugs to violent assault, and a small number of older prisoners. The goal of the program is to use experiences, structure, and discipline to transform these young men from being influenced (dominated) by their childhood traumas to being positive individuals. The program incorporates strict rules, incentives, work, and educational study to guide the young men through a transformational path in which they learn to confront their pasts, be vulnerable among their peers, use communication to resolve conflict, and learn basic life skills. The prisoners are out of their cells all day, going to classes and counseling. Among other aspects of the program, the men converted one cell into a yoga studio with a colorful mural to set the mood. While it is too soon to evaluate the success of the program, violence inside the prison has decreased. In the first two years of T.R.U.E., there were no fights or assaults on staff. Recognizing the positive nature of this model, other states are opening similar units.

Young Men Emerging Unit

In 2019, the Washington, DC, Jail created a Young Men Emerging (YME)[10] unit for eighteen- to twenty-five-year-old incarcerated men modeled on the T.R.U.E. unit in Connecticut. The unit creates a therapeutic and rehabilitative environment for young men who have experienced trauma related to exposure to and witnessing violence in their neighborhoods. With the facility's staff collaborating with mentors who are older incarcerated men serving life sentences, the program combines trauma treatment, counseling, life skills classes that teach accountability and responsibility, and "corrective behavior measures" within an atmosphere of love and caring. The transformation begins at orientation, when the Department of Correction staff and mentors interview candidates and decide who will be welcomed to the community. The program includes yoga, meditation, and Zumba classes, as well as partnerships with the community.

General Population Anticonflict Programs

Many of the anticonflict programs that are available to general population prisoners are designed to help incarcerated men connect to positive emotions and unlearn the toxic masculinity that led to their incarceration. In addition to the Alternatives to Violence Project, which is discussed in chapter 8, there are multiple successful programs that transform men. Two of those programs, the Guiding Rage into Power (GRIP) and Emotional Literacy Project for Prisoners, are discussed here.

GRIP: Guiding Rage into Power

GRIP, or **Guiding Rage into Power**, started at San Quentin State Prison in 2013 and has expanded to five state prisons across California. The goal of the program is to teach men about gender roles and how ideas of hypermasculinity have contributed to their violent crimes. During the trainings, the incarcerated men revisit their early childhood traumas, such as sexual assault, emotional abandonment, and domestic violence within their family. Becoming aware of the traumatic experiences is integral to the program, as it is those experiences that formed the basis of their coping mechanisms and survival tactics. Learning these lessons is transformative, which leads to positive changes in the men's lives.

T.R.U.E.
A prison anticonflict program that uses experiences, structure, and discipline to transform young men from being influenced (dominated) by their childhood traumas to being positive individuals.

GUIDING RAGE INTO POWER (GRIP)
Prison program that teaches men about gender roles and how ideas of hypermasculinity contributed to their violent crimes.

Emotional Literacy Project for Prisoners

One of the many prison programs that focus on emotional literacy is the Lionheart Foundation's **Emotional Literacy Project for Prisoners** awareness program based on the book *Houses of Healing: A Prisoner's Guide to Inner Power and Freedom*, which is used as the curriculum for prison-based discussion groups and facilitator-led classes in prisons throughout the United States. The goal is to teach incarcerated people to understand themselves, how the past impacts their present choices, and to forgive. It is centered on emotional intelligence, which is the ability to understand and manage emotions, which is necessary for personal growth. Research shows that emotional intelligence is related to aggression and offending. Program evaluations of the programs have shown a positive impact on those who have participated.

Work in the Gendered Cage

Just as incarcerated men are affected by gendered stereotypes, so are correctional officers, who are predominantly male. These correctional officers are expected to conform to the deeply masculine workplace culture that mirrors patriarchal society's hypermasculinity rules. Given the power differential between guards and prisoners, the male dominance hierarchy inside the prison has a profound impact on the day-to-day running of the prison. Assuming that all incarcerated men are dangerous predators, regardless of the crime or crimes they committed, prison administrators and staff believe in the need for inflexible regulation.

In the next chapter, we cover women; nonbinary, gender nonconforming, and intersex people in prison; parenting from behind bars; and the Prison Rape Elimination Act.

> **EMOTIONAL LITERACY PROJECT FOR PRISONERS** Lionheart Foundation's program centered on emotional intelligence that teaches incarcerated people to understand themselves, how the past impacts their present choices, and to forgive.

REVIEW AND STUDY QUESTIONS

1. Explain the meaning of the infantilization of incarcerated people. Since infantilization hinders successful reentry into free society, what programs and policies can be developed while the person is incarcerated?

2. Since early life traumas are the cornerstone of the pathway toward violence, what can be done to counteract their effects?

3. Given research that shows that family support is one of the most important factors for successful reentry into free society, what policies and programs (including those discussed here and others) should be instituted in carceral institutions and reentry programs?

4. What can be done to counter the negative effects of the prison-industrial complex?

Anderson, Elijah. *Code of the Street: Decency, Violence, and the Moral Life of the Inner City*. New York: Norton, 2000.

Davis, Angela Y. *Are Prisons Obsolete?* New York: Seven Stories Press, 2011.

Sabo, Don, Terry A. Kuper, and Willie London. *Prison Masculinities*. Philadelphia: Temple University Press, 2001.

Toews, Barb. *Little Book of Restorative Justice for People in Prison*. New York: Simon & Schuster, 2006.

Videos/Movies:

Gayles, Contessa. *The Feminist on Cellblock Y*. CNN, April 2018. https://www.cnn.com/videos/us/2018/04/18/the-feminist-on-cellblock-y-doc-orig.cnn.

Newsom, Jennifer Siebel. *The Mask You Live In*. The Representation Project, 2015. http://therepresentationproject.org/film/the-mask-you-live-in-film.

GOING FURTHER

Readings:

Alexander, Michelle. *The New Jim Crow: Mass Incarceration in the Age of Colorblindness*. New York: New Press, 2012.

KEY TERMS

code of the street A set of informal rules governing interpersonal public behavior, including violence.

Emotional Literacy Project for Prisoners Lionheart Foundation's program centered on emotional intelligence that teaches incarcerated people to understand themselves, how the past impacts their present choices, and to forgive.

fatherhood programs   Programs that connect fathers with their children and, if there is already contact, improve the father-child relationship.

First Step Act   Reform to the federal prison system in an effort to lower the number of people incarcerated in federal prisons and to reduce recidivism.

Guiding Rage into Power (GRIP)   Prison program that teaches men about gender roles and how ideas of hypermasculinity contributed to their violent crimes.

male prison code   Hierarchy based on forcing men to act in hypermasculine and dominating ways inside prisons and jails.

mask of masculinity   Maintaining a persona of hypermasculinity where acting tough and not showing any empathy enforces manhood.

prison-industrial complex   Prison system structure that connects economic and political interests, encouraging increased spending on incarceration.

returning community member   Nonstigmatizing term used for formerly incarcerated people.

T.R.U.E.   A prison anticonflict program that uses experiences, structure, and discipline to transform young men from being influenced (dominated) by their childhood traumas to being positive individuals.

NOTES

[1] Jennifer Gonnerman, "Before the Law," *New Yorker*, October 6, 2014.

[2] Gonnerman, "Before the Law."

[3] Terry A. Kupers, "Toxic Masculinity in and outside of Prison: The Same Dominance Hierarchy May Prevail in Prison and Outside," *Psychology Today*, April 8, 2019, https://www.psychologytoday.com/us/blog/prisons-and-prisms/201904/toxic-masculinity-in-and-outside-prison; Anna Curtis "'You Have to Cut It Off at the Knee': Dangerous Masculinity and Security inside a Men's Prison," *Men and Masculinities* 17, no. 2 (2014): 120–46.

[4] Terry A. Kupers, "Gender and Domination in Prison," *Western New England Law Review* 39 (2017), https://digitalcommons.law.wne.edu/lawreview/vol39/iss3/5; Terry A. Kupers, "Toxic Masculinity as a Barrier to Mental Health Treatment in Prison," *Journal of Clinical Psychology* 61, no. 6 (2005): 1–2.

[5] Elijah Anderson, *Code of the Street: Decency, Violence, and the Moral Life of the Inner City* (New York: Norton, 2005).

[6] Teresa Wilz, "Having a Parent behind Bars Costs Children, States," Pew Research Center, May 24, 2016, https://www.pewtrusts.org/en/research-and-analysis/blogs/stateline/2016/05/24/having-a-parent-behind-bars-costs-children-states.

[7] "Fathers behind Bars: The Problem & Solution for America's Children [Infographic]," National Fatherhood Initiative, October 16, 2014, https://www.fatherhood.org/fatherhood/fathers-behind-bars-the-problem-and-solution-for-americas-children-infographic.

[8] "Fathers behind Bars."

[9] "Prisoners Unlearn the Toxic Masculinity That Led to Their Incarceration," *HuffPost*, n.d., accessed November 1, 2019, https://www.huffpost.com/entry/prisoners-unlearn-the-toxic-masculinity-that-led-to-their-incarceration_n_5d406b9ce4b06e9f169f1247.

[10] Joel Castón and Michael Woody, "A DC Jail Unit Challenges the 'Warehouse,'" *Crime Report*, June 11, 2019, https://thecrimereport.org/2019/06/11/a-dc-jail-unit-challenges-the-warehouse-approach-to-corrections.

Unique Populations in Prison

In this chapter you will read about the experiences of women, girls, and trans, nonbinary, gender nonconforming, and intersex people who are incarcerated. The chapter highlights the unique problems that confront those who are extraordinary in the U.S. prison system.

LEARNING OBJECTIVES

After reading this chapter, you should be able to do the following:

- Identify the specific intersections of oppression that face transgender, nonbinary, and gender nonconforming communities and individuals.
- Explain the variety of external factors that may lead transgender individuals to face more violence, both in their private lives and in relation to public institutions.
- Identify the particular obstacles that face prisoners who are not cis men.

Case #13: CeCe McDonald

CeCe McDonald was born into a very large and religious African American family in Chicago, Illinois, in 1989. Early in her elementary school years, she was already experiencing opposition from her family because they felt that there was something wrong about her—in short, they thought she was a boy and should act like it. Instead, CeCe was a girl and wanted to act like a girl—she wanted to get dressed up and be glamorous, like her mother and the other older women in the family. She already knew that she had been assigned the wrong gender at birth, and she never felt comfortable with all the things she was "supposed" to be wearing and doing. Her family was angry and derisive, punishing her and instructing her to pray that this "deviation" would be washed out of her.

The constant opposition and derision from her family made her a rebellious child, and she had a hard time finding confidence and comfort. Her time at school was no easier. She was mercilessly bullied by classmates who passed harsh judgment on her rejection of what they thought of as her "correct" gender role. The taunting was not only verbal; in junior high, amid sexist taunts, she was beaten so badly that her teeth cut straight through her lip. She perpetually feared using the boys' bathroom because the confined space left her open to attack. Even still, she remained committed to being herself; this meant becoming a cheerleader and sneakily wearing her mother's clothes to school, though she would always change before getting home in order to prevent the further wrath of her family members. CeCe did want to be close to her mother, but her very identity drove a wedge between them. The final separation from her family occurred when an uncle discovered a romantic note that CeCe had written to a boy and attacked her in anger and disgust. She was fourteen when she was pushed out of her family.

At fourteen, as a homeless transgender girl, CeCe faced countless obstacles and dangers in the world. She encountered violence in the street time and time again, including physical and sexual assault. Left with no safe, reliable way to support herself financially, she began to sell marijuana in order to make ends meet, but she was still faced with constant instability and little to no access to physical safety or financial security. Every day was a struggle that presented not only the difficulties of making enough money to eat but the threat of a new assault; every morning she awoke with the knowledge that this day could be her last. Out of options, she turned to prostitution by the age of fifteen. Though this did present her with the chance to finally fully present as and live as a girl and even receive some affirmation for that choice, it was dubious affirmation; it involved, after all, exploitation and a large degree of physical vulnerability and risk of arrest. Feelings of fear, isolation, and uncertainty led CeCe to attempt suicide on several occasions; there seemed to be no promise of a better future to come.

After a few exhausting and painful years of this daily and dangerous grind, CeCe decided to take up a friend on an invitation to relocate to Minneapolis. This move set her on a new path and proved to be the change she needed to get herself on her feet. She worked toward and then passed her GED and began to attend Minneapolis Community and Technical College. She was also diagnosed with gender dysphoria, meaning that her biological sex and her gender identity were not aligned and that she experienced a great degree of emotional distress in response to that lack of alignment. She soon began to take estrogen as the first step in the transformation toward the body she had always felt she should have. Additionally, she initiated the bureaucratic process of legally changing her name and gender identity. Soon, she even had a boyfriend. She still endured taunts and discrimination, but things seemed to be falling into place.

On June 5, 2011, just a month after finally moving into a comfortable place of her own and beginning to enjoy her newfound stability, CeCe was walking with a few friends late on a warm night in Minneapolis; they were making a quick trip to the grocery store. CeCe was dressed casually, wearing denim shorts and a T-shirt. In front of a place called the Schooner Tavern, CeCe and her friends were confronted by a rowdy group of bar patrons. There were about four of them, all white, and they began to verbally assault CeCe and her friends with sexist and racist terms. Dean Schmitz, one of the people outside the bar, reportedly yelled, "Look at that boy dressed like a girl tucking her dick in" and told the group to "go back to Africa!"[1] CeCe and her friends, a couple of whom were gay men, seemed to be the perfect targets for the bigoted insults of Schmitz and his friends, who at first only yelled slurs. CeCe defensively stepped in front of her friends, with every intention of simply protecting herself and her friends and then walking on by. "Excuse me. We are people, and you need to respect us. . . . We're just trying to walk to the store,"[2] she said, as Schmitz and the others continued with their loud and abusive remarks and name-calling. The yelling was drawing onlookers out of the bar, and CeCe and her friends tried to simply carry on with their mission for groceries.

They were not permitted to simply walk on, however. A woman named Molly Flaherty, reportedly an ex-girlfriend of Schmitz, emerged from the group of bar-going antagonists and quickly approached CeCe, smashing a glass into CeCe's face; the broken glass cut into her cheek and through to her salivary gland and ultimately required eleven stitches. CeCe lashed back against Flaherty as the crowd outside the bar shouted further slurs, and her friends fought to escape from the group and get enough distance to defend themselves. CeCe and her friends finally managed to disentangle themselves and tried to make their escape. CeCe was covered in blood from the still-bleeding wound on her face, while Flaherty, also covered in blood and bits of broken glass, was convinced, wrongly, that she herself had been stabbed. As CeCe quickly tried to put distance between herself and the attackers, she heard her friends shout out a warning, and she turned to see that Schmitz, enraged, was rushing at her. She would find out later that he was on both cocaine and methamphetamines, that he had a swastika tattooed on his chest, and that this was not the first time he had engaged in an assault. In the moment, however, all CeCe knew with certainty was that she was in very real danger of being killed; Schmitz already hated her for who she was, and he was now also under the impression that she had stabbed his friend.

CeCe, because of her community college fashion courses, had a pair of scissors for cutting fabric in her purse, and she pulled them out to defend herself. Schmitz lunged at her. CeCe later reported that she was not aware in the fear and chaos of the moment that her scissors had actually made contact when she and Schmitz collided, let alone that she had stabbed him in the chest, but according to an eyewitness, Schmitz, upon being stabbed, drew back and said to CeCe, "You stabbed me in the chest," to which she responded, "Yes, I did."[3] CeCe and her boyfriend turned to run away from further danger as Schmitz turned to stumble back to his friends, and it was in fact CeCe and her boyfriend who attracted the attention of a police cruiser. They flagged down the police officers to attempt to report the attack they had just endured, but instead, CeCe found herself under arrest. She argued that she had been acting in self-defense against a sexist, homophobic, racist attack, but unbeknownst to her, she had stabbed Schmitz in the heart, and he had died almost immediately after she made her escape. Bleeding, shaken, and lucky to be alive, CeCe was all of a sudden facing a murder charge.

It took almost a year for her case to go to trial. During that time, for a full month, she was held in protective custody, otherwise known as solitary confinement. During this time, CeCe received very poor medical care, even for the deep laceration on her face. Those who supported her, particularly the Minneapolis organization Trans Youth Support Network, argued that she was not a murderer and was, in reality, "on trial for surviving a hate crime."[4] The prosecution was calling for a conviction for second-degree intentional murder, and in October 2011, CeCe was offered a plea deal: instead of second-degree murder, she could accept a conviction for first-degree manslaughter, which would carry a shorter sentence. She rejected the plea, however, maintaining that she had acted in self-defense. The prosecution reaffirmed their request for a second-degree murder conviction, and for the next several months, both defense and prosecution built their cases.

CeCe had faced violence for being Black and trans before; Schmitz himself had a record of violence. However, the judge ruling on her case, Daniel Moreno, was unwilling to accept evidence of acts of violence and racism in

Schmitz's past that might indicate that CeCe was defending herself against a hate crime. It was known to the judge that Schmitz had a swastika tattooed on his chest, a criminal record, and a brother who noted that Schmitz had been known to use racial slurs, but the judge deemed none of these things relevant in the case against CeCe. In addition, the fact that Schmitz had methamphetamines in his toxicology report was only partially allowed as evidence in the trial. The judge also rejected an attempt by the Legal Rights Center, CeCe's defense, to bring in an expert witness who could attest to the violence that transgender people have to face in their lives, as well as evidence of the disproportionate prevalence of attacks on and incarceration of trans women in particular. The strength of CeCe's claims of self-defense began to crumble as all these factors were excluded from the case. CeCe's defense depended on an acknowledgment that gender, race, and sexual orientation were in fact central features of the initial altercation and the subsequent events that had led to Schmitz's death, but the Hennepin County attorney's office plainly stated that "gender, race, sexual orientation and class are not part of the decision-making process. The charges filed took into account the evidence in this case."[5]

Not only CeCe's legal team, but also the growing number of people who were becoming aware of the case over the next several months, argued that it was clear that gender and race were a factor in several levels of decision making, from Schmitz and Flaherty's initial decision to accost CeCe and her friends to the decision to disallow evidence in the trial that would point to the likelihood that the attack constituted a racist and heterosexist hate crime. Support for CeCe began to emerge from many directions; alongside the Trans Youth Support Network in Minneapolis, there were statements and movements from public officials, the National Center for Transgender Equality, the CeCe Support Committee, and a widespread international grassroots "Free CeCe" campaign, as well as online petitions and the support of celebrities, who used their position in the public eye to bring CeCe's case to the attention of an even larger audience. Supporters came to court in purple to show their support for her as her trial neared.

On May 11, 2012, Molly Flaherty was convicted of second-degree assault with a deadly weapon and third-degree assault. While this may seem to suggest that CeCe was indeed acting in self-defense, just a week before Flaherty's conviction, as CeCe's trial was set to begin and a jury was selected and ready, CeCe took a plea deal, pleading guilty to second-degree manslaughter. A second-degree intentional murder conviction would mean up to forty years in prison, while a second-degree manslaughter conviction would mean a sentence of only a few years. CeCe took the deal because she was not convinced, given the limited evidence that would be allowed in court, that a jury would agree that her act had been one of self-defense. There were numerous eyewitnesses who corroborated her account of the evening and confirmed that Schmitz, Flaherty, and their friends had instigated the attack, as well as clear medical evidence that CeCe herself had been a victim, but she knew that a jury might still be convinced to see her as the aggressor. On June 4, 2012, for second-degree manslaughter, she was sentenced to forty-one months in prison, less the 275 days she had already spent in custody awaiting trial. This plea deal and the court's willingness to so drastically reduce the conviction indicated to the Legal Rights Center that the court recognized to some degree that self-defense was a large part of what made CeCe act that night and that a conviction for murder would be inappropriate. Despite this perhaps tacit recognition of the validity of CeCe's self-defense claim, she still could not escape being convicted as a felon.

Before her sentencing, CeCe had been held under house arrest and in solitary confinement, and her legal team was concerned about where she would be sent for incarceration. As a trans woman, they felt that it was unlikely she would be sent to a women's prison but that a men's prison would be far more dangerous for her physical safety. Though CeCe identifies as a woman and had legally transitioned, the Minnesota State Department of Corrections did indeed send her to a men's prison. Sarah Russell, a spokesperson for the Department of Corrections, said, "We will intake him as a male at St. Cloud prison. . . . We will assess him as any other offender would be assessed. . . . The assessments include, but are not limited to, screening for potential vulnerability to sexual assaults, tendencies to act out with sexually aggressive behavior and any disabilities."[6] It is clear in Russell's language that the state had already determined that CeCe was a "him." This misgendering of CeCe had occurred throughout the trial as well, and it did not bode well for her ability to have her gender acknowledged and respected while incarcerated.

Ultimately, she was sent to the Minnesota Correctional Facility at St. Cloud. She had not had gender confirmation surgery, and the state determined that this was the correct placement for her. This placement of CeCe in a men's prison also threw into question her ability to continue hormone therapy. CeCe was determined to make her time in prison as mild as possible, and she reports that she was able to stay on her hormones and generally keep to herself and that there was not much physical violence during her incarceration. However, verbal assaults and harassment and her absolute vulnerability in such a space did take a toll on her. In addition, she was required to participate in a drug rehabilitation program, despite the fact that it was irrelevant to her case or the event that had landed her in prison in the first place. She was eventually barred from the drug rehabilitation program because of her refusal to follow the dress code the prison imposed on her; they were trying to force her to wear clothing that was far too large for her in order to cover up the fact that she had curves.

CeCe was released in January 2014 after nineteen months in prison, plus the initial nine months she had been in custody prior to her sentencing. She was released into the arms of a small group of friends—among them was trans actress Laverne Cox, who has been instrumental in bringing CeCe's story to the public. CeCe's time and experience in prison, as well as the public debate that surrounded it, inspired Cox's portrayal of a transgender prisoner in the Netflix original series *Orange Is the New Black*, which features Cox's character, Sophia Burset, a trans woman who must fight for her right to appropriate medical care and the hormones she needs while incarcerated. Sophia, like CeCe, is a trans woman, but unlike CeCe, Sophia is in a women's prison. Cox had been researching CeCe and the particular difficulties that face transgender prisoners for the role, and her acclaimed performance has brought the particular considerations of transgender prisoners to a popular audience.

Despite the fact that CeCe never intended to become a spokesperson for the plight of transgender folks and their disproportionate experiences of violence and incarceration, she and Laverne Cox continue to be at the forefront of public discussions around violence against and criminalization of trans folks. Cox says, "I very easily could have been CeCe. Many times I've walked down the streets of New York and I've experienced harassment. I was kicked once on the street, and very easily that could have escalated into a situation that CeCe faced. And it's a situation that too many trans women of color face all over this country."[7] They both agree that one of the keys to making sure that trans individuals do not have to endure this kind of discrimination in prisons is to find ways to prevent them from being criminalized and put into prison in the first place; this requires creating, nurturing, and protecting communities that support them and do not see their identities as inherently criminal or deviant.

In various interviews, CeCe has shared the idea that it is unusual to hear stories of trans women who just lived happily ever after; there is always some violent or traumatic part of their story. Now, with her public profile, she can issue warnings to others, make them aware of the dangers, and tell them how imperative it is that they watch out for themselves in a world that is all too ready to tear them down. To that end, in addition to being a public figure, she remains an active and crucial member of the local community in Minneapolis and St. Paul, which continues to work to create a community where people can support each other and find some relief from lifetimes of bullying, abuse, and fear. However, though she is a heroine to many, CeCe still suffers from posttraumatic stress disorder and depression from the violence she has faced, and now, with a felony on her record, she faces continuing financial instability because of her difficulty in securing dependable employment and housing. She reports that she still has nightmares about being in prison, nightmares in which she is naked and people are ogling her as she walks by. She may be out of prison, but she is still not able to be fully free.

THINKING CRITICALLY ABOUT THE CASE

1. What are the variety of factors that led to the altercation between CeCe, Schmitz, and others?

2. For what reason did the court consider Schmitz's past inadmissible evidence?

3. Would being in a women's prison have made prison easier for CeCe? Why or why not?

REFERENCES

This case is adapted from the following sources:

"'Black Trans Bodies Are under Attack': Freed Activist CeCe McDonald, Actress Laverne Cox Speak Out." *Democracy Now!*, February 19, 2014. https://www.youtube.com/watch?v=kOuH43-_4Yo.

Cowan, Samantha. "Laverne Cox and CeCe McDonald Discuss the Epidemic of Violence against Trans Women." *Take Part*, June 3, 2016. http://www.takepart.com/article/2016/06/03/free-cece.

Erdely, Sabrina Rubin. "The Transgender Crucible." *Rolling Stone*, July 30, 2014. https://www.rollingstone.com/culture/culture-news/the-transgender-crucible-114095.

Hill, Marc Lamont. "Why Aren't We Fighting for CeCe McDonald?" *Ebony*, June 11, 2012. https://www.ebony.com/news/why-arent-we-fighting-for-cece-mcdonald.

"In Conversation: Alok Vaid-Menon and CeCe McDonald." *Nepantla: A Journal Dedicated to Queer Poets of Color* 2 (September 9, 2015). https://www.lambdaliterary.org/wp-content/uploads/2015/09/alok.cece_.pdf.

Molloy, Parker Marie. "Going to a Prison Made CeCe McDonald Want to Fix Them." *Advocate*, July 30, 2014. https://www.advocate.com/40-under-40-emerging-voices/2014/07/30/40-under-40-prison-turned-cece-mcdonald-activist.

Pasulka, Nicole. "The Case of CeCe McDonald—Murder, or Self-Defense against a Hate Crime?" *Mother Jones*, May 22, 2012. https://www.motherjones.com/politics/2012/05/cece-mcdonald-transgender-hate-crime-murder.

Pearce, Matt. "Transgender Woman Sentenced to Men's Prison in Minnesota Killing." *Los Angeles Times*, June 18, 2012. https://www.latimes.com/nation/la-xpm-2012-jun-18-la-na-nn-transgender-woman-sentenced-to-mens-prison-20120618-story.html.

Rivas, Jorge. "Black Transgender Woman CeCe McDonald to Be Housed in Male Prison." *Colorlines*, June 4, 2012. https://www.colorlines.com/articles/black-transgender-woman-cece-mcdonald-be-housed-male-prison.

Solomon, Akiba. "CeCe McDonald: Attacked for Her Identity, Incarcerated for Surviving." *Ebony*, May 4, 2012. https://www.ebony.com/news/cece-mcdonald-bias-attack.

CONTEXT AND ANALYSIS

Men make up the vast majority of people in prison in the United States—nearly 90 percent—but women (including, of course, trans women) are the fastest-growing prison population. Despite this, and despite the popularity of shows such as *Orange Is the New Black* and *Girls Incarcerated*, the experiences of women, girls, and nonbinary, gender nonconforming, and intersex individuals during and after incarceration are often made peripheral in discussions of prison in general.

A Brief History of Women in Prison

Prior to 1873, there were no dedicated women's prisons in the United States; women were held in special units in men's prisons. In 1873, the Indiana Women's Prison became the first prison in the nation specifically for women. Since then, women's facilities have opened steadily across the country. Currently, women are incarcerated in both dedicated women's prisons and in women's units in larger facilities that have populations of all genders, including twenty-nine facilities within the Federal Bureau of Prisons, as well as in state prisons and local jails.

At the federal, state, and local levels, there is widespread acknowledgment that imprisonment for women differs from imprisonment for men. The Federal Bureau of Prisons recognizes that women are more likely to face economic instability and have histories of trauma and abuse, both of which require particular efforts and programming that address such issues and provide further support upon release. Over the last two decades, there have also been increased federal efforts to curb the sexual abuse and assault of incarcerated women. Despite the attention paid to the particular vulnerabilities of incarcerated women, however, rates of incarceration for women and girls have risen sharply in the last few decades, eliciting arguments from prison policy experts and advocates for greater attention to programs and treatment for women (both those considered "at risk" and those who have been or are currently incarcerated), as well as a reexamination of the state and local policies that are leading to higher arrest, conviction, and incarceration rates.

Since 1980, the number of incarcerated women and girls has risen by approximately 700 percent overall, with the most dramatic rise in state prisons. This rate of increase is double the rate of increase of the population of men in prison during that time. National and state efforts to decrease—or at least slow the rise of—incarceration rates have primarily resulted in lower incarceration rates for men but stable or even increasing incarceration rates for women.[8] Drug offenses and property crimes are the majority of convictions among women in prison, and women are much more likely than men to be incarcerated for these types of nonviolent offenses. Because of this, the bulk of the rise of incarceration rates for women is in local jails and state prisons rather than federal prisons; only about 7 percent of incarcerated women are in the Federal Bureau of Prisons,[9] compared to about 45 percent in state prisons and 40 percent in local jails. Significantly, the majority of women in local jails have not yet been convicted and are awaiting trial. The fact that most incarcerated women are in state prisons and local jails is an indication that local and state policies are primarily responsible for the rise in rates of incarceration for women. In several other chapters (3, 7, 9, 11, and 14), we see further forms of criminalization that lead to higher rates of incarceration among women, such as women's responses to gender-based violence and abuse, as well as the treatment of women and girls who are involved in the sex trades and trafficking.

Race and Female Incarceration

Currently, Black women are approximately twice as likely to be imprisoned as white women. Nevertheless, while the rate of imprisonment for Black women has been decreasing slightly over the past two decades, the rate of imprisonment for white women is climbing. Rates of imprisonment for Latina and Hispanic women have also been on the rise; they are currently approximately 1.3 times more likely than white women to be imprisoned. For indigenous women, the rates of incarceration are approximately six times that of white women.[10]

For girls, rates of incarceration are similarly skewed based on race and ethnicity. Black and indigenous girls are 3.5 to 4 times more likely to be incarcerated than white girls, and Latina and Hispanic girls approximately 1.4 times more likely. Further information about children and the criminal/legal system may be found in chapter 6.

Immigration Detention

Data from 2018 indicates that there are approximately seven thousand women held in immigration detention in the United States, and a further five thousand women held in local jails for **Immigration and Customs Enforcement (ICE)** violations.[11] In 2015, the U.S. Commission on Civil Rights released a lengthy report noting that some facilities displayed "torture-like conditions," insufficient medical and mental health care, and sexual assault, accompanied by poor adherence to Prison Rape Elimination Act standards (discussed below).[12] In February 2019, over seventy-five thousand people were taken into custody, and in March 2019, ICE reported nearly fifty thousand people in detention, indicating that the numbers of those detained fluctuates quickly in response to release and deportation.[13] The numbers being held are rising, however, and estimates of how many people are currently in holding centers, immigration detention centers (both public and private), local jails, and private detention centers are currently approximate, given that the Department of Homeland Security and Immigration and Customs Enforcement are rarely transparent regarding processes, data, facilities, and conditions and that private companies operate approximately two-thirds of the facilities.[14]

Mothers in Prison and Children with Mothers in Prison

Approximately 80 percent of women incarcerated in the United States are mothers or are pregnant when they are first incarcerated. As the majority of these women are primary caretakers of their children, this presents unique problems for both parents and children.

The **Rebecca Project for Human Rights** and the **National Women's Law Center** have found that the vast majority of states do not provide sufficient prenatal and basic health care; do not have sufficient, medically approved guidelines regarding restraints and shackling for labor and delivery; and do not have sufficient recording and reporting policies for pregnancy, labor, and restraints.

The **National Commission on Correctional Health Care**'s position statement and recommendations highlight the need for deeper and more expansive care, treatment, and programming for those who are incarcerated while pregnant or parenting. They find that specialists in obstetrics and gynecology are not available in all facilities, leading to a greater risk for cervical, ovarian, and breast cancer, as regular checkups and screenings are not provided. They also find that just over half of those who are pregnant while incarcerated are provided with prenatal care,[15] despite the fact that many who are pregnant during intake are high risk because of mental and physical health conditions or drug use.

Despite prohibitions at the federal level and in some states, incarcerated people giving birth and in transit to and from medical facilities are routinely shackled and restrained, even in instances where prohibitions exist.[16] Arguments against this practice assert that the pain and all-encompassing experience of childbirth preclude the possibility that the person in labor will be a pronounced flight risk or present physical danger to others, particularly given the fact that the vast majority of incarcerated women have not been charged or convicted for violent crimes. Further, there is physical, mental, and emotional risk associated with shackling. As described by one woman who gave birth while incarcerated,

> when they shackled me I had 2 handcuffs. One was on my wrist and the other one was attached to the bed. And then I had another shackle and my legs—my ankles were so swollen, I don't even know how they got it closed around my ankle and then

IMMIGRATIONS AND CUSTOMS ENFORCEMENT (ICE) Federal law enforcement agency responsible for immigration enforcement.

REBECCA PROJECT FOR HUMAN RIGHTS Legal and policy organization that advocates for justice and reforms for vulnerable women and girls in the United States and Africa.

NATIONAL WOMEN'S LAW CENTER Legal organization that fights for gender justice, especially for women and girls facing multiple forms of discrimination.

NATIONAL COMMISSION ON CORRECTIONAL HEALTH CARE Mission is to improve the quality of health care in jails, prisons, and juvenile detention facilities.

attached to the bed too. So my leg and my arm were attached to the bed so there was no way for me to move and to try and deal with the labor pains. And the metal, 'cuz when you're swollen, it would just cut into your skin. I had bruises after the fact that stood on me for 3 weeks. I mean, purple bruises from my ankle and my wrist from them having them shackles and handcuffs on me. Even when I had to get an epidural, they didn't take the shackles and the handcuffs off. I just had to bend over and just pray that I could stay in that position while they were putting that needle in my back through the whole procedure. Not once did he try and loosen them. And the doctor asked him, you know, "Can't you take them off of her? She can't go nowhere. She can't walk. She's not goin' nowhere." It's procedure and policy. Can't do it. . . . I had a lot of complications when I gave birth to her. I guess maybe from the trauma of being shackled and handcuffed and being incarcerated—I had . . . I started hemorrhaging on the table before I had her. I broke some blood vessels in my uterus and they had to rush me and do a—they had to burn 'em really really fast before I had her otherwise I would of hemorrhaged to death. And because of that I was more fortunate than some of the other females. I got to stay in the hospital for five days with my daughter because of that. They had to make sure I was healing and I wasn't gonna start hemorrhaging once they let me—released me. So, I got to stay with her for 5 days, I got to bathe her, I got to feed her, well I got to breast feed her. I got a chance to spend some time with her and the other women don't get that. You are in there 24 hours and you're tooken back to the jail.[17]

In addition to not providing sufficient prenatal and basic health care, most states do not offer prison nurseries, despite the fact that accessibility of prison nursery programs has been shown to greatly reduce the chances that a participant will reoffend.[18]

Trauma and Care

Several studies have shown that the majority of incarcerated women have histories of trauma and abuse. This creates a multidirectional problem: not only do histories of trauma and symptoms of posttraumatic stress disorder (PTSD) have a bearing on offending behavior,[19] but the experience of incarceration may exacerbate PTSD while offering insufficient treatment and support. Though facilities themselves do not generally screen for posttraumatic stress disorder, many studies suggest that 50 percent or more of incarcerated women could be diagnosed with PTSD and that the vast majority—more than 80 percent—experience intermittent symptoms of PTSD.[20] These symptoms are often accompanied by physical and mental health conditions, and symptoms of all sorts are particularly pronounced in women who experienced childhood or sexual abuse. We have seen in previous chapters that prison itself often exacerbates symptoms of trauma and other forms of anxiety and depression and that prisons are seldom well equipped to offer timely and effective treatment to those suffering from PTSD and other forms of poor physical and mental health.

We have discussed some of the effects of trauma and PTSD (for instance, in chapters 4 and 9), and the interaction between trauma, PTSD, and imprisonment creates a highly volatile dynamic. According to the *Diagnostic and Statistical Manual of Mental Disorders* (*DSM*), the American Psychiatric Association's standard tool for diagnosis and recommendations for treatment, symptoms of PTSD may include hypervigilance, lack of impulse control, angry outbursts, and exaggerated responses to feelings of fear or being startled, all of which may be particularly problematic for those who are incarcerated. Angry outbursts and an inability to rein in such responses may lead to conflict with other prisoners or officers, which may lead to being placed in solitary confinement, which itself has negative impacts on mental health (as described in chapter 12). Histories of childhood trauma among incarcerated women lead to a rise in suicidal ideation and suicide attempts.[21] Panic disorder, agoraphobia, depression, various manifestations of obsessive-compulsive disorder, and substance-related disorders or drug use are also commonly experienced by those with histories of traumatic intimate partner violence.[22] This is particularly notable because drug convictions are a leading factor in women's incarceration. Since drug use is often used as a form of self-medication when no other assistance is forthcoming, treatment for both drug use and PTSD may ultimately be more beneficial than incarceration. Substance-related and mental health disorders, often occurring in tandem, have in fact resulted in greater disciplinary action, such as placement in solitary confinement.[23]

Posttraumatic stress disorder also involves physical ailments, such as an increased risk of diabetes, hypertension, chronic pain, cardiovascular diseases, a weakened immune system, and many other symptoms.[24] Because these conditions may be attributed to simply poor physical health rather than complications of PTSD, prisoners may not be able to receive proper treatment. However, even when the symptoms are seen as related to poor physical health, as we saw in the preceding section, there is often insufficient medical care.

Prison Rape Elimination Act

In 2003, Congress passed the **Prison Rape Elimination Act (PREA)**. The objective of the act is to "provide for the analysis of the incidence and effects of prison rape in Federal, State, and local institutions and to provide information, resources, recommendations and funding to protect individuals from prison rape."[25] It further created the National Prison Rape Elimination Commission and called for greater research on the prevalence of rape in prison, recommendations to prevent rape, national standards, and trainings for relevant officials and officers.

The impetus for the act was the lack of research and data on the prevalence of rape in prison. The act indicates that at least 13 percent of prisoners in the United States have been sexually assaulted, that most incidents are not reported, and that inadequate training and response on the part of correctional officers exacerbates the problem. It also estimates that those with mental illness and juveniles are at higher risk for assault and that sexual assault increases not only the risk of further violence between and among officers and prisoners but also the likelihood of recidivism due to the trauma that victimized prisoners experience and its effects on their likelihood to reoffend. Finally, the act notes that sexual assault while in prison violates the Eighth Amendment to the Constitution, which prohibits "cruel and unusual punishments."

The act falls under the purview of the Department of Justice, and there are several other official bodies coordinating the implementation and maintenance of PREA standards. The Bureau of Justice Statistics is primarily responsible for research and data, the National Institute of Corrections is responsible for trainings in facilities and producing further data, and the Bureau of Justice Assistance and the National Institute of Justice are responsible for the funds and grants needed to implement and maintain PREA mandates.

The national standards were created in 2009 and approved by the Department of Justice in 2012. The standards cover many areas: recommendations that every facility have a designated PREA point person; recommendations for supervision, monitoring, and staffing of facilities, including juvenile facilities, with special attention to juveniles incarcerated in adult facilities; recommendations for treatment of LGBTQ, intersex, and gender nonconforming individuals; recommendations for the treatment of individuals with disabilities or limited proficiency in English; and guidelines for reporting and investigation, including a prohibition against retaliation against those who cooperate with investigations. As of 2017, all U.S. states and territories had adopted PREA, with the exception of Arkansas and Utah, which have declined to implement PREA policies and standards in their state and local facilities.

The implementation and effects of PREA are yet unclear. Some standards did not go into effect until 2017, and much of the impetus for facilities to comply rests on the threat of a 5 percent reduction in funding for noncompliant facilities. Further, numerous PREA-compliant facilities still have high rates of sexual assault, and documented instances of retaliation against those who report sexual assault continue, indicating that PREA compliance in itself does not preclude the continued prevalence of sexual assault

PRISON RAPE ELIMINATION ACT (PREA)
The first federal law intended to deter the sexual assault and rape of incarcerated persons, established in 2003. It has set standards to prevent, detect, reduce, and respond to sexual abuse in prisons, jails, and juvenile detention facilities.

within facilities.[26] This may be attributed to several factors, including policies that are either unclear or unavailable to officers, lack of clarity around reporting and further steps, and unclear approaches to defining sexual assault versus "willing" sexual activity between officers and prisoners.

In 2010, the Sylvia Rivera Law Project, an organization engaged in organizing, advocacy, and legal assistance for trans, nonbinary, gender nonconforming, and intersex individuals and communities, released recommendations for the national standards. Their recommendations called for stronger independent oversight, deeper training of officers and other relevant figures, greater attention to the complications of reporting and confidentiality, and safeguards against the conflation of sexual activity with sexual assault, particularly in the case of TGNCI prisoners, who are already targeted for their sexuality and gender expression.[27]

Trans, Gender Nonconforming, and Intersex (TGNCI) in Prison

The situation for trans, gender nonconforming, and intersex (**TGNCI**) prisoners is perhaps yet more complicated than the situation for **cisgender** women. Black trans women in particular are incarcerated at approximately 10 times the rate of the general population. Moreover, they may be placed in a men's prison, where they experience very targeted forms of harassment and suffer from the environment of prison in general and misgendering in particular. As a result, it becomes clear that incarceration for TGNCI prisoners is especially fraught.

As we saw, CeCe was put in solitary confinement, which is a common practice when prisoners are transgender. The argument is that it is protective rather than punitive, though solitary confinement itself is an experience that often results in trauma and mental disturbances (as we saw in chapter 12). For TGNCI prisoners, the increased prevalence of strip searches, reduced access to medical and mental health care, and reduced visitation rights exacerbates the isolation of solitary confinement and may lead to an even greater risk of suicidal ideation than for cis prisoners.

The danger for TGNCI prisoners is heightened both in solitary confinement and in the general prison population. A 2007 study in California prisons, in a random sampling, revealed that nearly 60 percent of trans prisoners had experienced sexual assault in prison, compared to less than 5 percent of non-trans prisoners. The study also showed that trans prisoners were more likely to experience other forms of unwanted sexual contact, that weapons were more likely to be used in attacks on trans prisoners, and that trans prisoners were less likely to be able to receive medical care after an assault than other prisoners. Because of the increased risk for TGNCI prisoners, PREA contains a number of specific recommendations regarding TGNCI prisoners. Here are some examples:

- In deciding whether to assign a transgender or intersex inmate to a facility for male or female inmates, and in making other housing and programming assignments, the agency shall consider on a case-by-case basis whether a placement would ensure the inmate's health and safety, and whether the placement would present management or security problems.

- Placement and programming assignments for each transgender or intersex inmate shall be reassessed at least twice each year to review any threats to safety experienced by the inmate.

- A transgender or intersex inmate's own views with respect to his or her own safety shall be given serious consideration.

- Transgender and intersex inmates shall be given the opportunity to shower separately from other inmates.[28]

TGNCI
A contemporary acronym used to refer to trans, gender nonconforming, and intersex people.

CISGENDER
An adjective denoting that a person's gender identity corresponds with the gender they were assigned at birth; often expressed simply as "cis."

Despite this, in 2018, the Federal Bureau of Prisons stated that initial decisions about placement would rest on sex assigned at birth.

CeCe was not placed in a women's prison because she had not yet had gender affirmation surgery. Variously referred to as gender affirmation surgery, gender confirmation surgery, gender reassignment surgery, or "bottom surgery," this surgery is meant to help individuals physically transition from their birth-assigned sex to their gender. For trans people who suffer from **gender dysphoria**, this surgery may be a life-saving procedure because it is crucial in reversing the emotional, psychological, and physical distress that arises from dysphoria. Nearly half of those who experience gender dysphoria have accompanying suicidal ideation,[29] and for trans women who are assigned to a men's prison, the placement itself—to say nothing of the treatment that they may face inside—may severely aggravate their gender dysphoria. CeCe was placed in a men's prison because the Minnesota State Department of Corrections classified her according to her birth-assigned sex—in other words, according to her genitalia. In other states, such as Illinois and Massachusetts, trans prisoners have successfully petitioned to be incarcerated in facilities that reflect their gender identity, but the case-by-case nature of these determinations generally means that such placements are rare.

Fortunately, CeCe was able to continue taking her hormones while in prison, but the ability to continue with hormone therapy is not a given for TGNCI prisoners. The Federal Bureau of Prison's *Transgender Offender Manual* states, "Hormone or other necessary medical treatment may be provided after an individualized assessment of the requested inmate by institution medical staff. Medical staff should request consultation from Psychology Services regarding the mental health benefits of hormone or other necessary medical treatment. If appropriate for the inmate, hormone treatment will be provided."[30] While this may seem to suggest that hormone therapy will be made available, individualized assessments have a number of outcomes, and hormone therapy is not guaranteed. Very recently, however, the U.S. Ninth Circuit Court of Appeals issued a decision that stated that denying those in prison gender affirmation surgery violates the Eighth Amendment to the Constitution, which prohibits "cruel and unusual punishment."[31]

CeCe has consistently highlighted that, because of disproportionately high transgender incarceration rates, their treatment in prisons, health care, and more, she would have been likely to face discrimination regardless of the facility in which she was imprisoned, as neither a women's prison nor a men's prison is safe for transgender individuals, or indeed for anyone incarcerated. However, she also acknowledges that transgender prisoners have to face a particular form of punishment: "They wanted me to hate myself as a trans woman, they wanted to force me to be someone that I wasn't, they wanted me to . . . delegitimize myself as a trans woman, and I was not taking that, as a trans woman, as a proud Black trans woman, I was not going to allow the system to delegitimize and hypersexualize and take my identity away from me."[32]

Programs Designed for Women and TGNCI Prisoners

Though women, nonbinary, gender nonconforming, and intersex prisoners are somewhat peripheral in the popular imagination, there are a number of programs, organizations, and coalitions that are focused on support and advocacy for such populations.

There are too many programs to highlight here, but many of them have the broad mission of support and advocacy for those inside, with specific campaigns and efforts that respond to the particular difficulties for incarcerated women and TGNCI individuals. The Women's Prison Association in New York was established in the mid-nineteenth century and continues to work with women, not only within the criminal/legal system but also with support and community-based programs that act as alternatives to incarceration. To that end, they assist with such things as job training, access to physical and mental health treatment, and housing, in addition to their work with those who have been or are currently incarcerated. The California Coalition for Women Prisoners runs several programs that are meant to attend to the personal and legal needs of those incarcerated.

GENDER DYSPHORIA
Discomfort or distress when there is a mismatch between a person's biological sex and gender identity.

TRANSGENDER OFFENDER MANUAL
Federal Bureau of Prisons manual that provides guidance to staff for unique issues of transgender people in prison.

Through visiting programs, they are able to monitor conditions inside facilities, provide legal advocacy support for appeals and release, and assist formerly incarcerated individuals with reentry processes and community building. They also read and respond to letters from those inside, work to address the sexual assault and abuse of those incarcerated, and advocate for the end to sentences of life without parole. Their work is national as well as international.

In addition, there are several national organizations engaged in legal representation and advocacy for lesbian, gay, bisexual, queer, and TGNCI individuals who are criminalized and incarcerated. The Transgender Law Center, the Sylvia Rivera Law Project (mentioned above), and GLAD (GLBTQ Legal Advocates & Defenders) all focus on legal advocacy and support for those who are currently or have been incarcerated, and each of these projects highlights the intersection between the violence that LGBTQ, nonbinary, and gender nonconforming individuals and communities face in their day-to-day lives and in their encounters with the criminal/legal system.

There are also several nonprofit programs focused on trauma and healing for incarcerated populations. A small organization called Dance to Be Free, for example, offers dance classes inside women's prisons. In the last few years, they have also offered trainings for aspiring dance instructors who are currently imprisoned. In this way, individuals who complete the training can continue to offer classes on a regular basis to others inside. The teacher trainings began at La Vista Correctional Facility in Pueblo, Colorado, and have now been held in several other states and facilities. Founder Lucy Wallace explains the crux of the idea behind the project: "Whether they were sexually abused, verbally, physically, there's so much trauma in the body. You can't cognitively heal something that was so physically violating. You have to work it through the physical body."[33] Similarly, the Prison Yoga Project, operating in both women's and men's facilities, takes yoga, mindfulness, and books inside, with the understanding that trauma-informed restorative bodywork is a key part of restorative justice.[34]

Further projects devoted to supporting women, nonbinary, gender nonconforming, and intersex prisoners are highlighted in chapter 14 under "Trending Issues and Future Directions." Chapter 14 also discusses the movement for criminal justice reform as well as the alternative paradigms of restorative and transformative justice.

REVIEW AND STUDY QUESTIONS

1. What factors seem to be leading to the rise in incarceration rates for women, girls, trans, and nonbinary individuals?

2. What may account for the higher rates of incarceration of women of color as compared to white women?

3. What factors may be decreasing the efficacy of PREA?

GOING FURTHER

Readings:

Haley, Sarah. *No Mercy Here: Gender, Punishment, and the Making of Jim Crow Modernity.* Chapel Hill: University of North Carolina Press, 2016.

Law, Victoria. *Resistance behind Bars: The Struggles of Incarcerated Women.* Oakland, CA: PM Press, 2009.

Stanley, Eric, Nat Smith, and CeCe McDonald. *Captive Genders: Trans Embodiment and the Prison Industrial Complex.* Chico, CA: AK Press, 2015.

Videos/Movies:

Girls, Incarcerated. Netflix, 2018.

Kohan, Jenji. *Orange Is the New Black.* Netflix, 2013.

KEY TERMS

cisgender An adjective denoting that a person's gender identity corresponds with the gender they were assigned at birth; often expressed simply as "cis."

gender dysphoria Discomfort or distress when there is a mismatch between a person's biological sex and gender identity.

Immigrations and Customs Enforcement (ICE) Federal law enforcement agency responsible for immigration enforcement.

National Commission on Correctional Health Care Mission is to improve the quality of health care in jails, prisons, and juvenile detention facilities.

National Women's Law Center Legal organization that fights for gender justice, especially for women and girls facing multiple forms of discrimination.

Prison Rape Elimination Act (PREA) The first federal law intended to deter the sexual assault and rape of incarcerated persons, established in 2003. It has set standards to prevent, detect, reduce, and respond to sexual abuse in prisons, jails, and juvenile detention facilities.

Rebecca Project for Human Rights Legal and policy organization that advocates for justice and reforms for vulnerable women and girls in the United States and Africa.

TGNCI A contemporary acronym used to refer to trans, gender nonconforming, and intersex people.

Transgender Offender Manual Federal Bureau of Prisons manual that provides guidance to staff for unique issues of transgender people in prison.

NOTES

[1] Sabrina Rubin Erdely, "The Transgender Crucible," *Rolling Stone*, July 30, 2014, https://www.rollingstone.com/culture/culture-news/the-transgender-crucible-114095.

[2] Erdely, "The Transgender Crucible."

[3] Matt Pearce, "Transgender Woman Sentenced to Men's Prison in Minnesota Killing," *Los Angeles Times*, June 18, 2012, https://www.latimes.com/nation/la-xpm-2012-jun-18-la-nann-transgender-woman-sentenced-to-mens-prison-20120618-story.html.

[4] Nicole Pasulka, "The Case of CeCe McDonald—Murder, or Self-Defense against a Hate Crime?," *Mother Jones*, May 22, 2012.

[5] Pasulka, "The Case of CeCe McDonald."

[6] Jorge Rivas, "Black Transgender Woman CeCe McDonald to Be Housed in Male Prison," *Colorlines*, June 4, 2012, https://www.colorlines.com/articles/black-transgender-woman-cece-mcdonald-be-housed-male-prison.

[7] "'Black Trans Bodies Are under Attack': Freed Activist CeCe McDonald, Actress Laverne Cox Speak Out," *Democracy Now!*, February 19, 2014, https://www.youtube.com/watch?v=kOuH43-_4Yo.

[8] Wendy Sawyer, "The Gender Divide: Tracking Women's State Prison Growth," Prison Policy Initiative, January 9, 2018, https://www.prisonpolicy.org/reports/women_overtime.html.

[9] "Inmate Gender," Federal Bureau of Prisons, accessed July 9, 2019, https://www.bop.gov/about/statistics/statistics_inmate_gender.jsp.

[10] "Native Lives Matter," Lakota People's Law Project, February 2015, https://s3-us-west-1.amazonaws.com/lakota-peoples-law/uploads/Native-Lives-Matter-PDF.pdf; "Incarcerated Women and Girls," Sentencing Project, June 6, 2019, https://www.sentencingproject.org/publications/incarcerated-women-and-girls.

[11] Aleks Kajstura, "Women's Mass Incarceration: The Whole Pie," Prison Policy Initiative, November 13, 2018, https://www.prisonpolicy.org/reports/pie2018women.html; "With Liberty and Justice for All: The State of Civil Rights at Immigration Detention Facilities," U.S. Commission on Civil Rights, September 2015, https://www.usccr.gov/pubs/docs/Statutory_Enforcement_Report2015.pdf.

[12] "With Liberty and Justice for All."

[13] Nick Miroff and Maria Sacchetti, "U.S. Has Hit 'Breaking Point' at Border amid Immigration Surge, Customs and Border Protection Chief Says," *Washington Post*, March 27, 2019.

[14] Tara Tidwell Cullen, "ICE Released Its Most Comprehensive Immigration Detention Data Yet. It's Alarming," National Immigrant Justice Center, March 13, 2018, https://immigrantjustice.org/staff/blog/ice-released-its-most-comprehensive-immigration-detention-data-yet.

[15] Laura M. Maruschak, "Medical Problems of Prisoners," U.S. Department of Justice, Bureau of Justice Statistics, April 1, 2008, https://www.bjs.gov/index.cfm?ty=pbdetail&iid=1097.

[16] Jennifer G. Clarke and Rachel E. Simon. "Shackling and Separation: Motherhood and Prison," *AMA Journal of Ethics*, September 2013, https://journalofethics.ama-assn.org/article/shackling-and-separation-motherhood-prison/2013-09.

[17] Diana Delgado, "Interview with Diana Delgado," Women and Prison, accessed July 1, 2019, http://womenandprison.org/interviews/view/interview_with_diana_delgado.

[18] Laurie S. Goshin, Mary W. Byrne, and Alana M. Henninger, "Recidivism after Release from a Prison Nursery Program," *Public Health Nursing* 31 (2013): 109–17.

[19] K. P. Moloney, B. J. van den Burgh, and L.F. Moller, "Women in Prison: The Central Issues of Gender Characteristics and Trauma History," *Public Health* 123, no. 6 (2009): 426–30.

[20] Holly M. Harner, Mia Budescu, Seth J. Gillihan, Suzanne Riley, and Edna B. Foa, "Posttraumatic Stress Disorder in Incarcerated Women: A Call for Evidence-Based Treatment," *Psychological Trauma: Theory, Research, Practice, and Policy* 7, no. 1 (2015): 58–66, https://doi.apa.org/doiLanding?doi=10.1037%2Fa0032508; Jessica Reichert and Lindsay Bostwick, "Post-traumatic Stress Disorder and Victimization among Female Prisoners in Illinois," Illinois Criminal Justice Information Authority, November 2010, http://www.icjia.state.il.us/assets/pdf/ResearchReports/PTSD_Female_Prisoners_Report_1110.pdf.

[21] Kristen Clements-Nolle, Matthew Wolden, and Jessey Bargmann-Losche, "Childhood Trauma and Risk for Past and Future Suicide Attempts among Women in Prison," *Women's Health Issues* 19 (2009): 185–92.

[22] Donna Scott-Tilley, Abigail Tilton, and Mark Sandel, "Biologic Correlates to the Development of Posttraumatic Stress Disorder in Female Victims of Intimate Partner Violence: Implication for Practice," *Perspectives in Psychiatric Care* 46, no. 1 (2010): 26–36.

23 Kimberly Houser and Steven Belenko, "Disciplinary Responses to Misconduct among Female Prison Inmates with Mental Illness, Substance Use Disorders, and Co-occurring Disorders," *Psychiatric Rehabilitation Journal* 38, no. 1 (2015): 24–34, http://dx.doi.org/10.1037/prj0000110; "Still Worse Than Second-Class: Solitary Confinement of Women in the United States," American Civil Liberties Union, 2019, https://www.aclu.org/report/worse-second-class-solitary-confinement-women-united-states.

24 Alexander C. McFarlane, "The Long-Term Costs of Traumatic Stress: Intertwined Physical and Psychological Consequences," *World Psychiatry: Official Journal of the World Psychiatric Association (WPA)* 9, no. 1 (2010): 3–10; Scott-Tilley et al., "Biological Correlates."

25 Prison Rape Elimination Act of 2003, Pub. L. No. 108-79 (2003), https://www.prearesourcecenter.org/sites/default/files/library/prea.pdf.

26 Victoria Law, "For People behind Bars, Reporting Sexual Assault Leads to More Punishment," Just Detention International, September 30, 2018, https://justdetention.org/for-people-behind-bars-reporting-sexual-assault-leads-to-more-punishment.

27 "RE: Docket No. OAG-131; AG Order No. 3143-2010 National Standards to Prevent, Detect, and Respond to Prison Rape," Sylvia Rivera Law Project, May 10, 2010, https://srlp.org/files/SRLP%20PREA%20comment%20Docket%20no%20OAG-131.pdf.

28 Prison Rape Elimination Act National Standards, 28 CFR Part 115, accessed June 15, 2019, https://www.law.cornell.edu/cfr/text/28/part-115.

29 Elena García-Vega, Aida Camero, María Fernández, and Ana Villaverde, "Suicidal Ideation and Suicide Attempts in Persons with Gender Dysphoria," *Psicothema* 30, no. 3 (2018): 283–88, http://doi.org/10.7334/psicothema2017.438.

30 "Transgender Offender Manual: Change Notice," Federal Bureau of Prisons, May 11, 2018, https://www.documentcloud.org/documents/4459297-BOP-Change-Order-Transgender-Offender-Manual-5.html.

31 Chris Johnson, "9th Circuit: Gender Reassignment Surgery Must Be Granted to Trans Inmates," *Washington Blade*, August 23, 2019, https://www.washingtonblade.com/2019/08/23/9th-circuit-gender-reassignment-surgery-must-be-granted-to-trans-inmates.

32 "No One Can 'Take My Identity Away from Me,'" MSNBC, January 19, 2014, https://www.msnbc.com/melissa-harris-perry/watch/how-the-system-treats-trans-people-121475139959.

33 "How Dance Helps Prisoners," Dance to Be Free, accessed June 15, 2019, https://dancetobefree.org/gallery.

34 "Philosophy," Prison Yoga Project, accessed July 1, 2019, https://prisonyoga.org/our-mission/philosophy.

Trending Issues and Future Directions

In this chapter you will read about many of the current movements to reform or radically alter the criminal/legal system. We begin by returning to a case about IPV and its aftermath. After that you will read about a range of creative and innovative models of protest and change. We conclude with a discussion of restorative justice and some specific restorative justice programs.

LEARNING OBJECTIVES

After reading this chapter, you should be able to do the following:

- Identify and explain intersectional forms of oppression, as well as dynamics and factors within the criminal/legal system that seem to exacerbate intersectional forms of oppression.

- Identify several different projects and initiatives that are attempting to confront or reform such aspects of the criminal/legal system.

- Consider and articulate the ways in which such projects coalesce, as well as the obstacles they may face.

Case #14: Marissa Alexander

On August 1, 2010, in fear for her life, Marissa Alexander fired a warning shot into the air; the shot was meant to deter her husband, with whom she was estranged and at whose hands she had suffered years of domestic abuse.

When police came to the house, Alexander discovered that she was not to be considered a victim of abuse who had acted in self-defense. On the contrary, she was arrested and charged with aggravated assault.

Alexander grew up first on military bases and then in Jacksonville, Florida. As a child, she was an athlete with an inquiring mind and a strong sense of justice, and she was often seen as "difficult" because of her willingness to question authority.

She met her first husband during her senior year in high school. He appreciated her will and her independence, and though he was a few years older than she was, they eventually got married and had twins. Both Marissa and her husband were ambitious, and they focused on advancing their careers. This, however, came at the expense of a healthy relationship. They eventually separated and then finally divorced, but they remained friends and coparents.

Marissa continued to advance in her career. To her BA in Information technology, she added a master's in Business administration, despite her full-time work in a payroll company. Her work life started to suffer, however—she discovered, through murmurs and through direct feedback, that she was once again being perceived as "difficult." She was rattled; she had worked so hard, only to have old familiar judgments thrown in her face. She vowed to fit into the desired mold of her company, to exceed their expectations, and to stop being so "difficult."

Around this time, she began to date a new man. He was also a single parent, and his humor and good nature was a relief to Marissa in the face of her new troubles at work. Their relationship grew serious quickly, and his behavior soon began to change—he was jealous and possessive, no longer the sweet, funny man that she had first met. He soon became abusive, both verbally and physically.

Marissa tried to tune out the moments of abuse and focus instead on the good times. There was a cycle: "tension, abuse, reconciliation, peace . . . and then repeat," over and over and back to the beginning. Though Marissa tried not to see herself as a victim of intimate partner violence, she began to understand that this cycle had no end unless she ended it herself. On a particularly bad night, the police were called, which resulted in her partner receiving an order of no contact. At this point, Marissa had a decision to make: pursue criminal charges against him, which might result in his separation from his children, or file for a permanent no-contact order and forgo the criminal charges. Opting for the latter, Marissa felt that she had moved on, that she had ended the cycle.

She was wrong. She had feelings of failure at work, and she did not want to have a feeling of failure in her relationship. She wanted to return to the honeymoon period, to somehow transform him and their relationship into its initial incarnation of laughter, attention, and love. They began to have contact again, to see each other, and eventually she became pregnant. She felt that this, perhaps, was the key to a harmonious relationship, and as a gesture of trust, she reduced the no-contact order to a no-violent-contact order; she hoped that those days were behind them.

The violence, however, returned. When her newborn daughter was barely more than a week old, he flew into a rage; he had seen that her first husband had sent her a text with a photo of one of their children, and this was enough to bring the jealousy and the verbal and physical abuse back to the surface. This time he threatened to kill her. Flooded with terror, she responded by firing a single warning shot.

Remembering this moment, Marissa says, "Just when I thought that I was breaking the shackles of psychological abuse by defending myself, I had no idea that I would be shackled and become one of the growing numbers of survivor-defendants." She reports that the vast majority of women who are killed by a romantic partner are killed when they are trying to exit the relationship, explaining that, "for many women, ending the cycle of abuse means choosing between life and death, or prison and freedom."

Marissa chose life; this does not mean that she chose prison. That is, however, what she got. While awaiting trial, she was offered a three-year plea deal; she maintained her innocence, however, continuing to argue that she had acted in self-defense, and she refused the plea deal. She finally went to trial in the summer of 2012, where she was prosecuted and convicted after the jury deliberated for only twelve minutes; she was sentenced to twenty years in prison.

In the fall of 2013, an appeals court ordered that Marissa's case get a new trial; her first trial, they determined, had to be reversed because "the trial court abused its discretion in giving a self-defense instruction to the jury that, among other things, improperly shifted the burden to her to establish, beyond a reasonable doubt, that Mr. Gray was committing or was about to commit an aggravated battery when she discharged her pistol. At trial, the only real issue was whether she had acted in self-defense when she fired the gun." Awaiting a new trial, Marissa was placed under house arrest for several months, eventually taking the three-year plea deal that had originally been offered to her. This meant that, in addition to her time already served, she spent sixty-five more days in prison and was finally released into monitored probation in January 2015. Two years later, in January 2017, she was finally released.

This is not, however, the story of a single woman's abuse, trial, imprisonment, and release. Instead, it is a story at the center of a movement. The Free Marissa Now campaign was born around her, and out of that grew the Marissa Alexander Justice Project. Marissa tours, speaks, writes, and supports the work of other groups and organizations that have similar aims and analyses. Her project and others, such as Survived & Punished, work to support survivor-defendants and bring more awareness to the layers of both interpersonal and state violence that result in survivors having to choose, as Marissa says, "between life and death, or prison and freedom." These newer projects join more established projects—such as INCITE! Women, Gender Non-Conforming, and Trans People of Color against Violence—to try to affect policy, change social and legal norms, create and sustain networks of support, and advocate for those who exist at dangerous and particularly vulnerable intersections.

In this final chapter, we explore several projects that embody trending issues, future directions, and new approaches to gender and justice.

THINKING CRITICALLY ABOUT THE CASE

1. Why did Marissa choose not to pursue criminal charges against her abuser?

2. What exactly does Marissa mean when she says, "For many women, ending the cycle of abuse means choosing between life and death, or prison and freedom"?

3. What made the jury decide that Marissa was guilty of aggravated assault, rather than seeing her act as one of self-defense?

REFERENCES

This case is adapted from the following sources:

Alexander, Marissa. "Not Another Victim—I'm an Empowered Survivor Defendant: Marissa Alexander; TEDxFSCJ." Survived & Punished. Accessed June 1, 2019. https://survivedandpunished .org/2019/06/01/marissa-alexander-ted-talk.

Alexander v. State of Florida, No. 1D12–2469 (Fla. 2013).

CONTEXT AND ANALYSIS

The Marissa Alexander Justice Project[1] is part of a growing wave of organizations and coalitions that place their work at the intersection of gender, sexuality, race, class, nationality, and the criminal/legal system. At the same time, long-established projects such as the Sylvia Rivera Law Project and the Transgender Law Center continue to deepen their work and claim a more central place in a popular consciousness that continues to grow increasingly aware of intersecting structures of oppression. Though there is not enough space here to highlight every project that has emerged from this increasing awareness, in this final chapter, we explore several projects and organizations that are foregrounding such work.

Projects at the Intersections

Over the last several years, and often highly inspired by Dr. Kimberlé Crenshaw's formulation of intersectional forms of oppression (in which, as discussed in previous chapters, "the experiences of women of color are frequently the product of intersecting patterns of racism and sexism"),[2] many projects and organizations focusing on the specific obstacles faced by women of color have been established or continue to grow. As Crenshaw points out, intersectional forms of oppression are varied and can manifest in different ways. She describes three frameworks through which intersectional forms of oppression may be read: **structural-dynamic discrimination**, or a type of discrimination that exists because certain hierarchies make women and girls of color disproportionately likely to experience many forms of punishment, which create patterns that reinforce these hierarchies; **intersectional subordination**, or the negative social and material outcomes that come from discriminatory patterns and arise out of the collusion of the market and the state; and **discursive intersections**, or the ways in which our narrative and discussion about structures of oppression marginalize particular groups facing complex and intersecting structures of oppression that belie simple interpretations.[3] This analysis grew out of Crenshaw's attention to the ways in which women are elided in discussions about mass incarceration. Many recent projects, programs, and organizations, including the Marissa Alexander Justice Project, focus on precisely this intersection.

Alexander founded the Marissa Alexander Justice Project (MAJP) in 2016 with the aim of providing support and advocacy for survivor-defendants, for survivors of domestic and sexual violence, and for many other populations facing both interpersonal and institutional violence, paying particular attention to the ways in which racial discrimination at school, in sentencing, and in perceptions of criminality affect the likelihood that individuals and populations will face multiple manifestations of private and state violence.

Appearing at around the same time as MAJP, Survived & Punished[4] is a growing and dynamic organization focused on support and advocacy for survivor-defendants, as well as policy change. Alexander's case was a key foundation for the creation of Survived & Punished; the Chicago Alliance to Free Marissa Alexander (part of the Free Marissa Now Mobilization Campaign), the Stand with Nan-Hui coalition (based in the San Francisco area, with participation from the Asian Law Caucus and KACEDA, the Korean American Coalition to End Domestic Abuse), and the California Coalition for Women Prisoners all came together in 2015 at the Color of Violence 4 conference, organized by **INCITE! Women, Gender Non-Conforming, and Trans People of Color against Violence**.[5] Nan-Hui Jo, like Alexander, was criminalized for defending herself and her daughter from domestic violence; Nan-Hui, in an attempt to remove herself and her daughter from an abusive partner/father, was charged with kidnaping, and because of her immigration status, Nan-Hui was placed in immigration detention for many months and her partner was given custody of their daughter. The Stand with Nan-Hui Campaign formed to organize around her case, to educate the public about the multiple forms of victimization that Nan-Hui was facing, and to provide legal and personal support for her, so it was only natural that the central figures in the campaigns around Alexander and Nan-Hui would come together. Their projects, after all, are not only about specific individuals; they are about the

STRUCTURAL-DYNAMIC DISCRIMINATION
Form of institutional discrimination against individuals of a given race or gender that has the effect of restricting their opportunities.

INTERSECTIONAL SUBORDINATION
Negative social and material outcomes resulting from discriminatory patterns from the collusion of the market and the state.

DISCURSIVE INTERSECTIONS
Narratives and discussion about structures of oppression that marginalize those who face complex and intersecting structures of oppression.

INCITE! WOMEN, GENDER NON-CONFORMING, AND TRANS PEOPLE OF COLOR AGAINST VIOLENCE
National activist organization of radical feminists of color organizing a movement to end violence against women, gender nonconforming, and trans people of color and their communities.

systems that place women at intersections with no way out, where the choices available are, as Alexander says, "life and death, or prison and freedom."[6]

Mimi Kim and Emi Kane of INCITE!, Alisa Bierria of the Free Marissa Now Mobilization Campaign, and Hyejin Shim of the Stand with Nan-Hui Campaign came together in 2015 to discuss their individual campaigns and the particular intersections, obstacles, and forms of oppression faced by survivor-defendants. Reflecting on the parallels in their work and the inspiration that the Stand with Nan-Hui Campaign took from organizing work that was already being done by such groups as INCITE!, Shim said,

> The work that Free Marissa Now did, and the work that Black women and women of color have been doing around domestic violence and criminalization for decades, made it apparent that this was connected to a larger pattern of survivors being targeted by the system. They are targeted by a racist, sexist system for their survival strategies, particularly with the idea that a survivor must always be a perfect victim. There's this belief that a domestic violence survivor must always be the victim of crime, and the abuser is always the perpetrator of crime. So in a way there's not that much room or analysis about what happens when the survivor is actually considered the "perpetrator of a crime," even in the anti-violence movement. Instead, we're taking cues from the state to tell us who real "victims" and "perpetrators" are. In this case you had "domestic violence experts" like the district attorney saying that this was not a domestic violence case. So then what? We needed to organize.[7]

To Bierria, another salient obstacle is the difficulty that arises when organizations—even antiviolence organizations—are unwilling or unable to support survivors who have been criminalized for their acts of self-defense:

> Domestic violence organizations were actually pressured by State Attorney Angela Corey [Alexander's prosecutor] to not publicly support Marissa Alexander. So, there's not only an imagination problem but also a real material problem, because people are worried about their funding. One argument was that groups couldn't risk their funding to support one person when they have this whole other group of victims to support. But my pushback was, well, who gets to be part of the larger set of victims that they're serving? It's not just about Marissa not having support, it is also about any survivor who is being prosecuted having access to full support. As long as organizations make choices based on what Angela Corey or other prosecutors want, they're never going to have autonomy in terms of who they support. There will always be this barrier to services for survivors who are more vulnerable to criminalization—that is to say, Black women. It's so important to not only understand the ways that court system and police and prisons are impacting survivors of domestic violence, devastating people's lives and so on, but also the ways that many service organizations are prevented—or prevent themselves—from supporting criminalized survivors.[8]

Both Bierria and Shim point to the racist and nationalist tropes that were used in the cases against Alexander and Nan-Hui. Though the tropes were very different, in both cases they prevented the survivors from being perceived as "victims" and instead framed them as agents of their own abuse. Their situations and the narratives that were built around them clearly display both the structural-dynamic discrimination and discursive intersections described by Crenshaw. Survived & Punished continues to stand at the meeting of these intersections. INCITE! Women, Gender Non-Conforming, and Trans People of Color against Violence (formerly called INCITE! Women of Color against Violence) remains very active. The network held their first Color of Violence: Violence against Women of Color conference in 2000. Since then, they have been a key source of space, support, and resources for radical feminists of color engaged in a variety of campaigns, projects, and programs that center principles of transformative justice and antiviolence.

Though the **Black Lives Matter (BLM)** movement has been largely positioned as a movement focusing on state violence against Black individuals and communities, the movement also stands at the intersection of many forms of oppression, including gendered oppression. Founded in 2013 by three women—Alicia Garza, Patrisse Khan-Cullors, and Opal Tometi—Black Lives Matter's early and highly visible focuses were on the killings of Trayvon Martin in Sanford, Florida, and Mike Brown in Ferguson, Missouri. Their work has continued to grow in scope and support, particularly when national attention to the 2020 killings of George Floyd, Breonna Taylor, and others led to widespread calls to #DefundThePolice and establish alternative models of community support and protection.

The focus of BLM is incredibly expansive and responds to both the external and internal work of liberation. Their beliefs state, in part,

> We are guided by the fact that all Black lives matter, regardless of actual or perceived sexual identity, gender identity, gender expression, economic status, ability, disability, religious beliefs or disbeliefs, immigration status, or location.
>
> We make space for transgender brothers and sisters to participate and lead.
>
> We are self-reflexive and do the work required to dismantle cisgender privilege and uplift Black trans folk, especially Black trans women who continue to be disproportionately impacted by trans-antagonistic violence.
>
> We build a space that affirms Black women and is free from sexism, misogyny, and environments in which men are centered.
>
> We practice empathy. We engage comrades with the intent to learn about and connect with their contexts.
>
> We make our spaces family-friendly and enable parents to fully participate with their children. We dismantle the patriarchal practice that requires mothers to work "double shifts" so that they can mother in private even as they participate in public justice work.
>
> We disrupt the Western-prescribed nuclear family structure requirement by supporting each other as extended families and "villages" that collectively care for one another, especially our children, to the degree that mothers, parents, and children are comfortable.
>
> We foster a queer-affirming network. When we gather, we do so with the intention of freeing ourselves from the tight grip of heteronormative thinking, or rather, the belief that all in the world are heterosexual (unless s/he or they disclose otherwise).
>
> We cultivate an intergenerational and communal network free from ageism. We believe that all people, regardless of age, show up with the capacity to lead and learn.
>
> We embody and practice justice, liberation, and peace in our engagements with one another.[9]

Black Lives Matter, like Survived & Punished and so many other movements, projects, and campaigns, is deeply invested in creating deeper narratives that do not leave anyone to drown in discursive intersections. In particular, there has been greater attention to the disproportionate likelihood of Black women, and particularly Black trans women, to experience both interpersonal and state violence. #SayHerName, both a report and a hashtag, was created to draw attention to the invisibility of violence against Black women; it asks that Black women not be erased in public discussions of racialized violence that often center on men. The hashtag and the report (created by the African American Policy Forum, the Center for Intersectionality and Social Policy Studies at Columbia Law School, Kimberlé Crenshaw, and lawyer and activist Andrea Ritchie) emerged in 2015, partially in response to and in honor of Sandra Bland, who died in police custody in July 2015 after having been held for three days following a traffic stop in which she allegedly assaulted an officer. The report clearly names the intersections to which it is responding:

> The resurgent racial justice movement in the United States has developed a clear frame to understand the police killings of Black men and boys, theorizing the ways

BLACK LIVES MATTER (BLM)
Movement focusing on state violence against Black people, standing at the intersection of many forms of oppression, including gendered oppression.

in which they are systematically criminalized and feared across disparate class backgrounds and irrespective of circumstance. Yet Black women who are profiled, beaten, sexually assaulted, and killed by law enforcement officials are conspicuously absent from this frame even when their experiences are identical. When their experiences with police violence are distinct—uniquely informed by race, gender, gender identity, and sexual orientation—Black women remain invisible.[10]

Similarly, the African American Policy Forum, the Center for Intersectionality and Social Policy Studies, Crenshaw, Priscilla Ocen, and Jyoti Nanda collaborated on a report titled *Black Girls Matter: Pushed Out, Overpoliced, and Underprotected*, also released in 2015. As with #SayHerName, this report is meant to highlight the ways in which girls are often pushed to the background in discussions of institutional racism and the justice system, this time in relation to education:

> It is well-established in the research literature and by educational advocates that there is a link between the use of punitive disciplinary measures and subsequent patterns of criminal supervision and incarceration. Commonly understood as the "school-to-prison pipeline," this framework highlights the ways that punitive school policies lead to low achievement, system involvement, and other negative outcomes. Efforts to reverse the consequences of this pipeline have typically foregrounded boys of color, especially Black boys, who are suspended or expelled more than any other group. . . . [However,] punitive disciplinary policies also negatively impact Black girls and other girls of color. Yet much of the existing research literature excludes girls from the analysis, leading many stakeholders to infer that girls of color are not also at risk.[11]

Again, this report is meant to counteract the forms of structural-dynamic discrimination and discursive intersections that are too often present even in projects and movements that focus on forms of oppression in ways that may be too narrow and, as a result, omit impacted populations from their analysis and their efforts.

Movements and projects led by and centering indigenous women and communities also continue to become more visible. Many of these projects, like Survived & Punished, INCITE!, and Black Lives Matter, sit at the intersections of community and state violence. The hashtag #MMIWG, for instance, draws attention to the vast numbers of Missing and Murdered Indigenous Women and Girls, whose deaths and disappearances have for too long been unrecognized in mainstream popular consciousness. Explaining the need for such a hashtag and the greater attention to this epidemic, the **Coalition to Stop Violence against Native Women**[12] connects the disproportionate likelihood that indigenous women will be killed to the histories of genocide in North America and the continued prevalence of poverty, state violence, and marginalization among indigenous communities. According to a 2018 report created by the Urban Indian Health Institute, murder is the third-leading cause of death for indigenous women (here defined as American Indian or Alaska Native). Nevertheless, only a very small percentage of reports of the disappearances and murders of indigenous women and girls are recorded by the U.S. Department of Justice.[13] Alongside #MMIWG, projects like Walk4Justice draw attention to the multiple dangers faced by indigenous women. Two First Nations women, Gladys Radek (Gitxsan/Wet'suwet'en) and Bernie Williams (Haida), launched the first Walk4Justice in 2008, and since then, the walk has crisscrossed Canada several times. The long walk is meant to draw attention to the deadly spaces in which indigenous women go missing, spaces both physical and discursive. As Radek says, "I want people to pay attention when a woman goes missing, investigate all disappearances and murders equally, including those of sex workers, and have a national symposium, as well as a public inquiry, into how and why these women go missing."[14] This and other projects continue to insist that these deadly spaces and their particular intersections are long overdue attention and transformative intervention.

COALITION TO STOP VIOLENCE AGAINST NATIVE WOMEN
Connects the disproportionate number of indigenous women killed to the history of genocide as well as the continued prevalence of poverty, state violence, and marginalization among indigenous communities.

Indigenous women are also at the center of large national and international projects and movements focused on the intersection of environmental justice and social justice. Recently, these intersections became vividly visible during the protests against the Dakota Access Pipeline in the area of the Standing Rock Sioux. The protests, which lasted for nearly a year between 2016 and 2017, drew attention not only to land rights and the importance of clean water, but to the continued marginalization of indigenous peoples and the centrality of women in anticolonial, indigenous, and environmental justice movements. From the local to the international, indigenous women are organizing around these intersections with increasing support. The Women's Earth & Climate Action Network, International (WECAN), founded first as the Women's Earth and Climate Caucus by Osprey Orielle Lake at the 2013 International Women's Earth and Climate Summit, articulates these intersections clearly:

> It is clear that women experience climate change with disproportionate severity precisely because their basic rights continue to be denied in varying forms and intensities across the world. Enforced gender inequality reduces women's physical and economic mobility, voice, and opportunity in many places, making them more vulnerable to mounting environmental stresses. . . . Indigenous women, women from low-income communities, and women from the Global South bear an even heavier burden from the impacts of climate change because of the historic and continuing impacts of colonialism, racism and inequality; and in many cases, because they are more reliant upon natural resources for their survival and/or live in areas that have poor infrastructure. Drought, flooding, and unpredictable and extreme weather patterns present life or death challenges for many women, who are most often the ones responsible for providing food, water and energy for their families. In many frontline communities, gendered and sexual violence against women is added on top of other dire impacts perpetuated by the extractive industries that bear down on their homelands.[15]

WECAN contains both national and international groups and projects within its network and allies, and there are many smaller organizations and projects operating at the local level across the country that similarly highlight the connection between gender justice, racial justice, and environmental justice. More and more, projects, campaigns, and organizations are bridging the seeming gaps between their work to create coalitions that are committed to standing at these intersections.

There are several prominent organizations that have been working on legal support and advocacy for LGBTQ individuals and communities for many years, including the GLBTQ Legal Advocates & Defenders (GLAD, established in 1978),[16] the Sylvia Rivera Law Project (established in 2002),[17] and the Transgender Law Center (established in 2002).[18] As we saw in chapter 10, the rise of the movement against homophobia originally centered primarily on gay men and, to some extent, lesbians during the era of the Stonewall riots, but over the last couple of decades, the fight against transphobia and for trans rights has become firmly embedded in LGBTQ activism and organization. GLAD, for example, was originally called Gay & Lesbian Advocates & Defenders, but just as with INCITE!, GLAD changed their name to reflect inclusion of trans and nonbinary folks. GLAD, the Sylvia Rivera Law Project, and the Transgender Law Center all focus on support, social and legal advocacy, and policy change, and all of them work against the multiple obstacles that arise at the intersection of gender, sexuality, race, nationality, immigration, detention, imprisonment, education, and economic class.

A newer organization, **Black and Pink** was founded by Jason Lydon between 2005 and 2006. Their first and longest-running project is a pen-pal project, connecting incarcerated individuals who are LGBTQ with pen pals on the outside, and over the years, their capacity for new projects has grown as new chapters have been created across the country. Newsletters, public actions and events, educational and training workshops, and programs offering reentry support to those coming out of prison were added to the pen-pal project, and as an explicitly abolitionist organization, Black and Pink is committed to

BLACK AND PINK
Advocacy and pen-pal project connecting incarcerated LGBTQ people with pen pals on the outside.

making sure that they are led by those who have been most impacted by systems of mass incarceration, both organizationally and philosophically. In 2015, Black and Pink released a report, *Coming Out of Concrete Closets*, that presented data collected over several months and representing the experiences of nearly 1,200 incarcerated members of Black and Pink. This report makes it clear that the intersections of marginalized genders and sexuality, race, and economic class create conditions wherein there is a greater likelihood of homelessness, unemployment, survival through illicit trades, multiple instances of incarceration (often starting in youth), and disproportionately longer sentences in higher-security facilities and/or solitary confinement. It is also clear that those caught at these intersections are disproportionately likely to experience sexual assault and abuse while incarcerated, and that they do not have reliable and affordable access to health care.[19] For all of these reasons, Black and Pink continues to stand out as an organization committed not only to supporting and advocating for those inside and those who have been released but also to transformative justice practices and to the effort to abolish the penal system altogether.

Restorative and Transformative Justice

Restorative justice/practices come out of indigenous justice traditions used in cultures all over the world. In modern times, restorative justice began in the 1970s as mediation and reconciliation between victims and offenders who were dissatisfied with the criminal/legal system in an effort to transform the way justice is achieved. Since that time, restorative justice has been on the rise throughout the United States and worldwide. It is used when harm comes from simple assault and criminal property damage to more serious harms, including death due to drunk driving, sexual assault, and murder. New Zealand and others have made restorative justice the center of their juvenile justice systems.

To understand restorative justice, it is important to frame it as an alternative paradigm to retributive criminal justice. In the criminal/legal system, a criminal law is violated, a judicial process to determine guilt ensues, and punishment is given if there is a conviction. Victims, offenders, and community members often feel that this retributive criminal/legal system does not meet their needs. Moreover, many people feel that the process deepens society's conflicts and wounds instead of contributing to healing and peace.

In contrast, restorative justice is a victim/survivor-centered alternative to the retributive criminal/legal system, which aims only to punish the offender. Restorative justice perceives crime as a wound in the community that tears apart the web of relationships, and it seeks to repair that harm and to restore the peace, trust, and sense of safety that was destroyed. It focuses on the harm, emphasizing accountability of the offender and promoting engagement of those who are affected by the harm, including victims, offenders, and community members. The goal of restorative justice is to bring about healing and reconciliation in those communities harmed by crime and to offer offenders an opportunity for atonement and a path toward redemption.

Transformative justice, like restorative justice, includes strategies for responding to conflicts. However, it differs from restorative justice because it rejects the involvement of the police, the law, the government, or any other institution with punitive practices. Instead, it relies on community support networks and facilitators and seeks to change the larger social structures that allow harm to occur in the first place. As transformative justice practitioner Mia Mingus writes, transformative justice

> is not simply the absence of the state and violence, but the *presence* of the values, practices, relationships and world that we want. It is not only identifying what we don't want, but proactively practicing and putting in place things we want, such as healthy relationships, good communication skills, skills to de-escalate active or "live" harm and violence in the moment, learning how to express our anger in ways that are not destructive, incorporating healing into our everyday lives.[20]

There is no one-size-fits-all version of transformative justice; instead, it is a framework that must respond to the needs of the particular group or community that chooses to implement it.

Restorative Justice for Oakland Youth

Restorative Justice for Oakland Youth (RJOY) is a community-based restorative/transformative justice organization in Oakland, California's schools and community. It utilizes restorative justice philosophy and principles to respond to conflict and engage in community building. Instead of seeking to punish those who do harm, RJOY convenes community circles in order to heal a broken bond or system by focusing on the wrongdoing and finding a resolution that involves all affected stakeholders and community members.[21]

RJOY works with the Oakland Unified School District to shift away from a punitive approach toward a policy of restorative justice as the official disciplinary policy of the school district. As a result, suspensions and expulsions have been reduced and GPAs increased in the schools where RJOY has been involved. RJOY is expanding its program to change the juvenile justice system and introduce restorative practices and principles to the juvenile hall, juvenile court judges, elected officials, and the mayor's office.

Transformative Practices in Carceral Institutions

There are several restorative and transformative justice programs that exist in carceral institutions. In addition to the Alternatives to Violence Project, discussed in chapter 8, there are many other programs based on restorative and transformative justice. One such program is the Lionheart Foundation's **Houses of Healing in Prison**, which is a trauma-informed emotional literacy program that provides incarcerated people with the tools to recognize and heal unresolved traumas, effectively manage emotions, be accountable for offending behavior, and change lifelong patterns of violence and addiction in order to build productive lives.[22] It focuses on the necessity of self-forgiveness and forgiveness of others, which are essential to the fostering of empathy and emotional and spiritual maturity.

Restorative Justice in Other Criminal/Legal Agencies/Organizations

In addition to the programs discussed above, restorative justice is being used in courts, police departments, prosecutor offices, reentry programs, juvenile justice agencies, and legal cases, among others. This is a cutting-edge alternative to a criminal/legal system that is rife with racial, ethnic, and economic inequalities as well as high recidivism rates. Global communities, including ones across the United States, are creating restorative justice programs to build strong communities and to enhance the safety and well-being of all those involved.

Other Trends and Projects

There are many more projects centered on the reform or abolition of the penal system, as well as support for those most impacted, that are not explicitly focused on gender but that nevertheless present progressive and transformative alternatives to the punitive measures of the criminal/legal system.

As we have seen in previous chapters, prison education and programming are available in some facilities. From community colleges to well-funded universities such as Cornell, NYU, and Stanford to projects such as the Inside-Out Prison Exchange Program, institutions and organizations are increasingly offering prison education programs to facilities across the country that are amenable to programming.

There are also campaigns and projects, both local and national, advocating for systemic change, such as abolishing cash bail, sentences of life without parole, the death sentence,

RESTORATIVE JUSTICE FOR OAKLAND YOUTH (RJOY)
Community-based restorative/transformative justice organization in Oakland, California's schools and community.

HOUSES OF HEALING IN PRISON
Trauma-informed emotional literacy program focusing on healing unresolved traumas and the necessity of self-forgiveness and forgiveness of others, which are essential to the fostering of empathy and emotional and spiritual maturity.

and solitary confinement. These campaigns and projects continue to grow as the realities of mass incarceration become increasingly visible to a mainstream audience through such venues as Michelle Alexander's 2010 book *The New Jim Crow: Mass Incarceration in the Age of Colorblindness* and Ava Duvernay's 2016 documentary *13th*, both of which highlight the relationship between the history of slavery in the United States and contemporary American incarceration. The growing attention to the United States' disproportionately large prison population and the disparities in arrests and sentencing have strengthened movements not only for reform but for penal abolition overall. Organizations such as the Vera Institute for Justice[23] engage in research, education, and advocacy for policy change, always with an eye on their three core priorities: to work toward a substantial decrease in the prison population through the reform of pretrial detention and the creation of alternatives to incarceration; to counter racialized and otherwise biased disparities in legal treatment of individuals and communities; and to fundamentally improve the conditions of incarceration through the abolition of solitary confinement, an increase in education and programming, and profound shifts in the treatment of incarcerated minors.

In another vein, organizations such as the **Innocence Project** focus on the prevalence of wrongful convictions and work to both exonerate the innocent as well as reform the systems that give rise to wrongful convictions in the first place. The Innocence Project in particular works to exonerate the wrongfully convicted via DNA testing and policy reform. Since their establishment in the early 1990s, their attorneys have successfully fought for the exonerations of hundreds of wrongfully convicted individuals, many of whom had already spent several years in incarceration.[24] Moreover, there are many other innocence projects throughout the nation.

Other programs and projects focus on release and reentry. The **Homecoming Project**, for example, is a new and small but growing project that aims to match individuals being released from prison with households that have both a spare room and a willingness to offer ongoing support to those who may find reentry difficult on logistical or personal levels. Currently operating in Alameda County, California, the Homecoming Project is proving successful at assisting participants in establishing stability and avoiding crucial reentry difficulties such as homelessness and unemployment.[25]

Many of the new projects, trends, and organizations are able to continue to grow because of a widening awareness of biases, failures, and obstacles within the criminal/legal system; the increasing access mainstream audiences have to media helps to spotlight the lived realities of those impacted by incarceration. The ***Ear Hustle* podcast**, for example, began airing in May 2017 from within San Quentin State Prison in California.[26] Produced and founded by then–San Quentin prisoners Antwan Williams and Earlonne Woods, along with nonincarcerated artist Nigel Poor, and hosted by Poor and Woods, the podcast has received national attention, and their listener base continues to grow. Woods was released from prison in late 2018 after his sentence was commuted by then-governor Jerry Brown, who said, "I believe Earlonne will continue to educate, enlighten and enrich the lives of his peers at San Quentin and the many, many people who listen faithfully to *Ear Hustle*."[27] Many people do listen, and as they listen, they are exposed to individual voices that describe the realities of life in prison—solitary confinement, the struggle to stay safe when one is gay or trans, the pain of separation from one's family, the psychological battle of looking down the road at many more years of incarceration, and much more. These individual voices describe their own lives as well as a larger system.

In all of these new and growing projects, organizations, and trends, there is attention to the intersections of race, gender, sexuality, nationality, economic status, and many more structures and categories that come together to create what appear to be insurmountable obstacles, and these projects aim to identify and dismantle those obstacles to effect both short- and long-term change.

INNOCENCE PROJECT
Focuses on the prevalence of wrongful convictions, exonerating the innocent and reforming the system.

HOMECOMING PROJECT
Matches individuals being released from prison with households that have both a spare room and a willingness to offer ongoing support.

***EAR HUSTLE* PODCAST**
Airs from within San Quentin State Prison in California.

REVIEW AND STUDY QUESTIONS

1. What factors—both arising from public institutions and from civil society—necessitated that these specific projects be formed? In other words, why do they need to sit so squarely at their particular intersections?

2. What does environmental justice have to do with social justice?

3. In what specific ways do restorative justice and transformative justice differ from the criminal/legal system? Why does it seem important to the projects highlighted in this chapter that alternatives to the criminal/legal system be sought and practiced?

GOING FURTHER

Readings:

Davis, Angela. *Are Prisons Obsolete?* New York: Seven Stories Press, 2003.

Kaba, Mariame, and Shira Hassan. *Fumbling towards Repair: A Workbook for Community Accountability Facilitators.* Chico, CA: AK Press, 2019.

Ritchie, Andrea J. *Invisible No More: Police Violence against Black Women and Women of Color.* Boston: Beacon, 2017.

Websites:

Restorative Justice for Oakland Youth. https://rjoyoakland.org.

Woods, Earlonne, Antwan Williams, and Nigel Poor. *Ear Hustle* (podcast), 2017. https://www.earhustlesq.com.

Videos/Movies:

DuVernay, Ava. *13th.* Kandoo Films and Netflix, 2016.

KEY TERMS

Black and Pink Advocacy and pen-pal project connecting incarcerated LGBTQ people with pen pals on the outside.

Black Lives Matter (BLM) Movement focusing on state violence against Black people, standing at the intersection of many forms of oppression, including gendered oppression.

Coalition to Stop Violence against Native Women Connects the disproportionate number of indigenous women killed to the history of genocide as well as the continued prevalence of poverty, state violence, and marginalization among indigenous communities.

discursive intersections Narratives and discussion about structures of oppression that marginalize those who face complex and intersecting structures of oppression.

***Ear Hustle* podcast** Airs from within San Quentin State Prison in California.

Homecoming Project Matches individuals being released from prison with households that have both a spare room and a willingness to offer ongoing support.

Houses of Healing in Prison Trauma-informed emotional literacy program focusing on healing unresolved traumas and the necessity of self-forgiveness and forgiveness of others, which are essential to the fostering of empathy and emotional and spiritual maturity.

INCITE! Women, Gender Non-Conforming, and Trans People of Color against Violence National activist organization of radical feminists of color organizing a movement to end violence against women, gender nonconforming, and trans people of color and their communities.

Innocence Project Focuses on the prevalence of wrongful convictions, exonerating the innocent and reforming the system.

intersectional subordination Negative social and material outcomes resulting from discriminatory patterns from the collusion of the market and the state.

Restorative Justice for Oakland Youth (RJOY) Community-based restorative/transformative justice organization in Oakland, California's schools and community.

structural-dynamic discrimination Form of institutional discrimination against individuals of a given race or gender that has the effect of restricting their opportunities.

NOTES

1 "About," Marissa Alexander Justice Project, accessed June 7, 2019, https://marissaalexander.org.

2 Kimberlé Crenshaw, "Mapping the Margins: Intersectionality, Identity Politics, and Violence against Women of Color," *Stanford Law Review* 43, no. 6 (1991): 1243.

3 Kimberlé Crenshaw, "From Private Violence to Mass Incarceration: Thinking Intersectionally about Women, Race, and Social Control," *UCLA Law Review* 59 (2012): 1426–27.

4 "About S&P," Survived & Punished, accessed June 7, 2019, https://survivedandpunished.org.

5 "About," INCITE! Women, Gender Non-Conforming, and Trans People of Color against Violence, accessed June 7, 2019, https://incite-national.org.

6 Marissa Alexander, "Not Another Victim—I'm an Empowered Survivor Defendant: Marissa Alexander; TEDxFSCJ," Survived & Punished, accessed June 1, 2019, https://survivedandpunished.org/2019/06/01/marissa-alexander-ted-talk.

7 Alisa Bierria, Hyejin Shim, Mimi Kim, and Emi Kane, "Free Marissa Now and Stand with Nan-Hui: A Conversation about Parallel Struggles," *Feminist Wire*, June 30, 2015, https://www.thefeministwire.com/2015/06/free-marissa-and-stand-with-nan-hui.

8 Bierria et al., "Free Marissa Now."

9 "What We Believe: Guiding Principles," Black Lives Matter, accessed July 15, 2019, https://blacklivesmatter.com/about/what-we-believe.

10 "Say Her Name: Resisting Police Brutality against Black Women," African American Policy Forum and the Center for Intersectionality and Social Policy Studies, 2015, accessed July 15, 2019, http://static1.squarespace.com/static/53f20d90e4b0b80451158d8c/t/560c068ee4b0af26f72741df/1443628686535/AAPF_SMN_Brief_Full_singles-min.pdf.

11 *Black Girls Matter: Pushed Out, Overpoliced and Underprotected*, African American Policy Forum and the Center for Intersectionality and Social Policy Studies, 2015, accessed July 15, 2019, https://static1.squarespace.com/static/53f20d90e4b0b80451158d8c/t/54dcc1ece4b001c03e323448/1423753708557/AAPF_BlackGirlsMatterReport.pdf.

12 "About Us," Coalition to Stop Violence against Native Women, accessed July 16, 2019, https://www.csvanw.org.

13 "Missing and Murdered Indigenous Women and Girls: A Snapshot of Data from 71 Urban Cities in the United States," Urban Indian Health Institute, 2018, accessed July 7, 2019, http://www.uihi.org/wp-content/uploads/2018/11/Missing-and-Murdered-Indigenous-Women-and-Girls-Report.pdf.

14 Christine McFarlane, "Gladys Radek: A Woman on a Mission," Aboriginal Multi-Media Society, 2011, accessed July 8, 2019, https://ammsa.com/publications/ravens-eye/gladys-radek-woman-mission.

15 "Why Women?," Women's Earth & Climate Action Network International, accessed July 15, 2019, https://www.wecaninternational.org/why-women.

16 "Mission and Values," GLBTQ Legal Advocates & Defenders (GLAD), accessed July 14, 2019, https://www.glad.org.

17 "About SRLP," Sylvia Rivera Law Project, accessed July 14, 2019, https://srlp.org.

18 "About Us," Transgender Law Center, accessed July 15, 2019, https://transgenderlawcenter.org.

19 Jason Lydon, Kamaria Carrington, Hana Low, Reed Miller, and Mahsa Yazdy, *Coming Out of Concrete Closets: A Report on Black & Pink's National LGBTQ Prisoner Survey*, Black and Pink, 2015, accessed July 20, 2019, https://docs.wixstatic.com/ugd/857027_fcd066f0c450418b95a18ab34647bd15.pdf.

20 Mia Mingus, "Transformative Justice: A Brief Description," TransformHarm.org, accessed May 21, 2021, https://transformharm.org/transformative-justice-a-brief-description.

21 "About RJOY," Restorative Justice for Oakland Youth, accessed July 10, 2019, https://rjoyoakland.org.

22 "The Prison Project," Lionheart Foundation, accessed July 10, 2019, https://lionheart.org/prison/project.

23 "About Us," Vera Institute of Justice, accessed July 12, 2019, https://www.vera.org.

24 "About," Innocence Project, accessed July 12, 2019, https://www.innocenceproject.org.

25 "About Us," Homecoming Project, accessed July 12, 2019, https://impactjustice.org/impact/homecoming-project.

26 Earlonne Woods, Antwan Williams, and Nigel Poor, *Ear Hustle* (podcast), 2017, https://www.earhustlesq.com.

27 John Meyers and Jazmine Ulloa, "Immigrants Facing Deportation, Drug Offenders and a Former State Lawmaker Receive Pardons from Gov. Jerry Brown," *Los Angeles Times*, November 21, 2018, https://www.latimes.com/politics/la-pol-ca-thanksgiving-pardons-jerry-brown-20181121-story.html.

A

ableism   Discrimination against people with physical, intellectual, or psychiatric disabilities.

absolute deprivation   A term used to describe a situation when a person is so poor they are unable to obtain such basic necessities as food and shelter.

adversarial system   A system, as the U.S. legal system, where the judge acts as a referee between the prosecution and the defense, who zealously represent their party's case.

age of consent   Age when a person is considered to be legally competent to consent to sexual acts.

aggravated assault   Use of physical force or threatened use of physical force against another person.

aggrieved entitlement   Term coined by Michael Kimmel to describe white male resistance to perceived challenges against masculinity and historical experiences of privilege.

alimony   Also referred to as spousal support, payments ordered by a court in the aftermath of a divorce or separation; generally ordered when the parties have widely disparate income and earning potential, and typically time limited.

Alternatives to Violence Project (AVP)   Anticonflict program in prisons and the community that builds on respect for all, community, cooperation, and trust, leading to transformation.

anomie   A state of social unrest or rapid social change, when social norms are unclear or not enforced.

Anti–Drug Abuse Act of 1986   Created strict punishment in the form of prosecution, sentencing, and incarceration, including mandatory minimum sentences, for drug use.

antisubordination theory   An early critical legal theory that law should be used to reform institutions of oppression.

asylum   Protection granted to someone who has left their native country because they suffered persecution due to violence, race, religion, or political opinion, among other reasons.

attachment theory   Infants need to develop a relationship with at least one parent for successful social and emotional development.

B

battered woman syndrome   A term coined by Leonore Walker to explain why some women remained in abusive relationships.

battered women's movement   A movement that began in the 1970s to protect the rights and interests of women in abusive relationships, often combined with victims of sexual assault.

batterers intervention programs (BIPs)   Programs designed to prevent batterers from reoffending; typically court mandated.

Black and Pink   Advocacy and pen-pal project connecting incarcerated LGBTQ people with pen pals on the outside.

Black Lives Matter (BLM)   Movement focusing on state violence against Black people, standing at the intersection of many forms of oppression, including gendered oppression.

C

causation   Legal concept that requires a direct link from the act committed to the harm caused.

chattel slavery   System where people are treated as the owner's chattel, or personal property, and are bought and sold as possessions.

child support   Money paid by one parent to another for the care and support of their child or children.

chronic frustration syndrome   A theory that expands upon the idea of status frustration, suggesting that when all avenues of success or power are consistently denied, the response may be social anger.

cisgender   An adjective denoting that a person's gender identity corresponds with the gender they were assigned at birth; often expressed simply as "cis."

civil asset forfeiture   Allows police to seize property believed to be associated with a crime, whether or not a crime has actually been committed.

civil injunction   A court ruling ordering an individual to do or not do some specific act.

clear and convincing evidence   Standard of proof that is more stringent than the preponderance of the evidence but not as high as beyond a reasonable doubt.

cliques or sets   Smaller street gangs, usually in one neighborhood, that operate independently.

Coalition to Stop Violence against Native Women   Connects the disproportionate number of indigenous women killed to the history of genocide as well as the continued prevalence of poverty, state violence, and marginalization among indigenous communities.

code of the street   A set of informal rules governing interpersonal public behavior, including violence.

coercive authority   Refers to motivation by threat of punishment to mandate treatment.

consent decree   An agreement between parties to a legal action that resolves the underlying complaint.

conspiracy   Occurs when two or more people reach an agreement to commit a crime.

coordinated community response teams   A model of intervention to address IPV through the coordination of various services for victims and offenders, including police, courts, and service providers.

corporate crime   Refers to crimes committed by a corporation or other business entity, or by individuals acting on behalf of a corporation or business.

coverture   A legal doctrine that said that when a man and woman married, they became one legal person: the man. Therefore, a married woman had no independent legal identity to sue or be sued, contract, or retain or control finances.

crack cocaine   Smokable form of cocaine, marketable in smaller, less expensive quantities than powder cocaine.

criminal homicide   Killing that includes unjustified murder and non-negligent homicide.

critical race feminism   Legal theory that recognizes the intersection of race, gender, class, and age when analyzing oppression.

critical race theory   A collection of theories that examine the relationships of race, racism, and power.

cult of domesticity   Another term for the sphere occupied by women.

curtain rule   A legal idea that reinforces separate spheres (chapter 1) by ensuring that the court will not interfere with that which happens in the private sphere.

cycle of violence   A pattern of behaviors, sometimes used by abusers, where harm is followed by apologies and contrition, followed in turn by a repeat of the harmful acts.

D

decriminalize   To eliminate penalties for the use and possession of drugs for personal use, as well as penalties for possession of equipment used to transfer drugs into the body.

Deferred Action for Childhood Arrivals   An immigration policy that allows some individuals who were brought to the United States without documentation as children to receive deferred action from deportation for a two-year period.

deviant   A term used to describe anyone who deviates or differs from the social norm.

difference feminism   A response to equality theory, difference theory posits that only by recognizing gender differences, or what makes us unique, can we address gender inequality.

discursive intersections   Narratives and discussion about structures of oppression that marginalize those who face complex and intersecting structures of oppression.

domestic terrorism   Violence committed by those in the United States who espouse extremist ideologies of a political, religious, social, racial, or environmental nature.

dominance theory   Similar to radical theory, this theory suggests that to transform law, we need radical restructuring; in this case, we need to remove constructs of control or dominance.

DREAM Act   Proposed legislation that would grant temporary residency to young people who were sixteen or younger when they arrived in the United States without documents, have been residents for at least five consecutive years, and have completed a high school education.

Duluth model   Otherwise known as the power and control wheel, this has become the generally accepted model for education regarding IPV and for creating curricula for BIPs.

E

Ear Hustle **podcast**   Airs from within San Quentin State Prison in California.

embezzlement   Taking assets, money, or property that belongs to another but over which one has control and using it for personal gain.

Emotional Literacy Project for Prisoners   Lionheart Foundation's program centered on emotional intelligence that teaches incarcerated people to understand themselves, how the past impacts their present choices, and to forgive.

epistemology   The philosophy of knowledge or how we acquire and make sense of what we learn; how we know what we know.

equality theory   A theory that states that all people should be treated equally, no matter one's gender.

eugenics   The belief that we can improve the genetic quality of the human race by controlling who is able to reproduce.

F

failure to protect laws   Laws created to protect children from the influence of intimate violence by criminalizing those who fail to remove a child from any home where violence is occurring.

Fair Sentencing Act   2010 act that changed the sentencing ratio of crack and powder cocaine from a 100:1 to an 18:1 disparity.

fatherhood programs   Programs that connect fathers with their children and, if there is already contact, improve the father-child relationship.

femicide   The killing of women; originally used to mean the killing of women by men as an act of hatred toward women.

feminist methodology   A model of epistemology that suggests we give voice to that which we seek to understand.

feminist pathways theory   A theory that explores how our lived experiences impact our life course or path.

fetal alcohol syndrome   A condition that results from alcohol exposure during a mother's pregnancy, which is believed to cause brain damage and other possible birth defects.

First Step Act   Reform to the federal prison system in an effort to lower the number of people incarcerated in federal prisons and to reduce recidivism.

first-wave feminism   If the movement known as "feminism" could be defined by points in time, or waves, the first wave began with the Seneca Falls Convention in 1848 and continued into the 1920s.

fourth-wave feminism   The contemporary feminist movement, emphasizing empowerment, inclusion, and activism.

fraud   Wrongful deception intended for financial or personal gain.

G

gay panic and trans panic defenses   Legal strategy used to bolster other defenses that argues that a defendant's violence is due to the victim's sexual orientation or gender identity/expression.

gender dysphoria   Discomfort or distress when there is a mismatch between a person's biological sex and gender identity.

gender identity   Personal sense of one's own gender; can be the same or different from their sex assigned at birth.

gender stratified   Refers to inequalities between women and men regarding wealth, power, and privilege.

Girls Educational and Mentoring Services (GEMS)   Nonprofit organization that provides services to sexually exploited and domestically trafficked girls and young women.

Graham v. Florida   U.S. Supreme Court decision that juvenile offenders cannot be sentenced to life imprisonment without parole for nonhomicide offenses.

green criminology   Synergy between criminological theory and environment harms.

Guiding Rage into Power (GRIP)   Prison program that teaches men about gender roles and how ideas of hypermasculinity contributed to their violent crimes.

H

harm reduction   Practical strategies aimed at reducing the negative consequences of drug use.

hedonistic   A person who seeks only to maximize pleasure and minimize pain.

heteronormativity   The belief that heterosexuality, or relations between people of the opposite sex, is the cultural norm.

hierarchy   Any system of dominance that prioritizes one thing, or one person, over another.

Homecoming Project   Matches individuals being released from prison with households that have both a spare room and a willingness to offer ongoing support.

Houses of Healing in Prison   Trauma-informed emotional literacy program focusing on healing unresolved traumas and the necessity of self-forgiveness and forgiveness of others, which are essential to the fostering of empathy and emotional and spiritual maturity.

I

id, ego, and superego   A concept developed by Sigmund Freud that describes three elements that together comprise the human personality.

identity performance   A theory that explores the ways that discrimination can target certain individuals within a group more so than others on the basis of their conduct, dress, and self-presentation.

Immigrations and Customs Enforcement (ICE)   Federal law enforcement agency responsible for immigration enforcement.

In re Gault   U.S. Supreme Court decision granting juvenile defendants due process rights, including notice of the charges against the young person, the right to legal counsel, the right against self-incrimination, and the right to confront and cross-examine witnesses.

In re Winship   U.S. Supreme Court decision extending the standard of proof for a juvenile accused of a crime to beyond a reasonable doubt instead of a preponderance of the evidence.

incel community   Men called "involuntary celibates" who are an online subculture that define themselves as unable to find a romantic or sexual partner. They have increasingly become more extremist, often focusing on violence in recent years.

incest   The crime of having sexual intercourse with a parent, child, sibling, or grandchild.

INCITE! Women, Gender Non-Conforming, and Trans People of Color against Violence   National activist organization of radical feminists of color organizing a movement to end violence against women, gender nonconforming, and trans people of color and their communities.

Innocence Project   Focuses on the prevalence of wrongful convictions, exonerating the innocent and reforming the system.

intersectional subordination   Negative social and material outcomes resulting from discriminatory patterns from the collusion of the market and the state.

intersectional theories   Theories that recognize that our lives are shaped by many aspects of our identification, including race, class, gender, and heteronormativity.

interspousal immunity rule   A legal rule that prevents one spouse from testifying against the other, effectively restricting one spouse from seeking legal assistance when the other spouse is abusive.

intimate partner violence (IPV)   Replaces the term "domestic violence," especially among researchers and scholars. This is the terminology we will use in this text whenever it makes sense to do so.

intimate terrorism   Primarily perpetrated by a male against a female partner, intimate terrorism is rooted in a general pattern of control, jealousy, patriarchal beliefs, power, and stalking, whereas situational couple violence, in which either partner can be the aggressor, is embedded in a specific situation where conflict is settled with violence.

L

labeling   A theory that says that someone who is identified by those in authority—teacher, parent, police—as criminal is likely to incorporate that identity.

larceny   Theft of personal property.

learned helplessness   An element of battered woman syndrome that explained the state where a person might try, repeatedly, to break a pattern of abuse, to change a partner's behaviors, or to modify their own to reduce what they perceived as their chance of being harmed, only to find that their actions did not reduce those harms.

M

#MeToo   Reference to sexual harassment and assault used to highlight the depth and pervasiveness of the problem.

male code   Related to toxic masculinity, its expectations are strength, control, power, and the silencing of emotion, as well as fearlessness through risk-taking behavior and dominance through aggressive and violent behavior.

male prison code   Hierarchy based on forcing men to act in hypermasculine and dominating ways inside prisons and jails.

marital rape   Sexual intercourse with one's spouse without the spouse's consent.

marital rape exemption   Recognizes the "conjugal right" of the husband, or his absolute right to sexual relations with his wife.

mask of masculinity   Maintaining a persona of hypermasculinity where acting tough and not showing any empathy enforces manhood.

mass killing   Killing of at least four people in a single event.

mediation   A model of alternative conflict resolution that requires a neutral party to aid those in conflict in a conversation to resolve the underlying conflict.

Miller v. Alabama   U.S. Supreme Court ruling that mandatory sentences for life without parole, even in cases of murder, are unconstitutional for juvenile offenders. Federal and state courts are required to consider unique circumstances when determining individualized sentences for juvenile defendants.

Minneapolis domestic violence experiment   The first large-scale experiment to test the impact of arrest on repeated incidents of domestic violence. There have been numerous follow-up studies, and the results remain controversial.

misogyny   Refers to prejudice, anger, hatred of, or contempt for women and girls.

Montgomery v. Louisiana   The Supreme Court held that *Miller v. Alabama* must be applied retroactively.

mutual arrest   A concept employed by some police departments where, rather than determining who was the person who initiated the violence or presented the greatest threat, both parties are subject to arrest.

N

National Commission on Correctional Health Care   Mission is to improve the quality of health care in jails, prisons, and juvenile detention facilities.

National Incident-Based Reporting System (NIBRS)   FBI statistics that go into much greater detail than the UCR.

National Intimate Partner and Sexual Violence Survey (NISVS)   A unit of the national Centers for Disease Control, NISVS is an ongoing survey that collects state and national data about intimate partner and sexual violence.

National Women's Law Center   Legal organization that fights for gender justice, especially for women and girls facing multiple forms of discrimination.

neoliberalism   A social and economic philosophy that advocates for an extreme version of free-market capitalism, deregulation of markets, and elimination of the role of government, as in welfare.

neurobiology of trauma   Scientific study of how stress changes a person's neurobiology, including the brain.

Nineteenth Amendment   The amendment to the U.S. Constitution that gave women the right to vote.

O

ontology   A branch of philosophy that studies the nature of existence, things, and their being or identity.

P

panopticon Literally meaning "all seeing," it is a building created with a central observation tower and surrounding wings that can be observed from the central point. Today it is a model for jails and prisons, but also schools and other institutional buildings.

parens patriae The principle that the government or other political authority has the responsibility to protect those who are unable to protect themselves, including children.

patriarchy A system in which men hold primary authority and control over role definitions and power; a system that perpetuates oppressive and limiting gender roles.

phrenology A branch of science that examines cranial (skull) structure to determine a range of characteristics; at one time used to determine a predisposition to crime, also used by the Nazis to determine ethnicity.

policing power Absent a federal law, the fundamental authority of a state government to make laws to control and regulate behavior and enforce order; often manifested and abused by the police.

posttraumatic stress disorder (PTSD) A mental disability resulting from prolonged or severe trauma.

preponderance of the evidence Standard of legal proof used in non-criminal cases, where the evidence indicates that the fact is more likely than not (more than 50 percent likely) to be true.

prison-industrial complex Prison system structure that connects economic and political interests, encouraging increased spending on incarceration.

Prison Rape Elimination Act (PREA) The first federal law intended to deter the sexual assault and rape of incarcerated persons, established in 2003. It has set standards to prevent, detect, reduce, and respond to sexual abuse in prisons, jails, and juvenile detention facilities.

Prohibition The Eighteenth Amendment banned the "manufacture, sale, or transportation of intoxicating liquors"; ended in 1933 when the Twenty-First Amendment was passed.

psychopathy Believed to be a genetic predisposition resulting in under-developed brain regulation of emotions. As a consequence, psychopaths have little or no ability to form emotional attachments or feel empathy. They can often appear to be living within social norms. While some of the most well-known serial killers are believed to be psychopaths, some are CEOs of major corporations.

punitive damages Legal damages that punish the litigant for bad behavior.

Q

quality-of-life offenses Acts such as loitering, graffiti, public drinking, and panhandling.

quality-of-life policing Heavily policing normally noncriminal activities and minor offenses (congregating, drinking in public spaces, graffiti, public urination, panhandling, littering, and unlicensed street vending), theorizing that those behaviors will lead to serious crime.

queer legal theory A body of scholarship that gives a voice to the interests of sexual minorities in the pursuit of ending sex/gender subordination and to help promote egalitarianism and equality.

quid pro quo harassment When an employer requires an employee to submit to unwelcome sexual advances, requests for sexual favors, or other verbal or physical conduct of a sexual nature as a condition of employment, either implicitly or explicitly.

R

radical feminism A theory suggesting that without radically altering society and social relations, gender equality can never be achieved.

Rebecca Project for Human Rights Legal and policy organization that advocates for justice and reforms for vulnerable women and girls in the United States and Africa.

red flag law A gun control law that permits police or family members to petition a court to order temporary confiscation of firearms from a person who allegedly presents a danger to others or themselves.

refugee A person who has been forced to leave their country in order to escape war, persecution, or natural disaster.

relative deprivation A term used to describe a situation when, in an affluent society, a person does not have access to the measures of comfort or affluence available to many.

restorative justice A victim-centered response to harm that seeks accountability and responsibility from perpetrators of harm rather than punishment.

Restorative Justice for Oakland Youth (RJOY) Community-based restorative/transformative justice organization in Oakland, California's schools and community.

restraining order Like a civil injunction, but with possible criminal penalties; a court order requiring one person to stop an action or stay away from another person or persons.

returning community member Nonstigmatizing term used for formerly incarcerated people.

right to privacy The right to privacy, as defined by *Griswold v. Connecticut*, says that the state may not unreasonably interfere with an individual's right to make a choice about matters considered private, such as health care and sexuality.

robbery Taking of property from another person by force or threat of force.

Roper v. Simmons U.S. Supreme Court decision that the death penalty cannot be used against someone who committed murder before they were eighteen years old.

S

safe harbor laws Laws that prevent a minor from being prosecuted for prostitution.

Safe Harbour for Exploited Children Act Law that defines a sexually exploited child as someone under eighteen years old who has been subjected to sexual exploitation.

school resource officer (SRO) A law enforcement officer with sworn authority who is stationed in a school.

school-to-prison pipeline The process of criminalizing students through overzealous disciplinary practices that push students out of schools and put them in contact with law enforcement, thus leading to later involvement in the criminal/legal system.

second-wave feminism The period of the feminist movement from the 1920s through the 1970s.

Seneca Falls Convention This convention brought together three hundred men and women who rallied for the equality of women to be recognized.

separate sphere A social construct that separates the public parts of life from the private and, by definition, restricts women, and whatever occurs within a family, to the private sphere.

shaken baby syndrome A brain injury diagnosed in infants and toddlers who are injured or die as a result of forceful shaking.

sociopathy Considered to be the result of environmental factors, sociopaths tend to be erratic and impulsive and have difficulty forming attachments. Sociopaths have difficulty holding down a job and conforming to societal norms.

Southern Poverty Law Center (SPLC) An organization that monitors hate groups and other extremists throughout the United States, exposing their activities.

Southerners on New Ground (SONG) Social justice advocacy organization supporting LGBTQ people, primarily in the South.

standpoint theory A theory that suggests we need to change the lens through which we view, describe, and understand the world from a patriarchal or hierarchical lens to one that is more accepting of differences.

status frustration An expression to describe when a person, especially youth, are unable to obtain status in a manner that is socially acceptable.

status offender A young person who is under court jurisdiction for noncriminal behavior that is considered a law violation merely because of the youth's age, such as truancy, running away, violating curfew, underage use of alcohol, or general ungovernability.

strain The anxiety or uncertainty an individual might experience in a state of anomie.

structural-dynamic discrimination Form of institutional discrimination against individuals of a given race or gender that has the effect of restricting their opportunities.

subprime mortgages Deceptive lending practices, including loans with higher fees or loans incapable of being repaid, which end in foreclosure.

T

TGNCI A contemporary acronym used to refer to trans, gender nonconforming, and intersex people.

third-wave feminism A period of feminism beginning in the 1980s that decentered the movement, recognizing racial and gender diversity.

Time's Up Movement against sexual harassment founded by Hollywood celebrities to provide legal support for victims, particularly victims who lack resources.

Title IX Law that states that no person can be discriminated against by a federally funded education program on the basis of sex.

toxic masculinity Traditional and stereotypical patriarchal masculinity norms that emphasize strength, power, control, and aggression.

toxic shame Feeling of worthlessness, humiliation, and self-loathing emanating from trauma.

transformative justice An extension of restorative justice that focuses on healing harms within the community, including racism, gender-based oppression, and environmental harms, among others.

transforming power AVP core, which is centered on the belief that behavior cannot be effectively altered unless emotions are changed.

Transgender Law Center (TLC) Largest national trans-led organization advocating self-determination for transgender and gender nonconforming people; grounded in legal expertise and committed to racial justice.

Transgender Offender Manual Federal Bureau of Prisons manual that provides guidance to staff for unique issues of transgender people in prison.

T.R.U.E. A prison anticonflict program that uses experiences, structure, and discipline to transform young men from being influenced (dominated) by their childhood traumas to being positive individuals.

U

Uniform Crime Reporting (UCR) Summary-based reporting of crimes to the FBI from law enforcement agencies that voluntarily participate.

V

Voting Rights Act An act signed into law in 1965 to prohibit discriminatory voting practices.

W

war on drugs Government-led campaign to stop illegal drug use and distribution by enforcing and increasing penalties.

white-collar crime A broad term that typically refers to any crime associated with work or the workplace.

Z

zero-tolerance policies School policies that mandate expulsion or referral to juvenile or criminal court regardless of the circumstances or nature of the offense.

BIBLIOGRAPHY

"About." INCITE! Women, Gender Non-Conforming and Trans People of Color against Violence. Accessed June 7, 2019. https://incite-national.org.

"About." Innocence Project. Accessed July 12, 2019. https://www.innocenceproject.org.

"About." Marissa Alexander Justice Project. Accessed June 7, 2019. https://marissaalexander.org.

"About DES." U.S. Department of Health and Human Services, Centers for Disease Control and Prevention. Accessed October 3, 2019. https://www.cdc.gov/des/consumers/about/index.html.

"About RJOY." Restorative Justice for Oakland Youth. Accessed July 10, 2019. https://rjoyoakland.org.

"About S&P." Survived & Punished. Accessed June 7, 2019. https://survivedandpunished.org.

"About SRLP." Sylvia Rivera Law Project. Accessed July 14, 2019. https://srlp.org.

"About Us." Coalition to Stop Violence against Native Women. Accessed July 16, 2019. https://www.csvanw.org.

"About Us." Homecoming Project. Accessed July 12, 2019. https://impactjustice.org/impact/homecoming-project.

"About Us." Transgender Law Center. Accessed July 15, 2019. https://transgenderlawcenter.org.

"About Us." Vera Institute of Justice. Accessed July 12, 2019. https://www.vera.org.

"ACLU Comment on New Trump Asylum Restrictions." American Civil Liberties Union. Accessed July 18, 2019. https://www.aclu.org/press-releases/aclu-comment-new-trump-asylum-restrictions.

"The Advocates for Human Rights: Stop Violence against Women." Stop Violence against Women. Accessed August 1, 2018. http://www.stopvaw.org/state_and_federal_domestic_violence_laws_in_the_united_states.

"Annual Report on Sexual Assault in the Military." Department of Defense, fiscal year 2017. http://www.sapr.mil/public/docs/reports/FY17_Annual/DoD_FY17_Annual_Report_on_Sexual_Assault_in_the_Military.pdf.

"APA Review Confirms Link between Playing Violent Video Games and Aggression." American Psychological Association. Accessed August 13, 2015. https://www.apa.org/news/press/releases/2015/08/violent-video-games.

"Are U.S. Girls Becoming More Violent?" Population Reference Bureau. Accessed September 12, 2017. https://www.prb.org/areusgirlsbecomingmoreviolent.

"Arrests by Sex, 2017." FBI, Uniform Crime Reporting, Crime in the United States. Table 42. 2017. Accessed October 16, 2019. https://ucr.fbi.gov/crime-in-the-u.s/2017/crime-in-the-u.s.-2017/topic-pages/tables/table-42.

"Assembly Speaker Sheldon Silver Press Release: Assembly Passes 'Safe Harbour' Legislation." New York State Assembly. Accessed July 1, 2019. https://assembly.state.ny.us/Press/20080619.

"Asylum Eligibility and Procedural Modifications." U.S. Homeland Security Department and the Executive Office for Immigration Review. Accessed July 17, 2019. https://www.federalregister.gov/documents/2019/07/16/2019-15246/asylum-eligibility-and-procedural-modifications.

"Black Boys Viewed as Older, Less Innocent than Whites, Research Finds." American Psychological Association, 2014. https://www.apa.org/news/press/releases/2014/03/black-boys-older.

"Black Disparities in Youth Incarceration." Accessed September 12, 2017. https://www.sentencingproject.org/publications/black-disparities-youth-incarceration.

Black Girls Matter: Pushed Out, Overpoliced and Underprotected. African American Policy Forum and the Center for Intersectionality and Social Policy Studies, 2015. Accessed July 15, 2019. https://static1.squarespace.com/static/53f20d90e4b0b80451158d8c/t/54dcc1ece4b001c03e323448/1423753708557/AAPF_BlackGirlsMatterReport.pdf.

"'Black Trans Bodies Are Under Attack': Freed Activist CeCe McDonald, Actress Laverne Cox Speak Out." *Democracy Now!,* February 19, 2014. https://www.youtube.com/watch?v=kOuH43-_4Yo.

"A Brief History of the Drug War." Drug Policy Alliance. Accessed October 19, 2019. http://www.drugpolicy.org/issues/brief-history-drug-war.

"The Central Park Jogger: After 14 Years, Woman at Center of Famous Case Reveals Identity." *Dateline NBC,* December 8, 2003. http://www.nbcnews.com/id/3080050/ns/dateline_nbc-newsmakers/t/central-park-jogger/#.XPaY6ohKg2x.

"Crack Babies: Twenty Years Later." NPR, May 3, 2010. https://www.npr.org/templates/story/story.php?storyId=126478643.

"Crime in the United States, 2016." FBI, Uniform Crime Reporting. https://ucr.fbi.gov/crime-in-the-u.s/2016/crime-in-the-u.s.-2016.

"Crime in the United States, 2017." FBI, Uniform Crime Reporting. https://ucr.fbi.gov/crime-in-the-u.s/2017/crime-in-the-u.s.-2017.

"Crime Trends: 1990–2016." Brennan Center for Justice. https://www.brennancenter.org/publication/crime-trends1990-2016.

"Crime Victimization 2018." NCJ 253043. Bureau of Justice Statistics, September 2019. https://www.bjs.gov/content/pub/pdf/cv18.pdf.

"Declaration on the Elimination of Violence against Women," United Nations General Assembly, 1993, https://www.un.org/en/genocideprevention/documents/atrocity-crimes/Doc.21_declaration%20elimination%20vaw.pdf.

"Defend Our Online Communities." Stop SESTA & FOSTA, 2018. Accessed May 19, 2019. https://stopsesta.org.

"Department of Justice Takes Legal Action to Address Pattern and Practice of Excessive Force and Violence at NYC Jails on Rikers Island that Violates the Constitutional Rights of Young Male Inmates." U.S. Department of Justice, December 18, 2014.

"Domestic Violence Arrest Policies by State." American Bar Association, June 2011. https://www.americanbar.org/content/dam/aba/images/domestic_violence/Domestic%20Violence%20Arrest%20Policies%20by%20State%202011%20(complete).pdf.

"Dorothy Gaines." Sentencing Project. http://www.sentencingproject.org/stories/dorothy-gaines.

"Drug Courts." NCJ 238527. National Institute of Justice, U.S. Department of Justice, May 2018. https://www.ncjrs.gov/pdffiles1/nij/238527.pdf.

"Drug Decriminalization in Portugal: Learning from a Health and Human-Centered Approach." Drug Policy Alliance. Accessed October 20, 2019. http://www.drugpolicy.org/sites/default/files/dpa-drug-decriminalization-portugal-health-human-centered-approach_0.pdf.

"Enhanced Resource Guidelines." National Council of Juvenile and Family Court Judges, May 26, 2016. https://www.ncjfcj.org/enhancedresourceguidelines.

"Fact Sheet: Drug-Related Crime." Drugs & Crime, Bureau of Justice Statistics. Accessed February 16, 2016. https://www.bjs.gov/content/pub/pdf/DRRC.PDF.

"Fatal Force." *Washington Post*. Last updated May 17, 2021. https://www.washingtonpost.com/graphics/investigations/police-shootings-database.

"Fathers behind Bars: The Problem & Solution for America's Children [Infographic]." National Fatherhood Initiative, October 16, 2014. https://www.fatherhood.org/fatherhood/fathers-behind-bars-the-problem-and-solution-for-americas-children-infographic.

"Frequently Asked Questions about the Change in the UCR Definition of Rape." FBI, December 11, 2014. https://ucr.fbi.gov/recent-program-updates/new-rape-definition-frequently-asked-questions.

"Getting the Facts Straight about Girls in the Juvenile Justice System." National Council on Crime & Delinquency, 2009. https://www.nccdglobal.org/node/440.

"Global Report on Trafficking in Persons." United Nations Office on Drugs and Crime, 2014. https://www.unodc.org/res/cld/bibliography/global-report-on-trafficking-in-persons_html/GLOTIP_2014_full_report.pdf.

"Global Report on Trafficking in Persons Executive Summary." United Nations Office on Drugs and Crime, 2009. https://www.unodc.org/documents/humantrafficking/Executive_summary_english.pdf.

"The Grapevine: A Southern Trans Report." Southerners on New Ground and the Transgender Law Center, 2019. http://transgenderlawcenter.org/wpcontent/uploads/2019/05/grapevine_report_eng-FINAL.pdf.

"Harmful Masculinity and Violence." *In the Public Interest*. American Psychological Association. Accessed September 10, 2018. https://www.apa.org/pi/about/newsletter/2018/09/harmful-masculinity.

"Hate Crimes." FBI. Accessed June 1, 2019. https://www.fbi.gov/investigate/civil-rights/hate-crimes.

"Health, Rights and Drugs: Harm Reduction, Decriminalization and Zero Discrimination for People Who Use Drugs." UNAIDS, 2019. https://www.unaids.org/sites/default/files/media_asset/JC2954_UNAIDS_drugs_report_2019_en.pdf.

"How Dance Helps Prisoners." Dance to Be Free. Accessed June 15, 2019. https://dancetobefree.org/gallery.

"'I So Wish the Case Hadn't Been Settled': 1989 Central Park Jogger Believes More than 1 Person Attacked Her." ABC News, May 23, 2019. https://abcnews.go.com/US/case-settled-1989-central-park-jogger-believes-person/story?id=63077131.

"In Conversation: Alok Vaid-Menon and CeCe McDonald." *Nepantla: A Journal Dedicated to Queer Poets of Color* 2 (September 9, 2015). https://www.lambdaliterary.org/wp-content/uploads/2015/09/alok.cece_.pdf.

"Incarcerated Women and Girls." Sentencing Project, 2015. Accessed August 23, 2019. http://www.sentencingproject.org/doc/publications/Incarcerated-Women-and-Girls.pdf.

"Incarcerated Women and Girls." Sentencing Project, June 6, 2019. https://www.sentencingproject.org/publications/incarcerated-women-and-girls.

"Information on the Legal Rights Available to Immigrant Victims of Domestic Violence in the United States and Facts about Immigrating on a Marriage-Based Visa." U.S. Citizenship and Immigration Services. Accessed July 1, 2019. https://www.uscis.gov/sites/default/files/document/brochures/IMBRA%20Pamphlet%20Final%2001-07-2011%20for%20Web%20Posting.pdf.

"Inmate Gender." Federal Bureau of Prisons. Accessed July 9, 2019. https://www.bop.gov/about/statistics/statistics_inmate_gender.jsp.

"Law Enforcement Misconduct." U.S. Department of Justice. Accessed October 7, 2019. https://www.justice.gov/crt/law-enforcement-misconduct.

"Law School Data, Class Enrollment by Gender and Race/Ethnicity (Aggregate)." American Bar Association, Fall 2018. https://www.americanbar.org/groups/legal_education/resources/statistics.

"Leading Causes of Death in Males, United States." Centers for Disease Control and Prevention. Last updated November 20, 2019. https://www.cdc.gov/healthequity/lcod/index.htm.

"Leading Causes of Death (LCOD) in Females United States, 2015." Centers for Disease Control and Prevention, 2015. Accessed July 7, 2019. https://www.cdc.gov/women/lcod/2015/index.htm.

"LGBTQ Youth in the Foster Care System." Human Rights Campaign. Accessed September 12, 2019. https://assets2.hrc.org/files/assets/resources/HRC-YouthFosterCare-IssueBrief-FINAL.pdf.

"Major Criminal Cases." U.S. Environmental Protection Agency. Accessed September 17, 2019. https://www.epa.gov/enforcement/2016-major-criminal-cases.

"The Manifesto of Elliot Rodger." *New York Times*, May 25, 2014. https://www.nytimes.com/interactive/2014/05/25/us/shooting-document.html?_r=0.

"Map of Marijuana Legality by State." DISA. Accessed October 20, 2019. https://disa.com/map-of-marijuana-legality-by-state.

"Mapping Police Violence." Accessed October 7, 2019. https://mappingpoliceviolence.org.

"Missing and Murdered Indigenous Women and Girls: A Snapshot of Data from 71 Urban Cities in the United States." Urban Indian Health Institute, 2018. Accessed July 7, 2019. http://www.uihi.org/wp-content/uploads/2018/11/Missing-and-Murdered-Indigenous-Women-and-Girls-Report.pdf.

"Mission and Values." GLBTQ Legal Advocates & Defenders (GLAD). Accessed July 14, 2019. https://www.glad.org.

"Mothers against Senseless Killing." Accessed October 25, 2019. http://ontheblock.org.

"Mothers Demand Action." Accessed October 25, 2019. https://momsdemandaction.org.

"National Domestic Violence Hotline." Accessed October 12, 2013. https://www.thehotline.org/is-this-abuse.

"Native Lives Matter." Lakota People's Law Project, February 2015. https://s3-us-west-1.amazonaws.com/lakota-peoples-law/uploads/Native-Lives-Matter-PDF.pdf.

"No One Can 'Take My Identity Away from Me.'" MSNBC, January 19, 2014. https://www.msnbc.com/melissa-harris-perry/watch/how-the-system-treats-trans-people-121475139959.

"November Coalition Letter on the Passing of Alva Mae Groves." November Coalition, July 30, 2008. http://www.november.org/thewall/cases/groves-a/groves-a.html.

"Number of Mass Shootings in the United States between 1982 and August 2019, by Mass Shooter's Race and Ethnicity." Statista. Accessed October 31, 2019. https://www.statista.com/statistics/476456/mass-shootings-in-the-us-by-shooter-s-race.

"Operation Lipstick." Accessed October 25, 2019. https://www.operationlipstick.org.

"Painting the Current Picture: A National Report on Drug Courts and Other Problem-Solving Courts in the US." National Drug Court Institute, June 2016. https://www.ndci.org/wp-content/uploads/2016/05/Painting-the-Current-Picture-2016.pdf.

"Philosophy." Prison Yoga Project. Accessed July 1, 2019. https://prisonyoga.org/our-mission/philosophy.

"Position Statement: Criminal Justice System." TheArc.org. Accessed June 1, 2019. https://www.thearc.org/who-we-are/position-statements/rights/criminal-justice.

"Prison Policy Initiative." Accessed September 12, 2017. https://www.prisonpolicy.org/research/youth.

"The Prison Project." Lionheart Foundation. Accessed July 10, 2019. https://lionheart.org/prison/project.

"Prisoners Unlearn the Toxic Masculinity That Led to Their Incarceration." *HuffPost*, n.d. Accessed November 1, 2019. https://www.huffpost.com/entry/prisoners-unlearn-the-toxic-masculinity-that-led-to-their-incarceration_n_5d406b9ce4b06e9f169f1247.

"Protection for Private Blocking and Screening of Offensive Material." 47 U.S. Code § 230 of the Communications Act of 1934. Accessed July 1, 2019. https://www.law.cornell.edu/uscode/text/47/230.

"Protocol to Prevent, Suppress and Punish Trafficking in Persons Especially Women and Children, supplementing the United Nations Convention against Transnational Organized Crime." United Nations Human Rights Office of the High Commissioner, 2000. Accessed July 1, 2019. https://www.ohchr.org/Documents/ProfessionalInterest/ProtocolonTrafficking.pdf.

"The Psychology of Hate Crimes." APA.org. Accessed June 1, 2019. https://www.apa.org/advocacy/civil-rights/hate-crimes.pdf.

"Quick Facts: Women in the Federal Offender Population." U.S. Sentencing Commission. Accessed October 16, 2019. https://www.ussc.gov/sites/default/files/pdf/research-and-publications/quick-facts/Female_Offenders_FY18.pdf.

"RE: Docket No. OAG-131; AG Order No. 3143-2010 National Standards to Prevent, Detect, and Respond to Prison Rape." Sylvia Rivera Law Project, May 10, 2010. https://srlp.org/files/SRLP%20PREA%20comment%20Docket%20no%20OAG-131.pdf.

"Recent Immigration Policies Negatively Affect Women." Women's Legal Defense and Education Fund. Accessed July 3, 2019. https://www.legalmomentum.org/blog/recent-immigration-policies-negatively-affect-women.

"Report and Recommendations concerning the Use of Restrictive Housing." U.S. Department of Justice, January 2016.

"Report on Torture." Duckworth and Amnesty International Publications, 1973.

"Say Her Name: Resisting Police Brutality against Black Women." African American Policy Forum and the Center for Intersectionality and Social Policy Studies, 2015. Accessed July 15, 2019. http://static1.squarespace.com/static/53f20d90e4b0b80451158d8c/t/560c068ee4b0af26f72741df/1443628686535/AAPF_SMN_Brief_Full_singles-min.pdf.

"School Climate and Safety." 2015–16 Civil Rights Data Collection, U.S. Department of Education Office for Civil Rights, April 2018. https://www2.ed.gov/about/offices/list/ocr/docs/school-climate-and-safety.pdf.

"The Secret Life of Elliot Rodger." ABC News. Accessed June 1, 2019. https://abcnews.go.com/US/fullpage/secret-life-elliot-rodger-24322227.

"Smaller, Safer, Fairer: A Roadmap to Closing Rikers Island." City of New York Office of the Mayor, June 22, 2017.

"State Laws on Fetal Homicide and Penalty-Enhancement for Crimes against Pregnant Women." National Conference of State Legislatures, May 1, 2018. http://www.ncsl.org/research/health/fetal-homicide-state-laws.aspx.

"Statistical Briefing Book." Office of Juvenile Justice and Delinquency Program. Accessed July 1, 2019. https://www.ojjdp.gov/ojstatbb/crime/qa05101.asp.

"Still Worse than Second-Class: Solitary Confinement of Women in the United States." American Civil Liberties Union, 2019. https://www.aclu.org/report/worse-second-class-solitary-confinement-women-united-states?

"Terrorism." FBI. Accessed November 1, 2019. https://www.fbi.gov/investigate/terrorism.

"Toolkit 2017." Protected Innocence Challenge. Accessed July 1, 2019. https://sharedhope.org/wp-content/uploads/2017/11/2017-PIC-Fact-Sheet_2.pdf.

"Transgender Offender Manual: Change Notice." Federal Bureau of Prisons, May 11, 2018. https://www.documentcloud.org/documents/4459297-BOP-Change-Order-Transgender-Offender-Manual-5.html.

"U.S.A. FOSTA Legislation." Briefing note. Global Network of Sex Work Projects (NSWP), 2018. https://www.nswp.org/sites/nswp.org/files/fosta_briefing_note_2018.pdf.

"Victims of Criminal Activity: U Nonimmigrant Status." U.S. Citizenship and Immigration Services. Accessed July 1, 2019. https://www.uscis.gov/humanitarian/victims-of-human-trafficking-and-other-crimes/victims-of-criminal-activity-u-nonimmigrant-status.

"Victims of Human Trafficking: Nonimmigrant Status." U.S. Citizenship and Immigration Services. Accessed July 19, 2019. https://www.uscis.gov/humanitarian/victims-human-trafficking-other-crimes/victims-human-trafficking-t-nonimmigrant-status.

"War on Drugs." History.com. Accessed October 19, 2019. https://www.history.com/topics/crime/the-war-on-drugs.

"What We Believe: Guiding Principles." Black Lives Matter. Accessed July 15, 2019. https://blacklivesmatter.com/about/what-we-believe.

"Why Women?" Women's Earth & Climate Action Network International. Accessed July 15, 2019. https://www.wecaninternational.org/why-women.

"With Liberty and Justice for All: The State of Civil Rights at Immigration Detention Facilities." U.S. Commission on Civil Rights, September 2015. https://www.usccr.gov/pubs/docs/Statutory_Enforcement_Report2015.pdf.

"Wrongfully Convicted 'Central Park Five' Defendant Makes Gift Renaming Innocence Project." University of Colorado Law School, December 9, 2015. https://www.colorado.edu/law/2015/12/09/wrongfully-convicted-central-park-five-defendant-makes-gift-renaming-innocence-project.

"Youth Risk Behavior Survey: Data Summary and Trends Report, 2007–2017." Centers for Disease Control and Prevention. Accessed February 18, 2019. https://www.cdc.gov/healthyyouth/data/yrbs/pdf/trendsreport.pdf.

Abad-Santos, Alexander. "Everything You Need to Know about Steubenville High School's 'Rape Crew.'" *The Atlantic*, January 3, 2013.

———. "Look Who's Already in Trouble over the Steubenville Rape Case." *The Atlantic*, January 4, 2013.

Abad-Santos, Alexander, and Matt Sullivan. "Enter the Trial in Steubenville, Where the Cast Is Not Merely Football Players." *The Atlantic*, March 13, 2013.

Acoca, Leslie. "Are Those Cookies for Me or My Baby? Understanding Detained and Incarcerated Teen Mothers and Their Children." *Juvenile and Family Court Journal*, Spring 2004.

Alexander v. State of Florida, No. 1D12–2469. (Fla. 2013).

Alexander, Marissa. "Not Another Victim—I'm an Empowered Survivor Defendant: Marissa Alexander; TEDxFSCJ." Survived & Punished. Accessed June 1, 2019. https://survivedandpunished.org/2019/06/01/marissa-alexander-ted-talk.

Ali, Russlyn. "'Dear Colleague' Notice from the U.S. Department of Education Office for Civil Rights." U.S. Department of Education Office for Civil Rights, April 4, 2011. https://www2.ed.gov/about/offices/list/ocr/letters/colleague-201104.pdf.

Alianza Nacional de Campesinas. "Dear Sisters." *Time*, November 10, 2017. https://time.com/5018813/farmworkers-solidarity-hollywood-sexual-assault.

Allyn, Bobby. "Amber Guyger, Ex-Officer Who Killed Man in His Apartment, Given 10 Years in Prison." NPR, October 2, 2019. https://

www.npr.org/2019/10/02/766454839/amber-guyger-ex-officer -who-killed-man-in-his-apartment-given-10-years-in-prison.

Alternatives to Violence Project, Britain, 2007.

Alvarez, Priscilla. "When Sex Trafficking Goes Unnoticed in America." *The Atlantic*, February 23, 2016. https://www.theatlantic.com /politics/archive/2016/02/how-sex-trafficking-goes-unnoticed-in -america/470166.

American Immigration Council. Accessed October 5, 2019. https:// www.americanimmigrationcouncil.org/research/us-citizen-child ren-impacted-immigration-enforcement.

Anderson, Craig A., Nobuko Ihori, Brad J. Bushman, Hannah R. Rothstein, Akiko Shibuya, Edward L. Swing, Akira Sakamoto, and Muniba Saleem. "Violent Video Game Effects on Aggression, Empathy, and Prosocial Behavior in Eastern and Western Countries." *Psychological Bulletin* 136, no. 2 (2010): 151–73. http://doi.org /10.1037/a0018251.

Anderson, Elijah. *Code of the Street: Decency, Violence, and the Moral Life of the Inner City*. New York: Norton, 2005.

Angelari, Marguerite. "Hate Crime Statutes: A Promising Tool for Fighting Violence against Women." *American University Journal of Gender, Social Policy & the Law* 2, no. 1 (1993).

Arnold, Regina A. "Processes of Victimization and Criminalization of Black Women." *Social Justice* 17 (1990): 153–66.

Aviv, Rachel. "What If Your Abusive Husband Is a Cop?" *New Yorker*, October 7, 2019.

Badger, Emily. "The Dramatic Racial Bias of Subprime Lending during the Housing Boom." City Lab, August 16, 2013. https:// www.citylab.com/equity/2013/08/blacks-really-were-targeted-bo gus-loans-during-housing-boom/6559.

Balkin, Jack M., and Reva B. Siegel. "American Civil Rights Tradition: Anticlassification or Antisubordination?" *University of Miami Law Review* 58, no. 9 (2003). https://law.yale.edu/system/files/docu ments/pdf/Faculty/Siegel_TheAmericanCivilRightsTraditionAnti classificationOrAntisubordination.pdf.

Barry, Kathleen. *Female Sexual Slavery*. New York: New York University Press, 1979.

———. *The Prostitution of Sexuality*. New York: New York University Press, 1995.

Barry, Margaret M., Jon C. Dubin, and Peter A. Joy. "The Development of Legal Education in the United States." PILnet. Accessed February 16, 2016. https://www.pilnet.org/resource /the-development-of-legal-education-in-the-united-states.

Baum, Dan. "Legalize It All: How to Win the War on Drugs." *Harper's Magazine*, April 2016. https://harpers.org/archive/2016/04 /legalize-it-all.

Beccaria, Cesare. *On Crimes and Punishments*. Indianapolis, IN: Hackett, 1986.

Belknap, Joanne. *The Invisible Woman: Gender, Crime and Justice*. 4th ed. Stamford, CT: Cengage Learning, 2015.

Belknap, Joanne, and Kristi Holsinger. "The Gendered Nature of Risk Factors for Delinquency." *Feminist Criminology* 1 (2006): 48–71.

Bentham, Jeremy. *Proposal for a New and Less Expensive Mode of Employing and Reforming Convicts*. London, n.d.

Bhargava, Shalini. "Challenging Punishment and Privatization: A Response to the Conviction of Regina McKnight." *Harvard Civil Rights–Civil Liberties Law Review* 39 (2004): 513–42.

Bierria, Alisa, Hyejin Shim, Mimi Kim, and Emi Kane. "Free Marissa Now and Stand with Nan-Hui: A Conversation about Parallel Struggles." *Feminist Wire*, June 30, 2015. https://www.thefeminist wire.com/2015/06/free-marissa-and-stand-with-nan-hui.

Blake, Andrew. "Deric Lostutter, Hacker, Sentenced to 2 Years in Prison for Crimes Tied to Steubenville Rape Case." *Washington Times*, March 8, 2017.

Bowlby, John. "Attachment and Loss." In *Attachment*, vol. 1. New York: Basic Books, 1969.

Bradwell v. The State, 83 U.S. 130, 141–42 (S.Ct. 1873).

Brandenburg v. Ohio, 395 U.S. 444 (S.Ct. 1969).

BreakOUT! "We Deserve Better: A Report on Policing in New Orleans by and for Queer and Trans Youth of Color." National Council on Crime & Delinquency, October 24, 2014.

Brock, Eleanor. "The Truth about Women of Color behind Bars." Accessed October 21, 2019. https://www.logikcull.com/blog /women-color-behind-bars.

Bronski, Michael. "Stonewall Was a Riot." *ZNet*, June 10, 2009. http:// zcomm.org/znetarticle/stonewall-was-a-riot-by-michael-bronski.

Browne, Angela. *When Battered Women Kill*. New York: Free Press, 1987.

Browning, Christopher R., Margo Gardner, David Maimon, and Jeanne Brooks-Gunn. "Collective Efficacy and the Contingent Consequences of Exposure to Life-Threatening Violence." *Developmental Psychology* 50, no. 7 (2014): 1878–90. https://doi.org /10.1037/a0036767.

Brownmiller, Susan. *Against Our Will: Men, Women, and Rape*. New York: Bantam, 1976.

Brugger, Kelsey. "Elliot Rodger Report Details Long Struggle with Mental Illness." *Santa Barbara Independent*, February 20, 2015. https://www.independent.com/2015/02/20/elliot-rodger-report -details-long-struggle-mental-illness.

Bruno v. Codd, 396 N.Y.S.2d 974 (S.Ct. 1977).

Buka, Stephen L., Theresa L. Stichick, Isolde Birdthistle, and Fenton J. Earls. "Youth Exposure to Violence: Prevalence, Risks, and Consequences." *American Journal of Orthopsychiatry* 71, no. 3 (2001): 298–310. https://doi.org/10.1037/0002-9432.71.3.298.

Bundy v. Jackson, 641 F.2d 934 (D.C. Cir. 1981).

Burroughs, Gaylynn. "Carswell Prison Blues." *HuffPost*, November 29, 2008. http://www.huffingtonpost.com/entry/carswell-prison -blues_b_138999.html.

Butler, Cheryl Nelson. "The Racial Roots of Human Trafficking." *UCLA Law Review* 62 (2015): 1464–514. https://www.uclalaw review.org/racial-roots-human-trafficking.

Buttenweiser, Sarah Werthan. "Fathers' Fight: What Every Mother Should Know about the Fathers' Rights Movement." Mothers Movement. Accessed September 19, 2019. http://www.mothers movement.org/features/05/fathers_fight/buttenwieser_0605_1.htm.

California Penal Code § 192. Accessed June 1, 2019. https://leginfo .legislature.ca.gov/faces/printCodeSectionWindow.xhtml?lawCode =PEN&sectionNum=192.&op_statues=2014&op_chapter=684 &op_section=1.

Campbell, Alex. "Woman Sent to Prison for Failing to Protect Toddler Is Up for Parole." *BuzzFeed*, December 30, 2015. https://www .buzzfeednews.com/article/alexcampbell/woman-sent-to-prison -for-failing-to-protect-toddler-is-up-fo#.ktj2V7q6n.

Capehart, Jonathan. "It's Tamir Rice's Fault." *Washington Post*, March 2, 2015. http://www.washingtonpost.com/blogs/post-partisan /wp/2015/03/02/its-tamir-rices-fault.

Carey, Shannon M., Kimberly Pukstas, Mark S. Waller, Richard J. Mackin, and Michael W. Finigan. "Drug Courts and State Mandated Drug Treatment Programs: Outcomes, Costs, and Consequences." March 2008. https://www.ncjrs.gov/pdffiles1/nij/grants /223975.pdf.

Carrington, Kerry. "Girls and Violence: The Case for a Feminist Theory of Female Violence." *International Journal for Crime, Justice and Social Democracy* 2, no. 2 (2013): 63–79. https://doi .org/10.5204/ijcjsd.v2i2.101.

Carson, E. Ann. "Prisoners in 2014." Department of Justice, Bureau of Justice Statistics, September 2015. https://www.bjs.gov/content/pub/pdf/p14.pdf.

Castón, Joel, and Michael Woody. "A DC Jail Unit Challenges the 'Warehouse.'" *Crime Report*, June 11, 2019. https://thecrimereport.org/2019/06/11/a-dc-jail-unit-challenges-the-warehouse-approach-to-corrections.

Cauffman, Elizabeth, Shirley Feldman, Jaime Watherman, and Hans Steiner. "Posttraumatic Stress Disorder among Female Juvenile Offenders." *Journal of the American Academy of Child & Adolescent Psychiatry* 37, no. 11 (November 1998): 1209–16. https://doi.org/10.1097/00004583-199811000-00022.

Cepla, Zuzana. "Fact Sheet: U.S. Asylum Process." National Immigration Forum, January 10, 2019. https://immigrationforum.org/article/fact-sheet-u-s-asylum-process.

Cioca v. Rumsfeld, No. 12-1065 (4th Circuit 2013).

Clarke, Jennifer G., and Rachel E. Simon. "Shackling and Separation: Motherhood and Prison." *AMA Journal of Ethics*, September 2013. https://journalofethics.ama-assn.org/article/shackling-and-separation-motherhood-prison/2013-09.

Clarke, Matthew. "'Shaken Baby Syndrome' Diagnoses Discredited, Convictions Questioned." *Criminal Legal News*, May 15, 2018. https://www.criminallegalnews.org/news/2018/may/15/shaken-baby-syndrome-diagnoses-discredited-convictions-questioned.

Clements-Nolle, Kristen, Matthew Wolden, and Jessey Bargmann-Losche. "Childhood Trauma and Risk for Past and Future Suicide Attempts among Women in Prison." *Women's Health Issues* 19 (2009): 185–92.

Cobb, Jelani. "The Central Park Five, Criminal Justice, and Donald Trump." *New Yorker*, April 19, 2019. https://www.newyorker.com/news/daily-comment/the-central-park-five-criminal-justice-and-donald-trump.

Columbia et al. v. Heller, 554 U.S. 570 (S.Ct. 2008).

Commission on Women in the Profession. *A Current Glance at Women in the Law*. American Bar Association, April 2019. https://www.americanbar.org/content/dam/aba/administrative/women/current_glance_2019.pdf.

Coulter, Martha L., Abigail Alexander, and Victoria Harrison. "Specialized Domestic Violence Courts: Improvement for Women Victims?" *Women & Criminal Justice* 16, no. 3 (n.d.): 91–106. https://doi.org/10.1300/J012v16n03_05.

Cowan, Samantha. "Laverne Cox and CeCe McDonald Discuss the Epidemic of Violence against Trans Women." *Take Part*, June 3, 2016. http://www.takepart.com/article/2016/06/03/free-cece.

Crenshaw, Kimberlé Williams. "From Private Violence to Mass Incarceration: Thinking Intersectionally about Women, Race, and Social Control." *UCLA Law Review* 59 (2012): 1426–27.

———. "Mapping the Margins: Intersectionality, Identity Politics, and Violence against Women of Color." *Stanford Law Review* 43, no. 6 (July 1991): 1241–99. https://doi.org/10.2307/1229039.

Cullen, Tara Tidwell. "ICE Released Its Most Comprehensive Immigration Detention Data Yet. It's Alarming." National Immigrant Justice Center, March 13, 2018. https://immigrantjustice.org/staff/blog/ice-released-its-most-comprehensive-immigration-detention-data-yet.

Curtis, A. "'You Have to Cut It off at the Knee': Dangerous Masculinity and Security inside a Men's Prison." *Men and Masculinities* 17, no. 2 (2014): 120–46.

Cutuli, J. J., Robert M. Goerge, Claudia Coulton, Maryanne Schretzman, David Crampton, Benjamin J. Charvat, Nina Lalich, Jessica A. Raithel, Cristobal Gacitua, and Eun Lye Lee. "From Foster Care to Juvenile Justice: Exploring Characteristics of Youth in Three Cities." *Children and Youth Services Review* 68 (August 2016): 84–94. https://doi.org/10.1016/j.childyouth.2016.06.001.

Danilina, S. "Who Was Myra Bradwell: America's First Woman Lawyer." The Law Dictionary. Accessed February 16, 2016. https://thelawdictionary.org/article/who-was-myra-bradwell-americas-first-woman-lawyer.

Dawson, Ruth. "Trump Administration's Domestic Gag Rule Has Slashed the Title X Network's Capacity by Half." Guttmacher Institute. Updated April 15, 2021. https://www.guttmacher.org/article/2020/02/trump-administrations-domestic-gag-rule-has-slashed-title-x-networks-capacity-half.

Decrim NY. "Our Goals." Accessed July 1, 2019. https://www.decrimny.org.

Delgado, Diana. "Interview with Diana Delgado." Women and Prison. Accessed July 1, 2019. http://womenandprison.org/interviews/view/interview_with_diana_delgado.

Della Giustina, Jo-Ann. *Why Women Are Beaten and Killed: Sociological Predictors of Femicide*. New York: Edwin Mellen Press, 2010.

Della Giustina, Jo-Ann, and Jennifer Hartsfield. "Evaluation of the Alternatives to Violence Project in Massachusetts." Unpublished paper, 2019.

DePrince, Anne P., Joanne Belknap, Jennifer S. Labus, Susan E. Buckingham, and Angela R. Gover. "The Impact of Victim-Focused Outreach on Criminal Legal System Outcomes Following Police-Reported Intimate Partner Abuse." *Violence against Women* 18, no. 8 (2012): 861–81. https://doi.org/10.1177/1077801212456523.

Dick, Kirby. *The Invisible War*. Produced by Amy Ziering, Tanner King Barklow, and Chain Camera Pictures, 2012.

Dorf, Michael C., and Jeffrey Fagan. "Problem-Solving Courts: From Innovation to Institutionalization—Forward." *American Criminal Justice Review* 40, no. 40 (2003): 1501–12.

Duberman, Martin. *Stonewall*. New York: Penguin, 1993.

Dunlap, David W. "Stonewall, Gay Bar that Made History, Is Made a Landmark." *New York Times*, June 26, 1999. http://www.nytimes.com/1999/06/26/nyregion/stonewall-gay-bar-that-made-history-is-made-a-landmark.html.

Duran v. Missouri, 439 U.S. 357 (S.Ct. 1979).

Eisenstadt v. Baird, 405 U.S. 438 (S.Ct. 1972).

Elizabeth Goodwin, Administrator of the *Estate of Tamir Rice Plaintiff v. Timothy Loehmann et al. Defendants*. Case No. 1:14-CV-2670. *Time*, February 27, 2015. http://www.time.com/wp-content/uploads/2015/03/rice-answer.pdf.

Ellis, Katie. "Contested Vulnerability: A Case Study of Girls in Secure Care." *Children and Youth Services Review* 88 (May 2018): 156–63. https://doi.org/10.1016/j.childyouth.2018.02.047.

Erdely, Sabrina Rubin. "The Transgender Crucible." *Rolling Stone*, July 30, 2014. https://www.rollingstone.com/culture/culture-news/the-transgender-crucible-114095.

Estes, Richard J., and Neil Alan Weiner. "The Commercial Sexual Exploitation of Children in the U.S., Canada and Mexico." National Institute of Justice, September 18, 2001. https://abolitionistmom.org/wp-content/uploads/2014/05/Complete_CSEC_0estes-weiner.pdf.

Ewen, B. M. "Failure to Protect Laws: Protecting Children or Punishing Mothers?" *Journal of Forensic Nursing* 3, no. 2 (2007): 84–86.

Fagan, Kevin. "The Execution of Stanley Tookie Williams/Eyewitness: Prisoner Did Not Die Meekly, Quietly." *San Francisco Chronicle*, December 14, 2005. http://www.sfgate.com/news/article/THE-EXECUTION-OF-STANLEY-TOOKIE-WILLIAMS-2588632.php.

Faragher v. City of Boca Raton, 524 U.S. 775 (1998).

Feres v. United States, 340 U.S. 135 (S.Ct. 1950).

Ferrise, Adam. "Cleveland Officer Timothy Loehmann Fired in Wake of Tamir Rice Shooting." Cleveland.com, May 30, 2017. http://www.cleveland.com/metro/2017/05/cleveland_officer_tim othy_loeh_1.html.

———. "Cleveland's Critical Incident Review Committee Found No Violations in Officers' Response to Tamir Rice Shooting." Cleveland.com, April 28, 2017. http://www.cleveland.com /metro/2017/04/clevelands_critical_incident_r.html.

———. "Fired Cleveland Cop Timothy Loehmann, Who Shot Tamir Rice, Set for Arbitration." Cleveland.com, January 9, 2018. http://www.cleveland.com/metro/2018/01/fired _cleveland_cop_timothy_lo.html.

———. "Tamir Rice's Sister: Cleveland Police Officer 'Attacked Me.'" Cleveland.com, December 14, 2014. http://www.cleveland.com /metro/2014/12/tamir_rices_sister_cleveland_p.html.

Fiss, Owen M. "Groups and the Equal Protection Clause." *Philosophy and Public Affairs* 5, no. 2 (Winter 1976): 107–77.

Fitzgerald, Erin, Sarah Elspeth, Sarah Elspeth Patterson, Darby Hickey, Cherno Biko, and Harper Jean Tobin. "Meaningful Work: Transgender Experiences in the Sex Trade." National Transgender Discrimination Survey, Red Umbrella Project.org, Best Practices Policy Project.org, and National Center for Transgender Equality. org, December 2015. https://www.transequality.org/sites/default /files/Meaningful%20Work-Full%20Report_FINAL_3.pdf.

Flynn, Sean. "The Tamir Rice Story: How to Make a Police Shooting Disappear." *Gentlemen's Quarterly*, July 14, 2016. https://www .gq.com/story/tamir-rice-story.

Frantz, Ashley, Steve Almasy, and Catherine E. Shoichet. "Tamir Rice Shooting: No Charges for Officers." CNN, December 28, 2015. http://www.cnn.com/2015/12/28/us/tamir-rice-shooting/index .html.

Frazer, Somjen, and Erin Howe. "Transgender Health and Economic Insecurity: A Report from the 2015 LGBT Health and Human Services Needs Assessment Survey." New York: Empire State Pride Agenda, 2015.

Friedmann, Sarah. "Why Marshae Jones Was Charged with Manslaughter after She Was Shot & Lost Her Pregnancy." *Bustle*, June 27, 2019. https://www.bustle.com/p/why-marshae-jones-was-charged -with-manslaughter-after-she-was-shot-lost-her-pregnancy-1815 1897.

Funk, Rus Ervin. "Biderman's Chart of Coercion." National Center on Domestic and Sexual Violence. Accessed July 1, 2019. http:// www.ncdsv.org/images/Chart%20of%20Coercion1.pdf.

Gallagher, Janet. "Prenatal Invasions & Interventions: What's Wrong with Fetal Rights?" *Harvard Women's Law Journal* 10 (1987): 9–58.

Garbarino, James. *Lost Boys: Why Our Sons Turn Violent and How Can We Save Them*. New York: Anchor, 2000.

Garcia, Crystal A., and Jodi Lane. "Dealing with the Fall-Out: Identifying and Addressing the Role That Relationship Strain Plays in the Lives of Girls in the Juvenile Justice System." *Journal of Criminal Justice* 40, no. 3 (June 2012): 259–67.

García-Vega, Elena, Aida Camero, María Fernández, and Ana Villaverde. "Suicidal Ideation and Suicide Attempts in Persons with Gender Dysphoria." *Psicothema* 30, no. 3. (2018): 283–88. http:// doi.org/10.7334/psicothema2017.438.

Gates, Gary J. "LGBT Adult Immigrants in the United States." Williams Institute, UCLA School of Law, March 2013. https://williamsin stitute.law.ucla.edu/research/census-lgbt-demographics-studies/us -lgbt-immigrants-mar-2013.

Gerald Lynn Bostock v. Clayton County, Georgia, 590 U.S. ___ (2020).

Gerson, Kathleen. *No Man's Land: Men's Changing Commitments to Family and Work*. New York: Basic Books, 1994.

Giordano, Peggy C., and Jennifer E. Copp. "Girls' and Women's Violence: The Question of General versus Uniquely Gendered Causes." *Annual Review of Criminology* 2 (January 2019): 167–89. https://doi.org/10.1146/annurev-criminol-011518-024517.

Glaze, Lauren, and Danielle Kaeble. "Correctional Populations in the United States, 2013." Bureau of Justice Statistics, December 2014. https://www.bjs.gov/content/pub/pdf/cpus13.pdf.

Goldberg, Naomi G., Christy Mallory, Amira Hasenbush, Lara Stemple, and Ilan H. Meyer. "Police and the Criminalization of LGBT People." In *The Cambridge Handbook of Policing in the United States*, edited by Tamara Rice Lave and Eric J. Miller, 374–91. Cambridge: Cambridge University Press, 2019.

Goldstein, Dana. "Inexcusable Absences." *New Republic*, March 6, 2015. https://newrepublic.com/article/121186/truancy-laws-un fairly-attack-poor-children-and-parents.

Gonnerman, Jennifer. "Kalief Browder, 1993–2015." *New Yorker*, June 7, 2015.

———. "Before the Law." *New Yorker*, October 6, 2014.

Goodman, Amy. "A Conversation with Death Row Prisoner Stanley Tookie Williams from His San Quentin Cell." *Democracy Now!*, November 30, 2005. http://www.democracynow.org /2005/11/30/a_conversation_with_death_row_prisoner.

Goshin, Lorie S., Mary W. Byrne, and Alana M. Henninger. "Recidivism after Release from a Prison Nursery Program." *Public Health Nursing* 31 (2013): 109–17.

Graham v. Florida, 560 U.S. 48 (S.Ct. 2010).

Graham, David A. "'Probable Cause' in the Killing of Tamir Rice." *The Atlantic*, June 11, 2015. http://www.theatlantic.com/politics /archive/2015/06/tamir-rice-case-cleveland/395420.

Gramlich, John, and Katherine Schaeffer. "7 Facts about Guns in the U.S." Pew Research Center, October 22, 2019. https://www.pew research.org/fact-tank/2018/12/27facts-about-guns-in-united-states.

Green, Sharon. "Regina McKnight Released from Prison." ABC 15 WPDE, June 19, 2008. http://wpde.com/news/videos/regina -mcknight-released-from-prison.

Griswold v. Connecticut, 381 U.S. 479 (S.Ct. 1965).

Hagler, Jamal. "6 Things You Should Know about Women of Color and the Criminal Justice System." Center for American Progress, March 16, 2016. Accessed October 16, 2019. https://www.americanprogress.org/issues/criminal-justice/news /2016/03/16/133438/6-things-you-should-know-about-women-of -color-and-the-criminal-justice-system.

Hallinan, Joseph T. *Going Up the River: Travels in a Prison Nation*. New York: Random House, 2003.

Hampson, Rick. "The Metamorphosis of Hedda Nussbaum: 'Beyond Understanding.'" Associated Press, November 16, 1987. https:// apnews.com/2e647d4a1cf9394d2689bad7b47aa8d0.

Harding, Sandra. "Introduction: Is There a Feminist Method?" In *Feminism and Methodology: Social Science Issues*, edited by Sandra Harding, 1–14. Bloomington: Indiana University Press, 1987.

Harkinson, Josh. "Exclusive: Meet the Woman Who Kicked Off Anonymous' Anti-Rape Accusations." *Mother Jones*, May 13, 2013.

Harm Free Zone Movement. Accessed October 18, 2019. https:// forwardjustice.org/movement/harm-free-zone-movement.

Harner, Holly M., Mia Budescu, Seth J. Gillihan, Suzanne Riley, and Edna B. Foa. "Posttraumatic Stress Disorder in Incarcerated Women: A Call for Evidence-Based Treatment." *Psychological Trauma: Theory, Research, Practice, and Policy* 7, no. 1 (2015): 58–66. https://doi.apa.org/doiLanding?doi=10.1037%2Fa0032508.

Harrell, Adele, Christy Visher, Lisa Newmark, and Jennifer Yahner. "The Judicial Oversight Demonstration: Culminating Report on the Evaluation." NCJ 224201. National Institute of Justice, 2009. https://www.ncjrs.gov/pdffiles1/nij/224201.pdf.

Henry Wallace Police Crime Database. Accessed October 7, 2019. https://policecrime.bgsu.edu.

Herman, Judith Lewis. *Trauma and Recovery: The Aftermath of Violence—from Domestic Abuse to Political Terror*. New York: Basic Books, 1992.

Heron, Melonie. "Deaths: Leading Causes for 2017." *National Vital Statistics Reports* 68, no. 6 (June 24, 2019). https://www.cdc.gov/nchs/data/nvsr/nvsr68/nvsr68_06-508.pdf.

Hill, Marc Lamont. "Why Aren't We Fighting for CeCe McDonald?" *Ebony*, June 11, 2012. https://www.ebony.com/news/why-arent-we-fighting-for-cece-mcdonald.

Horowitz, Juliana Menasce. "Americans Narrowly Opposed Allowing Teachers and School Officials to Carry Guns." Pew Research Center, February 23, 2018. https://www.pewresearch.org/fact-tank/2018/02/23/in-2017-americans-narrowly-opposed-allowing-teachers-and-school-officials-to-carry-guns.

Hossain, Mazeda, Cathy Zimmerman, Melanie Abas, and Charlotte Watts. "The Relationship of Trauma to Mental Disorders among Trafficked and Sexually Exploited Girls and Women." *American Journal of Public Health* 100, no. 12 (2010): 2442–9. http://doi.org/10.2105/AJPH.2009.173229.

Houser, Kimberly, and Steven Belenko. "Disciplinary Responses to Misconduct among Female Prison Inmates with Mental Illness, Substance Use Disorders, and Co-occurring Disorders." *Psychiatric Rehabilitation Journal* 38, no. 1 (2015): 24–34. http://dx.doi.org/10.1037/prj0000110.

Hoyt v. Florida, 368 U.S. 57 (S.Ct. 1961).

Humm, Maggie. *The Dictionary of Feminist Theory*. Columbus: Ohio State University Press, 1990.

Hunter, Lea. "The U.S. Is Still Forcibly Sterilizing Prisoners." Associated Press, August 23, 2017. https://talkpoverty.org/2017/08/23/u-s-still-forcibly-sterilizing-prisoners.

In re Baby M, 537 A.2d 1227 (Supreme Court of New Jersey 1988).

In re Gault, 387 U.S. 1 (S.Ct. 1967).

In re Winship, 397 U.S. 358 (S.Ct. 1970).

Irvine, Angela. "Dispelling Myths: Understanding the Incarceration of Lesbian, Gay, Bisexual, and Gender Nonconforming Youth." Unpublished paper, National Council on Crime and Delinquency, Oakland, CA, 2014. As cited in Center for American Progress and MAP.

Jablonski, Ray. "Steubenville Rape Convict Trent Mays Released from Juvenile Detention." Cleveland.com, January 8, 2015. https://www.cleveland.com/metro/2015/01/steubenville_rape_convict_tren.html.

Johansen, Bruce E. "Americans and the 'Last Gasp of Eugenics.'" *Native Americas* 15, no. 4 (December 31, 1998): 45.

Johnson v. Calvert, 5 CAL. 4th 84 (California Supreme Court 1993).

Johnson, Chris. "9th Circuit: Gender Reassignment Surgery Must Be Granted to Trans Inmates." *Washington Blade*, August 23, 2019. https://www.washingtonblade.com/2019/08/23/9th-circuit-gender-reassignment-surgery-must-be-granted-to-trans-inmates.

Johnson, Leanor Boulin. *On the Front Lines: Police Stress and Family Well-Being*. Hearing before the Select Committee on Children, Youth, and Families, House of Representatives, 102d Congress, 1st Sess. (May 20, 1991), 32–48. https://eric.ed.gov/?id=ED338997.

Johnson, Michael. *A Typology of Domestic Violence: Intimate Terrorism, Violent Resistance, and Situational Couple Violence*. Boston, MA: Northeastern University Press, 2008.

Johnson, Michael, and Kathleen Ferraro. "Research on Domestic Violence in the 1990s: Making Distinctions." *Journal of Marriage and Family* 62, no. 4 (November 2000): 948–63.

Jones, Ann. *Next Time She'll Be Dead*. Boston, MA: Beacon, 1994.

Juvenile Justice and Delinquency Prevention Act, Pub. L. No. 93-415, § 5601, 42 U.S.C. (1974). https://ojjdp.ojp.gov/about/legislation.

Kajstura, Aleks. "Women's Mass Incarceration: The Whole Pie." Prison Policy Initiative, November 13, 2018. https://www.prisonpolicy.org/reports/pie2018women.html.

Kalish, Rachel, and Michael Kimmel. "Suicide by Mass Murder: Masculinity, Aggrieved Entitlement, and Rampage School Shootings." *Health Sociology Review* 19, no. 4 (2014): 451–64. http://doi.org/10.5172/hesr.2010.19.4.451.

Kanin, Eugene J. "False Rape Allegations." *Archives of Sexual Behavior* 23, no. 1 (1994): 81–92.

Kann, Laura, Steve Kinchen, Shari L. Shanklin, Katherine H. Flint, Joseph Hawkins, William A. Harris, Richard Lowry, et al. "Youth Risk Behavior Surveillance—United States, 2013." *Morbidity and Mortality Weekly Report*. Rockville, MD: Centers for Disease Control and Prevention, June 13, 2014. https://www.cdc.gov/mmwr/preview/mmwrhtml/ss6304a1.htm.

Kasino, Michael. "Pay It No Mind: The Life and Times of Marsha P. Johnson." 2012. http://www.youtube.com/watch?v=rjN9W2KstqE.

Kassle, Emily. "Sexual Assault Inside ICE Detention: 2 Survivors Tell Their Stories." *New York Times*, July, 17, 2018. https://www.nytimes.com/2018/07/17/us/sexual-assault-ice-detention-survivor-stories.html.

Katz, Jonathan. *The Macho Paradox: Why Some Men Hurt Women and How All Men Can Help*. Naperville, IL: Sourcebooks, 2006.

———. "Memo to Media: Manhood, Not Guns or Mental Illness, Should Be Central in Newton Shooting." *HuffPost*, December 18, 2012. https://www.huffingtonpost.in/jackson-katz/men-gender-gun-violence_b_2308522.html.

Kaufman, Leslie. "Determining the Future of a Girl with a Past: Is the Answer to Child Prostitution Counseling, or Incarceration?" *New York Times*, September 15, 2004.

Kayser, Terry, Laura Roberts, John Shuford, and John Michaelis. "Minnesota AVP Anger Study." *International Journal of Trauma Research and Practice* 1, no. 1 (2014): 2–13.

Keilitz, Susan. "Specialization of Domestic Violence Case Management in the Courts: A National Survey." NCJ 199724. National Institute of Justice, 2004.

Kessler-Harris, Alice. "The Long History of Workplace Sexual Harassment." *Jacobin*, March 2018. https://www.jacobinmag.com/2018/03/metoo-workplace-discrimination-sexual-harassment-feminism.

Kim, Mimi. "Alternative Interventions to Intimate Violence: Defining Political and Pragmatic Challenges." In *Restorative Justice and Violence against Women*, edited by James Ptacek, 193–217. New York: Oxford University Press, 2010.

Kingston, Sarah, and Terry Thomas. "No Model in Practice: A 'Nordic Model' to Respond to Prostitution?" *Crime, Law, and Social Change* 71, no. 4 (May 2019): 423–39. https://link.springer.com/article/10.1007/s10611-018-9795-6.

Kolata, Gina. "The Sad Legacy of the Dalkon Shield." *New York Times Magazine*, December 12, 1987. https://www.nytimes.com/1987/12/06/magazine/the-sad-legacy-of-the-dalkon-shield.html.

Kort-Butler, Lisa A. "Content Analysis in the Study of Crime, Media, and Popular Culture." In *Oxford Research Encyclopedia of Criminology*, September 29, 2016. https://oxfordre.com/criminology/view/10.1093/acrefore/9780190264079.001.0001/acrefore-9780190264079-e-23.

Kupers, Terry A. "Gender and Domination in Prison." *Western New England Law Review* 39 (2017). https://digitalcommons.law.wne.edu/lawreview/vol39/iss3/5.

———. "Toxic Masculinity as a Barrier to Mental Health Treatment in Prison." *Journal of Clinical Psychology* 61, no. 6 (2005): 713–24.

———. "Toxic Masculinity in and outside of Prison: The Same Dominance Hierarchy May Prevail in Prison and Outside." *Psychology Today*, April 8, 2019. https://www.psychology today.com/us/blog/prisons-and-prisms/201904/toxic-masculinity-in-and-outside-prison.

Kushner, David. "Anonymous vs. Steubenville." *Rolling Stone*, November 27, 2013.

Lane, Ben. "Finally: $8.5B Countrywide Mortgage Bond Settlement Gets Green Light." *Housing Wire*, May 13, 2016. Accessed September 17, 2019. https://www.housingwire.com/articles/37033-finally-85b-countrywide-mortgage-bond-settlement-gets-green-light.

Lapidus, Lenora, Namita Luthra, Anjuli Verma, Deborah Small, Patricia Allard, and Kirsten Levingston. "Caught in the Net: The Impact of Drug Policies on Women and Families." ACLU, 2004. https://www.aclu.org/sites/default/files/field_document/asset_up load_file431_23513.pdf.

Launer, Dale. "How I Tried to Help Elliot Rodger." BBC.com, July 9, 2014. https://www.bbc.com/news/magazine-28197785.

Law, Victoria. "For People behind Bars, Reporting Sexual Assault Leads to More Punishment." Just Detention International, September 30, 2018. https://justdetention.org/for-people-behind-bars-reporting-sexual-assault-leads-to-more-punishment.

Lee, Jaeah. "It's Been 6 Months since Tamir Rice Died, and the Cop Who Killed Him Still Hasn't Been Questioned." *Mother Jones*, May 15, 2015. http://www.motherjones.com/politics/2015/05/tamir-rice-investigation-cleveland-police.

Leigh, Carol. "Inventing Sex Work." In *Whores and Other Feminists*, edited by Jill Nagle, 226–31. New York: Routledge, 1997.

Lewis, Jone Johnson. "Separate Spheres Ideology: Women and Men in Their Own Places." ThoughtCo., September 11, 2019. https://www.thoughtco.com/separate-spheres-ideology-3529523.

Lisak, David, Lori Gardinier, Sarah C. Nicksa, and Ashley M. Cote. "False Allegations of Sexual Assault: An Analysis of Ten Years of Reported Cases." *Violence against Women* 16, no. 12 (2010): 1318–34.

Lisak, David, and Paul M. Miller. "Repeat Rape and Multiple Offending among Undetected Rapists." *Violence and Victims* 17, no. 1 (2002): 73–84.

Liu, Katherine A., and Natalie A. Dipietro Mager. "Women's Involvement in Clinical Trials: Historical Perspective and Future Implications." *Pharmacy Practice* 14, no. 1 (2016): 708. http://doi.org/10.18549/PharmPract.2016.01.708.

Lizotte, Alan, and David Sheppard. "Gun Use by Male Juveniles: Research and Prevention." Office of Juvenile Justice and Delinquency Prevention, July 2001. https://ojjdp.ojp.gov/library/publications/gun-use-male-juveniles-research-and-prevention.

Lloyd, Rachel. *Girls like Us: Fighting for a World Where Girls Are Not for Sale; An Activist Finds Her Calling and Heals Herself*. New York: HarperCollins, 2011.

Locke, Mandy. "Tight-Lipped 'Granny' Dies in Prison." *November Coalition*, August 17, 2007. http://www.november.org/stayinfo/breaking07/GrannyAlvaMae.html.

Lonsway, Kimberly A., and Joanne Archambault. "The 'Justice Gap' for Sexual Assault Cases: Future Directions for Research and Reform." *Violence against Women* 18, no. 2 (2012): 145–68.

Lucas, Ann M. "Race, Class, Gender, and Deviancy: The Criminalization of Prostitution." *Berkeley Journal of Gender, Law & Justice* 10, no. 1 (1995): 47–60.

Lydon, Jason, Kamaria Carrington, Hana Low, Reed Miller, and Mahsa Yazdy. *Coming Out of Concrete Closets: A Report on Black & Pink's National LGBTQ Prisoner Survey*. Black and Pink, 2015. Accessed July 20, 2019. https://docs.wixstatic.com/ugd/857027 _fcd066f0c450418b95a18ab34647bd15.pdf.

Lynch, Michael J. "Acknowledging Female Victims of Green Crimes: Environmental Exposure of Women to Industrial Pollutants." *Feminist Criminology* 13, no. 4 (2018): 404–27.

MacKinnon, Catharine. *Women's Lives, Men's Laws*. Cambridge, MA: Harvard University Press, 2005.

Macur, Juliet, and Nate Schweber. "Rape Case Unfolds on Web and Splits City." *New York Times*, December 16, 2012. https://www.youtube.com/watch?v=1wfuy-vnpWY.

Maher, Lisa, and Suzie Hudson. "Women in the Drug Economy: A Metasynthesis of the Qualitative Literature." *Journal of Drug Issues* 37 (2007): 805–26. http://doi.org/10.1177/002204260703700404.

Males, Mike, and Meda-Chesney Lind. "The Myth of Mean Girls." *New York Times*, April 2, 2010. http://www.nytimes.com/2010/04/02/opinion/02males.html.

Mallicoat, Stacey. *Women, Gender and Crime*. 3rd ed. Los Angeles: Sage, 2019.

Martin, Dell. "The Historical Roots of Domestic Violence." In *Domestic Violence on Trial*, edited by D. J. Sonkin. New York: Springer, 1990.

Maruschak, Laura M. "Medical Problems of Prisoners." U.S. Department of Justice, Bureau of Justice Statistics, April 1, 2008. https://www.bjs.gov/index.cfm?ty=pbdetail&iid=1097.

Matal v. Tam, 582 U.S.___ (S.Ct. 2017).

Mathias, Christopher. "Here's Kalief Browder's Heartbreaking Research Paper on Solitary Confinement." *HuffPost*, June 23, 2015.

Mattera, Phil. "17 of the Worst Corporate Crimes of 2015." *AlterNet*, December 18, 2015. https://www.alternet.org/2015/12/17-worst-corporate-crimes-2015.

Maynard, Mary. "Methods, Practice and Epistemology: The Debate about Feminism and Research." In *Researching Women's Lives from a Feminist Perspective*, edited by Mary Maynard and June Purvis, 27–48. Bristol, PA: Taylor & Francis, 1994.

Mayo-Coleman v. American Sugars Holdings Inc., No. 1:2014cv00079—Document 195 (S.D.N.Y. 2018).

McFarlane, Alexander C. "The Long-Term Costs of Traumatic Stress: Intertwined Physical and Psychological Consequences." *World Psychiatry: Official Journal of the World Psychiatric Association (WPA)* 9, no. 1 (2010): 3–10.

McFarlane, Christine. "Gladys Radek: A Woman on a Mission." *Aboriginal Multi-Media Society*, 2011. Accessed July 8, 2019. https://ammsa.com/publications/ravens-eye/gladys-radek-woman -mission.

McKinley, Jesse. "Could Prostitution Be Next to Be Decriminalized?" *New York Times*, May 31, 2019. https://www.nytimes.com/2019/05/31/nyregion/presidential-candidates-prostitution.html.

McWhorter, Stephanie K., Valerie A. Stander, Lex L. Merrill, Cynthia J. Thomsen, and Joel S. Milner. "Reports of Rape Reperpetration by Newly Enlisted Male Navy Personnel." *Violence and Victims* 24, no. 2 (2009): 204–18.

Mehren, Elizabeth. "A 6-Year-Old's Tragic Death." *Los Angeles Times*, November 25, 1987. https://www.latimes.com/archives/la-xpm -1987-11-25-vw-16336-story.html.

Meritor Savings Bank v. Vinson, 477 U.S. 57, (1986).

Merton, Robert K. "Social Structure and Anomie." *American Sociological Review* 3 (October 1938): 672–82.

Metzl, Jonathan M., and Kenneth T. MacLeish. "Mental Illness, Mass Shootings, and the Politics of American Firearms." *American Journal of Public Health* 105, no. 2 (2015): 240–49. http://doi.org/10.2105/AJPH.2014.302242.

Meyers, John, and Jazmine Ulloa. "Immigrants Facing Deportation, Drug Offenders and a Former State Lawmaker Receive Pardons from Gov. Jerry Brown." *Los Angeles Times*,

November 21, 2018. https://www.latimes.com/politics/la-pol-ca-thanksgiving-pardons-jerry-brown-20181121-story.html.

Miller v. Alabama, 567 U.S. 460 (S.Ct. 2012).

Miller, Marsha L., and John A. Shuford. *The Alternatives to Violence Project in Delaware: A Three-Year Cumulative Recidivism Study.* Alternatives to Violence Project, 2005. http://www.avpav.org/files/res-avp-rpteval-delaware-2005.pdf.

Mingus, Mia. "Transformative Justice: A Brief Description." TransformHarm.org. Accessed May 21, 2021. https://transformharm.org/transformative-justice-a-brief-description.

Miroff, Nick, and Maria Sacchetti. "U.S. Has Hit 'Breaking Point' at Border amid Immigration Surge, Customs and Border Protection Chief Says." *Washington Post*, March 27, 2019.

Mock, Brentin. "What New Research Says about Race and Police Shootings." City Lab, August 6, 2019. https://www.citylab.com/equity/2019/08/police-officer-shootings-gun-violence-racial-bias-crime-data/595528.

Mogul, Joey L., Andrea J. Ritchie, and Kay Whitlock. *Queer (In)justice: The Criminalization of LGBT People in the United States.* Boston: Beacon, 2011.

Molloy, Parker Marie. "Going to a Prison Made CeCe McDonald Want to Fix Them." *Advocate*, July 30, 2014. https://www.advocate.com/40-under-40-emerging-voices/2014/07/30/40-under-40-prison-turned-cece-mcdonald-activist.

Moloney, K. P., B. J. van den Burgh, and L. F. Moller. "Women in Prison: The Central Issues of Gender Characteristics and Trauma History." *Public Health* 123, no. 6 (2009): 426–30.

Montgomery v. Louisiana, 577 U.S. ___ (S.Ct. 2016).

Moran, Rachel. *Paid For: My Journey through Prostitution.* New York: Norton, 2013.

Morello, Karen Berger. *The Invisible Bar: The Woman Lawyer in America, 1638 to the Present.* New York: Random House, 1986.

Morgan, Rachel E., and Jennifer L. Truman. "Criminal Victimization, 2017." Bureau of Justice Statistics. Accessed July 1, 2019. https://www.bjs.gov/content/pub/pdf/cv17.pdf.

Mozingo, Joe. "Frantic Parents of Shooting Suspect Raced to Isla Vista during Rampage." *Los Angeles Times*, May 25, 2014. https://www.latimes.com/local/lanow/la-me-ln-frantic-parents-isla-vista-shootings-20140525-story.html.

Mullen, Katherine, and Rachael Lloyd. "The Passage of the Safe Harbor Act and the Voices of Sexually Exploited Youth." In *Lawyer's Manual on Human Trafficking: Pursuing Justice for Victims*, edited by Jill Laurie Goodman and Dorchen A. Leidholdt, 129–40. Supreme Court of the State of New York, Appellate Division, First Department, and New York State Judicial Committee on Women in the Courts, 2011.

Murray, Christine E., and A. Keith Mobley. "Empirical Research about Same-Sex Intimate Partner Violence: A Methodological Review." *Journal of Homosexuality* 56, no. 3 (2009): 361–86.

Muskal, Michael. "School Superintendent, 3 Others Charged in Steubenville Rape Case." *Los Angeles Times*, November 25, 2013.

Natapoff, Alexandra. "The Cost of 'Quality of Life' Policing: Thousands of Young Black Men Coerced to Plead Guilty to Crimes They Didn't Commit." *Washington Post*, November 11, 2015. https://www.washingtonpost.com/news/the-watch/wp/2015/11/11/the-cost-of-quality-of-life-policing-thousands-of-young-black-men-coerced-to-plead-guilty-to-crimes-they-didnt-commit.

Nelson-Butler, Cheryl. "The Racial Roots of Human Trafficking." SMU Dedman School of Law Legal Studies Research Paper No. 179. *UCLA Law Review* 62, no. 1494 (2015): 51. https://www.uclalawreview.org/racial-roots-human-trafficking.

Nolan, James L. "Redefining Criminal Courts: Problem-Solving and the Meaning of Justice." *American Criminal Justice Review* 40, no. 14 (2003): 1541–65.

Obama, Barack. "Why We Must Rethink Solitary Confinement: Its Overuse Leads to Tragic Results." *Washington Post*, January 26, 2016.

Olsen, Fran. "The Sex of Law." In *The Politics of Law: A Progressive Critique*, 2nd ed., edited by David Kairys. New York: Basic Books, 1998.

Oudekerk, Barbara. "Hate Crime Statistics: Briefing Prepared for the Virginia Advisory Committee." U.S. Commission on Civil Rights, Panel 1: Hate Crime History in VA, Current Legal Framework, Enforcement and Data. 2017 Hate Crime Statistics. FBI, March 29, 2019. https://www.bjs.gov/content/pub/pdf/hcs1317pp.pdf.

Page, Dana. "The Homicide by Child Abuse Conviction of Regina McKnight." *Howard Law Journal* 46 (2003): 363–403.

Paltrow, Lynn, and Jeanne Flavin. "Arrests of and Forced Interventions on Pregnant Women in the United States (1973–2005): The Implications for Women's Legal Status and Public Health." *Journal of Health Politics, Policy and Law* 38, no. 2 (2013): 299–343.

Paltrow, Lynn, and Tony Newman. "South Carolina Supreme Court Reverses 20-Year Homicide Conviction of Regina McKnight." Drug Policy Alliance Press Release, May 11, 2008. http://www.drugpolicy.org/news/2008/05/south-carolina-supreme-court-reverses-20-year-homicide-conviction-regina-mcknight.

Pasulka, Nicole. "The Case of CeCe McDonald—Murder, or Self-Defense against a Hate Crime?" *Mother Jones*, May 22, 2012. https://www.motherjones.com/politics/2012/05/cece-mcdonald-transgender-hate-crime-murder.

Patino, Vanessa, Lawanda Ravoira, and Angela Wolf. "A Rallying Cry for Change." National Council on Crime and Delinquency, 2006. https://www.nccdglobal.org/sites/default/files/publication_pdf/cry-for-change.pdf.

Patton, Dana, and Joseph L. Smith. "Lawyer, Interrupted: Gender Bias in Oral Arguments at the US Supreme Court." *Journal of Law and the Courts* 5, no. 2 (Fall 2017). https://doi.org/10.1086/692611.

Pavan v. Smith, 137 S.Ct. 2075 (S.Ct. 2017).

Pearce, Matt. "Transgender Woman Sentenced to Men's Prison in Minnesota Killing." *Los Angeles Times*, June 18, 2012. https://www.latimes.com/nation/la-xpm-2012-jun-18-la-na-nn-transgender-woman-sentenced-to-mens-prison-20120618-story.html.

Penal Reform International. 2016. https://www.penalreform.org.

Penny, Laurie. "Laurie Penny on Misogynist Extremism: Let's Call the Isla Vista Killings What They Were." *New Statesman*, May 25, 2014. https://www.newstatesman.com/lifestyle/2014/05/lets-call-isla-vista-killings-what-they-were-misogynist-extremism.

People v. Liberta, 64 N.Y.2d 152 (New York State Court of Appeals 1984).

Persky, Anna Stolley. "Reproductive Technology and the Law." *Washington Lawyer*, July/August 2012. https://www.dcbar.org/bar-resources/publications/washington-lawyer/articles/july-august-2012-reproductive-tech.cfm.

Pierce, Jennifer L. *Gender Trials: Emotional Lives in Contemporary Law Firms.* Berkeley, CA: University of California Press, 1995.

Potter, Hillary. "An Argument for Black Feminist Criminology: Understanding African American Women's Experiences with Intimate Partner Abuse Using an Integrated Approach." *Feminist Criminology* 1, no. 2 (2006): 106–24.

Prezepiorski, Lemos. "What Is Queer Criminology?" *University of Oxford Faculty of Law* (blog), June 19, 2018. Accessed August 29, 2019. https://www.law.ox.ac.uk/centres-institutes/centre-criminology/blog/2018/06/what-queer-criminology.

Prison Rape Elimination Act National Standards, 28 CFR Part 115. Accessed June 15, 2019. https://www.law.cornell.edu/cfr/text/28/part-115.

Prison Rape Elimination Act of 2003. Pub. L. No. 108-79 (2003). https://www.prearesourcecenter.org/sites/default/files/library/prea.pdf.

Pupovac, Jessica. "Crack Users Do More Time than People Convicted of Manslaughter." *AlterNet*, October 16, 2007. http://www.alternet.org/story/65406/crack_users_do_more_time_than_people_convicted_of_manslaughter.

Queen, Carol. *Real Live Nude Girl: Chronicles of Sex-Positive Culture*. Jersey City, NJ: Cleis Press, 1997.

Quezada, Janet Arelis. "Transgender Immigrants Not Safe in Detention Centers." GLAAD, September 22, 2015. https://www.glaad.org/blog/transgender-immigrants-not-safe-us-detention-centers.

Quinby v. Westlb AG, 245 F.R.D. 94 (S.D.N.Y. 2006).

Rampton, Martha. "Four Waves of Feminism." *Pacific Magazine*, 2008. https://www.pacificu.edu/about/media/four-waves-feminism.

Reeves, Richard V., and Joanna Venator. "Gender Gaps in Relative Mobility." Brookings Institute, November 13, 2013. https://www.brookings.edu/blog/social-mobility-memos/2013/11/12/gender-gaps-in-relative-mobility.

Reichert, Jessica, and Lindsay Bostwick. "Post-traumatic Stress Disorder and Victimization among Female Prisoners in Illinois." Illinois Criminal Justice Information Authority, November 2010. http://www.icjia.state.il.us/assets/pdf/ResearchReports/PTSD_Female_Prisoners_Report_1110.pdf.

Riera, Antonio, and David M. Walker. "The Impact of Race and Ethnicity on Care in the Pediatric Emergency Department." *Current Opinion in Pediatrics* 22, no. 3 (2010): 284–89.

Rivas, Jorge. "Black Transgender Woman CeCe McDonald to Be Housed in Male Prison." *Colorlines*, June 4, 2012. https://www.colorlines.com/articles/black-transgender-woman-cece-mcdonald-be-housed-male-prison.

Roberts, Dorothy E. "Racism and Patriarchy in the Meaning of Motherhood." *Faculty Scholarship at Penn Law* 595 (1993). http://scholarship.law.upenn.edu/faculty_scholarship/595.

Roe v. Wade, 410 U.S. 113 (S.Ct. 1973).

Rollè, Luca, Angela M. Caldarera, Eva Gerino, and Piera Brustia. "When Intimate Partner Violence Meets Same Sex Couples: A Review of Same Sex Intimate Partner Violence." *Frontiers in Psychology* 9 (2018): 1506. http://doi.org/10.3389/fpsyg.2018.01506.

Roper v. Simmons, 543 U.S. 551 (S.Ct. 2005).

Ross, Lee. "The Intuitive Psychologist and His Shortcomings: Distortions in the Attribution Process." *Advances in Experimental Social Psychology* 10 (1977): 184.

Russell, Katheryn K. "Development of a Black Criminology and the Role of the Black Criminologist." *Justice Quarterly* 9, no. 4 (1992): 667–83.

Russo, Francine. "The Faces of Hedda Nussbaum." *New York Times*, March 30, 1997. https://www.nytimes.com/1997/03/30/magazine/the-faces-of-hedda-nussbaum.html.

Ryan, Caitlin, and Rafael Diaz. "Family Responses as a Source of Risk & Resiliency for LGBT Youth." Child Welfare League of America Preconference Institute, February 2005. http://www.cwla.org.

Ryan, Rebecca M. "The Sex Right: A Legal History of the Marital Rape Exemption." *Law and Social Inquiry* 29, no. 4 (1995): 941–1001.

Salerno, Jessica M., Cynthia J. Najdowski, Bette L. Bottoms, Evan Harrington, Gretchen Kemner, and Dave Reetu. "Excusing Murder? Conservative Jurors' Acceptance of the Gay-Panic Defense." *Psychology, Public Policy, and Law* 21, no. 1 (2015): 24–34. https://doi.org/10.1037/law0000024.

Santoro, Taylor N., and Jonathan D. Santoro. "Racial Bias in the US Opioid Epidemic: A Review of the History of Systemic Bias and Implications for Care." *Cureus* 10, no. 12 (2018): e3733. http://doi.org/10.7759/cureus.3733.

Sarrio, Jaime. "Student Truancy Can Spell $1000 Fine, Jail for Parents." *Atlanta Journal-Constitution*, December 18, 2011. https://www.ajc.com/news/local/student-truancy-can-spell-000-fine-jail-for-parents/kqr39rIYWqELUedZmC4hlI.

Saunders, Debra J. "Why Clinton Should Pardon Dorothy Gaines." *SFGate*, September 26, 2000. http://www.sfgate.com/opinion/saunders/article/Why-Clinton-Should-Pardon-Dorothy-Gaines-3316047.php.

Sawyer, Wendy. "The Gender Divide: Tracking Women's State Prison Growth." Prison Policy Initiative, January 9, 2018. https://www.prisonpolicy.org/reports/women_overtime.html.

Schisgall, David, and Nina Alvarez, dirs. *Very Young Girls*. Showtime and Swinging T Productions, 2007.

Schneider, Elizabeth M. *Battered Women & Feminist Lawmaking*. New Haven, CT: Yale University Press, 2000.

Schultz, Connie. "A City of Two Tales." *Politico*, February 23, 2015. https://www.politico.com/magazine/story/2015/02/tamir-rice-cleveland-police-115401.

Scott v. Hart, No. C-76-2395 (N.D, Cal., filed Oct. 28, 1976).

Scott-Tilley, Donna, Abigail Tilton, and Mark Sandel. "Biologic Correlates to the Development of Posttraumatic Stress Disorder in Female Victims of Intimate Partner Violence: Implication for Practice." *Perspectives in Psychiatric Care* 46, no. 1 (2010): 26–36.

Senate Bill S1998A. New York State Senate. Accessed October 15, 2019. https://www.nysenate.gov/legislation/bills/2017/S1998.

Sharp, Susan F., B. Mitchell Peck, and Jennifer Hartsfield. "Childhood Adversity and Substance Use of Women Prisoners: A General Strain Theory Approach." *Journal of Criminal Justice* 40, no. 3 (June 2012): 202–11.

Sherbill, Sara. "Thirty Years Later, Can We Finally Forgive Hedda Nussbaum?" *Slate*, October 24, 2018. https://slate.com/human-interest/2018/10/hedda-nussbaum-joel-steinberg-abuse-trial-anniversary.html.

Sherman, Lawrence W., and Ellen G. Cohn. "The Impact of Research on Legal Policy: The Minneapolis Domestic Violence Experiment." *Law & Society Review* 23, no. 1 (1989): 117–44.

Siemsen, Cynthia. *Emotional Trials: The Moral Dilemmas of Women Criminal Defense Attorneys*. Northeastern Series on Gender, Crime, and Law. Boston, MA: Northeastern University Press, 2004.

Silbert, Mimi H., and Ayala M. Pines. "Sexual child abuse as an antecedent to prostitution". *Child Abuse & Neglect* 5, no. 4 (1981): 407–11. https://doi.org/10.1016/0145-2134(81)90050-8.

Simpson, Connor. "The Steubenville Verdict Is in, and These Boys Are Guilty." *The Atlantic*, March 17, 2013.

———. "The Steubenville Victim Tells Her Story." *The Atlantic*, March 16, 2013.

Smalley, Suzanne. "This Could Be Your Kid." *Newsweek*, August 17, 2003. https://www.newsweek.com/could-be-your-kid-135949.

Smith, P. "Drug War Prisoners: 86-Year-Old Alva Mae Groves Dies behind Bars." Stop the Drug War, August 23, 2007. http://www.stopthedrugwar.org/chronicle/2007/aug/23/drug_war_prisoners_86yearold_alv.

Smith, Sharon G., Xinjian Zhang, Kathleen C. Basile, Melissa T. Merrick, Jing Wang, Marcie-jo Kresnow, and Jieru Chen. "The National Intimate Partner and Sexual Violence Survey (NISVS): 2015 Data Brief—Updated Release." National Center for Injury Prevention and Control, Centers for Disease Control and Prevention, 2018. https://www.cdc.gov/violenceprevention/pdf/2015data-brief508.pdf.

Solis, Marie. "The Feminist Divide over Decriminalizing Sex Work." *Vice*, March 12, 2019. https://www.vice.com/en/article/vbwjp4/sex-work-decriminalization-new-%09york-feminist-movement.

Solomon, Akiba. "CeCe McDonald: Attacked for Her Identity, Incarcerated for Surviving." *Ebony*, May 4, 2012. https://www.ebony.com/news/cece-mcdonald-bias-attack.

South Carolina Code of Laws Title 16—Crimes and Offenses. Ch. 3: Offenses against the Person, Article 1: Homicide, § 16-3-85. Accessed September 10, 2019. https://www.scstatehouse.gov/code/t16c003.php.

Sprinkle, Annie. *Hardcore from the Heart: The Pleasures, Profits, and Politics of Sex in Performance*. New York: Continuum, 2001.

Stanford v. Kentucky, 492 U.S. 361 (S.Ct. 1989).

State v. Oliver, 70 N.C. 60 (N.C. *1874*).

Stickle, Ben. "A National Examination of the Effect of Education, Training and Pre-Employment Screening on Law Enforcement Use of Force." *Justice Policy Journal* 13, no. 1 (Spring 2016): 1–15. http://www.cjcj.org/uploads/cjcj/documents/jpj_education_use_of_force.pdf.

Stinson, Philip M. "Police Shootings Data: What We Know and What We Don't Know." *Criminal Justice Faculty Publications* 78 (2017). https://scholarworks.bgsu.edu/crim_just_pub/78.

Stoltz, Jo-Anne Madeleine, Kate Shannon, Thomas Kerr, Ruth Zhang, Julio S. Montaner, and Evan Wood. "Associations between Childhood Maltreatment and Sex Work in a Cohort of Drug-Using Youth." *Social Science & Medicine* 65, no. 6 (1982). http://doi.org/10.1016/j.socscimed.2007.05.005.

Stone, Michael H. "Mass Murder, Mental Illness, and Men." *Violence and Gender* 2, no. 1 (March 2015): 51–86. http://doi.org/10.1089/vio.2015.0006.

Strauder v. West Virginia, 100 U.S. 303 (S.Ct. 1879).

Swaine, Jon, and Daniel McGraw. "Tamir Rice: Judge Finds Cause for Murder Charge over Police Killing of 12-Year-Old." *The Guardian*, June 11, 2015. http://www.theguardian.com/us-news/2015/jun/11/tamir-rice-police-officer-murder-charge.

Sweet, Leonard I. "The Female Seminary Movement and Women's Mission in Antebellum America." *Church History* 54, no. 1 (March 1985): 41–55.

Talley, Tim. "Group Takes Aim of Oklahoma Failure-to-Protect Law." AP News, September 29, 2018. https://www.apnews.com/45a6f24af72c4750ac141f3fe10b3bc9.

Tamburin, Adam. "Federal Court Order Officially Ends Tennessee 'Inmate Sterilization' Program." *The Tennessean*, May 20, 2019. https://www.tennessean.com/story/news/2019/05/20/tennessee-inmate-sterilization-program/3748232002.

Terveer v. Billington, Civil Action No. 2012-1290 (D.D.C. 2014).

Thompson v. Oklahoma, 487 U.S. 815 (S.Ct. 1988).

Thurman v. City of Torrington, Conn., 595 F.Supp 1521 (Dist. Conn. 1984).

Time's Up. "Letter of Solidarity." January 1, 2018. https://www.timesupnow.com.

Tomlinson, Kathryn. "A Review of Literature concerning the Alternatives to Violence Project." http://www.avpav.org/files/2007-Tomlinson_AVPBritain_Lit_Review.pdf.

Truth, Sojourner. "Ain't I a Woman?" In *Feminism: The Essential Historical Writings*, edited by Miriam Schneir. New York: Random House, 1972.

United States v. Ricky Lee Groves, 89 F.3d 830 (Court of Appeals, 4th Circuit 1996). http://www.law.resource.org/pub/us/case/reporter/F3/089/89.F3d.830.95-5173.95-5172.html.

United States v. Willie Lee Strickland, 89 F.3d 830 (Court of Appeals, 4th Circuit 1996). http://www.law.resource.org/pub/us/case/reporter/F3/089/89.F3d.830.95-5173.95-5172.html.

Unnever, James, and Shaun L. Gabbidon. *A Theory of African American Offending: Race, Racism, and Crime*. New York: Taylor & Francis, 2011.

Van Dieten, Marilyn, Natalie J. Jones, and Monica Rondon. "Working with Women Who Perpetrate Violence: A Practice Guide." National Resource Center on Justice Involved Women, April 2014. http://cjinvolvedwomen.org/wp-content/uploads/2015/09/Working-With-Women-Who-Perpetrate-Violence-A-Practice-Guide6-23.pdf.

Victims of Trafficking and Violence Protection Act. Pub. L. No. 106-386 (2000), 106th Congress. Accessed June 15, 2019. https://www.govinfo.gov/content/pkg/PLAW-106publ386/pdf/PLAW-106publ386.pdf.

Wagner, Venise. "Tookie Williams." *Mother Jones*, May 5, 2001. http://www.motherjones.com/politics/2001/03/tookie-williams.

Walrath, Christine. "Evaluation of an Inmate-Run Alternatives to Violence Project: The Impact of Inmate-to-Inmate Intervention." *Journal of Interpersonal Violence* 16, no. 7 (2001): 697–711.

Ward, Martha C. *Poor Women, Powerful Men: America's Great Experiment in Family Planning*. Boulder, CO: Westview Press, 1986.

Warsinskey, Tim. "Steubenville Rape Case: Ma'lik Richmond Returns to Football Field and Hears Cheers." Cleveland.com, August 28, 2014. https://www.cleveland.com/metro/2014/08/steubenville_rape_case_malik_r.html.

Watson, Liz, and Peter Edelman. "Improving the Juvenile Justice System for Girls: Lessons from the States." Georgetown Center on Poverty, Inequality and Public Policy, October 2012. https://nationalcrittenton.org/wp-content/uploads/2015/03/1-Improving-the-Juvenile-Justice-System-for-Girls.pdf.

Weiser, Benjamin. "New York City Settles Suit over Abuses at Rikers Island." *New York Times*, June 22, 2015.

Weiss, Debra Cassens. "'After the JD' Study Shows Many Leave Law Practice." *ABA Journal Magazine*, April 1, 2014. http://www.abajournal.com/magazine/article/after_the_jd_study_shows_many_leave_law_practice.

Weiss, Karen Wigle. "A Review of the New York State Safe Harbor Law." End Child Prostitution and Trafficking (ECPAT). Accessed July 1, 2019. https://d2jug8yyubo3yl.cloudfront.net/26999B2F-7C10-4962-918C-E964709E745D/8d5cfab4-a75e-4dd6-97c8-2f9752d16b5d.pdf.

Welsh, Susan, Keren Schiffman, and Enjoli Francis. "Looking Back at the 1989 Central Park Jogger Rape Case That Led to 5 Teens' Conviction, Later Vacated." ABC News, May 24, 2019. https://abcnews.go.com/US/back-1989-central-park-jogger-rape-case-led/story?id=63084663.

West, Cornell. Foreword to *Critical Race Theory: The Key Writings That Formed the Movement*, edited by Kimberlé Crenshaw, Kendall Thomas, Gary Peller, and Neil Gotanda. New York: New Press, 1995.

Williams v. Saxbe, 413 F.Supp. 654 (1976).

Williams, Monnica T., Isha W. Metzger, Chris Leins, and Celenia DeLapp. "Assessing Racial Trauma within a DSM–5 Framework: The UConn Racial/Ethnic Stress & Trauma Survey." *Practice Innovations* 3, no. 4 (2018): 242–60. https://doi.org/10.1037/pri0000076.

Williams, Patricia J. *The Alchemy of Race and Rights*. Cambridge, MA: Harvard University Press, 1991.

———. *Blue Rage, Black Redemption*. New York: Touchstone, 2004.

Williams, Stanley Tookie. "The Tookie Protocol for Peace: A Local Street Peace Initiative." Underground Guerrilla. http://undergroundguerrilla.tripod.com/sitebuildercontent/sitebuilderfiles/tookie_peace_protocol.pdf.

Willoughby-Nason, Julia. *Time: The Kalief Browder Story*. Roc Nation, the Weinstein Company, and Cinemart, 2017.

Wilson, Bianca D. M., Khush Cooper, Angeliki Kastanis, and Sheila Nezhad. "Sexual and Gender Minority Youth in Foster Care: Assessing Disproportionality and Disparities in Los Angeles." Social Services & Child Welfare, Williams Institute, UCLA School of Law, August 2014. https://williamsinstitute.law.ucla.edu/publications/sgm-youth-la-foster-care.

Wilson, Reid. "In Major Cities, Murder Rates Drop Precipitously." *Washington Post*, January 2, 2015. https://www.washingtonpost.com/blogs/govbeat/wp/2015/01/02/in-major-cities-murder-rates-drop-precipitously/?utm_term=.e2c5bf86a4ab.

Wilz, Teresa. "Having a Parent behind Bars Costs Children, States." Pew Research Center, May 24, 2016. https://www.pewtrusts.org/en/research-and-analysis/blogs/stateline/2016/05/24/having-a-parent-behind-bars-costs-children-states.

Woffard, Ben. "The NRA's Most Wanted Customer: Women." *Glamour*, June 28, 2018. https://www.glamour.com/story/how-the-nra-is-trying-to-reach-women.

Woods, Earlonne, Antwan Williams, and Nigel Poor. *Ear Hustle* (podcast), 2017. https://www.earhustlesq.com.

Woolf, Nicky. "'PUAhate' and 'ForeverAlone': Inside Elliot Rodger's Online Life." *Guardian*, May 30, 2014. https://www.theguardian.com/world/2014/may/30/elliot-rodger-puahate-forever-alone-reddit-forums.

ABOUT THE AUTHORS

Jo-Ann Della Giustina, Esq., is a professor in the Bridgewater State University (BSU) Department of Criminal Justice. She received her JD from Chicago Kent College of Law and her PhD in criminal justice from John Jay College (Graduate Center). Dr. Della Giustina's research/publication interests include alternatives to incarceration; restorative and transformative justice; masculinity; violence; and femicide, which is the topic of her book *Why Women Are Beaten and Killed*. She received the BSU Award for Academic Excellence in multiple years and the 2014 BSU Office of Teaching and Learning Award.

Erin Katherine Krafft is an assistant professor in the Department of Crime and Justice Studies at the University of Massachusetts, Dartmouth, as well as director of the Urban Studies Program. She received her PhD in Slavic studies from Brown University, where her interdisciplinary work focused on gender and women's movements in the context of the changing state. Her areas of teaching and research include transnational feminisms, relationships between state structures and private life, and education and pedagogy.

Susan T. Krumholz received her JD from Seattle University and her PhD in law, policy, and society from Northeastern University. She is professor emerita in the Department of Crime and Justice Studies at the University of Massachusetts, Dartmouth. Her research/publication interests include intimate violence, alternatives to the criminal/legal system, and women as students and practitioners of the law. Dr. Krumholz received the 2008 UMass President's Public Service Award for her work bringing the Inside Out Prison Exchange program to the University of Massachusetts.